CAMBODIA

COUNTRY STUDY GUIDE

International Business Publications, USA
Washington, DC, USA - Cambodia

CAMBODIA

COUNTRY STUDY GUIDE

Editorial content: International Business Publications, USA

Editor-in-Chief: Dr. Igor S. Oleynik
Editor: Natasha Alexander
Managing Editor: Karl Cherepanya

Published by
International Business Publications, USA
P.O.Box 15343, Washington, DC 20003
Phone: (202) 546-2103, Fax: (202) 546-3275.
E-mail: rusric@erols.com

UPDATED ANNUALLY

We express our sincere appreciation to all government agencies and international organizations which provided information and other materials for this guide

Databases & Information: International Business Publications, USA
Cover Design: International Business Publications, USA

ISBN 0-7397-0745-0

For customer service and information, please contact:

in the USA: **International Business Publications, USA**
P.O.Box 15343, Washington, DC 20003
Phone: (202) 546-2103, Fax: (202) 546-3275.
E-mail: rusric@erols.com

Printed in the USA

CAMBODIA

COUNTRY STUDY GUIDE

TABLE OF CONTENTS

STRATEGIC AND DEVELOPMENT PROFILES

STRATEGIC PROFILES

Official name: Preah Réachéanachâkr Kâmpuchéa (The Kingdom of Cambodia)
Head of State: King Norodom Sihanouk
Head of government: Prime Minister Hun Sen (leader of CPP); Speaker of the National Assembly: Prince Norodom Ranariddh (since Nov 1998)
Ruling party: Coalition government: Cambodian People's Party (Kanakpak Pracheachon Kâmpuchéa) (KPK) and United National Front for an Independent, Neutral, Peaceful and Co-operative Cambodia (Funcinpec) (since Nov 1998)
Area: 181,035 square km
Population: 13.10 million (2000)
Capital: Phnom Penh
Official language: Khmer (French also spoken)
Currency: Riel (R) = 100 sen
Exchange rate: R3,835.00 per US$ (May 2002)
GDP per capita: US$289 (2000)
GDP real growth: 5.40% (2000); 5.3% (2001)
Inflation: -0.80% (2000); -0.6% (2001)
Balance of trade: -US$198.00 million (2000); -US$225.0 million (2001)*
Foreign debt: US$2.36 billion (2000)
Annual FDI: US$110.00 million (2000); US$120.0 million (2001)*
* estimated figure

GEOGRAPHY

Location: Southeastern Asia, bordering the Gulf of Thailand, between Thailand, Vietnam, and Laos
Geographic coordinates: 13 00 N, 105 00 E
Map references: Southeast Asia

Area:
total: 181,040 sq km
land: 176,520 sq km
water: 4,520 sq km

Area—comparative: slightly smaller than Oklahoma
Land boundaries:
total: 2,572 km
border countries: Laos 541 km, Thailand 803 km, Vietnam 1,228 km

Coastline: 443 km

Maritime claims:
contiguous zone: 24 nm
continental shelf: 200 nm
exclusive economic zone: 200 nm
territorial sea: 12 nm

Climate: tropical; rainy, monsoon season (May to November); dry season (December to April); little seasonal temperature variation

Terrain: mostly low, flat plains; mountains in southwest and north
Elevation extremes:
lowest point: Gulf of Thailand 0 m
highest point: Phnum Aoral 1,810 m

Natural resources: timber, gemstones, some iron ore, manganese, phosphates, hydropower potential

Land use:
arable land: 13%
permanent crops: 0%
permanent pastures: 11%
forests and woodland: 66%
other: 10% (1993 est.)

Irrigated land: 920 sq km (1993 est.)

Natural hazards: monsoonal rains (June to November); flooding; occasional droughts

Environment—current issues: illegal logging activities throughout the country and strip mining for gems in the western region along the border with Thailand are resulting in habitat loss and declining biodiversity (in particular, destruction of mangrove swamps threatens natural fisheries); soil erosion; in rural areas, a majority of the population does not have access to potable water; toxic waste delivery from Taiwan sparked unrest in Kampong Saom (Sihanoukville) in December 1998

Environment—international agreements:
party to: Biodiversity, Climate Change, Desertification, Endangered Species, Marine Life Conservation, Ship Pollution, Tropical Timber 94 signed, but not ratified: Law of the Sea, Marine Dumping

Geography—note: a land of paddies and forests dominated by the Mekong River and Tonle Sap

PEOPLE

Population: 11,626,520

Age structure:
0-14 years: 45% (male 2,667,768; female 2,587,590)
15-64 years: 52% (male 2,821,772; female 3,197,604)
65 years and over: 3% (male 143,016; female 208,770)

Population growth rate: 2.49%
Birth rate: 41.05 births/1,000 population
Death rate: 16.2 deaths/1,000 population

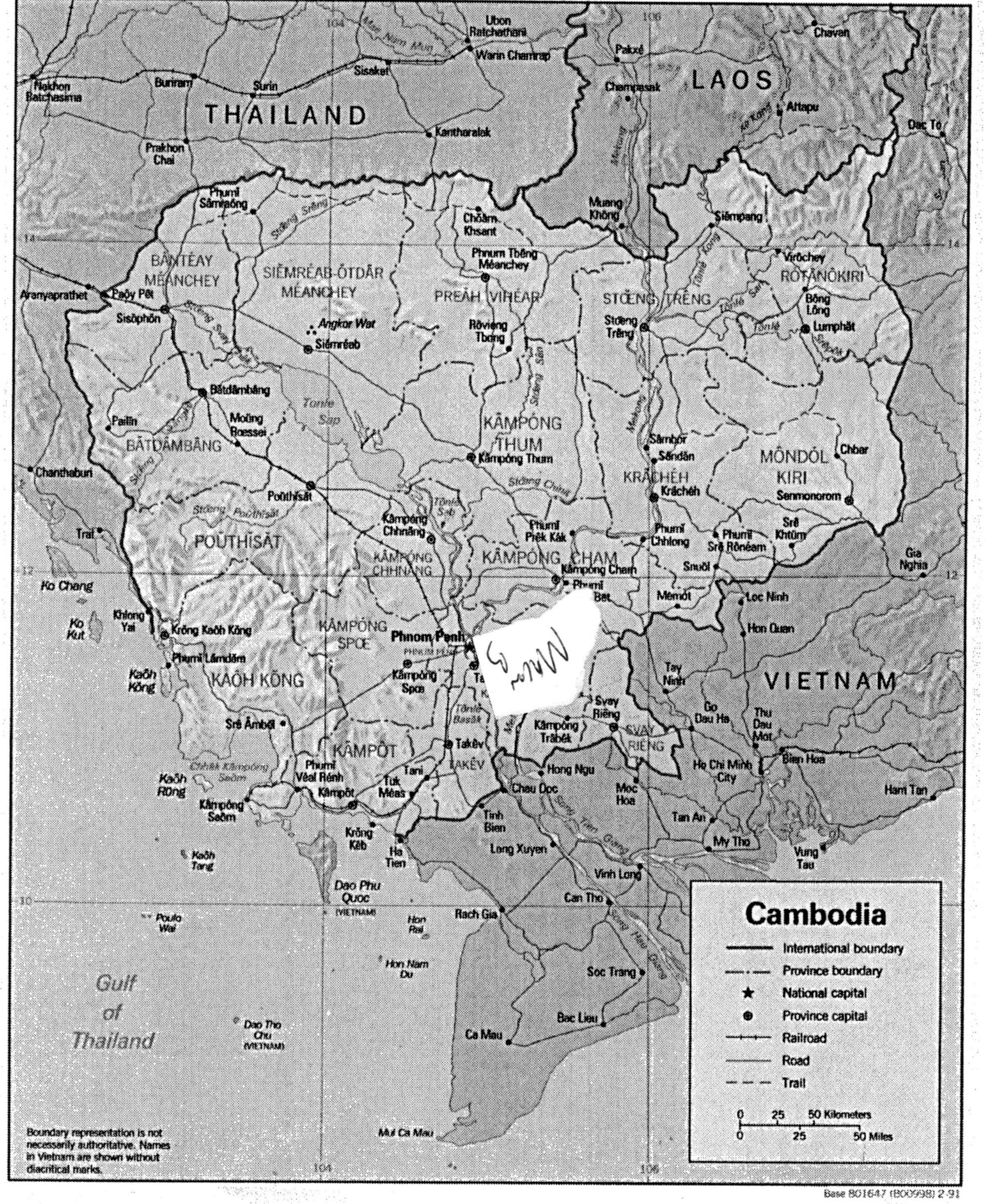
THAILAND
LAOS
VIETNAM
Cambodia
International boundary
Province boundary
National capital
Province capital
Railroad
Road
Trail
0 25 50 Kilometers
0 25 50 Miles
Boundary representation is not necessarily authoritative. Names in Vietnam are shown without diacritical marks.
Gulf of Thailand
Phnom Penh
Ubon Ratchathani
Warin Chamrap
Sisaket
Surin
Buriram
Nakhon Ratchasima
Pakxé
Champasak
Attapu
Chavan
Dac To
Kantharalak
Prakhon Chai
BANTÉAY MÉANCHEY
SIĔMRÉAB-ŎTDÂR MÉANCHEY
PREĂH VIHÉAR
STŒNG TRÊNG
RÔTÂNÔKIRI
Aranyaprathet
Paôy Pêt
Sisŏphŏn
Angkor Wat
Siĕmréab
Bătdâmbâng
Pailĭn
BĂTDÂMBÂNG
KÂMPÓNG THUM
Kâmpóng Thum
KRÂCHÉH
Krâchéh
MÔNDÓL KIRI
Senmonorom
Chanthaburi
Poŭthĭsăt
POŬTHĬSĂT
KÂMPÓNG CHHNĂNG
KÂMPÓNG CHAM
Kâmpóng Cham
Trat
Ko Chang
Ko Kut
Khlong Yai
Krŏng Kaôh Kŏng
KAÔH KŎNG
KÂMPÓNG SPŒ
Kâmpóng Spœ
Svay Riĕng
SVAY RIĔNG
KÂMPÔT
Kâmpôt
TAKÊV
Takêv
Srê Âmbĭl
Kâmpóng Saôm
Kaôh Rŏng
Kaôh Tang
Poulo Wai
Dao Phu Quoc
Hon Rai
Hon Nam Du
Dao Tho Chu
Mui Ca Mau
Ha Tien
Chau Doc
Hong Ngu
Long Xuyen
Rach Gia
Can Tho
Vinh Long
My Tho
Tan An
Ho Chi Minh City
Bien Hoa
Vung Tau
Ham Tan
Soc Trang
Bac Lieu
Ca Mau
Tay Ninh
Loc Ninh
Hon Quan
Gia Nghia
Mekong
Tonle Sap
Base 801647 (B00998) 2-91

Net migration rate: 0 migrant(s)/1,000 population

Sex ratio:
at birth: 1.05 male(s)/female
under 15 years: 1.03 male(s)/female
15-64 years: 0.88 male(s)/female
65 years and over: 0.69 male(s)/female
total population: 0.94 male(s)/female

Infant mortality rate: 105.06 deaths/1,000 live births

Life expectancy at birth:
total population: 48.24 years
male: 46.81 years
female: 49.75 years

Total fertility rate: 5.81 children born/woman
Nationality:
noun: Cambodian(s)
adjective: Cambodian

Ethnic groups: Khmer 90%, Vietnamese 5%, Chinese 1%, other 4%
Religions: Theravada Buddhism 95%, other 5%
Languages: Khmer (official), French

Literacy:
definition: age 15 and over can read and write
total population: 35%
male: 48%
female: 22% (1990 est.)

GOVERNMENT

Country name:
conventional long form: Kingdom of Cambodia
conventional short form: Cambodia
local long form: Preahreacheanachakr Kampuchea
local short form: Kampuchea

Data code: CB

Government type: multiparty liberal democracy under a constitutional monarchy established in September 1993

Capital: Phnom Penh

Administrative divisions: 20 provinces (khett, singular and plural) and 3 municipalities* (krong, singular and plural); Banteay Mean Cheay, Batdambang, Kampong Cham,

Kampong Chhnang, Kampong Spoe, Kampong Thum, Kampot, Kandal, Kaoh Kong, Keb*, Krachen, Mondol Kiri, Otdar Mean Cheay, Phnum Penh*, Pouthisat, Preah Seihanu* (Sihanoukville), Preah Vihear, Prey Veng, Rotanah Kiri, Siem Reab, Stoeng Treng, Svay Rieng, Takev
note: there may be a new municipality called Pailin

Independence: 9 November 1953 (from [illegible]nce)
National holiday: Independence Da[illegible]mber (1953)
Constitution: promulgated 21 Septe[illegible]

Legal system: primarily a civil law mi[illegible] of French-influenced codes from the United Nations Transitional Authority in Camb[illegible]ia (UNTAC) period, royal decrees, and acts of the legislature, with influences of customary law and remnants of communist legal theory; increasing influence of common law in recent years

Suffrage: 18 years of age; universal

Executive branch:

King	**Norodom SIHAMONI**
Pres., National Assembly	**Norodom RANARIDDH,** *Prince*
Prime Minister	**HUN SEN**
Dep. Prime Min.	**SAR KHENG**
Dep. Prime Min.	**Norodom SIRIVUDH,** *Prince*
Dep. Prime Min.	**SOK AN**
Dep. Prime Min.	**LU LAY SRENG**
Dep. Prime Min.	**TEA BANH**
Dep. Prime Min.	**HOR NAMHONG**
Dep. Prime Min.	**NHEK BUNCHHAY**
Min. of Agriculture, Forestry, & Fishing	**CHAN SARUN**
Min. in the Council of Ministers	**SOK AN**
Min. of Cults & Religious Affairs	**KHUN HAING**
Min. of Culture & Fine Arts	**Sisowath PANARA SIRIVUDH,** *Prince*
Min. of Economy & Finance	**KEAT CHHON**
Min. of Education, Youth, & Sport	**KOL PHENG**
Min. of Environment	**MOK MARET**
Min. of Foreign Affairs & Intl. Cooperation	**HOR NAMHONG**
Min. of Industry, Mines, & Energy	**SUY SEM**
Min. of Information	**KHIEU KANHARITH**
Co-Min. of Interior	**SAR KHENG**
Co-Min. of Interior	**Norodom SIRIVUDH,** *Prince*

Min. of Justice	**ANG VONG VATTANA**
Min. of Labor & Vocational Training	**NHEB BUN CHIN**
Min. of Land Management, Urbanization, & Construction	**IM CHHUN LIM**
Co-Min. of National Defense	**NHEK BUNCHHAY**
Co-Min. of National Defense	**TEA BANH,** *Gen.*
Min. of Planning	**CHHAY THAN**
Min. of Posts & Telecommunications	**SO KHUN**
Min. of Public Health	**NUTH SOKHOM**
Min. of Public Works & Transportation	**SUN CHANTHOL**
Min. of Relations With the National Assembly, Senate, & Inspection	**MEN SAM AN**
Min. of Rural Development	**LU LAY SRENG**
Min. of Social Affairs, War Veterans, & Youth Rehabilitation	**IT SAM-HENG**
Min. of Tourism	**LAY PROHAS**
Min. of Trade	**CHAM PRASIT**
Min. of Water Resources & Meteorology	**LIM KEAN-HAO**
Min. of Women's Affairs	**UNG KUNTHA PHAVY**
Governor, State Bank	**CHEA CHANTO**
Ambassador to the US	**ROLAND ENG**
Permanent Representative to the UN, New York	**CHEM WIDHYA**

Legislative branch: unicameral National Assembly (122 seats; members elected by popular vote to serve five-year terms)
elections: last held 26 July 1998 (next to be held NA 2003)
election results: percent of vote by party—CPP 41%, FUNCINPEC 32%, SRP 14%, other 13%; seats by party—CPP 64, FUNCINPEC 43, SRP 15
note: pursuant to the coalition agreement signed in November 1998, a Senate is being created and the legislature will thus become bicameral

Judicial branch: Supreme Council of the Magistracy, provided for in the constitution, was formed in December 1997; a Supreme Court and lower courts exercise judicial authority

Political parties and leaders: National United Front for an Independent, Neutral, Peaceful, and Cooperative Cambodia or FUNCINPEC [Prince NORODOM RANARIDDH]; Cambodian Pracheachon Party or Cambodian People's Party or CPP [CHEA SIM]; Sam Rangsi Party or SRP (formerly Khmer Nation Party or KNP) [SAM RANGSI]; Buddhist Liberal Party or BLP [IENG MOULY]; Populist Party [UNG HUOT]; Khmer Citizen Party or KCP [NGUON SOEUR]

International organization participation: ACCT, AsDB, ASEAN (observer), CP, ESCAP, FAO, G-77, IAEA, IBRD, ICAO, ICRM, IDA, IFAD, IFC, IFRCS, ILO, IMF, IMO, Intelsat (nonsignatory user), Interpol, IOC, ISO (subscriber), ITU, NAM, OPCW, PCA, UN, UNCTAD, UNESCO, UNIDO, UPU, WFTU, WHO, WIPO, WMO, WToO, WTrO (applicant)

Diplomatic representation in the US:
chief of mission: Ambassador VAR HUOTH
chancery: 4500 16th Street NW, Washington, DC 20011
telephone: [1] (202) 726-7742
FAX: [1] (202) 726-8381

Diplomatic representation from the US:
chief of mission: Ambassador Kenneth M. QUINN
embassy: 27 EO Street 240, Phnom Penh
mailing address: Box P, APO AP 96546
telephone: [855] (23) 216-436, 216-438
FAX: [855] (23) 216-811

Flag description: three horizontal bands of blue (top), red (double width), and blue with a white three-towered temple representing Angkor Wat outlined in black in the center of the red band

ECONOMY

Economy—overview: After four years of solid macroeconomic performance, Cambodia's economy slowed dramatically in 1997-98 due to the regional economic crisis, civil violence, and political infighting. Foreign investment fell off, and tourism has declined from 1996 levels. Also, in 1998 the main harvest was hit by drought. The long-term development of the economy after decades of war remains a daunting challenge. Human resource levels in the population are low, particularly in the poverty-ridden countryside. The almost total lack of basic infrastructure in the countryside will continue to hinder development. Recurring political instability and corruption within government discourage foreign investment and delay foreign aid. Even so, growth may resume in 1999 at, say, 2%.

GDP: purchasing power parity—$7.8 billion
GDP—real growth rate: 0%

GDP—per capita: purchasing power parity—$700

GDP—composition by sector:
agriculture: 51%
industry: 15%
services: 34% (1997 est.)

Population below poverty line: NA%

Household income or consumption by percentage share:
lowest 10%: NA%

highest 10%: NA%

Inflation rate (consumer prices): 15%
Labor force: 2.5 million to 3 million

Labor force—by occupation: agriculture 80% (1997 est.)
Unemployment rate: NA%

Budget:
revenues: $261 million
expenditures: $496 million, including capital expenditures of $NA

Industries: rice milling, fishing, wood and wood products, rubber, cement, gem mining, textiles

Industrial production growth rate: 7%
Electricity—production: 195 million kWh (1996)

Electricity—production by source:
fossil fuel: 61.54%
hydro: 38.46%
nuclear: 0%
other: 0% (1996)

Electricity—consumption: 195 million kWh (1996)
Electricity—exports: 0 kWh (1996)
Electricity—imports: 0 kWh (1996)
Agriculture—products: rice, rubber, corn, vegetables
Exports: $736 million (f.o.b.)
Exports—commodities: timber, garments, rubber, soybeans, sesame
Exports—partners: Singapore, Japan, Thailand, Hong Kong, Indonesia, Malaysia, US
Imports: $1.1 billion (f.o.b
Imports—commodities: cigarettes, gold, construction materials, petroleum products, machinery, motorvehicles
Imports—partners: Singapore, Vietnam, Japan, Australia, Hong Kong, Indonesia, Thailand
Debt—external: $2.2 billion
Economic aid—recipient: $569.8 million
Currency: 1 new riel (CR) = 100 sen
Exchange rates: riels (CR) per US$1—3,772.0 (January 1999), 3,744.4 (1998), 2,946.3 (1997), 2,624.1 (1996), 2,450.8 (1995), 2,545.3 (1994)
Fiscal year: calendar year

COMMUNICATIONS

Telephones: 20,000 (est.)

Telephone system: adequate landline and/or cellular service in Phnom Penh and other provincial cities; rural areas have little telephone service

domestic: NA international: adequate but expensive landline and cellular service available to all countries from Phnom Penh and major provincial cities; satellite earth station—1 Intersputnik (Indian Ocean Region)
Radio broadcast stations: AM 7, FM 3, shortwave 3
Television broadcast stations: 1 government-operated station and four commercial stations broadcasting to Phnom Penh and major provincial cities via relay
Televisions: 800,000

TRANSPORTATION

RAILWAYS:

total: 603 km
narrow gauge: 603 km 1.000-m gauge

Highways:
total: 35,769 km
paved: 4,165 km
unpaved: 31,604 km (1997 est.)

Waterways: 3,700 km navigable all year to craft drawing 0.6 m; 282 km navigable to craft drawing 1.8 m

Ports and harbors: Kampong Saom (Sihanoukville), Kampot, Krong Kaoh Kong, Phnom Penh

Merchant marine:
total: 141 ships (1,000 GRT or over) totaling 598,867 GRT/841,240 DWT
ships by type: barge carrier 1, bulk 16, cargo 108, container 4, livestock carrier 2, multifunctional large-load carrier 1, oil tankers 1, refrigerated cargo 4, roll-on/roll-off cargo 4 note: a flag of convenience registry; includes ships of 8 countries: Aruba 1, Cyprus 7, Egypt 1, South Korea 1, Malta 1, Panama 1, Russia 5, Singapore 1

Airports: 20

Airports—with paved runways:
total: 7
2,438 to 3,047 m: 2
1,524 to 2,437 m: 2
914 to 1,523 m: 3

Airports—with unpaved runways:
total: 13
1,524 to 2,437 m: 3
914 to 1,523 m: 10

Heliports: 3

MILITARY

Military branches: Royal Cambodian Armed Forces (RCAF)—created in 1993 by the merger of the Cambodian People's Armed Forces and the two noncommunist resistance armies
note: there are also resistance forces comprised of the Khmer Rouge (also known as the National United Army or NUA) and a separate royalist resistance movement
Military manpower—military age: 18 years of age
Military manpower—availability:
males age 15-49: 2,562,112
Military manpower—fit for military service:
males age 15-49: 1,428,523
Military manpower—reaching military age annually:
males: 119,839
Military expenditures—dollar figure: $85.3 million
Military expenditures—percent of GDP: 2.4%

TRANSNATIONAL ISSUES

Disputes—international: offshore islands and sections of the boundary with Vietnam are in dispute; maritime boundary with Vietnam not defined; parts of border with Thailand are indefinite; maritime boundary with Thailand not clearly defined

Illicit drugs: transshipment site for Golden Triangle heroin; possible money laundering; narcotics-related corruption reportedly involving some in the government, military, and police; possible small-scale opium, heroin, and amphetamine production; large producer of cannabis for the international market.

NARCOTICS

Cambodia is not a major producer of narcotics or a center for narcotics-derived money laundering, although reports that narcotics proceeds are in fact laundered there persist. Huge amounts of marijuana are cultivated for export, reportedly in Koh Kong, Preah Vihear, Banteay Meanchey, Kampong Cham, Kratie, and Stung Treng provinces. Marijuana production and trafficking is not thought to have a major effect on the U.S. The country's principal involvement in the international narcotics trade is as a transit route for Southeast Asian heroin to overseas markets, including the United States. There are numerous reports that narcotics traffickers, alien smugglers, and other criminals have found refuge in Cambodia. Corruption and factionalism among Cambodia's police is also a continuing problem. One police unit attacked another earlier this year in an effort to intimidate the unit attacked.

Outward cooperation by Cambodian police officials with the Drug Enforcement Agency (DEA) however is excellent. Senior Government officials consistently responded to U.S. requests to make available persons wanted on U.S. arrest warrants, including in narcotics cases. The Royal Government of Cambodia (RGC) has established a National Authority for Combating Drugs (NACD) and a special drug enforcement unit in the Ministry of Interior, however; the effectiveness of these bodies has been limited by a lack of resources and training, corruption at various levels of the RGC, the country's geographical location adjacent to major narcotics producing areas, and involvement by some elements of the Royal Cambodian Armed Forces (RCAF) and the national police in narcotics trafficking. While there were several high profile arrests of narcotics traffickers in 1998,including one of two American citizens and another of an active-duty RCAF officer, the number of arrests and seizures fell off from 1997 levels. Cambodia is taking steps to become a party to the 1988 UN Drug Convention.

STATUS OF COUNTRY

Cambodia is not a major poppy producing country and, with no known heroin production, is not a major importer of precursor chemicals. Since Cambodia has only a small drug abuse problem and no indigenous chemical industry, it is also unlikely to become a major producer of amphetamines or other manufactured illegal drugs. consequently, chemical control is a low priority. Marijuana is grown in Cambodia, some for domestic consumption, but in large part for export. There is no accurate estimate of the amount of land committed to marijuana production.
Cambodia shares borders with Thailand, Laos and Vietnam and lies near the major trafficking routes for Southeast Asian heroin. The country's recently-formed enforcement agencies have very few resources, and generally lack even basic training in law enforcement techniques and drug enforcement measures, including drug identification.

The country's geographical location and the lack of funds for training and operations make Cambodia a vulnerable target for drug traffickers and money launderers operating in Southeast Asia.Anecdotal evidence and reports of seizures by the Cambodian authorities suggest that Cambodia is a viable trafficking route and may be emerging as a magnet for ethnic Chinese groups involved in drug trafficking, money laundering, and alien smuggling. However, little reliable information exists about the extent of money laundering in Cambodia, although most observers do not believe it is a major money-laundering center.

COUNTRY ACTIONS AGAINST DRUGS

Policy Initiatives. In 1998, the senior levels of the RGC were preoccupied with responding to political instability stemming from the July 1997 factional fighting and the July 26, 1998 national elections and political demonstrations that followed. Few major policy initiatives in any area were undertaken by the RGC in 1998, including narcotics control. Nonetheless, in 1998 the RGC translated into Khmer and forwarded to the Council of Ministers one of the two UN Drug Conventions it has not yet signed, and at year's end was searching for funds to have the remaining convention translated (translation into Khmer is a legal prerequisite for RGC action). Senior RGC officials remained committed to securing Cambodia's accession to all three UN conventions as soon as possible, and the NACD became operational for the first time, albeit with very thin resources.

Prior to the July 1997 factional fighting and the resulting political instability, the RGC made strides toward effective control of drug trafficking and transiting in Cambodia. In December 1996, the national assembly passed a comprehensive counter-narcotics law which was drafted with UNDCP assistance and advice and reviewed by the Departments of State and Justice. The law includes anti-money laundering provisions. Passage of the law has provided the police and the courts, previously hamstrung by lack of comprehensive legislation, with the legal basis to operate more effectively against narcotics traffickers. There have been no prosecutions for money laundering, and money laundering continues to be reported in Cambodia. There is unlikely to be any change in this situation, until the government takes steps to enforce the anti-money laundering legislation already in place. A second significant step towards controlling narcotics trafficking in Cambodia was the formation of a special, 40-person national anti-drug unit to replace the existing national anti-narcotics unit of the national police.

Accomplishments. In 1998, the National Bank of Cambodia strengthened its oversight of banks operating in Cambodia, for the first time suspending the license of a bank, which failed to meet regulatory requirements. Cambodian authorities also continued to cooperate with visits by U.S. drug enforcement agency officials based in Bangkok, including in the case of an arrest of marijuana traffickers and seizure of marijuana. However, as noted above, Cambodia's continuing political instability during the year slowed legal reform and blunted enforcement efforts.

Law Enforcement Efforts. Cambodian enforcement authorities have focused their efforts on heroin trafficking and the eradication of domestic marijuana, as well as the import and sale of "ecstasy" and methamphetamine. In 1998, authorities continued to target trafficking organizations rather than individuals, and maintained their policy of readily sharing intelligence and requests for assistance. According to figures supplied by the NACD, 34 individuals were arrested in 1998 for narcotics related crimes, down from 101 in 1997 but equal to the 34 persons arrested in 1996. The NACD reported seizing8,560 kilograms of marijuana, 1.3 kilograms of heroin, and 4.05 kilograms of opium in 1998, all of which were lower than the amounts seized in 1997. There were two high profile drug enforcement actions in 1998, one against two American citizens and a Thai citizen who were attempting to traffic a large quantity of marijuana from Koh Kong province, and one against an active-duty RCAF officer who was involved in heroin smuggling.

Corruption. While no new high-level corruption cases were exposed publicly in 1998, the arrest of the RCAF officer described above continued the government's apparent effort to identify and target corrupt military and police officials involved in drug trafficking. Clearly, though, corruption remains an important factor in the misuse of Cambodia by criminal elements.

Agreements and Treaties. In 1998, Cambodia took steps to become a party to the 1988 UN Drug Convention and the other two major UN drug treaties. While formal extradition cooperation with the U.S. in narcotics-related cases is not possible since there is no extradition treaty, senior Cambodian authorities have consistently responded positively to requests by the United States to render persons facing arrest warrants, including warrants issued in narcotics cases.

Cultivation/Production. As noted above, significant amounts of marijuana are grown in Cambodia, although estimates of the amount of land under cultivation vary widely, and there is no reliable basis for concluding that it equals or exceeds 5000 hectares. Government authorities and most outside observers do not believe that opium poppy is cultivated in Cambodia. With the exception of a laboratory reportedly producing amphetamines in Koh Kong province, drugs such as heroin, cocaine, and "ecstasy" are not believed to be produced in the country. Domestic narcotics use is not a major problem, although anecdotal evidence suggests that narcotics use by foreigners is significant. Abuse of pharmaceutical drugs, which are not presently regulated in an effective manner, is common in Phnom Penh. Non-governmental organizations operate a few small demand reduction programs targeted at street children and other "at-risk" children.

UNITED STATES POLICY INITIATIVES AND PROGRAMS

Bilateral Cooperation. All U.S. Government non-humanitarian assistance to the Cambodian Government, including in the anti-narcotics area, was frozen after the July 1997 factional fighting. Hopes last year that a elections would quickly produce a new coalition government which would focus on narcotics and crime issues proved to be premature. A new coalition government resulted from the elections, but only after another year passed without adequate government attention to Cambodia's pressing crime and narcotics problems. As a result, a drug-testing laboratory funded by the Department of State and delivered to Cambodia in 1997 could not be turned over to the RGC during 1998, and the technician trained to operate the laboratory was forced to find employment elsewhere.

Despite the restrictions on U.S. assistance, the RCG continues to welcome bilateral cooperation with DEA and other U.S. Government agencies. DEA personnel continued to visit Cambodia regularly in 1998 and received excellent cooperation from the RGC. The U.S. Embassy in Phnom Penh accepted a number of drug samples from the RGC for transport to the U.S. for identification and analysis by the DEA. The RCG continued cooperation with its neighbors in Southeast Asia by attending regional conferences, and a representative from the Cambodian Embassy in Thailand attended the opening of the International Law Enforcement Academy (ILEA) in Bangkok at the invitation of Thailand.

The Road Ahead. After nearly 18 months of political turmoil in Cambodia, a new broad-based coalition government has been formed, following elections held on November 30, 1998. The new government, like its predecessor, is headed by Prime Minister Hun Sen. With the establishment of the new government, the U.S. is reviewing its restrictions on non-humanitarian assistance to the RGC. Besides establishing the drug testing laboratory and resuming training activities, there is a critical need for a policy dialogue on counternarcotics issues with the RGC, perhaps in conjunction with the UN Drug Control Program. Establishment of the new government may also make possible more rapid progress on ratifying the applicable UN conventions on illicit drugs and modifying existing narcotics laws and regulations, especially the expansion of the list of illicit narcotics as well as the strengthening of enforcement of money laundering legislation.

GEOGRAPHY AND NATURE

Cambodia covers 181,040 square kilometers in the southwestern part of the Indochina peninsula. It lies completely within the tropics; its southernmost points are only slightly more than 10° above the equator. Roughly square in shape, the ountry is bounded on the north by Thailand and by Laos, on the east and southeast by Vietnam, and on the west by the Gulf of Thailand and by Thailand. Much of the country's area consists of rolling plains. Dominant features are the large, almost centrally located, Tonle Sap (Great Lake) and the Mekong River, which traverses the country from north to south.

The climate is monsoonal and has marked wet and dry seasons of relatively equal length. Both temperature and humidity generally are high throughout the year. Forest covers about two-thirds of the country, but it has been somewhat degraded in the more readily accessible areas by burning (a method called slash-and-burn agriculture), and by shifting agriculture.

TOPOGRAPHY

Cambodia falls within several well-defined geographic regions. The largest part of the country-about 75 percent of the total- consists of the Tonle Sap Basin and the Mekong Lowlands. To the southeast of this great basin is the Mekong Delta, which extends through Vietnam to the South China Sea. The basin and delta regions are rimmed with mountain ranges to the southwest (the Cardamom Mountains the Elephant Range) and to the north (Dangrek Mountains). Higher land to the northeast and to the east merges into the Central Highlands of southern Vietnam.

The Tonle Sap Basin-Mekong Lowlands region consists chiefly of plains with elevations generally of less than 100 meters. As the elevation increases, the terrain becomes more rolling and dissected.

The Cardamom Mountains in the southwest, oriented generally in a northwest-southeast direction, rise to more than 1,500 meters. The highest mountain in Cambodia-Phnom Aural, at 1,771 meters-is in the eastern part of this range. The Elephant Range, an extension running toward the south and the southeast from the Cardamom Mountains, rises to elevations of between 500 and 1,000 meters. These two ranges are bordered on the west by a narrow coastal plain that contains Kampong Saom Bay, which faces the Gulf of Thailand. This area was largely isolated until the opening of the port of Kampong Saom (formerly called Sihanoukville) and the construction of a road and railroad connecting Kampong Saom, Kampot, Takev, and Phnom Penh in the 1960s.

The Dangrek Mountains at the northern rim of the Tonle Sap Basin consist of a steep escarpment with an average elevation of about 500 meters, the highest points of which reach more than 700 meters. The escarpment faces southward and is the southern edge of the Korat Plateau in Thailand. The watershed along the escarpment marks the boundary between Thailand and Cambodia. The main road through a pass in the Dangrek Mountains at O Smach connects northwestern Cambodia with Thailand. Despite this road and those running through a few other passes, in general the escarpment impedes easy communication between the two countries. Between the western part of the Dangrek and the northern part of the Cardamom ranges, however, lies an extension of the Tonle Sap Basin that merges into lowlands in Thailand, which allows easy access from the border to Bangkok.

The Mekong Valley, which offers a communication route between Cambodia and Laos, separates the eastern end of the Dangrek Mountains and the northeastern highlands. To the southeast, the basin joins the Mekong Delta, which, extending into Vietnam, provides both water and land communications between the two countries.

CLIMATE

Cambodia's climate-like that of the rest of Southeast Asia-is dominated by the monsoons, which are known as tropical wet and dry because of the distinctly marked seasonal differences. The monsoonal airflows are caused by annual alternating high pressure and low pressure over the Central Asian landmass. In summer, moisture-laden air-the southwest monsoon-is drawn landward from the Indian Ocean. The flow is reversed during the winter, and the northeast monsoon sends back dry air.

The southwest monsoon brings the rainy season from mid-May to mid-September or to early October, and the northeast monsoon flow of drier and cooler air lasts from early November to March. The southern third of the country has a two-month dry season; the northern two-thirds, a four-month one. Short transitional periods, which are marked by some difference in humidity but by little change in temperature, intervene between the alternating seasons. Temperatures are fairly uniform throughout the Tonle Sap Basin area, with only small variations from the average annual mean of around 25°C.

The maximum mean is about 28°C; the minimum mean, about 22°C. Maximum temperatures of higher than 32°C, however, are common and, just before the start of the rainy season, they may rise to more than 38°C. Minimum temperatures rarely fall below 10°C. January is the coldest month, and April is the warmest. Typhoons-tropical cyclones-that often devastate coastal Vietnam rarely cause damage in Cambodia.

The total annual rainfall average is between 100 and 150 centimeters, and the heaviest amounts fall in the southeast. Rainfall from April to September in the Tonle Sap Basin-Mekong Lowlands area averages 130 to 190 centimeters annually, but the amount varies considerably from year to year. Rainfall around the basin increases with elevation.

It is heaviest in the mountains along the coast in the southwest, which receive from 250 to more than 500 centimeters of precipitation annually as the southwest monsoon reaches the coast. This area of greatest rainfall, however, drains mostly to the sea; only a small quantity goes into the rivers flowing into the basin. The relative humidity is high at night throughout the year; usually it exceeds 90 percent. During the daytime in the dry season, humidity averages about 50 percent or slightly lower, but it may remain about 60 percent in the rainy period.

DRAINAGE

Except for the smaller rivers in the southeast, most of the major rivers and river systems in Cambodia drain into the Tonle Sap or into the Mekong River. The Cardamom Mountains and Elephant Range form a separate drainage divide. To the east the rivers flow into the Tonle Sap, while on the west they flow into the Gulf of Thailand. Toward the southern end of the Elephant Mountains, however, because of the topography, some small rivers flow southward on the eastern side of the divide.

The Mekong River in Cambodia flows southward from the CambodiaLaos border to a point below Kracheh city, where it turns west for about 50 kilometers and then turns southwest to Phnom Penh. Extensive rapids run above Kracheh city. From Kampong Cham the gradient slopes very gently, and inundation of areas along the river occurs at flood stage-June through November-through breaks in the natural levees that have built up along its course. At Phnom Penh four major water courses meet at a point called the Chattomukh (Four Faces). The Mekong River flows in from the northeast and the Tonle Sab-a river emanating from the Tonle Sap-flows in from the northwest. They divide into two parallel channels, the Mekong River proper and the Basak River, and flow independently through
the delta areas of Cambodia and Vietnam to the South China Sea.

The flow of water into the Tonle Sab is seasonal. In September or in October, the flow of the Mekong River, fed by monsoon rains, increases to a point where its outlets through the delta cannot handle the enormous volume of water. At this point, the water pushes northward up the Tonle Sab and empties into the Tonle Sap, thereby increasing the size of the lake from about 2,590 square kilometers to about 24,605 square kilometers at the height of the flooding. After the Mekong's waters crest-when its downstream channels can handle the volume of
water-the flow reverses, and water flows out of the engorged lake.

As the level of the Tonle Sap retreats, it deposits a new layer of sediment. The annual flooding, combined with poor drainage immediately around the lake, transforms the surrounding area into marshlands unusable for agricultural
purposes during the dry season. The sediment deposited into the lake during the Mekong's flood stage appears to be greater than the quantity carried away later by the Tonle Sab River. Gradual silting of the lake would seem to be occurring; during low-water level, it is only about 1.5 meters deep, while at flood stage it is between 10 and 15 meters deep.

HISTORY

HISTORICAL PROFILE

1865 Cambodia was made a French Protectorate.

1954 Independence declared.

1970-75 Civil war and intensive American bombing caused widespread destruction.

1975-79 Under the Khmer Rouge regime more than one million people were killed and towns and industry destroyed.

1979 The Khmer Rouge were ejected by a Vietnamese invasion in January.

1989 Vietnam claimed to have withdrawn its remaining troops from the country.

1991 The signing of a peace agreement in October brought to an end 13 years of civil war.

1993 UN organised elections held in May. The Cambodian National Unity Party (Khmer Rouge) guerrilla group boycotted the poll. On 16 June, the two main parties, United National Front for an Independent, Neutral, Peaceful and Co-operative Cambodia (Funcinpec) and Cambodian People's Party (Kanakpak Pracheachon Kâmpuchéa (KPK), agreed on a joint government under which they would share power. On 21 September, parliament adopted a new democratic constitution signalling the end of the US$2 billion United Nations peace-keeping mandate and the return to the throne of King Norodom Sihanouk.

1997 In July, Second Prime Minister Hun Sen (KPK) seized power, removing First Prime Minister Prince Norodom Ranariddh (Funcinpec) from office, in a move condemned by the international community.

1998 The KPK, led by Hun Sen, won the July elections, but the opposition parties objected saying the election was fraudulent. A coalition government was formed with Funcinpec in November.

ANCIENT HISTORY AND EARLY KINGDOMS

Archaeological evidence indicates that parts of the region now called Cambodia were inhabited during the first and second millennia B.C. by peoples having a Neolithic culture. By the first century A.D., the inhabitants had developed relatively stable, organized societies, which had far surpassed the primitive stage in culture and technical skills. The most advanced groups lived along the coast and in the lower Mekong River valley and delta regions, where they cultivated irrigated rice and kept domesticated animals.

Scholars believe that these people may have been Austroasiatic in origin and related to the ancestors of the groups who now inhabit insular Southeast Asia and many of the islands of the Pacific Ocean. They worked metals, including both iron and bronze, and possessed navigational skills. Mon-Khmer people, who arrived at a later date, probably intermarried with them. The Khmer who now populate Cambodia may have migrated from southeastern China to the Indochinese Peninsula before the first century A.D. They are believed to have arrived before their present Vietnamese, Thai, and Lao neighbors.

EARLY INDIANIZED KINGDOM OF FUNAN

At about the time that the ancient peoples of Western Europe were absorbing the classical culture and institutions of the Mediterranean, the peoples of mainland and insular Southeast Asia were responding to the stimulus of a civilization that had arisen in northern India during the previous millennium. The Britons, Gauls, and Iberians experienced Mediterranean influences directly, through conquest by and incorporation into the Roman Empire. In contrast, the Indianization of Southeast Asia was a slower process than the Romanization of Europe because there was no period of direct Indian rule and because land and sea barriers that separated the region from the Indian subcontinent are considerable. Nevertheless, Indian religion, political thought, literature, mythology, and artistic motifs gradually became integral elements in local Southeast Asian cultures. The caste system never was adopted, but Indianization stimulated the rise of highly-organized, centralized states.

Funan, the earliest of the Indianized states, generally is considered by Cambodians to have been the first Khmer kingdom in the area. Founded in the first century A.D., Funan was located on the lower reaches of the Mekong River in the delta area. Its capital, Vyadhapura, probably was located near the present-day town of Phumi Banam in Prey Veng Province. The earliest historical reference to Funan is a Chinese description of a mission that visited the country in the third century A.D. The name Funan derives from the Chinese rendition of the old Khmer word bnam (meaning mountain). What the Funanese called themselves, however, is not known.

During this early period in Funan's history, the population was probably concentrated in villages along the Mekong River and along the Tonle Sab River below the Tonle Sap. Traffic and communications were mostly waterborne on the rivers and their delta tributaries. The area was a natural region for the development of an economy based on fishing and rice cultivation. There is considerable evidence that the Funanese economy depended on rice surpluses produced by an extensive inland irrigation system. Maritime trade also played an extremely important role in the development of Funan. The remains of what is believed to have been the kingdom's main port, Oc Eo (now part of Vietnam), contain Roman as well as Persian, Indian, and Greek artifacts.

By the fifth century A.D., the state exercised control over the lower Mekong River area and the lands around the Tonle Sap. It also commanded tribute from smaller states in the area now comprising northern Cambodia, southern

Laos, southern Thailand, and the northern portion of the Malay Peninsula.

Indianization was fostered by increasing contact with the subcontinent through the travels of merchants, diplomats, and learned Brahmans (Hindus of the highest caste traditionally assigned to the priesthood). Indian immigrants, believed to have arrived in the fourth and the fifth centuries, accelerated the process. By the fifth century, the elite culture was thoroughly Indianized. Court ceremony and the structure of political institutions were based on Indian models. The Sanskrit language was widely used; the laws of Manu, the Indian legal code, were adopted; and an alphabet based on Indian writing systems was introduced.

Funan reached its zenith in the fifth century A.D.. Beginning in the early sixth century, civil wars and dynastic strife undermined Funan's stability, making it relatively easy prey to incursions by hostile neighbors. By the end of the seventh century, a northern neighbor, the kingdom of Chenla, had reduced Funan to a vassal state.

THE SUCCESSOR STATE OF CHENLA

The people of Chenla also were Khmer. Once they established control over Funan, they embarked on a course of conquest that continued for three centuries. They subjugated central and upper Laos, annexed portions of the Mekong Delta, and brought what are now western Cambodia and southern Thailand under their direct control.

The royal families of Chenla intermarried with their Funanese counterparts and generally preserved the earlier political, social, and religious institutions of Funan. In the eighth century A.D., however, factional disputes at the Chenla court resulted in the splitting of the kingdom into rival northern and southern halves. According to Chinese chronicles, the two parts were known as Land (or Upper) Chenla and Water (or Lower) Chenla. Land Chenla maintained a relatively stable existence, but Water Chenla underwent a period of constant turbulence.

Late in the eighth century A.D., Water Chenla was subjected to attacks by pirates from Java, Sumatra, and the Malay Peninsula. By the beginning of the ninth century, it had apparently become a vassal of the Sailendra dynasty of Java. The last of the Water Chenla kings allegedly was killed around A.D. 790 by a Javanese monarch whom he had offended. The ultimate victor in the strife that followed was the ruler of a small Khmer state located north of the Mekong Delta. His assumption of the throne as Jayavarman II (ca. A.D. 802-50) marked the liberation of the Khmer people from Javanese suzerainty and the beginning of a unified Khmer nation.

THE ANGKORIAN PERIOD

The Angkorian period lasted from the early ninth century to the early fifteenth century A.D. In terms of cultural accomplishments and political power, this was the golden age of Khmer civilization. The great temple cities of the Angkorian region, located near the modern town of Siemreab, are a lasting monument to the greatness of Jayavarman II's

successors. (Even the Khmer Rouge, who looked on most of their country's past history and traditions with hostility, adopted a stylized Angkorian temple for the flag of Democratic Kampuchea. A similar motif is found in the flag of the PRK). The kingdom founded by Jayavarman II also gave modern-day Cambodia, or Kampuchea, its name. During the early ninth to the mid-fifteenth centuries, it was known as Kambuja, originally the
name of an early north Indian state, from which the current forms of the name have been derived.

Possibly to put distance between himself and the seaborne Javanese, Jayavarman II settled north of the Tonle Sap. He built several capitals before establishing one, Hariharalaya, near the site where the Angkorian complexes were built. Indravarman I (A.D. 877-89) extended Khmer control as far west as the Korat Plateau in Thailand, and he ordered the construction of a huge reservoir north of the capital to provide irrigation for wet rice cultivation. His son,
Yasovarman I (A.D. 889-900), built the Eastern Baray (reservoir or tank), evidence of which remains to the present time. Its dikes, which may be seen today, are more than 6 kilometers long and 1.6 kilometers wide. The elaborate
system of canals and reservoirs built under Indravarman I and his successors were the key to Kambuja's prosperity for half a millennium. By freeing cultivators from dependence on unreliable seasonal monsoons, they made possible
an early "green revolution" that provided the country with large surpluses of rice. Kambuja's decline during the thirteenth and fourteenth centuries probably was hastened by the deterioration of the irrigation system. Attacks by Thai and other foreign peoples and the internal discord caused by dynastic rivalries diverted human resources from the system's upkeep, and it gradually fell into disrepair.

Suryavarman II (1113-50), one of the greatest Angkorian monarchs, expanded his kingdom's territory in a series of successful wars against the kingdom of Champa in central Vietnam, the kingdom of Nam Viet in northern Vietnam,
and the small Mon polities as far west as the Irrawaddy River of Burma. He reduced to vassalage the Thai peoples who had migrated into Southeast Asia from the Yunnan region of southern China and established his suzerainty over
the northern part of the Malay Peninsula. His greatest achievement was the construction of the temple city complex of Angkor Wat. The largest religious edifice in the world, Angkor Wat is considered the greatest single architectural
work in Southeast Asia. Suryavarman II's reign was followed, however, by thirty years of dynastic upheaval and an invasion by the neighboring Cham, who destroyed the city of Angkor in 1177.

The Cham ultimately were driven out and conquered by Jayavarman VII, whose reign (1181-ca. 1218) marked the apogee of Kambuja's power. Unlike his predecessors, who had adopted the cult of the Hindu god-king, Jayavarman
VII was a fervent patron of Mahayana Buddhism. Casting himself as a bodhisattva, he embarked on a frenzy of building activity that included the Angkor Thom complex and the Bayon, a remarkable temple whose stone towers depict 216 faces of buddhas, gods, and kings. He also built over 200 rest houses and hospitals throughout his kingdom. Like the Roman emperors, he maintained a system of roads between his capital and provincial towns. According to historian George Coedès, "No other Cambodian king can

claim to have moved so much stone." Often, quality suffered for the sake of size and rapid construction, as is revealed in the intriguing but poorly constructed Bayon.

Carvings show that everyday Angkorian buildings were wooden structures not much different from those found in Cambodia today. The impressive stone buildings were not used as residences by members of the royal family.
Rather, they were the focus of Hindu or Buddhist cults that celebrated the divinity, or buddhahood, of the monarch and his family. Coedès suggests that they had the dual function of both temple and tomb. Typically, their dimensions reflected the structure of the Hindu mythological universe. For example, five towers at the center of the Angkor Wat complex represent the peaks of Mount Meru, the center of the universe; an outer wall represents the mountains that ring the world's edge; and a moat depicts the cosmic ocean. Like many other ancient edifices, the monuments of the Angkorian region absorbed vast reserves of resources and human labor and their purpose remains shrouded in mystery.

Angkorian society was strictly hierarchical. The king, regarded as divine, owned both the land and his subjects. Immediately below the monarch and the royal family were the Brahman priesthood and a small class of officials, who numbered about 4,000 in the tenth century. Next were the commoners, who were burdened with heavy corvée (forced labor) duties. There was also a large slave class that, like the nameless multitudes of ancient Egypt, built the enduring monuments.

After Jayavarman VII's death, Kambuja entered a long period of decline that led to its eventual disintegration. The Thai were a growing menace on the empire's western borders. The spread of Theravada Buddhism, which came to Kambuja from Sri Lanka by way of the Mon kingdoms, challenged the royal Hindu and Mahayana Buddhist cults. Preaching austerity and the salvation of the individual through his or own her efforts, Theravada Buddhism did not lend doctrinal support to a society ruled by an opulent royal establishment maintained through the virtual slavery of the masses.

In 1353 a Thai army captured Angkor. It was recaptured by the Khmer, but wars continued and the capital was looted several times. During the same period, Khmer territory north of the present Laotian border was lost to the Lao kingdom of Lan Xang. In 1431 the Thai captured Angkor Thom. Thereafter, the Angkorian region did not again encompass a royal capital, except for a brief period in the third quarter of the sixteenth century.

CAMBODIA'S STRUGGLE FOR SURVIVAL, 1432-1887

The more than four centuries that passed from the abandonment of Angkor around the mid-fifteenth century to the establishment of a protectorate under the French in 1863 are considered by historians to be Cambodia's "dark ages," a period of economic, social, and cultural stagnation when the kingdom's internal affairs came increasingly under the control of its aggressive neighbors, the Thai and the Vietnamese. By the mid-nineteenth century, Cambodia had become an almost helpless pawn in the power struggles between Thailand and Vietnam and probably would have been completely absorbed by one or the other if France had not intervened, giving Cambodia a colonially dominated "lease on life."

Fear of racial and cultural extinction has persisted as a major theme in modern Cambodian thought and helps to explain the intense nationalism and xenophobia of the Khmer Rouge during the 1970s. Establishment in 1979 of the People's Republic of Kampuchea, a Vietnamese-dominated satellite state, can be seen as the culmination of a process of Vietnamese encroachment that was already well under way by the seventeenth century.

The process of internal decay and foreign encroachment was gradual rather than precipitous and was hardly evident in the fifteenth century when the Khmer were still powerful. Following the fall of Angkor Thom, the Cambodian court abandoned the region north of the Tonle Sap, never to return except for a brief interlude in the late sixteenth century. By this time however, the Khmer penchant for monument building had ceased. Older faiths such as Mahayana Buddhism and the Hindu cult of the god-king had been supplanted by Theravada Buddhism, and the Cambodians had become part of the same religious and cultural cosmos as the Thai. This similarity did not prevent intermittent warfare between the two kingdoms, however. During the sixteenth century Cambodian armies, taking advantage of Thai troubles with the Burmese, invaded the Thai kingdom several times.

In the meantime, following the abandonment of the Angkorian sites, the Khmer established a new capital several hundred kilometers to the southeast on the site of what is now Phnom Penh. This new center of power was located at the confluence of the Mekong and the Tonle Sab rivers. Thus, it controlled the river commerce of the Khmer heartland and the Laotian kingdoms and had access, by way of the Mekong Delta, to the international trade routes that linked the China coast, the South China Sea, and the Indian Ocean.

A new kind of state and society emerged, more open to the outside world and more dependent on commerce as a source of wealth than its inland predecessor. The growth of maritime trade with China during the Ming dynasty (1368-1644) provided lucrative opportunities for members of the Cambodian elite who controlled royal trading monopolies. The appearance of Europeans in the region in the sixteenth century also stimulated commerce.

King Ang Chan (1516-66), one of the few great Khmer monarchs of the post-Angkorian period, moved the capital from Phnom Penh to Lovek. Portuguese and Spanish travelers who visited the city, located on the banks of the Tonle Sab, a river north of Phnom Penh, described it as a place of fabulous wealth. The products traded there included precious stones, metals, silk and cotton, incense, ivory, lacquer, livestock (including elephants), and rhinoceros horn (prized by the Chinese as a rare and potent medicine). By the late sixteenth and early seventeenth centuries, Lovek contained flourishing foreign trading communities of Chinese, Indonesians, Malays, Japanese, Arabs, Spanish, and Portuguese. They were joined later in the century by the English and the Dutch.

Because the representatives of practically all these nationalities were pirates, adventurers, or traders, this was an era of stormy cosmopolitanism. Hard-pressed by the Thai, King Sattha (1576-94) surrounded himself with a personal guard of Spanish and Portuguese mercenaries, and in 1593 asked the Spanish governor of the Philippines for aid. Attracted by the prospects of establishing a Spanish protectorate in Cambodia and of converting the monarch to Christianity, the governor sent a force of 120 men, but Lovek had already fallen to the Thai when they arrived the following year. The Spanish took advantage of the extremely confused situation to place one of Sattha's sons on the throne in 1597. Hopes of making the country a Spanish dependency were dashed, however, when the Spaniards were massacred two years later by an equally belligerent contingent of Malay mercenaries.

The Thai, however, had dealt a fatal blow to Cambodian independence by capturing Lovek in 1594. With the posting of a Thai military governor in the city, a degree of foreign political control was established over the kingdom for the first time. Cambodian chronicles describe the fall of Lovek as a catastrophe from which the nation never fully recovered.

DOMINATION BY THAILAND AND BY VIETNAM

More than their conquest of Angkor a century and a half earlier, the Thai capture of Lovek marked the beginning of a decline in Cambodia's fortunes. One possible reason for the decline was the labor drain imposed by the Thai conquerors as they marched thousands of Khmer peasants, skilled artisans, scholars, and members of the Buddhist clergy back to their capital of Ayutthaya. This practice, common in the history of Southeast Asia, crippled Cambodia's ability to recover a semblance of its former greatness. A new Khmer capital was established at Odongk (Udong), south of Lovek, but its monarchs could survive only by entering into what amounted to vassal relationships with the Thai and with the Vietnamese. In common parlance, Thailand became Cambodia's "father" and Vietnam its "mother."

By the late fifteenth century, the Vietnamese-who, unlike other Southeast Asian peoples, had patterned their culture and their civilization on those of China--had defeated the oncepowerful kingdom of Champa in central Vietnam. Thousands of Chams fled into Khmer territory. By the early seventeenth century, the Vietnamese had reached the Mekong Delta, which was inhabited by Khmer people. In 1620 the Khmer king Chey Chettha II (1618-28) married a daughter of Sai Vuong, one of the Nguyen lords (1558- 1778), who ruled southern Vietnam for most of the period of the restored Le dynasty (1428-1788). Three years later, Chey Chettha allowed the Vietnamese to establish a custom-house at Prey Nokor, near what is now Ho Chi Minh City (until 1975, Saigon). By the end of the seventeenth century, the region was under Vietnamese administrative control, and Cambodia was cut off from access to the sea. Trade with the outside world was possible only with Vietnamese permission.

There were periods in the seventeenth and the eighteenth centuries, when Cambodia's neighbors were preoccupied with internal or external strife, that afforded the beleaguered country a breathing spell. The Vietnamese were involved in a lengthy civil war until 1674, but upon its conclusion they promptly annexed sizable areas of contiguous Cambodian territory in the region of the Mekong Delta. For the next one hundred years they used the alleged mistreatment of Vietnamese colonists in the delta as a pretext for their continued expansion. By the end of the eighteenth century, they had extended their control to include the area encompassed in the late 1980s by the Socialist Republic of Vietnam (Vietnam).

Thailand, which might otherwise have been courted as an ally against Vietnamese incursions in the eighteenth century, was itself involved in a new conflict with Burma. In 1767 the Thai capital of Ayutthaya was besieged and destroyed. The Thai quickly recovered, however, and soon reasserted their dominion over Cambodia. The youthful Khmer king, Ang Eng (1779-96), a refugee at the Thai court, was installed as monarch at Odongk by Thai troops. At the same time, Thailand quietly annexed Cambodia's three northernmost provinces. In addition, the local rulers of the northwestern provinces of Batdambang and Siemreab (Siemreap) became vassals of the Thai king, and these areas came under the Thai sphere of influence.

A renewed struggle between Thailand and Vietnam for control of Cambodia in the nineteenth century resulted in a period when Vietnamese officials, working through a puppet Cambodian king, ruled the central part of the country and attempted to force Cambodians to adopt Vietnamese customs. Several rebellions against Vietnamese rule ensued. The most important of these occurred in 1840 to 1841 and spread through much of the country. After two years of fighting, Cambodia and its two neighbors reached an accord that placed the country under the joint suzerainty of Thailand and Vietnam. At the behest of both countries, a new monarch, Ang Duong (1848-59), ascended the throne and brought a decade of peace and relative independence to Cambodia.

In their arbitrary treatment of the Khmer population, the Thai and the Vietnamese were virtually indistinguishable. The suffering and the dislocation caused by war were comparable in many ways to similar Cambodian experiences in the 1970s. But the Thai and the Vietnamese had fundamentally different attitudes concerning their relationships with Cambodia. The Thai shared with the Khmer a common religion, mythology, literature, and culture. The Chakri kings at Bangkok wanted Cambodia's loyalty and tribute, but they had no intention of challenging or changing its people's values or way of life. The Vietnamese viewed the Khmer people as barbarians to be civilized through exposure to Vietnamese culture, and they regarded the fertile Khmer lands as legitimate sites for colonization by settlers from Vietnam.

THE FRENCH PROTECTORATE

France's interest in Indochina in the nineteenth century grew out of its rivalry with Britain, which had excluded it from India and had effectively shut it out of other parts of mainland Southeast Asia. The French also desired to establish commerce in a region that promised so much untapped wealth and to redress the Vietnamese state's persecution of Catholic converts, whose welfare was a stated aim of French overseas policy. The Nguyen dynasty's repeated refusal to establish diplomatic relations and the violently anti-Christian policies of the emperors Minh Mang (1820- 41), Thieu Tri (1841-47), and Tu Duc (1848-83) impelled the French to engage in gunboat diplomacy that resulted, in 1862, in the establishment of French dominion over Saigon and over the three eastern provinces of the Cochinchina (Mekong Delta) region.

In the view of the government in Paris, Cambodia was a promising backwater. Persuaded by a missionary envoy to seek French protection against both the Thai and the Vietnamese, King Ang Duong invited a French diplomatic mission to visit his court. The Thai, however, pressured him to refuse to meet with the French when they finally arrived at Odongk in 1856. The much-publicized travels of the naturalist Henri Mouhot, who visited the Cambodian court, rediscovered the ruins at Angkor, and journeyed up the Mekong River to the Laotian kingdom of Luang Prabang from 1859 to 1861, piqued French interest in the kingdom's alleged vast riches and in the value of the Mekong as a gateway to China's southwestern provinces.

In August 1863, the French concluded a treaty with Ang Duong's successor, Norodom (1859-1904). This agreement afforded the Cambodian monarch French protection (in the form of a French official called a résident-in French resident) in exchange for giving the French rights to explore and to exploit the kingdom's mineral and forest resources. Norodom's coronation, in 1864, was an awkward affair at which both French and Thai representatives officiated. Although the Thai attempted to thwart the expansion of French influence, their own influence over the monarch steadily dwindled. In 1867 the French concluded a treaty with the Thai that gave the latter control of Batdambang Province and of Siemreab Province in exchange for their renunciation of all claims of suzerainty over other parts of Cambodia. Loss of the northwestern provinces deeply upset Norodom, but he was beholden to the French for sending military aid to suppress a rebellion by a royal pretender.

In June 1884, the French governor of Cochinchina went to Phnom Penh, Norodom's capital, and demanded approval of a treaty with Paris that promised far-reaching changes such as the abolition of slavery, the institution of private land ownership, and the establishment of French résidents in provincial cities. Mindful of a French gunboat anchored in the river, the king reluctantly signed the agreement. Local elites opposed its provisions, however, especially the one dealing with slavery, and they fomented rebellions throughout the country during the following year. Though the rebellions were suppressed, and the treaty was ratified, passive resistance on the part of the Cambodians postponed implementation of the reforms it embodied until after Norodom's death.

THE FRENCH COLONIAL PERIOD, 1887-1953

In October 1887, the French proclaimed the Union Indochinoise, or Indochina Union, comprising Cambodia and the three constituent regions of Vietnam: Tonkin, Annam, and Cochinchina. (Laos was added to the Indochina Union after being separated from Thai suzerainty in 1893.) Cambodia's chief colonial official, responsible to the Union's governor general and appointed by the Ministry of Marine and Colonies in Paris, was a resident general (résident supérieur). Residents, or local governors, were posted in all the principal provincial centers.

In 1897 the incumbent resident general complained to Paris that Norodom was no longer capable of ruling and received permission to assume the king's authority to issue decrees, collect taxes, and appoint royal officials. Norodom and his successors were left with hollow, figurehead roles as head of state and as patron of the Buddhist religion. The colonial bureaucracy expanded rapidly. French nationals naturally held the highest positions, but even on the lower rungs of the bureaucracy Cambodians found few opportunities because the colonial government preferred to hire Vietnamese.

When Norodom died in 1904, the French passed over his sons and set his brother Sisowath (1904-27) on the throne. Sisowath's branch of the royal family was considered more cooperative than that of Norodom because the latter was viewed as partly responsible for the revolts of the 1880s and because Norodom's favorite son, Prince Yukanthor, had stirred up publicity abroad about French colonial injustices. During their generally peaceful reigns, Sisowath and his son Monivong (1927-41) were pliant instruments of French rule. A measure of the monarchs' status was the willingness of the French to provide them annually with complimentary rations of opium. One of the few highlights of Sisowath's reign was French success in getting Thailand's King Chulalongkorn to sign a new treaty in 1907 returning the northwestern provinces of Batdambang and Siemreab to Cambodia.

THE COLONIAL ECONOMY

Soon after establishing their protectorate in 1863, the French realized that Cambodia's hidden wealth was an illusion and that Phnom Penh would never become the Singapore of Indochina. Aside from collecting taxes more efficiently, the French did little to transform Cambodia's village-based economy. Cambodians paid the highest taxes per capita in Indochina, and in 1916 a nonviolent tax revolt brought tens of thousands of peasants into Phnom Penh to petition the king for a reduction. The incident shocked the French, who had lulled themselves into believing that the Cambodians were too indolent and individualistic to organize a mass protest. Taxes continued to be sorely resented by the Cambodians. In 1925 villagers killed a French resident after he threatened to arrest tax delinquents. For poor peasants, the corvée service-a tax substitute--of as many as ninety days a year on public works projects, was an onerous duty.

According to Hou Yuon (a veteran of the communist movement who was murdered by the Khmer Rouge after they seized power in 1975), usury vied with taxes as the chief burden upon the peasantry. Hou's 1955 doctoral thesis at the University of Paris was one of the earliest and most thorough studies of conditions in the rural areas during the French colonial era. He argued that although most landholdings were small (one to five hectares), poor and middleclass peasants were victims of flagrantly usurious practices that included effective interest rates of 100 to 200 percent. Foreclosure reduced them to the status of sharecroppers or landless laborers. Although debt slavery and feudal landholding patterns had been abolished by the French, the old elites still controlled the countryside. According to Hou, "the great feudal farms, because of their precapitalist character, are disguised as small and mediumsized farms, in the form of tenancies and share-farms, and materially are indistinguishable from other small and medium-seized farms." Whether or not the countryside was as polarized in terms of class (or property) as Hou argues is open to debate, but it is clear that great tension and conflict existed despite the smiles and the easygoing manner of Khmer villagers.

To develop the economic infrastructure, the French built a limited number of roads and a railroad that extended from Phnom Penh through Batdambang to the Thai border. The cultivation of rubber and of corn were economically important, and the fertile provinces of Batdambang and Siemreab became the rice baskets of Indochina. The prosperous 1920s, when rubber, rice, and corn were in demand overseas, were years of considerable economic growth, but the world depression after 1929 caused great suffering, especially among rice cultivators whose falling incomes made them more than ever the victims of moneylenders.

Industry was rudimentary and was designed primarily to process raw materials such as rubber for local use or export. There was considerable immigration, which created a plural society similar to those of other Southeast Asian countries. As in British Burma and Malaya, foreigners dominated the developed sectors of the economy. Vietnamese came to serve as laborers on rubber plantations and as clerical workers in the government. As their numbers increased, Vietnamese immigrants also began to play important roles in the economy as fishermen and as operators of small businesses. The Chinese had been in Cambodia for several centuries before the imposition of French rule, and they had dominated precolonial commerce. This arrangement continued under the French, because the colonial government placed no restrictions on the occupations in which they could engage. Chinese merchants and bankers in Cambodia developed commercial networks that extended throughout Indochina as well as overseas to other parts of Southeast Asia and to mainland China.

THE EMERGENCE OF NATIONALISM

In stark contrast to neighboring Cochinchina and to the other Vietnamese-populated territories of Indochina, Cambodia was relatively quiescent politically during the first four decades of the twentieth century. The carefully maintained fiction of royal rule was probably the major factor. Khmer villagers, long inured to abuses of power, believed that as long as a monarch occupied the throne "all was right with the world." Low literacy rates, which the French were extremely reluctant to improve, also insulated the great majority of the population from the nationalist currents that were sweeping other parts of Southeast Asia.

Nevertheless, national consciousness was emerging among the handful of educated Khmer who composed the urban-based elite. Restoration of the monuments at Angkor, which the historian David P. Chandler suggests was

France's most valuable legacy to the colony, awakened Cambodians' pride in their culture and in their past achievements. Many of the new elite were graduates of the Lycée Sisowath in Phnom Penh, where resentment of the favored treatment given Vietnamese students resulted in a petition to King Monivong during the 1930s.

Significantly, the most articulate of the early nationalists, were Khmer Krom members of the Cambodian minority who lived in Cochinchina. In 1936 Son Ngoc Thanh and another Khmer Krom named Pach Chhoeun, began publishing Nagaravatta (Angkor Wat), the first Khmerlanguage newspaper. In its editorials, Nagaravatta mildly condemned French colonial policies, the prevalence of usury in the rural areas, foreign domination of the economy, and the lack of opportunities for educated Khmer. Much of the paper's journalistic wrath was directed toward the Vietnamese for their past exploitation of Cambodia and for their contemporary monopolization of civil service and of professional positions.

The Khmer were fortunate in escaping the suffering endured by most other Southeast Asian peoples during World War II. After the establishment of the Vichy regime in France in 1940, Japanese forces moved into Vietnam and displaced French authority. In mid1941 , they entered Cambodia but allowed Vichy French colonial officials to remain at their administrative posts. The pro-Japanese regime in Thailand, headed by Prime Minister Field Marshal Luang Plaek Phibunsonggram, requested assurances from the Vicky regime that, in the event of an interruption of French sovereignty, Cambodian and Laotian territories formerly belong to Thailand would be returned to Bangkoh's authority.

The request was rejected. In January 1941, a Thai force invaded Cambodia. The land fighting was indecisive, but the Vichy French defeated the Thai navy in an engagement in the Gulf of Thailand. At this point, Tokyo intervened and compelled the French authorities to agree to a treaty ceding the province of Batdambang and part of the province of Siemreab to Thailand in exchange for a small compensation. The Cambodians were allowed to retain Angkor. Thai aggression, however, had minimal impact on the lives of most Cambodians outside the northwestern region.

King Monivong died in April 1941. Although his son, Prince Monireth, had been considered the heir apparent, the French chose instead Norodom Sihanouk, the great grandson of King Norodom. Sihanouk was an ideal candidate from their point of view because of his youth (he was nineteen years old), his lack of experience, and his pliability.

Japanese calls of "Asia for the Asiatics" found a receptive audience among Cambodian nationalists, although Tokyo's policy in Indochina was to leave the colonial government nominally in charge. When a prominent, politically active Buddhist monk, Hem Chieu, was arrested and unceremoniously defrocked by the French authorities in July 1942, the editors of Nagaravatta led a demonstration demanding his release. They as well as other nationalists apparently overestimated the Japanese willingness to back them, for the Vichy authorities quickly arrested the demonstrators and gave Pach Chhoeun, one of the

Nagaravatta editors, a life sentence. The other editor, Son Ngoc Thanh, escaped from Phnom Penh and turned up the following year in Tokyo.

In a desperate effort to enlist local support in the final months of the war, the Japanese dissolved the French colonial administration on March 9, 1945, and urged Cambodia to declare its independence within the Greater East Asia Co-Prosperity Sphere. Four days later, King Sihanouk decreed an independent Kampuchea (the original Khmer pronunciation of Cambodia). Son Ngoc Thanh returned from Tokyo in May, and he was appointed foreign minister. On August 15, 1945, the day Japan surrendered, a new government was established with Son Ngoc Thanh acting as prime minister. When an Allied force occupied Phnom Penh in October, Thanh was arrested for collaboration with the Japanese and was sent into exile in France to remain under house arrest. Some of his supporters went to northwestern Cambodia, then still under Thai control, where they banded together as one faction in the Khmer Issarak movement, originally formed with Thai encouragement in the 1940s.

THE STRUGGLE FOR INDEPENDENCE

Cambodia's situation at the end of the war was chaotic. The Free French, under General Charles de Gaulle, were determined to recover Indochina, though they offered Cambodia and the other Inchochinese protectorates a carefully circumscribed measure of self-government. Convinced that they had a "civilizing mission," they envisioned Indochina's participation in a French Union of former colonies that shared the common experience of French culture. Neither the urban professional elites nor the common people, however, were attracted by this arrangement. For Cambodians of practically all walks of life, the brief period of independence, from March to October of 1945, was an invigorating breath of fresh air. The lassitude of the Khmer was a thing of the past.

In Phnom Penh, Sihanouk, acting as head of state, was placed in the extremely delicate position of negotiating with the French for full independence while trying to neutralize party politicians and supporters of the Khmer Issarak and Viet Minh who considered him a French collaborator. During the tumultuous period between 1946 and 1953, Sihanouk displayed the remarkable aptitude for political survival that sustained him before and after his fall from power in March 1970. The Khmer Issarak was an extremely heterogeneous guerrilla movement, operating in the border areas. The group included indigenous leftists, Vietnamese leftists, antimonarchical nationalists loyal to Son Ngoc Thanh, and plain bandits taking advantage of the chaos to terrorize villagers. Though their fortunes rose and fell during the immediate postwar period (a major blow was the overthrow of a friendly leftist government in Bangkok in 1947), by 1954 the Khmer Issarak operating with the Viet Minh by some estimates controlled as much as 50 percent of Cambodia's territory.

In 1946 the French allowed the Cambodians to form political parties and to hold elections for a Consultative Assembly that would advise the monarch on drafting the country's constitution. The two major parties were both headed by royal princes. The Democratic Party, led by Prince Sisowath Yuthevong, espoused immediate independence, democratic reforms, and parliamentary government. Its supporters were teachers, civil servants, politically active members of the Buddhist priesthood, and others whose opinions had been greatly influenced by the nationalistic appeals of Nagaravatta before it was closed down by the French in 1942.

Many Democrats sympathized with the violent methods of the Khmer Issarak. The Liberal Party, led by Prince Norodom Norindeth, represented the interests of the old rural elites, including large landowners. They preferred continuing some form of the colonial relationship with France, and advocated gradual democratic reform. In the Consultative Assembly election held in September 1946, the Democrats won fifty out of sixty-seven seats.

With a solid majority in the assembly, the Democrats drafted a constitution modeled on that of the French Fourth Republic. Power was concentrated in the hands of a popularly elected National Assembly. The king reluctantly proclaimed the new constitution on May 6, 1947. While it recognized him as the "spiritual head of the state," it reduced him to the status of a constitutional monarch, and it left unclear the extent to which he could play an active role in the politics of the nation. Sihanouk would turn this ambiguity to his advantage in later years, however.

In the December 1947 elections for the National Assembly, the Democrats again won a large majority. Despite this, dissension within the party was rampant. Its founder, Prince Yuthevong, had died and no clear leader had emerged to succeed him. During the period 1948 to 1949, the Democrats appeared united only in their opposition to legislation sponsored by the king or his appointees. A major issue was the king's receptivity to independence within the French Union, proposed in a draft treaty offered by the French in late 1948. Following dissolution of the National Assembly in September 1949, agreement on the pact was reached through an exchange of letters between King Sihanouk and the French government. It went into effect two months later, though National Assembly ratification of the treaty was never secured.

The treaty granted Cambodia what Sihanouk called "fifty percent independence": by it, the colonial relationship was formally ended, and the Cambodians were given control of most administrative functions. Cambodian armed forces were granted freedom of action within a self-governing autonomous zone comprising Batdambang and Siemreab provinces, which had been recovered from Thailand after World War II, but which the French, hard-pressed elsewhere, did not have the resources to control.

Cambodia was still required to coordinate foreign policy matters with the High Council of the French Union, however, and France retained a significant measure of control over the judicial system, finances, and customs. Control of wartime military operations outside the autonomous zone remained in French hands. France was also permitted to maintain military bases on Cambodian territory. In 1950 Cambodia was accorded diplomatic recognition by the United States and by most noncommunist powers, but in Asia only Thailand and the Republic of Korea (South Korea) extended recognition.

The Democrats won a majority in the second National Assembly election in September 1951, and they continued their policy of opposing the king on practically all fronts. In an effort to win greater popular approval, Sihanouk asked the French to release nationalist Son Ngoc Thanh from exile and to allow him to return to his country. He made a triumphant entry into Phnom Penh on October 29, 1951. It was not long, however, before he began demanding withdrawal of French troops from Cambodia.

He reiterated this demand in early 1952 in Khmer Krok (Khmer Awake!) a weekly newspaper that he had founded. The newspaper was forced to cease publication in March, and Son Ngoc Thanh fled the capital with a few armed followers to join the Khmer Issarak. Branded alternately a communist and an agent of the United States Central Intelligence Agency (CIA) by Sihanouk, he remained in exile until Lon Nol established the Khmer Republic in 1970.

In June 1952, Sihanouk announced the dismissal of his cabinet, suspended the constitution, and assumed control of the government as prime minister. Then, without clear constitutional sanction, he dissolved the National Assembly and proclaimed martial law in January 1953. Sihanouk exercised direct rule for almost three years, from June 1952 until February 1955. After dissolution of the assembly, he created an Advisory Council to supplant the legislature and appointed his father, Norodom Suramarit, as regent.

In March 1953, Sihanouk went to France. Ostensibly, he was traveling for his health; actually, he was mounting an intensive campaign to persuade the French to grant complete independence. The climate of opinion in Cambodia at the time was such that if he did not achieve full independence quickly, the people were likely to turn to Son Ngoc Thanh and the Khmer Issarak, who were fully committed to attaining that goal. At meetings with the French president and with other high officials, the French suggested that Sihanouk was unduly "alarmist" about internal political conditions. The French also made the thinly veiled threat that, if he continued to be uncooperative, they might replace him. The trip appeared to be a failure, but on his way home by way of the United States, Canada, and Japan, Sihanouk publicized Cambodia's plight in the media.

To further dramatize his "royal crusade for independence," Sihanouk, declaring that he would not return until the French gave assurances that full independence would be granted, left Phnom Penh in June to go into self-imposed exile in Thailand. Unwelcome in Bangkok, he moved to his royal villa near the ruins of Angkor in Siemreab Province. Siemreab, part of the autonomous military zone established in 1949, was commanded by Lieutenant Colonel Lon Nol, formerly a right-wing politician who was becoming a prominent, and in time would be an indispensable, Sihanouk ally within the military. From his Siemreab base, the king and Lon Nol contemplated plans for resistance if the French did not meet their terms.

Sihanouk was making a high-stakes gamble, for the French could easily have replaced him with a more pliable monarch; however, the military situation was deteriorating throughout Indochina, and the French government, on July

3, 1953, declared itself ready to grant full independence to the three states of Cambodia, Vietnam, and Laos. Sihanouk insisted on his own terms, which included full control of national defense, the police, the courts, and financial matters. The French yielded: the police and the judiciary were transferred to Cambodian control at the end of August, and in October the country assumed full command of its military forces. King Sihanouk, now a hero in the eyes of his people, returned to Phnom Penh in triumph, and independence day was celebrated on November 9, 1953. Control of residual matters affecting sovereignty, such as financial and budgetary affairs, passed to the new Cambodian state in 1954.

CAMBODIA UNDER SIHANOUK, 1954-70

Sihanouk continues to be one of the most controversial figures in Southeast Asia's turbulent, and often tragic, postwar history. Admirers view him as one of the country's great patriots, whose insistence on strict neutrality kept Cambodia out of the maelstrom of war and out of the revolution in neighboring Vietnam for more than fifteen years before he was betrayed by his close associate, Lon Nol. Critics attack him for his vanity, eccentricities, and intolerance of any political views different from his own. One such critic, Michael Vickery, asserts that beneath the neutralist rhetoric Sihanouk presided over a regime that was oppressively reactionary and, in some instances, as violent in its suppression of political opposition as the Khmer Rouge. According to Vickery, the royal armed forces under Lon Nol slaughtered women and children in pro-Khmer Issarak regions of Batdambang in 1954 using methods that were later to become routine under Pol Pot. Another critical observer, Milton E. Osborne, writing as an Australian expatriate in Phnom Penh during the late 1960s, describes the Sihanouk years in terms of unbridled greed and corruption, of a foreign policy inspired more by opportunism than by the desire to preserve national independence, of an economy and a political system that were rapidly coming apart, and of the prince's obsession with making outrageously mediocre films-one of which starred himself and his wife, Princess Monique.

Sihanouk was all of these things-patriot, neutralist, embodiment of the nation's destiny, eccentric, rigid defender of the status quo, and promoter of the worst sort of patron-client politics. He believed that he single-handedly had won Cambodia's independence from the French. The contributions of other nationalists, such as Son Ngoc Thanh and the Viet Minh, were conveniently forgotten. Sihanouk also believed he had the right to run the state in a manner not very different from that of the ancient Khmer kings-that is, as an extension of his household. Unlike the ancient "god-kings," however, he established genuine rapport with ordinary Cambodians.

He made frequent, often impromptu, trips throughout the country, visiting isolated villages, chatting with peasants, receiving petitions, passing out gifts, and scolding officials for mismanagement. According to British author and journalist William Shawcross, Sihanouk was able to create a "unique brand of personal populism." To ordinary Cambodians, his eccentricities, volatility, short temper, sexual escapades, and artistic flights of fancy were an expression of royal charisma rather than an occasion for scandal. Sihanouk's delight in making life difficult for foreign diplomats and journalists, moreover, amused his subjects. Ultimately, the eccentric humanity of Sihanouk was to contrast poignantly with the random brutality of his Khmer Rouge successors.

THE GENEVA CONFERENCE

Although Cambodia had achieved independence by late 1953, its military situation remained unsettled. Noncommunist factions of the Khmer Issarak had joined the government, but communist Viet Minh activities increased at the very time French Union force were stretched thin elsewhere. In April 1954, several Viet Minh battalions crossed the border into Cambodia. Royalist forces engaged them but could not force their complete withdrawal. In part, the communists were attempting to strengthen their bargaining position at the Geneva Conference that had been scheduled to begin in late April.

The Geneva Conference was attended by representatives of Cambodia, North Vietnam, the Associated State of Vietnam (the predecessor of the Republic of Vietnam, or South Vietnam), Laos, the People's Republic of China, the Soviet Union, France, Britain, and the United States. One goal of the conference was to restore a lasting peace in Indochina. The discussions on Indochina began on May 8, 1954. The North Vietnamese attempted to get representation for the resistance government that had been established in the south, but failed. On July 21, 1954, the conference reached an agreement calling for a cessation of hostilities in Indochina. With respect to Cambodia, the agreement stipulated that all Viet Minh military forces be withdrawn within ninety days and that Cambodian resistance forces be demobilized within thirty days. In a separate agreement signed by the Cambodian representative, the French and the Viet Minh agreed to withdraw all forces from Cambodian soil by October 1954.

In exchange for the withdrawal of Viet Minh forces, the communist representatives in Geneva wanted full neutrality for Cambodia and for Laos that would prevent the basing of United States military forces in these countries. On the eve of the conference's conclusion, however, the Cambodian representative, Sam Sary, insisted that, if Cambodia were to be genuinely independent, it must not be prohibited from seeking whatever military assistance it desired (Cambodia had earlier appealed to Washington for military aid). The conference accepted this point over North Vietnam's strenuous objections. In the final agreement, Cambodia accepted a watered-down neutrality, vowing not to join any military alliance "not in conformity with the principles of the Charter of the United Nations" or to allow the basing of foreign military forces on its territory "as long as its security is not threatened."

The conference agreement established the International Control Commission (officially called the International Commission for Supervision and Control) in all the Indochinese countries. Made up of representatives from Canada, Poland, and India, it supervised the cease-fire, the withdrawal of foreign troops, the release of prisoners of war, and overall compliance with the terms of the agreement. The French and most of the Viet Minh forces were withdrawn on schedule in October 1954.

DOMESTIC DEVELOPMENTS

The Geneva agreement also stipulated that general elections should be held in Cambodia during 1955 and that the International Control Commission should monitor them to ensure fairness. Sihanouk was more determined than ever to defeat the Democrats (who, on the basis of their past record, were expected to win the election). The king attempted unsuccessfully to have the constitution amended. On March 2, 1955, he announced his abdication in favor of his father, Norodom Suramarit. Assuming the title of samdech (prince), Sihanouk explained that this action was necessary in order to give him a free hand to engage in politics.

To challenge the Democrats, Prince Sihanouk established his own political machine, the oddly named Sangkum Reastr Niyum (Popular Socialist Community), commonly referred to as the Sangkum. The name is odd because its most important components were right-wing parties that were virulently anticommunist. The Sangkum's emergence in early 1955 unified most right-wing groups under the prince's auspices. In the September election, Sihanouk's new party decisively defeated the Democrats, the Khmer Independence Party of Son Ngoc Thanh, and the leftist Pracheachon (Citizens') Party, winning 83 percent of the vote and all of the seats in the National Assembly.

Khmer nationalism, loyalty to the monarch, struggle against injustice and corruption, and protection of the Buddhist religion were major themes in Sangkum ideology. The party adopted a particularly conservative interpretation of Buddhism, common in the Theravada countries of Southeast Asia, that the social and economic inequalities among people were legitimate because of the workings of karma. For the poorer classes, virtuous and obedient conduct opened up the possibility of being born into a higher station in a future life. The appeal to religion won the allegiance of the country's many Buddhist priests, who were a particularly influential group in rural villages.

As the 1960s began, organized political opposition to Sihanouk and the Sangkum virtually had disappeared. According to Vickery, the Democratic Party disbanded in 1957 after its leaders-who had been beaten by soldiers-requested the privilege of joining the Sangkum.

Despite its defense of the status quo, especially the interests of rural elites, the Sangkum was not an exclusively right-wing organization. Sihanouk included a number of leftists in his party and government. Among these were future leaders of the Khmer Rouge. Hu Nim and Hou Yuon served in several ministries between 1958 and 1963, and Khieu Samphan served briefly as secretary of state for commerce in 1963.

Sihanouk's attitude toward the left was paradoxical. He often declared that if he had not been a prince, he would have become a revolutionary. Sihanouk's chronic suspicion of United States intentions in the region, his perception of revolutionary China as Cambodia's most valuable ally, his respect for such prominent and capable leftists as Hou, Hu, and Khieu, and his vague notions of "royal socialism" all impelled him to experiment with socialist policies. In

1963 the prince announced the nationalization of banking, foreign trade, and insurance as a means of reducing foreign control of the economy. In 1964 a state trading company, the National Export-Import Corporation, was established to handle foreign commerce.

The declared purposes of nationalization were to give Khmer nationals, rather than Chinese or Vietnamese, a greater role in the nation's trade, to eliminate middlemen and to conserve foreign exchange through the limiting of unnecessary luxury imports. As a result of this policy, foreign investment quickly disappeared, and a kind of "crony socialism" emerged somewhat similar to the "crony capitalism" that evolved in the Philippines under President Ferdinand Marcos. Lucrative state monopolies were parceled out to Sihanouk's most loyal retainers, who "milked" them for cash.

Sihanouk was headed steadily for a collision with the right. To counter charges of one-man rule, the prince declared that he would relinquish control of candidate selection and would permit more than one Sangkum candidate to run for each seat in the September 1966 National Assembly election. The returns showed a surprising upsurge in the conservative vote at the expense of more moderate and left-wing elements, although Hou, Hu, and Khieu were reelected by their constituencies. General Lon Nol became prime minister.

Out of concern that the right wing might cause an irreparable split within the Sangkum and might challenge his domination of the political system, Sihanouk set up a "counter government" (like the British "shadow cabinet") packed with his most loyal personal followers and with leading leftists, hoping that it would exert a restraining influence on Lon Nol. Leftists accused the general of being groomed by Western intelligence agencies to lead a bloody anticommunist coup d'état similar to that of General Soeharto in Indonesia. Injured in an automobile accident, Lon Nol resigned in April 1967. Sihanouk replaced him with a trusted centrist, Son Sann. This was the twenty-third successive Sangkum cabinet and government to have been appointed by Sihanouk since the party was formed in 1955.

NONALIGNED FOREIGN POLICY

Sihanouk's nonaligned foreign policy, which emerged in the months following the Geneva Conference, cannot be understood without reference to Cambodia's past history of foreign subjugation and its very uncertain prospects for survival as the war between North Vietnam and South Vietnam intensified. Soon after the 1954 Geneva Conference, Sihanouk expressed some interest in integrating Cambodia into the framework of the Southeast Asia Treaty Organization (SEATO), which included Cambodia, Laos, and South Vietnam within the "treaty area," although none of these states was a signatory. But meetings in late 1954 with India's Prime Minister Jawaharlal Nehru and Burma's Premier U Nu made him receptive to the appeal of nonalignment. Moreover, the prince was somewhat uneasy about a United States-dominated alliance that included one old enemy, Thailand, and encompassed another, South Vietnam, each of which offered sanctuary to anti-Sihanouk dissidents.

At the Bandung Conference in April 1955, Sihanouk held private meetings with Premier Zhou Enlai of China and Foreign Minister Pham Van Dong of North Vietnam. Both assured him that their countries would respect Cambodia's independence and territorial integrity. His experience with the French, first as a client, then as the self-proclaimed leader of the "royal crusade for independence," apparently led him to conclude that the United States, like France, would eventually be forced to leave Southeast Asia. From this perspective, the Western presence in Indochina was only a temporary interruption of the dynamics of the region-continued Vietnamese (and perhaps even Thai) expansion at Cambodia's expense. Accommodation with North Vietnam and friendly ties with China during the late 1950s and the 1960s were tactics designed to counteract these dynamics. China accepted Sihanouk's overtures and became a valuable counterweight to growing Vietnamese and Thai pressure on Cambodia.

Cambodia's relations with China were based on mutual interests. Sihanouk hoped that China would restrain the Vietnamese and the Thai from acting to Cambodia's detriment. The Chinese, in turn, viewed Cambodia's nonalignment as vital in order to prevent the encirclement of their country by the United States and its allies. When Premier Zhou Enlai visited Phnom Penh in 1956, he asked the country's Chinese minority, numbering about 300,000, to cooperate in Cambodia's development, to stay out of politics, and to consider adopting Cambodian citizenship. This gesture helped to resolve a sensitive issue--the loyalty of Cambodian Chinese--that had troubled the relationship between Phnom Penh and Beijing. In 1960 the two countries signed a Treaty of Friendship and Nonaggression. After the Sino-Soviet rift Sihanouk's ardent friendship with China contributed to generally cooler ties with Moscow.

China was not the only large power to which Sihanouk looked for patronage, however. Cambodia's quest for security and nation- building assistance impelled the prince to search beyond Asia and to accept help from all donors as long as there was no impingement upon his country's sovereignty. With this end in mind, Sihanouk turned to the United States in 1955 and negotiated a military aid agreement that secured funds and equipment for the Royal Khmer Armed Forces (Forces Armées Royales Khmères-FARK-see Appendix B). A United States Military Assistance Advisory Group (MAAG) was established in Phnom Penh to supervise the delivery and the use of equipment that began to arrive from the United States. By the early 1960s, aid from Washington constituted 30 percent of Cambodia's defense budget and 14 percent of total budget inflows.

Relations with the United States, however, proved to be stormy. United States officials both in Washington and in Phnom Penh frequently underestimated the prince and considered him to be an erratic figure with minimal understanding of the threat posed by Asian communism. Sihanouk easily reciprocated this mistrust because several developments aroused his suspicion of United States intentions toward his country.

One of these developments was the growing United States influence within the Cambodian armed forces. The processing of equipment deliveries and the training of Cambodian personnel had forged close ties between United States military advisers and their Cambodian counterparts. Military officers of both nations also shared apprehensions about the spread of communism in Southeast Asia.

Sihanouk considered FARK to be Washington's most powerful constituency in his country. The prince also feared that a number of high-ranking, rightist FARK officers led by Lon Nol were becoming too powerful and that, by association with these officers, United States influence in Cambodia was becoming too deeply rooted.

A second development included the repetition of overflights by United States and South Vietnamese military aircraft within Cambodian airspace and border incursions by South Vietnamese troops in hot pursuit of Viet Cong insurgents who crossed into Cambodian territory when military pressure upon them became too sustained. As the early 1960swore on, this increasingly sensitive issue contributed to the deterioration of relations between Phnom Penh and Washington.

A third development was Sihanouk's own belief that he had been targeted by United States intelligence agencies for replacement by a more pro-Western leader. Evidence to support this suspicion came to light in 1959 when the government discovered a plot to overthrow Sihanouk. The conspiracy involved several Khmer leaders suspected of American connections. Among them were Sam Sary, a leader of right-wing Khmer Serei troops in South Vietnam; Son Ngoc Thanh, the early nationalist leader once exiled into Thailand; and Dap Chhuon, the military governor of Siemreab Province. Another alleged plot involved Dap Chuon's establishment of a "free" state that would have included Siemreab Province and Kampong Thum (Kampong Thom) Province and the southern areas of Laos that were controlled by the rightist Laotian prince, Boun Oum.

These developments, magnified by Sihanouk's abiding suspicions, eventually undermined Phnom Penh's relations with Washington. In November 1963, the prince charged that the United States was continuing to support the subversive activities of the Khmer Serei in Thailand and in South Vietnam, and he announced the immediate termination of Washington's aid program to Cambodia. Relations continued to deteriorate, and the final break came in May 1965 amid increasing indications of airspace violations by South Vietnamese and by United States aircraft and of ground fighting between Army of the Republic of Vietnam (ARVN) troops and Viet Cong insurgents in the Cambodian border areas.

In the meantime, Cambodia's relations with North Vietnam and with South Vietnam, as well as the rupture with Washington, reflected Sihanouk's efforts to adjust to geopolitical realities in Southeast Asia and to keep his country out of the escalating conflict in neighboring South Vietnam. In the early to mid-1960s, this effort required a tilt toward Hanoi because the government in Saigon tottered on the brink of anarchy. In the cities, the administration of Ngo Dinh Diem and the military regimes that succeeded it had become increasingly ineffectual and unstable, while in the countryside the government forces were steadily losing ground to the Hanoi-backed insurgents. To observers in Phnom Penh, South Vietnam's short-term viability was seriously in doubt, and this compelled a new tack in Cambodian foreign policy. First, Cambodia severed diplomatic ties with Saigon in August 1963. The following March, Sihanouk announced plans to establish diplomatic relations with North Vietnam and to negotiate a border settlement directly with Hanoi.

These plans were not implemented quickly, however, because the North Vietnamese told the prince that any problem concerning Cambodia's border with South Vietnam would have to be negotiated directly with the National Front for the Liberation of South Vietnam (NFLSVN). Cambodia opened border talks with the front in mid-1966, and the latter recognized the inviolability of Cambodia's borders a year later. North Vietnam quickly followed suit. Cambodia was the first foreign government to recognize the NFLSVN's Provisional Revolutionary Government after it was established in June 1969. Sihanouk was the only foreign head of state to attend the funeral of Ho Chi Minh, North Vietnam's deceased leader, in Hanoi three months later.

In the late 1960s, while preserving relations with China and with North Vietnam, Sihanouk sought to restore a measure of equilibrium by improving Cambodia's ties with the West. This shift in course by the prince represented another adjustment to prevailing conditions in Southeast Asia. North Vietnamese and Viet Cong forces were increasing their use of sanctuaries in Cambodia, which also served as the southern terminus of the Ho Chi Minh Trail, their logistical resupply route originating in North Vietnam. Cambodian neutrality in the conflict thus was eroding, and China, preoccupied with its Cultural Revolution, did not intercede with Hanoi.

On Cambodia's eastern border, South Vietnam, surprisingly, had not collapsed, even in the face of the communist Tet Offensive in 1968, and President Nguyen Van Thieu's government was bringing a measure of stability to the war-ravaged country. As the government in Phnom Penh began to feel keenly the loss of economic and military aid from the United States, which had totaled about US$400 million between 1955 and 1963, it began to have second thoughts about the rupture with Washington. The unavailability of American equipment and spare parts was exacerbated by the poor quality and the small numbers of Soviet, Chinese, and French substitutes.

In late 1967 and in early 1968, Sihanouk signaled that he would raise no objection to hot pursuit of communist forces by South Vietnamese or by United States troops into Cambodian territory. Washington, in the meantime, accepted the recommendation of the United States Military Assistance Command-Vietnam (MACV) and, beginning in March 1969, ordered a series of airstrikes (dubbed the Menu series) against Cambodian sanctuaries used by the North Vietnamese and the Viet Cong. Whether or not these bombing missions were authorized aroused considerable controversy, and assertions by the Nixon administration that Sihanouk had "allowed" or even "encouraged" them were disputed by critics such as British journalist William Shawcross. On a diplomatic level, however, the Menu airstrikes did not impede bilateral relations from moving forward. In April 1969, Nixon sent a note to the prince affirming that the United States recognized and respected "the sovereignty, neutrality and territorial integrity of the Kingdom of Cambodia with its present frontiers." Shortly thereafter, in June 1969, full diplomatic relations were restored between Phnom Penh and Washington.

THE CAMBODIAN LEFT: THE EARLY PHASES

The history of the communist movement in Cambodia can be divided into six phases: the emergence of the Indochinese Communist Party, whose members were almost exclusively Vietnamese, before World War II; the ten-year struggle for independence from the French, when a separate Cambodian communist party, the Kampuchean (or Khmer) People's Revolutionary Party (KPRP), was established under Vietnamese auspices; the period following the Second Party Congress of the KPRP in 1960, when Saloth Sar (Pol Pot after 1976) and other future Khmer Rouge leaders gained control of its apparatus; the revolutionary struggle from the initiation of the Khmer Rouge insurgency in 1967-68 to the fall of the Lon Nol government in April 1975; the Democratic Kampuchea regime, from April 1975 to January 1979; and the period following the Third Party Congress of the KPRP in January 1979, when Hanoi effectively assumed control over Cambodia's government and communist party.

Much of the movement's history has been shrouded in mystery, largely because successive purges, especially during the Democratic Kampuchea period, have left so few survivors to recount their experiences. One thing is evident, however, the tension between Khmer and Vietnamese was a major theme in the movement's development. In the three decades between the end of World War II and the Khmer Rouge victory, the appeal of communism to Westerneducated intellectuals (and to a lesser extent its more inchoate attraction for poor peasants) was tempered by the apprehension that the much stronger Vietnamese movement was using communism as an ideological rationale for dominating the Khmer.

The analogy between the Vietnamese communists and the Nguyen dynasty, which had legitimized its encroachments in the nineteenth century in terms of the "civilizing mission" of Confucianism, was persuasive. Thus, the new brand of indigenous communism that emerged after 1960 combined nationalist and revolutionary appeals and, when it could afford to, exploited the virulent anti-Vietnamese sentiments of the Khmers. Khmer Rouge literature in the 1970s frequently referred to the Vietnamese as yuon (barbarian), a term dating from the Angkorian period.

In 1930 Ho Chi Minh founded the Vietnamese Communist Party by unifying three smaller communist movements that had emerged in Tonkin, in Annam, and in Cochinchina during the late 1920s. The name was changed almost immediately to the ICP, ostensibly to include revolutionaries from Cambodia and Laos. Almost without exception, however, all the earliest party members were Vietnamese. By the end of World War II, a handful of Cambodians hadjoined its ranks, but their influence on the Indochinese communist movement and on developments within Cambodia was negligible.

Viet Minh units occasionally made forays into Cambodia bases during their war against the French, and, in conjunction with the leftist government that ruled Thailand until 1947, the Viet Minh encouraged the formation of armed, left-wing Khmer Issarak bands. On April 17, 1950 (twenty-five years to the day before the Khmer Rouge captured Phnom Penh), the first nationwide congress of the Khmer Issarak groups convened, and the United Issarak Front was established. Its leader was Son Ngoc Minh (possibly a brother of the nationalist Son Ngoc Thanh), and a third of its leadership consisted of members of the ICP. According to the historian David P. Chandler, the leftist Issarak groups, aided by the Viet Minh, occupied a sixth of Cambodia's territory by 1952; and, on the eve of the Geneva Conference, they controlled as much as one half of the country.

In 1951 the ICP was reorganized into three national units--the Vietnam Workers' Party, the Lao Itsala, and the KPRP. According to a document issued after the reorganization, the Vietnam Workers' Party would continue to "supervise" the smaller Laotian and Cambodian movements. Most KPRP leaders and rank-and-file seem to have been either Khmer Krom, or ethnic Vietnamese living in Cambodia. The party's appeal to indigenous Khmers appears to have been minimal.

According to Democratic Kampuchea's version of party history, the Viet Minh's failure to negotiate a political role for the KPRP at the 1954 Geneva Conference represented a betrayal of the Cambodian movement, which still controlled large areas of the countryside and which commanded at least 5,000 armed men. Following the conference, about 1,000 members of the KPRP, including Son Ngoc Minh, made a "Long March" into North Vietnam, where they remained in exile. In late 1954, those who stayed in Cambodia founded a legal political party, the Pracheachon Party, which participated in the 1955 and the 1958 National Assembly elections. In the September 1955 election, it won about 4 percent of the vote but did not secure a seat in the legislature. Members of the Pracheachon were subject to constant harassment and to arrests because the party remained outside Sihanouk's Sangkum.

Government attacks prevented it from participating in the 1962 election and drove it underground. Sihanouk habitually labeled local leftists the Khmer Rouge (see Appendix B), a term that later came to signify the party and the state headed by Pol Pot, Ieng Sary, Khieu Samphan, and their associates.

During the mid-1950s, KPRP factions, the "urban committee" (headed by Tou Samouth), and the "rural committee" (headed by Sieu Heng), emerged. In very general terms, these groups espoused divergent revolutionary lines. The prevalent "urban" line, endorsed by North Vietnam, recognized that Sihanouk, by virtue of his success in winning independence from the French, was a genuine national leader whose neutralism and deep distrust of the United States made him a valuable asset in Hanoi's struggle to "liberate" South Vietnam. Champions of this line hoped that the prince could be persuaded to distance himself from the right wing and to adopt leftist policies.

The other line, supported for the most part by rural cadres who were familiar with the harsh realities of the countryside, advocated an immediate struggle to overthrow the "feudalist" Sihanouk. In 1959 Sieu Heng defected to the government and provided the security forces with information that enabled them to destroy as much as 90 percent of the party's rural apparatus. Although communist networks in Phnom Penh and in other towns under Tou Samouth's jurisdiction fared better, only a few hundred communists remained active in the country by 1960.

THE PARIS STUDENT GROUP

During the 1950s, Khmer students in Paris organized their own communist movement, which had little, if any, connection to the hard-pressed party in their homeland. From their ranks came the men and women who returned home and took command of the party apparatus during the 1960s, led an effective insurgency against Sihanouk and Lon Nol from 1968 until 1975, and established the regime of Democratic Kampuchea.

Pol Pot, who rose to the leadership of the communist movement in the 1960s, was born in 1928 (some sources say in 1925) in Kampong Thum Province, north of Phnom Penh. He attended a technical high school in the capital and then went to Paris in 1949 to study radio electronics (other sources say he attended a school for printers and typesetters and also studied civil engineering). Described by one source as a "determined, rather plodding organizer," he failed to obtain a degree, but, according to the Jesuit priest, Father François Ponchaud, he acquired a taste for the classics of French literature as well as for the writings of Marx.

Another member of the Paris student group was Ieng Sary. He was a Chinese-Khmer born in 1930 in South Vietnam. He attended the elite Lycée Sisowath in Phnom Penh before beginning courses in commerce and politics at the Institut d'Etudes Politiques in France. Khieu Samphan, considered "one of the most brilliant intellects of his generation," was born in 1931 and specialized in economics and politics during his time in Paris. In talent he was rivaled by Hou Yuon, born in 1930, who was described as being "of truly astounding physical and intellectual strength," and who studied economics and law. Son Sen, born in 1930, studied education and literature; Hu Nim, born in 1932, studied law.

These men were perhaps the most educated leaders in the history of Asian communism. Two of them, Khieu Samphan and Hou Yuon, earned doctorates from the University of Paris; Hu Nim obtained his degree from the University of Phnom Penh in 1965. In retrospect, it seems enigmatic that these talented members of the elite, sent to France on government scholarships, could launch the bloodiest and most radical revolution in modern Asian history. Most came from landowner or civil servant families. Pol Pot and Hou Yuon may have been related to the royal family. An older sister of Pol Pot had been a concubine at the court of King Monivong. Three of the Paris group forged a bond that survived years of revolutionary struggle and intraparty strife, Pol Pot and Ieng Sary married Khieu Ponnary and Khieu Thirith (also known as Ieng Thirith), purportedly relatives of Khieu Samphan. These two well-educated women also played a central role in the regime of Democratic Kampuchea.

The intellectual ferment of Paris must have been a dizzying experience for young Khmers fresh from Phnom Penh or the provinces. A number sought refuge in the dogma of orthodox Marxism-Leninism. At some time between 1949 and 1951, Pol Pot and Ieng Sary joined the French Communist Party, the most tightly disciplined and Stalinist of Western Europe's communist movements. In 1951 the two men went to East Berlin to participate in a youth festival. This experience is considered to have been a turning point in their ideological development. Meeting with Khmers who were fighting with the Viet Minh (and whom they subsequently judged to be too subservient to the Vietnamese), they became convinced that only a tightly disciplined party organization and a readiness for armed struggle could achieve revolution.

They transformed the Khmer Students' Association (KSA), to which most of the 200 or so Khmer students in Paris belonged, into a platform for nationalist and leftist ideas. In 1952 Pol Pot, Hou Yuon, Ieng Sary, and other leftists gained notoriety by sending an open letter to Sihanouk calling him the "strangler of infant democracy." A year later, the French authorities closed down the KSA. In 1956, however, Hou Yuon and Khieu Samphan helped to establish a new Marxist-oriented group, the Khmer Students' Union.

The doctoral dissertations written by Hou Yuon and Khieu Samphan express basic themes that were later to become the cornerstones of the policy adopted by Democratic Kampuchea. The central role of the peasants in national development was espoused by Hou Yuon in his 1955 thesis, "The Cambodian Peasants and Their Prospects for Modernization," which challenged the conventional view that urbanization and industrialization are necessary precursors of development. The major argument in Khieu Samphan's 1959 thesis, "Cambodia's Economy and Industrial Development," was that the country had to become self-reliant and had to end its economic dependency on the developed world. In its general contours, Khieu's work reflected the influence of a branch of the "dependency theory" school, which blamed lack of development in the Third World on the economic domination of the industrialized nations.

THE KPRP SECOND CONGRESS

After returning to Cambodia in 1953, Pol Pot threw himself into party work first in Kampong Cham Province (Kompong Cham) and then in Phnom Penh under Tou Samouth's "urban committee." His comrades, Ieng Sary and Hou Yuon, became teachers at a new private high school, the Lycée Kambuboth, which Hou Yuon helped to establish. Khieu Samphan returned from Paris in 1959, taught as a member of the law faculty of the University of Phnom Penh, and started a left-wing, French-language publication, L'Observateur. The paper soon acquired a reputation in Phnom Penh's small academic circle. The following year, the government closed the paper, and Sihanouk's police publicly humiliated Khieu by undressing and photographing him in public-as Shawcross notes, "not the sort of humiliation that men forgive or forget."

Yet the experience did not prevent Khieu from advocating cooperation with Sihanouk in order to promote a united front against United States activities in South Vietnam. As mentioned, Khieu Samphan, Hou Yuon, and Hu Nim tried to "work through the system" by joining the Sangkum and by accepting posts in the prince's government. Hardliners like Pol Pot, Ieng Sary, and Son Sen advocated resistance.

In late September, 1960, twenty-one leaders of the KPRP held a secret congress in a vacant room of the Phnom Penh railroad station. This pivotal event remains shrouded in mystery because its outcome has become an object of contention (and considerable historical rewriting) between pro-Vietnamese and anti-Vietnamese Khmer communist factions. The question of cooperation with, or resistance to, Sihanouk was thoroughly discussed. Tou Samouth, who advocated a policy of cooperation, was elected general secretary of the KPRP that was renamed the Workers' Party of Kampuchea (WPK).

His ally, Nuon Chea (also known as Long Reth), became deputy general secretary; however, Pol Pot and Ieng Sary were named to the Political Bureau to occupy the third and the fifth highest positions in the renamed party's hierarchy. The name change is significant. By calling itself a workers' party, the Cambodian movement claimed equal status with the Vietnam Workers' Party. The pro-Vietnamese regime of the People's Republic of Kampuchea (PRK) implied in the 1980s that the September 1960 meeting was nothing more than the second congress of the KPRP.

On July 20, 1962, Tou Samouth disappeared. He may have been the victim of Sihanouk's police, but some observers suggest that Pol Pot, who had built up a strong faction within the party, had him eliminated. In February 1963, at the WPK's second congress, Pol Pot was chosen to succeed Tou Samouth as the party's general secretary. Tou's allies, Nuon Chea and Keo Meas, were removed from the Central Committee and replaced by Son Sen and Vorn Vet. From then on, Pol Pot and loyal comrades from his Paris student days controlled the party center, edging out older veterans whom they considered excessively pro-Vietnamese.

In July 1963, Pol Pot and most of the central committee left Phnom Penh to establish an insurgent base in Rotanokiri (Ratanakiri) Province in the northeast. This is a region inhabited by tribal minorities, the Khmer Loeu, whose rough treatment (including resettlement and forced assimilation) at the hands of the central government made them willing recruits for a guerrilla struggle. In 1965 Pol Pot made a visit of several months duration to North Vietnam and China. He probably received some training in China, which must have enhanced his prestige when he returned to the WPK's liberated areas. Despite friendly relations between Sihanouk and the Chinese, the latter kept Pol Pot's visit a secret from Sihanouk. In September 1966, the party changed its name a second time, to the Kampuchean (or Khmer) Communist Party (KCP). Adopting the label "communist" suggested that the Cambodian movement was more advanced than Vietnam's (which was merely a "workers' party"), and was on the same level as China's.

INTO THE MAELSTROM: INSURRECTION AND WAR, 1967-75

By the mid-1960s, Sihanouk's delicate balancing act was beginning to go awry. Regionally, the presence of large-scale North Vietnamese and Viet Cong logistical bases on Cambodian territory and the use of Kampong Saom (then Sihanoukville) as a port of disembarkation for supplies being sent to communist troops, as well as the covert intelligence-gathering, sabotage missions, and overflights by South Vietnamese and United States teams had made a sham of Cambodian neutrality. Domestically, Sihanouk's sporadic harassment of the leftists and the withdrawal of his endorsement from all candidates in the 1966 elections cost the radicals their chance for victory and alienated them from the prince as well.

Sihanouk also lost the support of the rightists by his failure to come to grips with the deteriorating economic situation in the country and with the growing North Vietnamese and Viet Cong military presence in Cambodia. In addition to these regional developments and the clash of interests among Phnom Penh's politicized elite, social tensions also were creating a favorable environment for the growth of a domestic communist insurgency in the rural areas.

In early 1967, an insurrection broke out in the area around Samlot in Batdambang, a province long noted for the presence of large landowners and great disparities of wealth. Local resentment focused on tax collections and on the decision of the revenuestarved government to expropriate land to build a sugar refinery near Samlot. In January 1967, irate villagers attacked a tax collection brigade-an incident that recalled the 1925 murder of the French resident in the area. With the probable encouragement of local communist cadres, the insurrection quickly spread through the whole region. Sihanouk was on one of his frequent sojourns in France, and Lon Nol, the prime minister, responded harshly. After returning home in March 1967, Sihanouk personally supervised counterinsurgency measures. He later mentioned, in an offhand way, that the effectiveness of the royal armed forces had restored the peace but that approximately 10,000 people had died.

The insurgency was not suppressed completely. It spread rapidly from Batdambang to the southern and to the southwestern provinces of Pouthisat (Pursat), Kampong Chhnang (Kompong Chang), Kampong Cham, Kampong Spoe (Kompong Speu), Kampot, and the central province of Kampong Thum. By the end of 1968, unrest was reported in eleven of the country's eighteen provinces. The Khmer Loeu regions of Mondol Kiri (Mondolkiri) Province and Rotanokiri Province fell almost entirely under KCP control by the end of the decade.

In January 1968, the communists established the Revolutionary Army of Kampuchea (RAK). During Sihanouk's last two years in power, the RAK obtained minimal assistance from the North Vietnamese, the Viet Cong, and the Chinese. Although North Vietnam had established a special unit in 1966 to train the Cambodian communists, it was extremely reluctant to alienate Sihanouk at a time when vital supplies were passing through the port of Kampong Saom and along the Ho Chi Minh Trail to the Viet Cong bases along the CambodiaVietnam border. Beijing and Moscow also were providing Sihanouk with arms, many of which were being used against the insurgents. The indifference of the world communist movement to the Cambodian struggle from 1967 to 1969 made a permanent impression on Pol Pot and other Khmer Rouge leaders.

THE MARCH 1970 COUP D'ETAT

Sihanouk was away on a trip to Moscow and Beijing when General Lon Nol launched a successful coup d'état. On the morning of March 18, 1970, the National Assembly was hastily convened, and voted unanimously to depose Sihanouk as head of state. Lon Nol, who had been serving as prime minister, was granted emergency powers. Sirik Matak, an ultraconservative royal prince who in 1941 had been passed over by the French in favor of his cousin Norodom Sihanouk as king, retained his post as deputy prime minister. The new government emphasized that the transfer of power had been totally legal and constitutional, and it received the recognition of most foreign governments.

Most middle-class and educated Khmers in Phnom Penh had grown weary of Sihanouk and apparently welcomed the change of government. But he was still popular in the villages. Days after the coup, the prince, now in Beijing, broadcast an appeal to the people to resist the usurpers. Demonstrations and riots occurred throughout the country. In one incident on March 29, an estimated 40,000 peasants began a march on the capital to demand Sihanouk's reinstatement. They were dispersed, with many casualties, by contingents of the armed forces and the Khmer Serei.

From Beijing, Sihanouk proclaimed his intention to create a National United Front of Kampuchea (Front Uni National du Kampuchéa-FUNK). In the prince's words, this front would embrace "all Khmer both inside and outside the country- including the faithful, religious people, military men, civilians, and men and women who cherish the ideals of independence, democracy, neutrality, progressivism, socialism, Buddhism, nationalism, territorial integrity, and anti-imperialism." A coalition, brokered by the Chinese, was hastily formed between the prince and the KCP. On May 5, 1970, the actual establishment of FUNK and of the Royal Government of National Union of Kampuchea (Gouvernement Royal d'Union Nationale du Kampuchéa-GRUNK), were announced.

Sihanouk assumed the post of GRUNK head of state, appointing Penn Nouth, one of his most loyal supporters, as prime minister. Khieu Samphan was designated deputy prime minister, minister of defense, and commander in chief of the GRUNK armed forces (though actual military operations were directed by Pol Pot). Hu Nim became minister of information, and Hou Yuon assumed multiple responsibilities as minister of interior, communal reforms, and cooperatives. GRUNK claimed that it was not a government-in-exile because Khieu Samphan and the insurgents remained inside Cambodia.

For Sihanouk and the KCP, this was an extremely useful marriage of convenience. Peasants, motivated by loyalty to the monarchy, rallied to the FUNK cause. The appeal of the Sihanouk-KCP coalition grew immensely after October 9, 1970, when Lon Nol abolished the monarchy and redesignated Cambodia as the Khmer Republic. The concept of a republic was not popular with most villagers, who had grown up with the idea that something was seriously awry in a Cambodia without a monarch.

GRUNK operated on two tiers. Sihanouk and his loyalists remained in Beijing, although the prince did make a visit to the "liberated areas" of Cambodia, including Angkor Wat, in March 1973. The KCP commanded the insurgency within the country. Gradually, the prince was deprived of everything but a passive, figurehead role in the coalition. The KCP told people inside Cambodia that expressions of support for Sihanouk would result in their liquidation, and when the prince appeared in public overseas to publicize the GRUNK cause, he was treated with almost open contempt by Ieng Sary and Khieu Samphan. In June 1973, the prince told the Italian journalist Oriana Fallaci that when "they [the Khmer Rouge] no longer need me, they will spit me out like a cherry pit!" By the end of that year, Sihanouk loyalists had been purged from all of GRUNK's ministries.

THE WIDENING WAR

The 1970 coup d'état that toppled Sihanouk dragged Cambodia into the vortex of a wider war. The escalating conflict pitted government troops, now renamed the Khmer

National Armed Forces (Forces Armées Nationales Khmères-FANK), initially against the North Vietnamese and the Viet Cong, and subsequently against the old RAK, now revitalized and renamed the Cambodian People's National Liberation Armed Forces (CPNLAF).

As combat operations quickly disclosed, the two sides were mismatched. The inequality lay not so much in sheer numbers. Thousands of young urban Cambodians flocked to join FANK in the months following the coup and, throughout its five-year life, the republican government forces held a numerical edge over their opponents, the padded payrolls and the phantom units reported in the press notwithstanding. Instead, FANK was outclassed in training and leadership. With the surge of recruits, the government forces expanded beyond their capacity to absorb the new inductees.

Later, given the press of tactical operations and the need to replace combat casualties, there was insufficient time to impart needed skills to individuals or to units, and lack of training remained the bane of FANK's existence until its collapse. While individual soldiers and some government units fought bravely, their leaders- with notable exceptions-were both corrupt and incompetent. Arrayed against an armed force of such limited capability was arguably the best light infantry in the world at the time--the North Vietnamese and the Viet Cong. And when there forces were supplanted, it was by the tough, rigidly indoctrinated peasant army of the CPNLAF with its core of Khmer Rouge leaders.

With the fall of Sihanouk, the North Vietnamese and the Viet Cong became alarmed at the prospect of a pro-Western regime that might allow the United States to establish a military presence on their western flank. To prevent this from happening, they began transferring their military installations away from the border area to locations deeper within Cambodian territory. A new command center was established at the city of Kracheh (Kratié).

On April 29, 1970, South Vietnamese and United States units unleashed a multi-pronged offensive into Cambodia to destroy the Central Office for South Vietnam (COSVN), the headquarters for North Vietnamese and Viet Cong combat operations in South Vietnam. Extensive logistical installations and large amounts of supplies were found and destroyed, but as reporting from the United States MACV subsequently disclosed, still larger amounts of material already had been moved deeper into Cambodia.

The North Vietnamese army turned on the republican government forces, and by June 1970, three months after the coup, they and the CPNLAF had swept FANK from the entire northeastern third of the country. After defeating the government forces, they turned newly won territories over to the local insurgents. The Khmer Rouge also established "liberated areas" in the south and the southwestern parts of the country, where they operated independently of the Vietnamese. The KCP's debt to the North Vietnamese after March 1970 was one that Pol Pot was loath to acknowledge; however, it is clear that without North Vietnamese and Viet Cong assistance, the revolutionary struggle would have dragged on much longer than it did.

United States bombing of enemy troop dispositions in Cambodia- particularly in the summer of 1973, when intense aerial bombardment (known as Arclight) was used to halt a Khmer Rouge assault on Phnom Penh-bought time for the Lon Nol government, but did not stem the momentum of the communist forces. United States official documents give a figure of 79,959 sorties by B-52 and F-111 aircraft over the country, during which a total of 539,129 tons of ordnance were dropped, about 350 percent of the tonnage (153,000 tons) dropped on Japan during World War II. Many of the bombs that fell in Cambodia struck relatively uninhabited mountain or forest regions; however, as declassified United States Air Force maps show, others fell over some of the most densely inhabited areas of the country, such as Siemreab Province, Kampong Chhnang Province, and the countryside around Phnom Penh.

Deaths from the bombing are extremely difficult to estimate, and figures range from a low of 30,000 to a high of 500,000. Whatever the real extent of the casualties, the Arclight missions over Cambodia, which were halted in August 15, 1973, by the United States Congress, delivered shattering blows to the structure of life in many of the country's villages, and, according to some critics, drove the Cambodian people into the arms of the Khmer Rouge.

The bombing was by far the most controversial aspect of the United States presence in Cambodia. In his book Sideshow, William Shawcross provides a vivid image of the hellish conditions, especially in the months of January to August 1973, when the Arclight sorties were most intense. He claims that the bombing contributed to the forging of a brutal and singlemindedly fanatical Khmer Rouge movement. However, his arguments have been disputed by several United States officials-including the former ambassador to Cambodia, Emory C. Swank, and the former Air Force commander in Thailand, General John W. Vogt--in an appendix to the second volume of the memoirs of then Secretary of State, Henry Kissinger.

From the Khmer Rouge perspective, however, the severity of the bombings was matched by the treachery of the North Vietnamese. The Cambodian communists had refused to take part in the Paris peace talks. When North Vietnam and the United States signed the Paris Peace Accords on January 27, 1973, bombing missions over Vietnam and Laos were terminated. The fighter bombers and other aircraft thus released were diverted to strike Khmer Rouge positions in Cambodia.

EARLY KHMER ROUGE ATROCITIES

One of the earliest accounts of life under the Khmer Rouge was written in 1973 by a school administrator, Ith Sarin, who had joined the movement after becoming disillusioned with Lon Nol and the Khmer Republic, then rose to the status of candidate member of the KCP, but left the party and returned to Phnom Penh after nine months in the underground. His work, Regrets for the Khmer Soul (in Khmer, Sranaoh Pralung Khmer), it revealed the secrecy with which the Khmer Rouge concealed the existence of the communist party, which they referred to by the sinister term Angkar Loeu (High Organization), or simply, Angkar. The KCP Central Committee was referred to as the Kena Mocchhim (or Committee Machine, mocchhim being derived from the Western term, "machine").

Territories under Angkar control were well organized. Ith Sarin described a five-level hierarchy of Angkar-controlled bodies reaching from the six areas, or phumphaek (see Glossary) into which the country was divided down to the hamlet, or phum level. The Angkar imposed a grim regime in which hatred for Lon Nol, the Americans, and, at times, the North Vietnamese "allies" was assiduously cultivated. Expressions of support for Sihanouk were firmly discouraged and people were encouraged to spy on each other. Discipline was unremittingly harsh. Ith Sarin concluded from his experience that the great majority of the people did not like the Angkar and the collective way of life it imposed, that they despaired that Sihanouk would ever return to power, and that they would support the Khmer Republic if it carried out genuine reforms. Oddly, Lon Nol's security forces banned the book for a time on the grounds that it was "pro-communist." Although this was not true, it did provide a foretaste of what the entire Cambodian population would endure after April 1975.

Disturbing stories of Khmer Rouge atrocities began to surface as the communists prepared to deal the coup de grace to the Khmer Republic. In March 1974, they captured the old capital city of Odongk north of Phnom Penh, destroyed it, dispersed its 20,000 inhabitants into the countryside, and executed the teachers and civil servants. The same year, they brutally murdered sixty people, including women and children, in a small village called Sar Sarsdam in Siemreab Province. A similar incident was reported at Ang Snuol, a town west of the capital. Other instances of what one observer, Donald Kirk, described as a "sweeping, almost cosmic policy" of indiscriminate terror, were recounted by refugees who fled to Phnom Penh or across the Thai border. Kirk contrasted this behavior with the Viet Cong's use of "a modicum of care and precision" in applying terror in South Vietnam (for instance, assassination of landlords or of South Vietnamese officials). Atrocity stories, however, were considered to be anticommunist propaganda by many, if not most, Western journalists and other observers; nevertheless, Phnom Penh's populationswelled to as many as 2.5 million people as terrified refugees sought to escape not only the United States bombing and the ground fighting, but the harshness of life under the Angkar.

THE FALL OF PHNOM PENH

The Khmer Rouge initiated their dry-season offensive to capture the beleaguered Cambodian capital on January 1, 1975. Their troops controlled the banks of the Mekong River, and they were able to rig ingenious mines to sink convoys bringing relief supplies of food, fuel, and ammunition to the slowly starving city. After the river was effectively blocked in early February, the United States began airlifts of supplies. This was extremely risky because of Khmer Rouge rockets. The communists also fired rockets and shells into the city, causing many civilian deaths. Doomed units of republican soldiers dug in around the capital; many of them had run out of ammunition, and they were overrun as the Khmer Rouge advanced. American observers, who generally had little esteem for FANK officer corps, were impressed by the determination of the Khmer enlisted men to fight to the end.

On April 1, 1975, President Lon Nol resigned and left the country. His exit was prompted by fear of certain death if he fell into Khmer Rouge hands. The communists had included him among "seven traitors" who were marked for execution. (The others were non-communist, nationalist leaders Sirik Matak, Son Ngoc Thanh, In Tam, Prime Minister Long Boret, Cheng Heng, who became head of state after Sihanouk's ouster, and Sosthene Fernandez, the FANK commander in chief). Saukham Khoy became acting president of a government that had less than three weeks to live. Last-minute efforts on the part of the United States to arrange a peace agreement involving Sihanouk ended in failure. On April 12, United States embassy personnel were evacuated by helicopter. The ambassador, John Gunther Dean, invited high officials of the Khmer Republic to join them. But Sirik Matak, Long Boret, Lon Non (Lon Nol's brother), and most members of Lon Nol's cabinet declined. They chose to share the fate of their people. All were executed soon after Khmer Rouge units entered Phnom Penh on April 17, 1975.

DEMOCRATIC KAMPUCHEA, 1975-78

Mid-April is the beginning of the Cambodian new year, the year's most festive celebration. For many Cambodians, the fall of Phnom Penh promised both a new year and a new era of peace. The people of Phnom Penh and of other cities waited in anticipation for the appearance of their new rulers. The troops who entered the capital on April 17 were mostly grim-faced youths clad in black with the checkered scarves that had become the uniform of the movement. Their unsmiling demeanor quickly dispelled popular enthusiasm. People began to realize that, in the eyes of the victors, the war was not over; it was just beginning, and the people were the new enemy. According to Father Ponchaud, as the sense of consternation and dread grew, it seemed that "a slab of lead had fallen on the city."

Evacuation of Phnom Penh began immediately.The black-clad troops told the residents that they would move only about "two or three kilometers" outside the city and would return in "two or three days." Other witnesses report being told that the evacuation was because of the threat of an American bombing and that they did not have to lock their houses since the Khmer Rouge would "take care of everything" until they returned. The roads out of the city were clogged with evacuees. Phnom Penh-the population of which, numbering 2.5 million people, included as many as 1.5 million wartime refugees living with relatives or in shantytowns around the urban center-was soon emptied. Similar evacuations occurred at Batdambang, Kampong Cham, Siemreab, Kampong Thum, and the country's othertowns and cities.

There were no exceptions to the evacuation. Even Phnom Penh's hospitals were emptied of their patients. The Khmer Rouge provided transportation for some of the aged and the disabled, and they set up stockpiles of food outside the city for the refugees; however, the supplies were inadequate to sustain the hundreds of thousands of people on the road. Even seriously injured hospital patients, many without any means of conveyance, were summarily forced to leave regardless of their condition. According to Khieu Samphan, the evacuation of Phnom Penh's famished and disease-racked population resulted in 2,000 to 3,000 deaths, which is probably anunderstatement. The foreign community, about 800 persons, was quarantined in the French embassy compound, and by the end of the month the foreigners were taken by truck to the Thai border. Khmer women who were married to foreigners were allowed to accompany their husbands, but Khmer men were not permitted to leave with their foreign wives.

Promises that urban residents forced into the countryside would be allowed to return home were never kept. Instead, the town dwellers, regarded as politically unreliable "new people," were put to work in forced labor battalions throughout the country. One refugee, for example, recalled that her family was sent to the region around Moung Roessei in Batdambang Province to clear land and grow rice.

Aside from the alleged threat of United States air strikes, the Khmer Rouge justified the evacuations in terms of the impossibility of transporting sufficient food to feed an urban population of between 2 and 3 million people. Lack of adequate transportation meant that, instead of bringing food to the people (tons of it lay in storehouses in the port city of Kampong Saom, according to Father Ponchaud), the people had to be brought to (and had to grow) the food. But there were other, more basic motivations. The Khmer Rouge was determined to turn the country into a nation of peasants in which the corruption and parasitism of city life would be completely uprooted. In addition, Pol Pot wanted to break up the "enemy spy organizations" that allegedly were based in the urban areas. Finally, it seems that Pol Pot and his hard-line associates on the KCP Political Bureau used the forced evacuations to gain control of the city's population and to weaken the position of their factional rivals within the communist party. Had Phnom Penh been controlled by one of the more moderate communist leaders, the exodus might not have taken place when it did.

The regime immediately seized and executed as many Khmer Republic civil servants, police, and military officers as it could find. Evacuees who had been associated with the Lon Nol government had to feign peasant or working-class backgrounds to avoid certain death. One refugee wrote that she and her family, who came from the middle or upper middle class, dyed their city clothes black (like those of peasants) to help them escape detection. In one incident, soon after the fall of Phnom Penh, more than 300 former military officers were told to put on their dress uniforms in order to "meet Sihanouk." Instead, they were taken to a jungle clearing in Batdambang Province and were machine-gunned or clubbed to death. The wives and the children of people with government backgrounds were also killed, apparently to eliminate people who might harbor feelings of revenge toward the regime.

According to refugee accounts, the rate of killing had decreased by the summer of 1975. Some civil servants and educated people were sent to "reeducation centers" and, if they showed "genuine" contrition, were put in forced labor battalions. There were new killings, however, in late 1975 and in early 1976. Many of the victims were educated people, such as schoolteachers. During the entire Democratic Kampuchea period from 1975 to 1978, cadres exercised the power of life and death, especially over "new people," for whom threats of being struck with a pickax or an ax handle and of being "put in a plastic bag" were a part of everyday life. In order to save ammunition, firearms were rarely used. People were murdered for not working hard, for complaining about living conditions, for collecting or stealing food for their own use, for wearing jewelry, for having sexual relations, for grieving over the loss of relatives or friends, or for expressing religious sentiments. Sick people were often eliminated. The killings often, if not usually, occurred without any kind of trial, and they continued, uninterrupted, until the 1979 Vietnamese invasion. People who displeased the Angkar, or its local representatives, customarily received a formal warning (kosang) to mend their ways. More than two warnings resulted in being given an "invitation," which meant certain death. In 1977 and 1978 the violence reached a climax as the revolutionaries turned against each other in bloody purges.

REVOLUTIONARY TERROR

Estimates of the number of people who perished under the Khmer Rouge vary tremendously. A figure of three million deaths between 1975 and 1979 was given by the Vietnamese-sponsored Phnom Penh regime, the PRK. Father Ponchaud suggested 2.3 million. Amnesty International estimated 1.4 million dead; the United States Department of State, 1.2 million. Khieu Samphan and Pol Pot, who could be expected to give underestimations, cited figures of 1 million and 800,000, respectively. In 1962 the year of the last census taken before Cambodia was engulfed by war, the population of the country was cited at 5.7 million. Ten years later, in 1972, the population was estimated to have reached 7.1 million. Using Pol Pot's rather modest figure of 800,000 deaths, about 11 percent of
the population would have died from unnatural causes between 1975 and 1978. By contrast, Amnesty International's figure would yield a death rate of almost 20 percent of the population; Father Ponchaud's, of approximately 32 percent. The revolution was easily, in proportion to the size of the country's population, the bloodiest in modern Asian history.

As is evident from the accounts of refugees, the greatest causes of death were hunger, disease, and exposure. Many city people could not survive the rigors of life in the countryside, the forced marches, and the hard physical labor. People died from the bites of venomous snakes, drowned in flooded areas during the rainy season, and were killed by wild beasts in jungle areas. Many fell victim to malaria. Others died in the fighting between Vietnam and Cambodia in 1978 and in 1979. Nonetheless, executions accounted for hundreds of thousands of victims and perhaps for as many as 1 million. Western journalists have been shown "killing fields" containing as many as 16,000 bodies.

SOCIETY UNDER THE ANGKAR

The social transformation wrought by the Khmer Rouge, first, in the areas that they occupied during the war with Lon Nol and, then, in varying degrees, throughout the country, was far more radical than anything attempted by the
Russian, Chinese, or Vietnamese revolutions. According to Pol Pot, five classes existed in pre-Revolutionary Cambodia - peasants, workers, bourgeoisie, capitalists, and feudalists. Postrevolutionary society, as defined by the 1976 Constitution of Democratic Kampuchea, consisted of workers, peasants, and "all other Kampuchean working people." No allowance was made for a transitional stage such as China's "New Democracy" in which "patriotic" landlord or bourgeois elements were permitted to play a role in socialist construction. Sihanouk writes that in 1975 he, Khieu Samphan, and Khieu Thirith went to visit Zhou Enlai, who was gravely ill. Zhou warned them not to attempt to achieve communism suddenly by one "great leap forward" without intermediate steps, as China had done with disastrous results in the late 1950s. Khieu Samphan and Khieu Thirith "just smiled an incredulous and superior smile." Khieu

Samphan and Son Sen later boasted to Sihanouk that "we will be the first nation to create a completely communist society without wasting time on intermediate steps."

Although conditions varied from region to region, a situation that was, in part, a reflection of factional divisions that still existed within the KCP during the 1970s, the testimony of refugees reveals that the most salient social division was between the politically suspect "new people," those driven out of the towns after the communist victory, and the more reliable "old people," the poor and lower middle-class peasants who had remained in the countryside. Despite the ideological commitment to radical equality, KCP members and the armed forces constituted a clearly recognizable elite. The working class was a negligible factor because of the evacuation of the urban areas and the idling of most of the country's few factories. The one important working class group in pre-Revolutionary Cambodia-laborers on large rubber plantations-traditionally had consisted mostly of Vietnamese emigrants and thus was politically suspect.

The number of people, including refugees, living in the urban areas, on the eve of the communist victory probably was somewhat more than 3 million, in a wartime population that has been estimated at between 5.7 and 7.3 million. As mentioned, despite their rural origins, the refugees were considered "new people"- that is, people unsympathetic to Democratic Kampuchea. Some doubtless passed as "old people" after returning to their native villages, but the Khmer Rouge seem to have been extremely vigilant in recording and keeping track of the movements of families and of individuals. The lowest unit of social control, the krom (group), consisted of ten to fifteen nuclear families whose activities were closely supervised by a three-person committee. The committee chairman was selected by the KCP. This grass roots leadership was required to note the social origin of each family under its jurisdiction and to report it to persons higher up in the Angkar hierarchy. The number of "new people" may initially have been as high as 2.5 million.

The "new people" were treated as slave laborers. They were constantly moved, were forced to do the hardest physical labor, and worked in the most inhospitable, fever-ridden parts of the country, such as forests, upland areas, and swamps. "New people" were segregated from "old people," enjoyed little or no privacy, and received the smallest rice rations. When the country experienced food shortages in 1977, the "new people" suffered the most. The medical care available to them was primitive or nonexistent. Families often were separated because people were divided into work brigades according to age and sex and sent to different parts of the country. "New people"were subjected to unending political indoctrination and could be executed without trial. The creation of what amounted to a slave class suggests continuity between the Cambodian revolution and the country's ancient history. Like the Khmer Rouge leadership, the god-kings of Angkor had commanded armies of slaves. Pol Pot boasted in 1977 that "if our people can make Angkor, they can make anything."

The situation of the "old people" under Khmer Rouge rule was more ambiguous. Refugee interviews reveal cases in which villagers were treated as harshly as the "new people," enduring forced labor, indoctrination, the separation of children from parents, and executions; however, they were generally allowed to remain in their native villages.

Because of their age-old resentment of the urban and rural elites, many of the poorest peasants probably were sympathetic to Khmer Rouge goals. In the early 1980s, visiting Western journalists found that the issue of peasant support for the Khmer Rouge was an extremely sensitive subject that officials of the People's Republic of Kampuchea had little inclination to discuss.

On the basis of interviews with refugees from different parts of the country as well as other sources, Vickery has argued that there was a wide regional variation in the severity of policies adopted by local Khmer Rouge authorities.
Ideology had something to do with the differences, but the availability of food, the level of local development, and the personal qualities of cadres also were important factors. The greatest number of deaths occurred in undeveloped
districts, where "new people" were sent to clear land. While conditions were hellish in some localities, they apparently were tolerable in others. Vickery describes the Eastern Zone, which was dominated by pro-Vietnamese
cadres, as one in which the extreme policies of the Pol Pot leadership were not adopted (at least until 1978, when the Eastern leadership was liquidated in a bloody purge).

Executions were few, "old people" and "new people" were treated largely the same, and food was made available to the entire population. Although the Southwestern Zone was one original center of power of the Khmer Rouge, and cadres administered it with strict discipline, random executions were relatively rare, and "new people" were not persecuted if they had a cooperative attitude. In the Western Zone and in the Northwestern Zone, conditions were harsh. Starvation was widespread in the latter zone because cadres sent rice to Phnom Penh rather than distributed it to the local population. In the Northern Zone and in the Central Zone, there seem to have been more executions than there were victims of starvation. Little reliable information emerged on conditions in the Northeastern Zone, one of the most isolated parts of Cambodia.

On the surface, society in Democratic Kampuchea was strictly egalitarian. The Khmer language, like many in Southeast Asia, has a complex system of usages to define speakers' rank and social status. These usages were abandoned. People were encouraged to call each other "friend," or "comrade" (in Khmer, mit or met), and to avoid traditional signs of deference such as bowing or folding the hands in salutation. Language was transformed in other ways. The Khmer Rouge invented new terms. People were told they must "forge" (lot dam) a new revolutionary character, that they were the "instruments" (opokar) of the Angkar, and that nostalgia for prerevolutionary times (cchoeu sttak aram, or "memory sickness") could result in their receiving Angkar's "invitation."

As in other revolutionary states, however, some people were "more equal" than others. Members and candidate members of the KCP, local-level leaders of poor peasant background who collaborated with the Angkar, and members of the armed forces had a higher standard of living than the rest of the population. Refugees agree that, even during times of severe food shortage, members of the grass-roots elite had adequate, if not luxurious, supplies of food. One refugee wrote that "pretty new bamboo houses" were built for Khmer Rouge cadres along the river in Phnom Penh. According to Craig Etcheson, an authority on Democratic Kampuchea, members of the revolutionary army lived in self-contained colonies, and they had a "distinctive warrior-caste ethos." Armed forces units personally loyal to Pol Pot, known as the "Unconditional Divisions," were a privileged group within the military.

Given the severity of their revolutionary ideology, it is surprising that the highest ranks of the Khmer Rouge leadership exhibited a talent for cronyism that matched that of the Sihanouk- era elite. Pol Pot's wife, Khieu Ponnary,
was head of the Association of Democratic Khmer Women and her younger sister, Khieu Thirith, served as minister of social action. These two women are considered among the half-dozen most powerful personalities in Democratic
Kampuchea. Son Sen's wife, Yun Yat, served as minister for culture, education and learning. Several of Pol Pot's nephews and nieces were given jobs in the Ministry of Foreign Affairs. One of Ieng Sary's daughters was appointed
head of the Calmette Hospital although she had not graduated from secondary school. A niece of Ieng Sary was given a job as English translator for Radio Phnom Penh although her fluency in the language was extremely limited.
Family ties were important, both because of the culture and because of the leadership's intense secretiveness and distrust of outsiders, especially of pro-Vietnamese communists. Greed was also a motive. Different ministries, such
as the Ministry of Foreign Affairs and the Ministry of Industry, were controlled and exploited by powerful Khmer Rouge families. Administering the diplomatic corps was regarded as an especially profitable fiefdom.

RELIGIOUS AND MINORITY COMMUNITIES

Article 20 of the 1976 Constitution of Democratic Kampuchea guaranteed religious freedom, but it also declared that "all reactionary religions that are detrimental to Democratic Kampuchea and the Kampuchean People are strictly
forbidden." About 85 percent of the population follows the Theravada school of Buddhism. Before 1975 the Khmer Rouge tolerated the activities of the community of Buddhist monks, or sangha, in the liberated areas in order to win popular support. This changed abruptly after the fall of Phnom Penh. The country's 40,000 to 60,000 Buddhist monks, regarded by the regime as social parasites, were defrocked and forced into labor brigades. Many monks were executed; temples and pagodas were destroyed or turned into storehouses or jails. Images of the Buddha were defaced and dumped into rivers and lakes. People who were discovered praying or expressing religious sentiments in other ways were often killed. The Christian and Muslim communities also were persecuted. The Roman Catholic cathedral of Phnom Penh was completely razed. The Khmer Rouge forced Muslims to eat pork, which they regard as an abomination. Many of those who refused were killed. Christian clergy and Muslim leaders were executed.

The Khmer Rouge's treatment of minorities seems to have varied from group to group. The Vietnamese endured the greatest suffering. Tens of thousands were murdered in regime-organized massacres. Most of the survivors fled to Vietnam. The Cham, a Muslim minority who are the descendants of migrants from the old state of Champa, were forced to adopt the Khmer language and customs. Their communities, which traditionally had existed apart from Khmer villages, were broken up. Forty thousand Cham were killed in two districts of Kampong Cham Province alone. Thai minorities living near the Thai border also were persecuted.

Despite the fact that Chinese and Sino-Khmers had dominated the Cambodian economy for centuries and could be considered exploiters of the peasantry, the Khmer Rouge apparently did not single them out for harsh treatment. The war drove most rural Chinese into the cities, and after the forced evacuations they and their urban compatriots were regarded as "new people." They shared the same hardships as Khmers, however. Phnom Penh's close relationship with China was probably a factor in the regime's reluctance to persecute them openly.

In the late 1980s, little was known of Khmer Rouge policies toward the tribal peoples of the northeast, the Khmer Loeu. Pol Pot established an insurgent base in the tribal areas of Rotanokiri Province in the early 1960s, and he may have had a substantial Khmer Loeu following. Predominately animist peoples with few ties to the Buddhist culture of the lowland Khmers, the Khmer Loeu had resented Sihanouk's attempts to "civilize" them. Cambodia expert Serge Thion notes that marriage to a tribal person was considered "final proof of unconditional loyalty to the party." Khieu Samphan may have been married to a tribal woman.

EDUCATION AND HEALTH

Like the radical exponents of the Cultural Revolution in China during the 1960s, the Khmer Rouge regarded traditional education with unalloyed hostility. After the fall of Phnom Penh, they executed thousands of teachers. Those who had been educators prior to 1975 survived by hiding their identities. Aside from teaching basic mathematical skills and literacy, the major goal of the new educational system was to instill revolutionary values in the young. For a regime at war with most of Cambodia's traditional values, this meant that it was necessary to create a gap between the values of the young and the values of the nonrevolutionary old.

In a manner reminiscent of George Orwell's 1984, the regime recruited children to spy on adults. The pliancy of the younger generation made them, in the Angkar's words, the "dictatorial instrument of the party." In 1962 the communists had created a special secret organization, the Alliance of Democratic Khmer Youth, that, in the early 1970s, changed its name to the Alliance of Communist Youth of Kampuchea. Pol Pot considered Alliance alumni as his most loyal and reliable supporters, and used them to gain control of the central and of the regional KCP apparatus. The powerful Khieu Thirith, minister of social action, was responsible for directing the youth movement.

Hardened young cadres, many little more than twelve years of age, were enthusiastic accomplices in some of the regime's worst atrocities. Sihanouk, who was kept under virtual house arrest in Phnom Penh between 1976 and 1978, wrote in War and Hope that his youthful guards, having been separated from their families and given a thorough indoctrination, were encouraged to play cruel games involving the torture of animals. Having lost parents, siblings, and friends in the war and lacking the Buddhist values of their elders, the Khmer Rouge youth also lacked the inhibitions that would have dampened their zeal for revolutionary terror.

Health facilities in the years 1975 to 1978 were abysmally poor. Many physicians either were executed or were prohibited from practicing. It appears that the party and the armed forces elite had access to Western medicine and to a system of hospitals that offered reasonable treatment but ordinary people, especially "new people," were expected to use traditional plant and herbal remedies that usually were ineffective. Some bartered their rice rations and personal possessions to obtain aspirin and other simple drugs.

THE ECONOMY

In its general contours, Democratic Kampuchea's economic policy was similar to, and possibly inspired by, China's radical Great Leap Forward that carried out immediate collectivization of the Chinese countryside in 1958. During the early 1970s, the Khmer Rouge established "mutual assistance groups" in the areas they occupied. After 1973 these were organized into "low-level cooperatives" in which land and agricultural implements were lent by peasants to the community but remained their private property. "High-level cooperatives," in which private property was abolished and the harvest became the collective property of the peasants, appeared in 1974. "Communities," introduced in early 1976, were a more advanced form of high-level cooperative in which communal dining was instituted. State-owned farms also were established.

Far more than had the Chinese communists, the Khmer Rouge relentlessly pursued the ideal of economic self-sufficiency, in their case the version that Khieu Samphan had outlined in his 1959 doctoral dissertation. Extreme measures were taken. Currency was abolished, and domestic trade or commerce could be conducted only through barter. Rice, measured in tins, became the most important medium of exchange, although people also bartered gold, jewelry, and other personal possessions. Foreign trade was almost completely halted, though there was a limited revival in late 1976 and early 1977. China was the most important trading partner, but commerce amounting to a few million dollars was also conducted with France, with Britain, and with the United States through a Hong Kong intermediary.

From the Khmer Rouge perspective, the country was free of foreign economic domination for the first time in its 2,000-year history. By mobilizing the people into work brigades organized in a military fashion, the Khmer Rouge hoped to unleash the masses' productive forces. There was an "Angkorian" component to economic policy. That ancient kingdom had grown rich and powerful because it controlled extensive irrigation systems that produced surpluses of rice. Agriculture in modern Cambodia depended, for the most part, on seasonal rains. By building a nationwide system of irrigation canals, dams, and reservoirs, the leadership believed it would be possible to produce rice on a year-round basis. It was the "new people" who suffered and sacrificed the most to complete these ambitious projects.

Although the Khmer Rouge implemented an "agriculture first" policy in order to achieve self-sufficiency, they were not, as some observers have argued, "back-to-nature" primitivists. Although the 1970-75 war and the evacuation of the cities had destroyed or idled most industry, small contingents of workers were allowed to return to the urban areas to reopen some plants. Like their Chinese counterparts, the Cambodian communists had great faith in the inventive power and the technical aptitude of the masses, and they constantly published reports of peasants' adapting old mechanical parts to new uses. Much as the Chinese had attempted unsuccessfully to build a new steel industry based on backyard furnaces during the Great Leap Forward, the Khmer Rouge sought to move industry to the countryside. Significantly, the seal of Democratic Kampuchea displayed not only sheaves of rice and irrigation sluices, but also a factory with smokestacks.

POLITICS UNDER THE KHMER ROUGE

By the April 1975 communist victory, Pol Pot and his close associates occupied the most important positions in the KCP and in the state hierarchies. He had been KCP general secretary since February 1963. His associates functioned as the party's Political Bureau, and they controlled a majority of the seats on the Central Committee. Khieu Thirith's management of youth groups meant that Pol Pot had ample reserves of zealous young cadres, "the nucleus and wick of the struggle," committed to imposing the party center's will throughout the country. But his domination of the revolutionary movement was not complete. In different areas of the country, especially in the Eastern Zone, pro-Vietnamese and veteran Khmer Issarak commanders were jealous of their independence. They questioned, and at times openly defied, his policies of revolutionary terror and hostility toward Vietnam. The highest ranks of the party were not free of dissension.

Like Joseph Stalin in the late 1920s and in the 1930s, Pol Pot initiated a purge of his opponents, both imagined and real. In terms of the number of people liquidated in relation to the total population, the Khmer Rouge terror was far bloodier than Stalin's. Through the 1970s, and especially after mid-1975, the party was shaken by factional struggles. There were even armed attempts to topple Pol Pot. The resultant purges reached a crest in 1977 and 1978 when hundreds of thousands of people, including some of the most important KCP leaders, were executed.

ESTABLISHING DEMOCRATIC KAMPUCHEA

The communists had exercised real power behind the facade, since its establishment in 1970, of the Royal Government of National Union of Kampuchea, (Governement Royal d'Union Nationale du Kampuchéa-GRUNK). It remained formally in control of the country until the proclamation of the Constitution of Democratic Kampuchea on January 5, 1976. Three months later, on April 2, Sihanouk resigned as head of state. Sihanouk remained under comfortable, but insecure, house arrest in Phnom Penh, until he departed for China on the last flight before Vietnamese forces captured the city on January 7, 1979.

Khieu Samphan described the 1976 Constitution as "not the result of any research on foreign documents, nor...the fruit of any research by scholars. In fact the people-workers, peasants, and Revolutionary Army-wrote the Constitution with their own hands." It was a brief document of sixteen chapters and twenty-one articles that defined the character of the state; the goals of economic, social and cultural policies; and the basic tenets of foreign policy. The "rights and duties of the individual" were briefly defined in Article 12. They included none of what are commonlyregarded as guarantees of political human rights except the statement that "men and women are equal in every respect." The document declared, however, that "all workers" and "all peasants" were "masters" of their factories and fields. An assertion that "there is absolutely no unemployment in Democratic Kampuchea" rings true in light of the regime's massive use of forced labor.

The Constitution defined Democratic Kampuchea's foreign policy principles in Article 21, the document's longest, in terms of "independence, peace, neutrality, and nonalignment." It pledged the country's support to anti-imperialist struggles in the Third World. In light of the regime's aggressive attacks against Vietnamese, Thai, and Lao territory during 1977 and 1978, the promise to "maintain close and friendly relations with all countries sharing a common border" bore little resemblance to reality.

Governmental institutions were outlined very briefly in the Constitution. The legislature, the Kampuchean People's Representative Assembly (KPRA), contained 250 members "representing workers, peasants, and other working people and the Kampuchean Revolutionary army." One hundred and fifty KPRA seats were allocated for peasant representatives; fifty, for the armed forces; and fifty, for worker and other representatives. The legislature was to be popularly elected for a five-year term. Its first and only election was held on March 20, 1976. "New people" apparently were not allowed to participate.

The executive branch of government also was chosen by the KPRA. It consisted of a state presidium "responsible for representing the state of Democratic Kampuchea inside and outside the country." It served for a five-year term, and its president was head of state. Khieu Samphan was the first and only person to serve in this office, which he assumed after Sihanouk's resignation. The judicial system was composed of "people's courts," the judges for which were appointed by the KPRA, as was the executive branch.

The Constitution did not mention regional or local government institutions. After assuming power, the Khmer Rouge abolished the old provinces (khet) and replaced them with seven zones; the Northern Zone, Northeastern Zone, Northwestern Zone, Central Zone, Eastern Zone, Western Zone, and Southwestern Zone. There were also two other regional-level units: the Kracheh Special Region Number 505 and, until 1977, the Siemreab Special Region Number 106. The zones were divided into damban (regions) that were given numbers. Number One, appropriately, encompassed the Samlot region of the Northwestern Zone (including Batdambang Province), where the insurrection against Sihanouk had erupted in early 1967. With this exception, the damban appear to have been numbered arbitrarily.

The damban were divided into srok (districts), khum (subdistricts), and phum (villages), the latter usually containing several hundred people. This pattern was roughly similar to that which existed under Sihanouk and the Khmer Republic, but inhabitants of the villages were organized into krom (groups) composed of ten to fifteen families. On each level, administration was directed by a three-person committee (kanak, or kena). KCP members occupied committee posts at the higher levels. Subdistrict and village committees were often staffed by local poor peasants, and, very rarely, by "new people." Cooperatives (sahakor), similar in jurisdictional area to the khum, assumed local government responsibilities in some areas.

AN ELUSIVE PARTY

To most people inside and outside Democratic Kampuchea, the communist party was known simply as the Angkar Loeu. The party's commitment to revolution was expressed in the terminology of the 1976 Constitution, but no mention was made of a specifically Marxist-Leninist ideology. The KCP's real leaders and identity were kept closely guarded secrets from non-members until 1977. Head of state Khieu Samphan was a front-Sihanouk describes him as a "bit player"-for the most important leader, Saloth Sar, whose appearances and speeches were not publicized in the official media. Under the name Pol Pot, Saloth Sar was elected to a seat in the KPRA in March 1976 as a representative of rubber plantation workers, and he became Democratic Kampuchea's prime minister the following month.

The histories of most revolutionary movements contain a clandestine theme, but rarely have any approached the near-paranoia of the Cambodian communists. In part, this reflected the profound distrust with which Pol Pot and his associates regarded people outside their small, closed circle that had begun its association in Paris in the 1950s. Also, there may have been an unwillingness to risk the support of a still-conservative peasantry by publicly embracing Marxism-Leninism. The most important reason for the obsession with secrecy, however, was intraparty strife-the KCP's continuing failure to resolve factional differences and to achieve consensus on its mission and policies. Even more than the future, however, the past was a focus of bitter controversy: how much should the KCP acknowledge its debt to the Vietnamese communists?

On September 18, in a speech mourning the death of Mao Zedong, Pol Pot announced that the Angkar was "Marxist-Leninist" and that it enjoyed "fraternal relations" with the Chinese Communist Party. But it was not until a year later, in September 1977, that Pol Pot revealed the existence of the KCP and its history in a five-hour recorded radio speech. He stated that the KCP was seventeen years old and that its founding date had been September 30, 1960. He noted that the KCP's decision to disclose its real identity had been encouraged by "foreign friends" (the Chinese) who wanted the KCP to take credit for the revolutionary victory.

Pol Pot's mention of the September 1960 founding date was extremely significant. Within the party ranks, September 30, 1951, traditionally had been recognized as its founding date. This was the day when the Kampuchean (or Khmer) People's Revolutionary Party (KPRP) was established following the reorganization of the Indochinese Communist Party (ICP). The September 1960 meeting had been considered the KPRP's second congress, but in the September-October 1976 edition of the party's official journal, Tung Padevat (Revolutionary Flag), the date of birth of the KPRP was given as September 30, 1960. Tung Padevat declared that the new founding date was adopted because "we must arrange the history of the party into something clean and perfect, in line with our policies of independence and selfmastery ." Pol Pot's speech a year later gave official sanction to this view.

Another party journal, Tung Kraham (Red Flag), mentioned the traditional founding date, September 30, 1951, in its September 1976 issue. The argument over the birth date reflected deep factional divisions within the KCP. Backers of the 1951 birth date, if not pro-Vietnamese, were at least willing to recognize their movement's past dependence on Vietnamese support. Pol Pot and his associates adopted the 1960 birthday to emphasize the party's Cambodian identity and to distance it from any association with the Vietnamese communists. The party's official history, or "Black Book," published in 1978 after pro-Vietnamese elements had been liquidated, stated that the KCP had severed fraternal party relations with the Vietnam Workers' Party as early as 1973.

INTER-PARTY CONFLICT

On the eve of its 1975 victory against the Lon Nol forces, the KCP was, in terms of personnel, ideological viewpoints, and factional loyalties, quite heterogeneous. Etcheson, in The Rise and Demise of Democratic Kampuchea, identifies six factions: the Pol Pot group (members of which he labels "Stalinists"); internationalists (pro-Vietnamese elements who were based in Hanoi after 1954, and who returned to the country when the FUNK united front was declared in 1970); veterans of the leftist Khmer Issarak (who remained in the country after 1954, mostly in the southern and in western parts of the country); veterans of the Pracheachon Party founded in 1954 (which had contested Sihanouk's Sangkum openly until being driven underground in the 1960s); pro-Chinese or Maoist elements (including Paris-group intellectuals Hou Yuon and Hu Nim); and the pro-Sihanouk Khmer Rumdo. Ben Kiernan, another analyst of Cambodia, identifies three factions: the Pol Pot faction, the pro-Vietnamese communists, and the adherents of the Chinese Cultural Revolution model. The roles of ideology and of conflicting party lines in factional struggles, however, should not be overemphasized. Behind doctrinal differences lay the dynamics of personal rivalry and the strong sense of patron-client loyalty that has always characterized Cambodian politics.

Although the Revolutionary Army of Kampuchea (RAK) was "reestablished" in July 1975 to bring all Khmer Rouge units formally under central authority, real control of regional armed forces remained in the hands of the zone party committee heads. The most important center of regional resistance to the Pol Potdominated party center was the Eastern Zone, comprising part or all of the old provinces of Prey Veng, Svay Rieng, Kandal, and Kampong Cham that adjoined Vietnam. Its leader was So Phim, a proVietnamese internationalist.

Differences between the Eastern Zone revolutionaries and the other Khmer Rouge were readily apparent by 1975. While the uniforms of Pol Pot loyalists and their allies were black, the uniforms of the Eastern Zone were a distinctive green. In addition, cadre behavior toward the civilian population in the Eastern Zone was generally exemplary. It seems that some of the Eastern cadres were sympathetic to Sihanouk; refugee Molyda Szymusiak wrote that during the evacuation of Phnom Penh, a "Sihanouk Khmer" soldier advised her relatives (who were distantly related to the royal family) to accompany him to Prey Veng Province on Cambodia's southern border.

At least two coups d'état against the center were attempted--in July and in September, 1975. The latter incident involved Eastern Zone troops. After April 1975, Hou Yuon, one of the original Paris group, disappeared. His colleague, Hu Nim, who was tortured and killed in the Tuol Sleng detention center in 1977, indicated in his confession that Hou Yuon had been liquidated for opposing the extremism of the center's policies.

Pol Pot loyalists occupied most of the important positions in the new government that was formed after the March 20, 1976, elections; however, Vorn Vet, a pro-Vietnamese leader, was appointed second vice premier with responsibility over six ministry-level economic committees, and he also headed the special Phnom Penh capital zone. So Phim, a longtime rival of Pol Pot within the communist movement, was first vice president of the presidium and a member of the KCP Political Bureau. (The second vice president, Nhim Ros, was a Pol Pot loyalist who commanded the Northwestern Zone.) The year 1976 appears to have been a time initially of retreat for the faction led by Pol Pot. Many communists were alienated by his authoritarian behavior. Article 4 of the Constitution, "Democratic Kampuchea applies the collective principle in leadership and in work," apparently reflects this opinion. In relation to what had gone before and what was to come, policies during 1976 were moderate. The terror eased. Relations with Hanoi were placed on a friendlier footing. Trade and diplomatic relations were expanded.

On September 27, 1976, Pol Pot resigned as premier "for reasons of health." Nuon Chea, the pro-Vietnamese deputy premier, became acting premier. Little is known of the intense factional maneuvering that was occurring at this time, but by late October 1976, Pol Pot had regained his post. On October 22, his comeback was confirmed with his issuance of a statement in his capacity as prime minister condemning China's "counterrevolutionary Gang of Four," who had been arrested in Beijing on October 6.

The influence of China on Democratic Kampuchea's internal politics apparently was a crucial, though little understood, factor in Pol Pot's defeat of his pro-Vietnamese rivals. Etcheson and Kiernan have suggested, in separate articles, that radicals in the Chinese Communist Party may have backed pro-Vietnamese Internationalist elements in the KCP in 1976 because they were interested in preserving good relations with Hanoi. The fall of the radicals in October 1976, a month after Mao Zedong's death, brought in the moderates, led by Deng Xiaoping. As the subsequent break between Beijing and Hanoi shows, Deng was inclined to regard Vietnam as an agent of Soviet"hegemonism." Chinese support of the Pol Pot faction may have been a crucial element in its ability to triumph over the pro-Vietnamese communists in the fall of 1976. From an ideological standpoint, the pragmatic Deng Xiaoping and the ultra-radical Pol Pot were polar opposites, but from the geopolitical perspective, the post-Mao Zedong leadership recognized the value of having a well-armed Cambodian thorn in the side of Vietnam. Immediately after making his September 27, 1977, speech revealing the KCP's existence, Pol Pot, accompanied by Ieng Sary and Vorn Vet, visited Beijing, where he acknowledged the importance of Maoist thought to the Cambodian revolution. In early 1978, the Chinese sent substantial military aid, which included armor, artillery, and antitank guns.

THE PURGE

In 1975 Pol Pot concluded an alliance with the party head of the Southwestern Zone, Ta Mok, who was a Khmer Issarak veteran and, like Pol Pot, was strongly anti-Vietnamese. During 1977 and 1978, Ta Mok provided the backing that enabled Pol Pot to liquidate the opposition within the KCP and to initiate new terrorism against the local population. In February 1977, Southwestern cadres went into the Eastern, Northern, and Western zones to purge local Khmer Rouge. Four months later, the same process was begun in the Northwestern Zone. The purges intensified following an abortive coup d'état in August.

After the fall of the capital, Ta Mok's lieutenant, a former high school teacher who assumed the name Mit (Comrade) Deuch, became head of the secret police, and established the Tuol Sleng interrogation and detention center on the site of a former Phnom Penh high school. In the 1975 to 1976 period, Tuol Sleng's meticulous records show that 2,404 "antiparty elements" were tortured and executed. The terror escalated in 1977, when the number of victims rose to 6,330. In the first six months of 1978, records show that 5,765 people were killed; records for the latter half of that year have not been discovered. The victims who passed through Tuol Sleng from mid-1975 to January 1979 numbered about 20,000. Among those who met death in the infamous prison were Paris alumni Hu Nim and (presumably) Hou Yuon. Similar centers were set up throughout the country (Tuol Sleng's code designation, S-21, suggests that at least twenty other similar sites had been established).

Molyda Szymusiak writes that a new wave of terror began in the Batdambang region after cadres arrived from the south. The Sala Som Niat, a school for political education was converted into an extermination center where local communists were tortured and executed. The pattern in these centers was much the same: victims were tortured, forced to write often absurd confessions, and then killed. A young British teacher, captured in a yacht off the Cambodian coast, confessed at Tuol Sleng that he had been recruited by the Central Intelligence Agency (CIA) of the United States when he was twelve years old; he was subsequently murdered. Hu Nim was forced to confess that he had become a CIA agent in 1957.

The Eastern Zone apparently remained largely unaffected by the purge until May 1978, when So Phim led a revolt that provoked massive retaliation by Pol Pot and his Southwestern henchmen. In the bloodiest purge of the entire 1975 to 1978 period, as many as 100,000 people in the Eastern Zone-labeled people with "Khmer bodies but Vietnamese minds"-were liquidated or were deported to face certain death in other parts of the country. Most of the victims were political cadres, "new people," and Vietnamese or part-Vietnamese residents. So Phim reportedly committed suicide as he faced capture. Some of his subordinates, including Heng Samrin, the leader of the PRK after 1979, fled to Vietnam.

THE FALL OF DEMOCRATIC KAMPUCHEA

Immediately following the Khmer Rouge victory in 1975, there were skirmishes between their troops and Vietnamese forces. A number of incidents occurred in May 1975. The Cambodians launched attacks on the Vietnamese islands of Phu Quoc and Tho Chu and intruded into Vietnamese border provinces. In late May, at about the same time that the United States launched an air strike against the oil refinery at Kampong Saom, following the Mayaguez incident, Vietnamese forces seized the Cambodian island of Poulo Wai. The following month, Pol Pot and Ieng Sary visited Hanoi. They proposed a friendship treaty between the two countries, an idea that met with a cool reception from Vietnam's leaders. Although the Vietnamese evacuated Poulo

Wai in August, incidents continued along Cambodian's northeastern border. At the instigation of the Phnom Penh regime, thousands of Vietnamese also were driven out of Cambodia.

Relations between Cambodia and Vietnam improved in 1976, in part because of Pol Pot's preoccupation with intraparty challenges. In May Cambodian and Vietnamese representatives met in Phnom Penh in order to establish a commission to resolve border disagreements. The Vietnamese, however, refused to recognize the Brévié Line-the colonial-era demarcation of maritime borders between the two countries-and the negotiations broke down. In late September, however, a few days before Pol Pot was forced to resign as prime minister, air links were established between Phnom Penh and Hanoi.

With Pol Pot back in the forefront of the regime in 1977, the situation rapidly deteriorated. Incidents escalated along all of Cambodia's borders. Khmer Rouge forces attacked villages in the border areas of Thailand near Aranyaprathet. Brutal murders of Thai villagers, including women and children, were the first widely reported concrete evidence of Khmer Rouge atrocities. There were also incidents along the Laotian border. At approximately the same time, villages in Vietnam's border areas underwent renewed attacks. In turn, Vietnam launched air strikes against Cambodia. In September, border fighting resulted in as many as 1,000 Vietnamese civilian casualties. The following month, the Vietnamese counterattacked in a campaign involving a force of 20,000 personnel. Vietnamese defense minister General Vo Nguyen Giap underestimated the tenacity of the Khmer Rouge, however, and was obliged to commit an additional 58,000 reinforcements in December. On January 6, 1978, Giap's forces began an orderly withdrawal from Cambodian territory. The Vietnamese apparently believed they had "taught a lesson" to the Cambodians, but Pol Pot proclaimed this a "victory" even greater than that of April 17, 1975.

Faced with growing Khmer Rouge belligerence, the Vietnamese leadership decided in early 1978 to support internal resistance to the Pol Pot regime, with the result that the Eastern Zone became a focus of insurrection. War hysteria reached bizarre levels within Democratic Kampuchea. In May 1978, on the eve of So Phim's Eastern Zone uprising, Radio Phnom Penh declared that if each Cambodian soldier killed thirty Vietnamese, only 2 million troops would be needed to eliminate the entire Vietnamese population of 50 million. It appears that the leadership in Phnom Penh was seized with immense territorial ambitions, i.e., to recover the Mekong Delta region, which they regarded as Khmer territory.

Massacres of ethnic Vietnamese and of their sympathizers by the Khmer Rouge intensified in the Eastern Zone after the May revolt. In November, Vorn Vet led an unsuccessful coup d'état. There were now tens of thousands of Cambodian and Vietnamese exiles on Vietnamese territory. On December 3, 1978, Radio Hanoi announced the formation of the Kampuchean (or Khmer) National United Front for National Salvation (KNUFNS). This was a heterogeneous group of communist and noncommunist exiles who shared an antipathy to the Pol Pot regime and a virtually total dependence on Vietnamese backing and protection. The KNUFNS provided the semblance, if not the reality, of legitimacy for Vietnam's invasion of Democratic Kampuchea and for its subsequent establishment of a satellite regime in Phnom Penh).

In the meantime, as 1978 wore on, Cambodian bellicosity in the border areas surpassed Hanoi's threshold of tolerance. Vietnamese policy makers opted for a military solution and, on December 22, Vietnam launched its offensive with the intent of overthrowing Democratic Kampuchea. An invasion force of 120,000, consisting of combined armor and infantry units with strong artillery support, drove west into the level countryside of Cambodia's southeastern provinces. After a seventeen-day blitzkrieg, Phnom Penh fell to the advancing Vietnamese on January 7, 1979.

From new redoubts in the mountain and jungle fastness of Cambodia's periphery, Pol Pot and other Khmer Rouge leaders regrouped their units, issued a new call to arms, and reignited a stubborn insurgency against the regime in power as they had done in the late 1960s. For the moment, however, the Vietnamese invasion had accomplished its purpose of deposing an unlamented and particularly loathsome dictatorship. A new administration under the mentorship of Hanoi was quickly established, and it set about competing, both domestically and internationally, with the Khmer Rouge as the legitimate government of Cambodia. Peace still eluded the war-ravaged nation, however, and although the insurgency set in motion by the Khmer Rouge proved unable to topple the new Vietnamese-backed regime in Phnom Penh, it did nonetheless keep the country in a permanent state of insecurity. The fledgling Khmer administration, weak and lacking in manpower and in resources, was propped up by a substantial Vietnamese military force and civilian advisory effort.

In the 1980's, the government took steps to reduce its control of the economy. These included allowing Cambodians to own their own small businesses and farms. In addition, Vietnam gradually withdrew troops from Cambodia. In September 1989, Vietnam said that it had completed the withdrawal.

Also in 1989, Cambodia's government and opposition groups began negotiations to resolve the war. In October 1991, they signed a United Nations-sponsored peace treaty. Under the treaty, the United Nations (UN) took over administration of the Cambodian government in 1992 to guide Cambodia through a period of transition to democracy. The UN worked with a 12-member Supreme National Council made up of members of the former government and the three opposition groups.

In May 1993, democratic, multiparty elections were held for a 120-member assembly. A transitional government was formed by the parties that won the most seats. It governed until a constitution was put into effect in September 1993. A new democratically elected government headed by two prime ministers was established. The office of king was restored, but only as a ceremonial position. Sihanouk, who had been head of state in the transitional government, remained head of state and became king. The Khmer Rouge, though it had signed the UN peace treaty, boycotted the elections and did not become part of the new government. In the mid-1990's, however, many members of the Khmer Rouge began leaving the organization.

Relations between Hun Sen and Prince Norodom Ranariddh, the prime ministers who took power in 1993, were strained. In July 1997, Hun Sen forced Ranariddh from office and appointed another prime minister to replace him. Fighting between supporters of Hun Sen and Ranariddh continued.

POPULATION & SOCIETY

Nationality: Noun and adjective: Cambodian(s), Khmer.
Population (1995): 10.56 million.
Avg. annual growth rate: 4.1%. Births--44 births/1000 population. Deaths--16 deaths/1000 population. Health: Infant mortality--108 deaths/1000 live births. Life expectancy-- 48 years male/51 years female.
Ethnic groups: Cambodian 90%; Chinese and Vietnamese 5% each; small numbers of hill tribes, Chams, and Burmese.
Religions: Theravada Buddhism 95%; Islam; animism; atheism.
Languages: Khmer (official) spoken by more than 95% of the population, including minorities; some French still spoken; English increasingly popular as a second language.
Literacy: 35.2%.

ETHNIC GROUPS

THE CHAM

The Cham people in Cambodia descend from refugees of the kingdom of Champa, which once ruled much of Vietnam between Cao Ha in the north and Bien Hoa in the south. In 1471 Champa was conquered by the Vietnamese, and many Cham fled to Cambodia. Cham scholar Po Dharma points out that the Cham have lived in Cambodia since at least 1456. They settled along the Tonle Sap and Mekong rivers and in Batdambang, Pouthisat, Takev, Kampot, Kampong Cham, Kampong Thum, and Kampong Chhnang provinces. At some time before the seventeenth century, the Cambodian Cham and some of those in adjacent Vietnam converted to Islam, probably as a result of contacts with their Malay kin who had embraced that religion centuries earlier.

Friendly relations prevailed between the Cham and the Khmer for centuries even though, because of the Cham religion, little intermarriage occurred. Under the Khmer Republic of 1970 to 1975, one of the elite military units was made up of members of the Cham and other ethnic minorities. The Khmer Rouge tried, without much success, to recruit the Cham during the struggle with the Khmer Republic. The Cham were singled out for particularly brutal repression under the Khmer Rouge regime, and large numbers were killed. The PRK actively courted the Cham, and in 1987 a Cham was a member of the party Central Committee and minister of agriculture. Cham sources estimate that in the 1986, in addition to the Cham in Cambodia and in Vietnam, there were 3,000 Cham in Malaysia, 2,000 in the United States, 1,000 in Western Europe, 500 in Canada, and several hundred in Indonesia.

Po Dharma divides the Cambodian Cham into two groups-the orthodox and the traditional-based on their religious practices. The orthodox group, which makes up about one-third of the total number of Cham in the country, were located mainly in the Phnom Penh-Odongk area and in the provinces of Takev and Kampot. The traditional Cham were scattered throughout the midsection of the country in the provinces of Batdambang, Kampong Thum, Kampong Cham, and Pouthisat.

The Cham of both groups typically live in villages inhabited only by other Cham; the villages may be along the shores of water courses, or they may be inland. The Cham refer to the former as play krong (river villages) and to the latter as play ngok (upper villages). The inhabitants of the river villages engage in fishing, in raising rice, and in growing vegetables, especially onions. They trade fish to local Khmer for rice. The women in these villages earn money by weaving. The Cham who live inland support themselves by various means, depending on the village. Some villages specialize in metal working; others raise fruit trees or vegetables. The Cham also often serve as butchers of cattle for their Khmer Buddhist neighbors and are, in some areas, regarded as skillful water buffalo breeders.

Cham dress is distinctive. The main item of clothing for both sexes is a sarong-like garment called a batik, which is worn knotted at the waist. Men wear shirts over the batik, and women wear close-fitting blouses that are open at the throat and have tight sleeves. The characteristic headdress is a turban or scarf.

Cham society is matriarchal with matrilineal descent. There is some trace of an earlier clan system. Parents permit their daughters a considerable amount of freedom of choice in marriage. The parents of the girl usually make the marriage overtures to the boy. A Cham marriage involves little ceremony. Among the Muslim Cham, the girl's parents ask the groom if he accepts their daughter in marriage, and he is expected to answer yes. The imam acts as a witness. This simple ceremony is followed by a feast. Residence is matrilocal; the young man goes to live with his wife's family. Females inherit the family property.

THE KHMER LOEU

The Khmer Loeu are the non-Khmer highland tribes in Cambodia. Although the origins of this group are not clear, some believe that the Mon-Khmer-speaking tribes were part of the long migration of these people from the northwest. The Austronesian-speaking groups, Rade and Jarai, apparently came to coastal Vietnam and then moved west, forming wedges among some of the Mon-Khmer groups. The Khmer Loeu are found mainly in the northeastern provinces of Rotanokiri, Stoeng Treng, and Mondol Kiri. The Cambodian government coined the word Khmer Loeu-literally "Highland Khmer"-in the 1960s in order to create a feeling of unity between the highland tribal groups and the ruling lowland ethnic Khmer. Traditionally the Khmer have referred to these groups as phnong and samre, both of which have pejorative meanings. Some of the highland groups, in fact, are related in language to the Khmer, but others are from a very different linguistic and cultural background.

Khmer Loeu form the majority population in Rotanokiri and Mondulkiri provinces, and they also are present in substantial numbers in Kracheh and Stoeng Treng provinces. Their total population in 1969 was estimated at 90,000 persons. In 1971 the number of Khmer Loeu was estimated variously between 40,000 and 100,000 persons. Population figures were unavailable in 1987, but the total probably was nearly 100,000 persons.

Most Khmer Loeu live in scattered temporary villages that have only a few hundred inhabitants. These villages usually are governed by a council of local elders or by a village headman.

The Khmer Loeu cultivate a wide variety of plants, but the main crop is dry or upland rice grown by the slash-and-burn method. Hunting, fishing, and gathering supplement the cultivated vegetable foods in the Khmer Loeu diet. Houses vary from huge multifamily longhouses to small single-family structures. They may be built close to the ground or on stilts.

During the period of the French Protectorate, the French did not interfere in the affairs of the Khmer Loeu. Reportedly, French army commanders considered the Khmer Loeu as an excellent source of personnel for army outposts, and they recruited large numbers to serve with the French forces. Many Khmer Loeu continued this tradition by enlisting in the Cambodian army.

In the 1960s, the Cambodian government carried out a broad civic action program-for which the army had responsibility-among the Khmer Loeu in Mondol Kiri, Rotanokiri, Stoeng Treng, and Kaoh Kong provinces. The goals of this program were to educate the Khmer Loeu, to teach them Khmer, and eventually to assimilate them into the mainstream of Cambodian society. There was some effort at resettlement; in other cases, civil servants went out to live with individual Khmer Loeu groups to teach their members Khmer ways. Schools were provided for some Khmer Loeu communities, and in each large village a resident government representative disseminated information and encouraged the Khmer Loeu to learn the lowland Khmer way of life. Civil servants sent to work among the Khmer Loeu often viewed the assignment as a kind of punishment.

In the late 1960s, an estimated 5,000 Khmer Loeu in eastern Cambodia rose in rebellion against the government and demanded self-determination and independence. The government press reported that local leaders loyal to the government had been assassinated. Following the rebellion, the hill people's widespread resentment of ethnic Khmer settlers caused them to refuse to cooperate with the Cambodian army in its suppression of rural unrest. Both the Khmer and the Vietnamese communists took advantage of this disaffection, and they actively recruited Khmer Loeu into their ranks. In late 1970, the government forces withdrew from Rotanokiri and Mondol Kiri provinces and abandoned the area to the rapidly growing Khmer communist insurgent force, the Revolutionary Army of Kampuchea (RAK), and to its Vietnamese mentors. There is some evidence that in the 1960s and in the 1970s the Front Uni pour la Libération des Races Opprimés (FULRO--United Front for the Liberation of Oppressed Races) united tribes in the mountainous areas of southern Vietnam and had members from Khmer Loeu groups as well as from the Cham in Cambodia.

In the early 1980s, Khmer Rouge propaganda teams infiltrated the northeastern provinces and encouraged rebellion against the central government. In 1981 the government structure included four Khmer Loeu province chiefs, all reportedly from the Brao group, in the northeastern provinces of Mondol Kiri, Rotanokiri, Stoeng Treng, and Preah Vihear. According to a 1984 resolution of the PRK National Cadres Conference entitled "Policy Toward Ethnic Minorities," the minorities were considered an integral part of the Cambodian nation, and they were to be encouraged to participate in collectivization. Government policy aimed to transform minority groups into modern Cambodians. The same resolution called for the elimination of illiteracy, with the stipulations that minority languages be respected and that each tribe be allowed to write, speak, and teach in its own language.

The major Khmer Loeu groups in Cambodia are the Kuy, Mnong, Stieng, Brao, Pear, Jarai, and Rade. All but the last two speak Mon-Khmer languages.

In the mid 1990s, about 160,000 Kuy lived in the northern Cambodian provinces of Kampong Thum, Preah Vihear, and Stoeng Treng as well as in adjacent Thailand. Most of the Kuy have been assimilated into the predominant culture of the country in which they live. Many are Buddhists, and the majority practice wet-rice cultivation. They have the reputation of being skilled blacksmiths.

The Brao, including the Tampuon subgroup, inhabit northeastern Cambodia and adjacent Laos. In 1962 the Brao population in Laos was estimated at about 9,000 persons. In 1994 it was reported that the total Brao population was between 10,000 and 15,000 persons. About 3,000 Brao reportedly moved into Cambodia from Laos in the 1920s. The Brao live in large villages centered on a communal house. They cultivate dry-rice and produce some pottery. They appear to have a bilateral kinship system.

A total of 23,000 Mnong were thought to be living in Cambodia and in Vietnam in the early 1990s. In Cambodia the Mnong are found in Mondol Kiri, Kracheh, and Kampong Cham provinces in villages consisting of several longhouses each of which is divided into compartments that house can nuclear families. The Mnong practice dry-rice farming, and some also cultivate a wide variety of vegetables, fruits, and other useful plants as secondary crops. Some subgroups weave cloth. At least two of the Mnong subgroups have matrilineal descent. Monogamy is the predominant form of marriage, and residence is usually matrilocal. Wealth distinctions are measured by the number of buffalo that a notable person sacrifices on a funereal or ceremonial occasion as a mark of status and as a means of eliciting social approval. Slavery is known to have existed in the past, but the system allowed a slave to gain freedom. The Stieng are closely related to the Mnong. Both groups straddle the Cambodian-Vietnamese border, and their languages belong to the same subfamily of Mon-Khmer. In 1978 the Cambodian Stieng numbered about 20,000 persons in all. The Stieng cultivate dry-field rice. Their society is apparently patriarchal, residence after marriage and is patrilocal if a bride-price was paid. The groups have a very loose political organization; each village has its own leaders and tribunals.

Several small groups, perhaps totalling no more than 10,000 people in Cambodia and southeastern Thailand, make up the Pearic group. The main members are the Pear in Batdambang, Pouthisat, and Kampong Thum provinces; the Chong in Thailand and Batdambang Province; the Saoch in Kampot Province; the Samre in what was formerly Siemreab Province (now part of Siemreab-Otdar Meanchey Province); and the Suoi in Kampong Chhnang Province. Some believe that this group constitutes the remnant of the pre-Khmer population of Cambodia. Many members of the Pearic group grow dry-field rice, which they supplement by hunting and by gathering. They have totemic clans, each headed by a chief who inherited his office patrilineally. Marriage occurs at an early age; there is a small bride-price. Residence may be matrilocal until the birth of the first child, or it may be patrilocal as it is among the Saoch. The village headman is the highest political leader. The Saoch have a council of elders who judge infractions of traditional law. Two chief sorcerers, whose main function is to control the weather, play a major role in Pearic religion. Among the Saoch, a corpse is buried instead of being burned as among the Khmer.

The Austronesian groups of Jarai and Rade form two of the largest ethnic minorities in Vietnam. Both groups spill over into northeastern Cambodia, and they share many cultural similarities. The total Jarai population stands at about 200,000; the Rade number about 120,000. According to 1988 population figures, there were 10,000 Jarai and 15,000 Rade in Cambodia in the late 1970s. They live in longhouses containing several compartments occupied by matrilineally linked nuclear families. There may be twenty to sixty longhouses in one village. The Rade and Jarai cultivate dry-field rice and secondary crops such as maize. Both groups have exogamous matrilineal descent groups (consanguineous kin groups that acknowledge a traditional bond of common descent in the maternal line and within which they do not marry). Women initiate marriage negotiations, and residence is matrilocal. Each village has its own political hierarchy and is governed by an oligarchy of the leading families. In the past, sorcerers known as the "kings of fire and water" exerted political power that extended beyond an individual village. The Rade and the Jarai have been involved intimately in the FULRO movement, and many of the leaders in the movement are from these two groups.

THE CHINESE

The Chinese in Cambodia formed the country's largest ethnic minority in the late 1960s and in the early 1970s. In the late 1960s, an estimated 425,000 ethnic Chinese lived in Cambodia, but by 1994, as a result of warfare, Khmer Rouge and Vietnamese persecution, and emigration, only about 61,400 Chinese remained in the country. Sixty percent of the Chinese were urban dwellers engaged mainly in commerce; the other 40 percent were rural residents working as shopkeepers, as buyers and processors of rice, palm sugar, fruit, and fish, and as moneylenders. In 1963 90 percent of the Chinese in Cambodia were involved in commerce and that 92 percent of those involved in commerce in Cambodia were Chinese. The Chinese in Kampot Province and in parts of Kaoh Kong Province also cultivated black pepper and fruit (especially rambutans, durians, and coconuts), and they engaged in salt-water fishing. In rural Cambodia, the Chinese were moneylenders, and they wielded considerable economic power over the ethnic Khmer peasants through usury. Studies in the 1950s disclosed that Chinese shopkeepers would sell to peasants on credit at interest rates of from 10 to 20 percent a month. In 1952 according to Australian political analyst Ben Kiernan, the Colonial Credit Office found in a survey that 75 percent of the peasants in Cambodia were in debt. There seemed to be little distinction between Chinese and Sino-Khmer (offspring of mixed Chinese and Khmer marriages) in the moneylending and shopkeeping enterprises.

The Chinese in Cambodia represented to five major linguistic groups, the largest of which was the Teochiu (accounting for about 60 percent), followed by the Cantonese (accounting for about 20 percent), the Hokkien (accounting for about 7 percent), and the Hakka and the Hainanese (each accounting for about 4 percent). These belonging to certain Chinese linguistic groups in Cambodia tended to gravitate to certain occupations. The Teochiu, who made up about 90 percent of the rural Chinese population, ran village stores, controlled rural credit and rice-marketing facilities, and grew vegetables. In urban areas they were often engaged in such enterprises as the import-export business, the sale of pharmaceuticals, and street peddling. The Cantonese, who were the majority Chinese group before the Teochiu migrations began in the late 1930s, lived mainly in the city. Typically, the Cantonese engaged in transportation and in construction, for the most part as mechanics or carpenters. The Hokkien community was involved in import-export and in banking, and it included some of the country's richestChinese. The Hainanese started out as pepper growers in Kampot Province, where they continued to dominate that business. Many moved to Phnom Penh, where, in the late 1960s, they reportedly had a virtual monopoly on the hotel and restaurant business. They also often operated tailor shops and haberdasheries. In Phnom Penh, the newly-arrived Hakka were typically folk dentists, sellers of traditional Chinese medicines, and shoemakers.

Distinction by dialect group also has been important historically in the administrative treatment of the Chinese in Cambodia. The French brought with them a system devised by the Vietnamese Emperor Gia Long (1802-20) to classify the local Chinese according to areas of origin and dialect. These groups were called bang (or congregations by the French) and had their own leaders for law, order, and tax-collecting. In Cambodia every Chinese was required to belong to a bang. The head of a bang, known as the ong bang, was elected by popular vote; he functioned as an intermediary between the members of his bang and the government. Individual Chinese who were not accepted for membership in a bang were deported by the French authorities.

The French system of administering the Chinese community was terminated in 1958. During the 1960s, Chinese community affairs tended to be handled, at least in Phnom Penh, by the Chinese Hospital Committee, an organization set up to fund and to administer a hospital established earlier for the Chinese community. This committee was the largest association of Chinese merchants in the country, and it was required by the organization's constitution to include on its fifteen-member board six from the Teochiu dialect group, three from the Cantonese, two from the Hokkien, two from the Hakka, and two from the Hainanese. The hospital board constituted the recognized leadership of Phnom Penh's Chinese community. Local Chinese school boards in the smaller cities and towns often served a similar function.

In 1971 the government authorized the formation of a new body, the Federated Association of Chinese of Cambodia, which was the first organization to embrace all of Cambodia's resident Chinese. According to its statutes, the federation was designed to "aid Chinese nationals in the social, cultural, public health, and medical fields," to administer the property owned jointly by the Chinese community in Phnom Penh and elsewhere, and to promote friendly relations between Cambodians and Chinese. With leadership that could be expected to include the recognized leaders of the national Chinese community, the federation was believed likely to continue the trend, evident since the early 1960s, to transcend dialect group allegiance in many aspects of its social, political, and economic programs.

Generally, relations between the Chinese and the ethnic Khmer were good. There was some intermarriage, and a sizable proportion of the population in Cambodia was part Sino-Khmer, who were assimilated easily into either the Chinese or the Khmer community. Willmott assumes that a Sino-Khmer elite dominated commerce in Cambodia from the time of independence well into the era of the Khmer Republic.

The Khmer Rouge takeover was catastrophic for the Chinese community for several reasons. When the Khmer Rouge took over a town, they immediately disrupted the local market. According to Willmott, this disruption virtually eliminated retail trade "and the traders (almost all Chinese) became indistinguishable from the unpropertied urban classes." The Chinese, in addition to having their major livelihood eradicated, also suffered because of their class membership. They were mainly well-educated urban merchants, thus possessing three characteristics that were anathema to the Khmer Rouge. Chinese refugees have reported that they shared the same brutal treatment as other urban Cambodians under the Khmer Rouge regime and that they were not especially singled out as an ethnic group until after the Vietnamese invasion. Observers believe that the anti-Chinese stance, of the Vietnamese government and of its officials in Phnom Penh, makes it unlikely that a Chinese community on the earlier scale will reappear in Cambodia in the near future.

THE VIETNAMESE

Enmity has existed between the Khmer and the Vietnamese for centuries, but this antagonism did not hinder the growth of a sizable Vietnamese community scattered throughout southeastern and central Cambodia. An estimated 291,596 Vietnamese, constituting more than 7 percent at the total population, resided in Cambodia in 1950. They were concentrated in Phnom Penh, end in Kandal, Prey Veng, and Kampong Cham provinces.

The Khmer have shown more antipathy toward the Vietnamese than toward the Chinese or toward their other neighbors, the Thai. Several factors explain this attitude. The expansion of Vietnamese power has resulted historically in the loss of Khmer territory. The Khmer, in contrast, have lost no territory to the Chinese and little to the Thai. No close cultural or religious ties exist between Cambodia and Vietnam. The Vietnamese fall within the Chinese culture sphere, rather than within the Indian, where the Thai and the Khmer belong. The Vietnamese differ from the Khmer in mode of dress, in kinship organization, and in many other ways-for example the Vietnamese are Mahayana Buddhists. Although Vietnamese lived in urban centers such as Phnom Penh, a substantial number lived along the lower Mekong and Basak rivers as well as on the shores of the Tonle Sap, where they engaged in fishing. Much of the manpower on French-owned rubber plantations was provided by the Vietnamese, who also were employed by the French as lower level civil servants and as white collar workers in private businesses.

SOCIAL STRUCTURE

Cambodian society traditionally contains three main occupational segments : The government bureaucracy, the clergy, and the peasantry (with the king occupying the top position in both political and the religious hierarchies). While integrated, each has its separate functions, both socially and, to a large extent, politically. The society as a whole centers on these three segments and the way in which they relate to one another. Other occupational segments-commercial and professionals- are relatively peripheral. (The commercial segment has been concentrated for a long time in the hands of foreigners. But recently Cambodians have shown more interests in these activities by following business careers and professional trainings.)

There is also another important distinction in Cambodian society, the distinction between the royalty-nobility and the commoners. The royal family and the nobility form the core of the government and for the most part confine their occupational activities to government services.

The nobility, the government bureaucracy, and the clergy have distinct internal ranking systems, with different levels clearly defined and titled. Within the government, there is a distinction between the decision-making power level at the top and the large mass of administrative officials and lesser civil servants. Within the clergy, there are the permanent professional clergy and the temporary clergy. Certain ranks in the government or the nobility, and any given religious official, may be of superior or inferior rank to a particular government official or noble. These ranking systems are important to Cambodians, and relative rank is continually manifested in the use of titles and in rather highly formalized patterns of respect and differences.

Due to these ranking systems, there are several prescribed patterns of addresses, speeches, and manners to be observed among members of the three occupational groups and between nobles and commoners. As would be expected, religious and governmental officials have greater prestige that the peasants, and noble greater prestige than the commoners. (More prestige and power result from religious and governmental rank than from either economic or professional status). The peasants are also differential to their fellow commoners in the clergy or the government. A person's age or reputation for righteous conduct have a special prestige of their own. Difference in age is an especially important factor in social relationship, and greater age can offset the respect normally due to a person of superior task.

Another distinction could be made between the urban society, where the Cambodian elite class centers around the king, the royal family, and the royal court, and the village society, where the class distinctions are minimal and much less clearly defined than in the urban centers. This is due to the importance placed on family and communal interdependence, and the fact that the peasants own their own lands, houses, and kettles, etc...

Buddhism does not support the ultimate validity for such status differences and the individual Cambodian is encouraged to believe that, through the achievement of merit, any man can become a saint and reach the stage of perfection in his next life. But in Cambodian society, there is still this fact of superior and inferior social rank, and it is accepted by the Cambodians as one of the primary reference points for social relationships.

This class structure in the Cambodian society is not rigid and impermeable, especially in light of the evolution of ideas in modern times, In fact, since the country regained its independence recently, the tendencies toward social mobility have increased, especially through marriage between royalty and commoners, through advancement in governmental or religious ranking systems, and lately through education and betterment of economic status.

In short, one could say that Cambodians, in general, do not think in Maxist terms on an elite, a bourgeoisie and a proletariat which are in any way antagonistic to or in basic competition with each other. The various segment and classes of society are viewed as facts of life, and there was little concern with changing the social structure. The Cambodian, in general, is more concerned, either in this life or the next, through personal merit and individual achievement.

LANGUAGE

The majority of Cambodians, even those who are not ethnic Khmer, speak Khmer, the official language of the country. Ethnic Khmer living in Thailand, in Vietnam, and in Laos speak dialects of Khmer that are more or less intelligible to Khmer speakers from Cambodia. Minority languages include Vietnamese, Cham, several dialects of Chinese, and the languages of the various hill tribes.

AUSTROASIATIC-MON-KHMER

Khmer belongs to the Mon-Khmer family of the Austroasiatic phylum of languages. American linguists David Thomas and Robert Headley have divided the Mon-Khmer family into nine branches: Pearic in western Cambodia and eastern Thailand; Khmer in Cambodia, Thailand, Vietnam, and Laos; Bahnaric in Vietnam, Laos, and Cambodia; Katuic in Vietnam, Laos, and Cambodia; Khmuic in Laos, Thailand, and China; Monic in Burma and Thailand; Palaungic in Burma, China, and Thailand; Khasi in Assam (India); and Viet-Muong in Vietnam. Of the languages inthe Mon-Khmer family, Vietnamese has the largest number of speakers (about 47 million); Khmer, has the next largest (about 8 million).

Khmer, in contrast to Vietnamese, Thai, Lao, and Chinese, is nontonal. Native Khmer words may be composed of one or two syllables. Khmer is uninflected, but it has a rich system of affixes, including infixes, for derivation. Generally speaking, Khmer has nouns (including pronouns as a special subcategory), verbs (including stative verbs or adjectives), adverbs, and various kinds of words called particles (including verbal auxiliaries, prepositions, conjunctions, final particles, and interjections). Many Khmer words change, chameleon-like, from one part of speech to another, depending on the context. The normal word order is subject-verb-object. Adjectival modifiers follow the nouns they modify.

Khmer, like its neighbors, Thai, Lao, and Burmese, has borrowed extensively from other languages, especially the Indic languages of Sanskrit and Pali. Khmer uses Sanskrit and Pali roots much as English and other West European languages use Latin and Greek roots to derive new, especially scientific, words. Khmer has also borrowed terms-especially financial, commercial, and cooking terms-from Chinese. In the nineteenth and twentieth centuries, Khmer borrowed from French as well. These latter borrowings have been in the realm of material culture, especially the names for items of modern Western technology, such as buuzii (spark plug) from the French bougie.

Khmer is written in a script derived from a south Indian alphabet. The language has symbols for thirty-three consonants, twenty-four dependent vowels, twelve independent vowels, and several diacritic. Most consonants have reduced or modified forms, called subscripts, when they occur as the second member of a consonant cluster. Vowels may be written before, after, over, or under a consonant symbol.

Some efforts to standardize Khmer spelling have been attempted, but inconsistencies persist, and many words have more than one accepted spelling. A two-volume dictionary prepared under the direction of the Venerable Chuon Nath of the Buddhist Institute in Phnom Penh is the standard work on Khmer lexicography.

Khmer is divided into three stages-Old Khmer (seventh to twelfth century A.D.), Middle Khmer (twelfth to seventeenth century A.D.), and Modern Khmer (seventeenth century to the present). It is likely that Old Khmer was the language of Chenla. What the language of Funan was, but it was is not at all certain, probably a Mon-Khmer language. The earliest inscription in Khmer, found at Angkor Borei in Takev Province south of Phnom Penh, dates from A.D. 611.

AUSTRONESIAN

The Austronesian languages are spread over vast areas of Asia and the Pacific, from Madagascar to Easter Island and from Taiwan to Malaysia. Four Austronesian languages-Cham, Jarai, Rade, and Malay-are spoken in Cambodia. Cham is spoken by the largest number of people. Before 1975, there were about 100,000 speakers of Western Cham. Western Cham is the term used to distinguish (at least two mutually related dialects of) the Cham spoken in Cambodia and that used in adjacent inland Vietnam from Eastern Cham spoken in the coastal areas of central Vietnam. Western Cham is written in Arabic script, or, since the late 1960s and the early 1970s, in a romanized script devised by Protestant missionaries. The traditional

Cham script, based on an Indian script, is still known and used by the Eastern Cham in Vietnam, but it has been lost by the Western Cham.

The Cham language is also nontonal. Words may contain one, two, or three syllables. Cham contains much linguistic borrowing from Arabic, Malay, and Khmer. The normal word order is subject-verb-object, and, as in Khmer,
modifying adjectives follow the nouns that they modify. Most Cham in Cambodia are bilingual in Cham and in Khmer and many also know Arabic and Malay. Rade and Jarai, close relatives of Cham, are spoken by several thousand members of both ethnic groups in northeastern Cambodia. Both languages are written in romanized scripts based on the Vietnamese alphabet. Rade and Jarai have rich oral literatures, and the former has two epic tales that have been transcribed and published.

RELIGION

BUDDHISM

ORIGINS OF BUDDHISM ON THE INDIAN SUBCONTINENT

Theravada Buddhism is the religion of virtually all of the ethnic Khmer, who constitute about 90 percent or more of the Cambodian population. Buddhism originated in what are now north India and Nepal during the sixth century B.C.
It was founded by a Sakya prince, Siddhartha Gautama (563-483 B.C.; his traditional dates are 623-543 B.C., also called the Gautama Buddha), who, at the age of twenty-nine, after witnessing old age, sickness, death, and meditation, renounced his high status and left his wife and infant son for a life of asceticism. After years of seeking truth, he is said to have attained enlightenment while sitting alone under a bo tree. He became the Buddha-"the enlightened"-and formed an order of monks, the sangha, and later an order of nuns. He spent the remainder of his life as a wandering preacher, dying at the age of eighty.

Buddhism began as a reaction to Hindu doctrines and as an effort to reform them. Nevertheless, the two faiths share many basic assumptions. Both view the universe and all life therein as parts of a cycle of eternal flux. In each religion, the present life of an individual is a phase in an endless chain of events. Life and death are merely alternate aspects of individual existence marked by the transition points of birth and death. An individual is thus continually reborn, perhaps in human form, perhaps in some non-human form, depending upon his or her actions in the previous life. The endless cycle of rebirth is known as samsara (wheel of life).

Theravada Buddhism is a tolerant, non prescriptive religion that does not require belief in a supreme being. Its precepts require that each individual take full responsibility for his own actions and omissions. Buddhism is based on three concepts: dharma (the doctrine of the Buddha, his guide to right actions and belief); karma (the belief that one's life now and in future lives depends upon one's own deeds and misdeeds and that as an individual one is responsible for, and rewarded on the basis of, the sum total of one's acts and omissions in all one's incarnations past and present); and sangha, the ascetic community within which man can improve his karma.

The Buddha added the hope of escape-a way to get out of the endless cycle of pain and sorrow-to the Brahmanic idea of samsara. The Buddhist salvation is nirvana, a final extinction of one's self. Nirvana may be attained by achieving good karma through earning much merit and avoiding misdeeds. A Buddhist's pilgrimage through existence is a constant attempt to distance himself or herself from the world and finally to achieve complete detachment, or nirvana.

The fundamentals of Buddhist doctrine are the Four Noble Truths: suffering exists; craving (or desire) is the cause of suffering; release from suffering can be achieved by stopping all desire; and enlightenment-buddhahood-can be attained by following the Noble Eightfold Path (right views, right intention, right speech, right action, right livelihood, right effort, right mindfulness, and right concentration), which constitutes a middle way between sensuality and ascetism. Enlightenment consists of knowing these truths. The average layperson cannot hope for nirvana after the end of this life, but can-by complying, as best he or she is able to, with the doctrine's rules of moral conduct-hope to improve his or her karma and thereby better his condition in the next incarnation.

The doctrine of karma holds that, through the working of a just, automatic, and impersonal cosmic law, one's actions in this incarnation and in all previous ones will determine which position in the hierarchy of living things one will occupy in the next incarnation. An individual's karma can be improved through certain acts and omissions. By following the five precepts or commandments, a Buddhist can better his or her karma. These commandments are: do not kill, do not steal, do not indulge in forbidden sexual pleasures, do not tell lies, and do not take intoxicants or stupefying drugs or liquors.

The most effective way to work actively to improve one's karma is to earn merit. Any act of benevolence or generosity can gain merit for the doer. Cambodian Buddhists tend to regard opportunities for earning merit as primarily connected with interaction with the sangha, contributing to its support through money, goods, and labor, and participating in its activities. Some of the favorite ways for a male to earn merit are to enter the sangha as a monk (after the age of twenty) or as a novice, or to live in the wat as a temple servant; in the case of a female (usually the elderly), the favorite way is to become a nun. Other activities that gain merit include sponsoring a monk or novice, contributing to a wat, feeding members of the sangha at a public meal, and providing food for either of the two daily meals of the sangha.

In his first sermon to his followers, the Buddha described a moral code, the dharma, which the sangha was to teach after him. He left no designated successor. Indian emperor Asoka (273-232 B.C.) patronized the sangha and encouraged the teaching of the Buddha's philosophy throughout his vast empire; by 246 B.C., the new religion had reached Sri Lanka. The Tripitaka, the collection of basic Buddhist texts, was written down for the first time in Sri Lanka during a major Buddhist conference in the second or first century B.C. By the time of the conference, a schism had developed separating Mahayana (Greater Path) Buddhism from more conservative Theravada (Way of the Elders, or Hinayana-Lesser Path) faction or Buddhism. The Mahayana faction reinterpreted the original teachings of the Buddha and added a type of deity called a bodhisattva to large numbers of otherbuddhas. The Mahayana adherents believe that nirvana is available to everyone, not just to select holy men. Mahayana Buddhism quickly spread throughout India, China, Korea, Japan, Central Asia, and to some parts of Southeast Asia. According to the Venerable Pang Khat, Theravada Buddhism reached Southeast Asia as early as the second or third century A.D., while Mahayana Buddhism did not arrive in Cambodia until about A.D. 791. In Southeast Asia, Mahayana Buddhism carried many Brahman beliefs with it to the royal courts of Funan, of Champa, and of other states. At this time, Sanskrit words were added to the Khmer and to the Cham languages. Theravada Buddhism (with its scriptures in the Pali language), remained influential in Sri Lanka, and by the thirteenth century it had spread into Burma, Thailand, Laos, and Cambodia, where it supplanted Mahayana Buddhism.

CAMBODIAN ADAPTATIONS

Cambodian Buddhism has no formal administrative ties with other Buddhist bodies, although Theravada monks from other countries, especially Thailand, Laos, Burma, and Sri Lanka, may participate in religious ceremonies in order to make up the requisite number of clergy. Cambodian Buddhism is organized nationally in accordance with regulations formulated in 1943 and modified in 1948. During the monarchical period, the king led the Buddhist clergy. Prince Sihanouk continued in this role even after he had abdicated and was governing as head of state. He appointed both the heads of the monastic orders and other high-ranking clergy. After the overthrow of Sihanouk in 1970, the new head of state, Lon Nol, appointed these leaders.

Two monastic orders constituted the clergy in Cambodia. The larger group, to which more than 90 percent of the clergy belonged, was the Mohanikay. The Thommayut order was far smaller. The Thommayut was introduced into the ruling circles of Cambodia from Thailand in 1864; it gained prestige because of its adoption by royalty and by the aristocracy, but its adherents were confined geographically to the Phnom Penh area. Among the few differences between the two orders is stricter observance by the Thommayut bonzes (monks) of the rules governing the clergy. In 1961 the Mohanikay had more than 52,000 ordained monks in some 2,700 wats, whereas the Thommayut order had 1,460 monks in just over 100 wats. In 1967 more than 2,800 Mohanikay wats and 320 Thommayut wats were in existence in Cambodia. After Phnom Penh, the largest number of Thommayut wats were found in Batdambang, Stoeng Treng, Prey Veng, Kampot, and Kampong Thum provinces.

Each order has its own superior and is organized into a hierarchy of eleven levels. The seven lower levels are known collectively as the thananukram; the four higher levels together are called the rajagana. The Mohanikay order has thirty-five monks in the rajagana; the Thommayut has twentyone . Each monk must serve for at least twenty years to be named to these highest levels.

The cornerstones of Cambodian Buddhism are the Buddhist bonze and the wat. Traditionally, each village has a spiritual center-a wat-where from five to more than seventy bonzes reside. A typical wat in rural Cambodia consists of a walled enclosure containing a sanctuary, several residences for bonzes, a hall, a kitchen, quarters for nuns, and a pond. The number of monks varies according to the size of the local population. The sanctuary, which contains an altar with statues of the Buddha and, in rare cases, a religious relic, is reserved for major ceremonies and usually only for the use of bonzes. Other ceremonies, classes for monks and for laity, and meals take place in the hall. Stupas containing the ashes of extended family members are constructed near the sanctuary. Fruit trees and vegetable gardens tended by local children are also part of the local wat. The main entrance, usually only for ceremonial use, faces east; other entrances are located at other points around the wall. There are no gates.

Steinberg notes the striking ratio of bonzes to the total population of Cambodia. In the late 1950s, an estimated 100,000 bonzes (including about 40,000 novices) served a population of about 5 million. This high proportion undoubtedly was caused in large part by the ease with which one could enter and leave the sangha. Becoming a bonze and leaving the sangha are matters of individual choice although, in theory, nearly all Cambodian males over sixteen serve terms as bonzes. Most young men do not intend to become fully ordained bonzes (bhikkhu), and they remain as monks for less than a year. Even a son's temporary ordination as a bonze brings great merit to his parents, however, and is considered so important that arrangements are made at a parent's funeral if the son has not undergone the process while the parent was living. There are two classes of bonzes at a wat-the novices (samani or nen) and the bhikkhu. Ordination is held from mid-April to mid-July, during the rainy season.

Buddhist monks do not take perpetual vows to remain monks, although, in fact, some become monks permanently. Traditionally, they became monks early in life. It is possible to become a novice at as young an age as seven, but in practice thirteen is the earliest age for novices. A bhikkhu must be at least twenty. The monk's life is regulated by Buddhist law, and life in the wat adheres to a rigid routine. A bhikkhu follows 227 rules of monastic discipline as well as the 10 basic precepts. These include the five precepts that all Buddhists should follow. The five precepts for monastic asceticism prohibit eating after noon, participating in any entertainment (singing, dancing, and watching movies or television), using any personal adornments, sleeping on a luxurious bed, and handling money. In addition, a monk also is expected to be celibate. Furthermore, monks supposedly avoid all involvement in political affairs.
They are not eligible to vote or to hold any political office, and they may not witness a legal document or give testimony in court. Since the person of a monk is considered sacred, he is considered to be outside the normal civil laws and public duties that affect lay people. Some of these practices have changed in the modern period, however,and in the 1980s Buddhist monks have been active even in the PRK government.

Women are not ordained, but older women, especially widows, can become nuns. They live in wat and play an important role in the everyday life of the temple. Nuns shave their heads and eyebrows and generally follow the same precepts as monks. They may prepare the altars and do some of the housekeeping chores.

Role of Buddhism in Cambodian Life

Buddhist monks traditionally were called upon to perform a number of functions in Cambodian life. They participated in all formal village festivals, ceremonies, marriages, and funerals. They also might have participated in ceremonies to name infants and in other minor ceremonies or rites of passage. Monks did not lead the ceremonies, however, because that role was given to the achar, or master of ceremonies; the monk's major function was to say prayers of blessing. They were often healers and, in traditional Khmer culture, they were the practitioners whose role was closest to that of modern psychiatrists. They might also have been skilled in astrology. The monk traditionally occupied a unique position in the transmission of Khmer culture and values. By his way of life, he provided a living model of the most meritorious behavior a Buddhist could follow. He also provided the laity with many opportunities for gaining merit. For centuries monks were the only literate people residing in rural communities; they acted as teachers to temple servants, to novices, and to newly ordained monks. Until the 1970s, most literate Cambodian males gained literacy solely through the instruction of the sangha.

After independence from France, young Cambodian intellectuals changed their attitude toward the clergy. The Khmer Rouge was able to instill antireligious feelings in younger males because the latter were losing interest in becoming monks even during their teenage years, the traditional temporary period of service. The monks themselves had abandoned some of their traditional restrictions and had become involved in politics. At intervals during the colonial period, some monks had demonstrated or had rebelled against French rule, and in the 1970s monks joined pro- government demonstrations against the communists.

Anticlerical feelings reached their highest point among the Khmer Rouge, who at first attempted to indoctrinate monks and to force them to pass anticlerical ideas on to the laity. Under the Khmer Rouge regime, monks were expelled forcibly from the wats and were compelled to do manual labor. Article 20 of the 1976 Constitution of Democratic Kampuchea permitted freedom of religion but banned all reactionary religions, that were "detrimental to the country."

The minister of culture stated that Buddhism was incompatible with the revolution and was an instrument of exploitation. Under this regime, to quote the Finnish Inquiry Commission, "The practice of religion was forbidden and the pagodas were systematically destroyed." Observers estimated that 50,000 monks died during the Khmer Rouge regime. The status of Buddhism and of religion in general after the Vietnamese invasion was at least partially similar to its status in pre-Khmer Rouge times.

The few wats that were restored had only two or three old monks in residence and that public attendance was low. The monks were allowed to leave the wats only for an hour in the mornings, to collect their food, or during holy days. Lay people who practiced their faith were about the same ages as the monks, and they were allowed to visit the wats only in the evenings. A government circular had also instructed civil servants to stop celebrating the traditional New Year

Festival. Some traditional Buddhist festivals still were tolerated, but the state collected a 50 percent tithe ondonations. Martin believes that Buddhism was threatened externally by state repression and by nonsupport and internally by invalid clergy. She noted that the two Buddhist superiors, Venerable Long Chhim and Venerable Tep Vong, were both believed to be from Vietnam. Venerable Tep Vong was concurrently the superior of the Buddhistclergy, vice president of the PRK's Khmer National Assembly, and vice president of the KUFNCD National Council. She quoted a refugee from Batdambang as having said, "During the meetings, the Khmer administrative authorities, accompanied by the Vietnamese experts, tell you, `Religion is like poison, it's like opium; it's better to give the money to the military, so they can fight'."

Buddhism is still strong among the various Cambodian refugee groups throughout the world, although some younger monks, faced with the distractions of a foreign culture, have chosen to leave the clergy and have become laicized. In the United States in 1992, there were twelve Cambodian wats with about twenty-one monks. In the 1980s, a Cambodian Buddhist wat was constructed near Washington, D.C., financed by a massive outpouring of donations from Cambodian Buddhists throughout North America. This wat is one of the few outside Southeast Asia that has the consecrated boundary within which ordinations may be performed.

Most of the major Cambodian annual festivals are connected with Buddhist observances. The chol chnam (New Year Festival) takes place in mid-April; it was one of the few festivals allowed under the Khmer Rouge regime. The phchun ben, celebrated in September or in October, is a memorial day for deceased ancestors and for close friends. Meak bochea, in January or February, commemorates the last sermon of the Buddha. Vissakh bochea, in April or in May, is the triple anniversary of the birth, death, and enlightenment of the Buddha. The chol vossa takes place in June or in July; it marks the beginning of a penitential season during which the monks must remain within the temple compounds. The kathen marks the end of this season; celebrated in September, it features offerings, especially of robes, to the monks. The kathen was still celebrated in the PRK in the late 1980s.

Cambodian Buddhism exists side-by-side with, and to some extent intermingles with, pre-Buddhist animism and Brahman practices. Most Cambodians, whether or not they profess to be Buddhists (or Muslims), believe in a rich supernatural world. When ill, or at other times of crisis, or to seek supernatural help, Cambodians may enlist the aid of a practitioner who is believed to be able to propitiate or obtain help from various spirits. Local spirits are believed to inhabit a variety of objects, and shrines to them may be found in houses, in Buddhist temples, along roads, and in forests.

Several types of supernatural entities are believed to exist; they make themselves known by means of inexplicable sounds or happenings. Among these phenomena are khmoc (ghosts), pret and besach (particularly nasty demons, the spirits of people who have died violent, untimely, or unnatural deaths), arak (evil spirits, usually female), neak ta (tutelary spirits residing in inanimate objects), mneang phteah (guardians of the house), meba (ancestral spirits), and mrenh kongveal (elf-like guardians of animals).

All spirits must be shown proper respect, and, with the exception of the mneang phteah and mrenh kongveal, they can cause trouble ranging from mischief to serious life-threatening illnesses. An important way for living people to show respect for the spirits of the dead is to provide food for the spirits. If this food is not provided, the spirit can cause trouble for the offending person. For example, if a child does not provide food for the spirit of its dead mother, that spirit can cause misfortunes to happen to the child.

Aid in dealing with the spirit world may be obtained from a kru (shaman or spirit practitioner), an achar (ritualist), thmup (witch, sorcerer or sorceress), or a rup arak (medium, usually male). The kru is a kind of sorcerer who prepares charms and amulets to protect the wearer from harm. He can cure illnesses, find lost objects, and prepare magic potions. Traditionally, Cambodians have held strong beliefs about protective charms. Amulets are worn routinely by soldiers to ward off bullets, for example. The kru are believed to have the power to prepare an amuletand to establish a supernatural link between it and the owner. A kru may acquire considerable local prestige and power. Many kru are former Buddhist monks.

Another kind of magical practitioner is the achar, a specialist in ritual. He may function as a kind of master of ceremonies at a wat and as a specialist in conducting spirit worship rituals connected with life-cycle ceremonies.
Rup arak are mediums who can be possessed by supernatural beings and communicate with the spirit world. The thmup are sorcerers who cause illnesses.

Fortunetellers and astrologers-haor teay-are important in Cambodian life. They are consulted about important decisions such as marriages, building a new house, or going on a long journey. They are believed to be able to foretell future events and to determine lucky or unlucky days for various activities.

Villagers are sensitive to the power and to the needs of the spirit world. According to observations by an American missionary in the early 1970s, villagers consulted the local guardian spirit to find out what the coming year would bring, a new province chief held a ceremony to ask the protection of the spirits over the province, and soldiers obtained magic cloths and amulets from mediums and shamans to protect them from the bullets of the enemy. Before embarking on a mission against enemy forces, a province chief might burn incense and call on a spirit for aid in defeating the enemy. Examples of Brahman influences were various rituals concerned with the well-being of the nation carried out by the ruler and the baku (a Brahman priestly group attached to the royal court). These rituals were reportedly stopped after Sihanouk's ouster in 1970

CHINESE RELIGION

Mahayana Buddhism is the religion of the majority of Chinese and Vietnamese in Cambodia. Elements of other religious practices, such as veneration of folk heros and ancestors, Confucianism, and Taoism mix with Chinese and Vietnamese Buddhism.

In the Chinese home, ancestors and household gods are honored during prescribed times to help unite the extended family and to gain help from the dead, who can intercede for the living. Taoism teaches meditation and the use of magic to gain happiness, wealth, health, and immortality. Confucianism, part social philosophy and part religion, stresses religious ritual and pays great attention to the veneration of ancestors and of great figures of the past.

Chinese Mahayana Buddhism has become intertwined with Taoist and with Confucian beliefs. Adherents honor many buddhas, including the Gautama Buddha, and they believe in a paradise after death. They also believe in bodhisattvas-people who have nearly attained nirvana, but who stay back to help save others.

ISLAM

Islam is the religion of the Cham (also called Khmer Islam) and Malay minorities. According to Po Dharma, there were 150,000 to 200,000 Muslims in Cambodia as late as 1975. Persecution under the Khmer Rouge eroded their numbers, however, and by the late 1980s they probably had not regained their former strength. All of the Cham Muslims are Sunnis of the Shafii school. Po Dharma divides the Muslim Cham in Cambodia into a traditionalist branch and an orthodox branch.

The Cham have their own mosques. In 1962 there were about 100 mosques in the country. At the end of the nineteenth century, the Muslims in Cambodia formed a unified community under the authority of four religious dignitaries--mupti, tuk kalih, raja kalik, and tvan pake. A council of notables in Cham villages consisted of one hakem and several katip, bilal, and labi. The four high dignitaries and the hakem were exempt from personal taxes, and they were invited to take part in major national ceremonies at the royal court. When Cambodia became independent, the Islamic community was placed under the control of a five-member council that represented the community in official functions and in contacts with other Islamic communities.

Each Muslim community has a hakem who leads the community and the mosque, an imam who leads the prayers, and a bilal who calls the faithful to the daily prayers. The peninsula of Chrouy Changvar near Phnom Penh is considered the spiritual center of the Cham, and several high Muslim officials reside there. Each year some of the Cham go to study the Quran at Kelantan in Malaysia, and some go on to study in, or make a pilgrimage to, Mecca. According to figures from the late 1950s, about 7 percent of the Cham had completed the pilgrimage and could wear the fez or turban as a sign of their accomplishment.

The traditional Cham retain many ancient Muslim or pre-Muslim traditions and rites. They consider Allah as the all-powerful God, but they also recognize other non-Islamic deities. Their are closer, in many respects, to the Cham of coastal Vietnam than they are to other Muslims. The religious dignitaries of the traditional Cham (and of the Cham in Vietnam) dress completely in white, and they shave their heads and faces. These Cham believe in the power of magic and sorcery, and they attach great importance to magical practices in order to avoid sickness or slow or violent death. They believe in many supernatural powers. Although they show little interest in the pilgrimage to Mecca and in the five daily prayers, the traditional Cham do celebrate many Muslim festivals and rituals.

The orthodox Cham have adopted a more conformist religion largely because of their close contacts with, and intermarriages with, the Malay community. In fact, the orthodox Cham have adopted Malay customs and family organization, and many speak the Malay language. They send pilgrims to Mecca, and they attend international Islamic conferences. Conflicts between the traditional and the orthodox Cham increased between 1954 and 1975. For example, the two groups polarized the population of one village, and each group eventually had its own mosque and separate religious organization.

According to Cham sources, 132 mosques were destroyed during the Khmer Rouge era, many others were desecrated, and Muslims were not allowed to worship. In the PRK, Islam has been given the same freedom as Buddhism. Vickery believes that about 185,000 Cham lived in Cambodia in the mid-1980s and that the number of mosques was about the same then as it was before 1975. In early 1988, there were six mosques in the Phnom Penh area and a "good number" in the provinces, but Muslim dignitaries were thinly stretched; only 20 of the previous 113 most prominent Cham clergy in Cambodia survived the Khmer Rouge period.

OTHER RELIGIONS

Christianity, introduced into Cambodia by Roman Catholic missionaries in 1660, made little headway, at least among the Buddhists. In 1972 there were probably about 20,000 Christians in Cambodia, most of whom were Roman Catholics. Before the repatriation of the Vietnamese in 1970 and 1971, possibly as many as 62,000 Christians lived in Cambodia. According to Vatican statistics, in 1953, members of the Roman Catholic Church in Cambodia numbered 120,000, making it, at the time, the second largest religion in the country. In April 1970, just before repatriation, estimates indicate that about 50,000 Catholics were Vietnamese. Many of the Catholics remaining in Cambodia in 1972 were Europeans-chiefly French.

Steinberg reported, also in 1953, that an American Unitarian mission maintained a teacher-training school in Phnom Penh, and Baptist missions functioned in Batdambang and Siemreab provinces. A Christian and Missionary Alliance mission was founded in Cambodia in 1923; by 1962 the mission had converted about 2,000 people. American Protestant missionary activity increased in Cambodia, especially among some of the hill tribes and among the Cham, after the establishment of the Khmer Republic.

The 1962 census, which reported 2,000 Protestants in Cambodia, remains the most recent statistic for the group. In 1982 French geographer Jean Delvert reported that three Christian villages existed in Cambodia, but he gave no indication of the size, location, or type of any of them. Observers reported that in 1980 there were more registered Khmer Christians among the refugees in camps in Thailand than in all of Cambodia before 1970. Kiernan notes that, until June 1980, five weekly Protestant services were held in Phnom Penh by a Khmer pastor, but that they had been reduced to a single weekly service after police harassment. His estimates suggest that in 1987 the Christian community in Cambodia had shrunk to only a few thousand members.

Highland tribal groups, most with their own local religious systems, probably number fewer than 100,000 persons. The Khmer Loeu have been loosely described as animists, but most tribal groups have their own pantheon of local spirits. In general they see their world filled with various invisible spirits. They associate spirits with rice, soil, water, fire, stones, paths, and so forth. Sorcerers or specialists in each village contact these spirits and prescribe ways to appease them. In times of crisis or change, animal sacrifices may be made to placate the anger of the spirits.

Illness is often believed to be caused by evil spirits or sorcerers. Some tribes have special medicine men or shamans who treat the sick. In addition to belief in spirits, villagers believe in taboos on many objects or practices. Among the Khmer Loeu, the Rade and Jarai groups have a
well developed hierarchy of spirits with a supreme ruler at its head.

CULTURE

CUSTOMS AND TRADITIONS

In Cambodia, the given name of a person is chosen through a study of the horoscope by the astrologist. The names are personalized for each individual. This explains why, in Cambodia, a person is always called by his/her first name. For official purpose, she/he is called with the title or social rank first followed by the first name, always in this order. To call a person by his/her last name is considered impolite.

The full name is written in this order :

FAMILY NAME	FIRST NAME
DUONG	DARA
CHAN	RAKSMEY

The last name always comes first. If Dara is the husband and Raksmey is the wife, in many occasions, she would be referred to as Mrs Dara instead of her real name. This is very common in the urban areas. Other times, if a woman has a child named Davy, she would be referred to as Davy's mom and her first name would become easily forgotten.

It is said that the Cambodian are generally very formal people; they tend to appreciate more well-educated persons who are polite and possess good manners. In general, they warmly and positively respond to any friendly approach. They love to associate with those who speak with a soft tone with a cultured upbringing.

General Cambodians are not accustomed to shaking hands as a greeting, except those who have been exposed to Western influences. To greed they put their palms together and raise them to their mouth bowing at the same time their head.

Touching is different in Cambodia. Between friends of the same gender, touching is common and permitted; for instance, two girls walking hand-in-hand. This has nothing to do with sexual relationship; it is a sign to sincere friendship.

Touching a person's head is considered impolite because their heads are considered the alter of consciousness-the most sacred part of human being. This is permitted only for parents/grandparents on their little kids or between people of sincere relationship.

Cambodians refer among themselves as "older brother/sister, younger brother/sister, uncle, aunt, niece, and nephew, etc..." much more than the first name even if these persons are strangers to them. It is a sign of respect since they are not comfortable calling someone by first name,

Beckoning someone with a finger is considered impolite or with the palm upward because this is interpreted as calling a dog or calling for a fight. The palm should be downward when you do so.

In speaking to a family, the head of household is traditionally greeted first, then any elder, then his wife, and so on.

Cambodians are usually shy. If you invite them to eat, even if they are starving, they would still refuse. This is simply a "polite refusal" so as not to seem over-eager. It may be necessary to offer two or three times. If this is not done, they would think your invitation is just a "courteous invitation" .

Usually after lunch people have a nap. This can be understood because the weather in Cambodia is hot and humid. Noon temperature is to dangerous to be out working.

People tend to be superstitious, for instance, they might not want to be in a photo of 3 persons together. They believe the middle person is ill-starred. And if the picture is taken, the middle person will be disunited or separated.

As for food, they are used to eat a good deal of rice. Fish and rice are their basic foods. They also eat a lot of fresh vegetables, fish sauce, fish paste and soybean.

At the table, they generally use spoons and forks even though in some occasions, they would use chopsticks instead. Some still prefer eating with their fingers depending on what kind of dish they are having.

The most popular sports in Cambodia are soccer, boxing, basketball, volleyball, and boat races. One can usually see outdoor courts for these sports near any public school sites.

Generally, instead of using hats, men and women, especially in the countryside, they wear a losely-draped turban-like headgear as protection against the sun when they go outdoors.

Women, in general, wear a kind of skirt called "sampot" made from cotton for heavy labor work. For formal events and celebrations, they wear multi-colored silk skirt or, in urban areas, western-styled dresses. For men, in the countryside, wear "Ao hopao buon" (four-pocket shirt) and "kho cheo" (loose-legged pants). In the cities, they dress like most Westerners do.

When they smile and say "yes" to you, it doesn't mean they understand or agree with you. It means that they let you know they hear what you have said.

FAMILY

The ideal household consists of a married couple and their unmarried children of any age. This is very common in the urban districts. But in rural areas, a household includes, most of the time, married children and their families, cousins, nieces and nephews; some other times in-law members, because of economic factors, because there is more space available, because their households are always larger, or because they just want to live in close ties.

An average Cambodian family has 4-6 children in one household. Unlike many other Asians, the Cambodians do not want to have an unlimited number of offsprings, although they accept with genuine pleasure those who come. Because polygamy is legal, one wouldn't be surprised to see a father of a large number of children from different mothers.

Unlike the Chinese or the Hmong, the everage Cambodian does attach special importance to tracing descendants through the male line. The father in general prefers having more boys or to have boys first, so that when they grow up they could help their fathers on the farm or earn some other income to help the family. But the mother usually prefers having girls first so she could help manage the large household. It's usual and normal to see that grandparents or other senior relatives sharing the same household with their married children or grandchildren. The grandparents usually help with daily miscellaneous work in the household such as taking care of the house, providing child care for the grandchildren while their parents are at work, or just guarding and giving advice to teenagers so they wouldn't go off tracks after school. Just like many other Asians, the Cambodian would never sent their senior parents or relatives to a nursing home. Unlike the people in China where ancestors play a major family function, filial piety is a less compulsive moral obligation, but respect for one's elder is expected of everyone.

FAMILY LIFE

Generally each small family group may occupy a separate house, own farm land, raise cattle for field labor or for consumption, plans and operates as an independent unit. Major domestic, social, and religious activities, as well as the minor shared activities of daily life, are handled by the members of immediate family. This fact remains strong in the country as well as in the urban areas.

In the country, the houses of the peasants are built on stilts so that the cows or other livestock can be kept beneath the house. Crowded conditions are usual and since there is little privacy protection, everyone in the community knows a good deal about everyone else in the community. However, in the urban areas, the houses of wealthier families tend be large villas which may contain 4-5 bedrooms and usually with a large veranda at the front of the house.

In the rural Cambodian family, the husband does more arduous agricultural work such as hoeing, and preparing the field for seeding; but both husband and wife work together in the fields when the time comes for transplanting rice. Elsewhere, the husband may belong to the administrative bureaucracy, has and easier live, and spend more time outside of the house. But as a breadwinner, he remains normally the most powerful head of the household, has authority over all family members, and makes decisions on major affairs. His authority is more visible toward the children and, they normally feel a special fear of their father.

The Cambodian woman occupies a key position in the household, and in many ways, the prosperity, well-being and development of the family as a unit revolve around her. Her ethical influence over the younger minds is very important. As a carrier of basic social and moral values of Cambodian culture, she is highly regarded by the men in her own family and by the Cambodian community at large. In the circle of family activities, the wife stands on equal footing with her husband-in some matters she surpasses him in initiative. Generally, it is the wife who is the family treasurer, controlling the purses strings and budgeting the family assets.

Cambodian children are treated affectionately but not fussed over and are encouraged to take care of themselves from an early age. They are, at the same time, allowed to be "children" and are not constantly goaded into adopting adult attitudes or behavior. However, once the child begins to assert its own personality, parental attentiveness diminishes. They are subjected to a such stricter control in Cambodia than in any Western Countries.

A girl learns household duties from her mother-cooking, sewing, tending to younger siblings, etc... . She also joins the mother in trips to the market (daily shopping) and picks up fine points of the art of bargaining. A boy in rural areas learns the techniques of agriculture from his father and older brother. In urban areas, Cambodian boys and girls are more exposed to higher formal schooling and foreign influences including those from Western countries.

In principles, the authority of the parent is sacred and unqualified, but parents usually prefer to teach approved behavior by means of examples set by adults or older siblings. Sharp reprimand and physical punishment are avoided as much as possible, though in certain cases, physical punishment is still used to discipline a child.

Boys are, in general, more exempt from discipline than girls who receive stricter supervision. They must be above reproach if a favorable marriage is later to be arranged. Parental domination falls doubly hard on the daughter and her life is mapped out along the lines of the family advantage and interest. The parents still have another important duty: settling a son or daughter in a profitable marriage because, usually, advantages gained through marriage benefit the whole family. But the feature is diminishing in modern society even though it is not rare to see the practice still active in some families.

It is to be stressed that the family functions as a social security organization for its immediate relatives only. Financial assistance to an immediate family is a part of the Cambodian family system; aid to an intimate relative such as father, mother, brother, sister, etc... is regarded not as the sort of favor that warrants a debt of gratitude, but as a part of the natural order of things. Aid to distant relatives may be offered, as well as to close friends.

MARRIAGE AND SEXUAL BEHAVIOR

As general rules, a high value is placed on proper standards of sexual behavior and on premarital chastity. This is very true in the rural areas, but in urban society, it applies nearly solely to the girls, who are required to be above all approach in this matter. Premarital activities by girls is condemned; however many more men experience sexual relations, especially in the cities where prostitutes are found. In the rural areas, virginity of a bride is mandatory; in the cities, attitudes about this tend to be less rigid nowadays. In some villages, a bride who gets pregnant even by her betrothed, is considered the shame of the family or as an evil person who will attract bad fortune or evil spirits over the family, and therefore, she is ostracized from the family.

Marital fidelity is mandatory, too, but practically only for women. Polygamy is still legal but is diminishing significantly because of the economic pressure and general expansion of education among young generations.

In the rural areas, girls have to observe a strict code of conduct, a custom which is losing its influence in modern society. For instance, at the age of 12, there is a ceremony called "Kor Sork" or cutting the top tuft of hair; it is the puberty rite symbolizing the passage from childhood to adolescence. The onset of menstruation, ritually marked by the practice known as "chol mlub" or "entering the shade", is also disappearing in the modern societies, but is still found sometimes in some villages. This means that, at the first sign of menstruation, a girl is isolated from her family and from her community. The seclusion may last from several days to several months or years, depending on the socio-economic rank of the family. During this cloistered period, a girl is protected from all "desire" including the glances of any man, whether kin or stranger. The leaving of the "shade" is generally marked by a ceremony and the girl is henceforth eligible for marriage.

The young children are not permitted much knowledge of sex, because the parents feel that too much knowledge can lead to desire and eventually to trouble. Usually bits and pieces of information about sex are picked up from friends, but the parents tend to discourage curiosity and rather give inaccurate or fragmentary answers to direct questions. In practice, girls receive little information until the last night of the wedding feast, when the bride's parents take the bride aside and explain the basic facts of sex.

The Western concept of romantic love has caught the imagination of westernized Cambodians, but it is still a purely urban phenomenon. In Phnom Penh, there is some "dating" among college students, but this is usually done in a group of young people of both genders, rather than as separate couples. It is quite different from the way it is done in many westernized societies where generally boys and girls can go any where hand-in-hand. In public, physical contact is not permitted between both genders even hand-holding.

The rural patterns of courtship differ from those in the urban areas, too. In the country, a young man usually begins a flirtation by remarking about the captivation of beauty of the sky or the tree, because to speak directly of a girl's beauty or about her dress is considered blatant. But a sophisticated young man may write love letters. Later, if his intentions become serious, he could ask one of his elder relatives, as a go-between, to sound out the intentions of the girl's parents and eventually ask for her hand. But the general rule remains that the parents select the mates for their children, no matter what age they are.

A man generally marries between the age of 20-26, a girl between 16-22. Marriage within the circle of blood relatives is strictly forbidden (except for royalties) but first cousin marriage is permitted and occurs frequently.

A marriage project ripens slowly in the course of gossip and conservations with neighbors, relatives and friends. Festivals and weddings are considered appropriate occasions on which to bring up the subject and to move the project forward. The final decision remains with the families involved; however, neighbors and friends can still participate from the sidelines. During the first phase, the families "feel each other out"; the two prospective mother-in-law carefully search out good and bad points concerning character and the social status of the two families. It the girl's mother casually mentions that the girl is too young to marry, this is interpreted as disapproval and the project is therefore abandoned. But if the girl's mother seems favorably disposed, the proposition is brought forward. Throughout, there are exchanges of gifts, until, finally, the girls accepts a "box of betel nut". This symbolic act seals the engagement. After that before the wedding, there are other occasional gift exchanges of "sampot" (Cambodian skirt/wrap-around cloth) and "kanseng" (scarves) which has primarily the symbolic value to "fix the words and ties the hearts" of the engaged couple.

The wedding is a lavish and elaborate affair. It may last one, two or even three days, and consists primarily in feast offered at the bride's house. The custom currently remains strong and unchanged in the rural areas where rites are complicated and formalized. In the cities, marriage patterns tend to be more flexible and less complicated, but still strongly formalized.

Divorce is infrequent and frowned upon, maybe because of the existence of polygamy, and also because most of the time men can go out by themselves without their spouses.

IDENTITY

As characters of people differ from one individual to another, it would not be easily describe and stereotype the character of the Cambodians. Nevertheless, it is possible to see and catch the dominant features which reflects the general character of the whole group.

During the French domination, some Frenchmen used to say that Cambodians tended to be "lazy". Following the accession of the country to independence in 1953, the Cambodian government multiplied efforts to erase this image, urging the people to show they are the fruits of Angkorian ancestors, that they are willing and able to do better, and they are not "lazy" as they were noted by the French.

In fact, the Cambodians are generally gentle, sympathetic, polite, and reluctant to show anger or displeasure in a direct manner. Deeply religious, they tend to be more conservative and to have few ambitions to improve life in the material sense. Humble and submissive, they prefer usually to suffer in silence rather than to open their hearts to a stranger. And because they are Buddhists, they tend to be resigned to their fate and not to be aggressive.

They are known as a smiling people for they always smile. Their smile usually reflects their kind feelings, their sweet character, their good hearts, and the good life they are living. But their smile could also means their politeness or a desire to please, and does not usually mean the things it means here.

Another feature generally qualified as characteristic of Cambodians is that they tend to hold a grudge when they feel they have been humiliated or have suffered a loss of face, and the bitterness grows stronger if this happens in public. In this case it is difficult for them to forgive, for they never forget the shock, unless an apology is made.

Shyness is another dominant characteristic to them. It's sometimes associated with a kind of reserve, leading to the impression that they lack education or are not polite. Some of them are so shy they don't even feel comfortable in saying hello spontaneously, or expressing thanks in a proper way, but rather keep themselves in a very low, low profile. That does not mean they forget a good deed they have received. As the matter of fact, they are deeply sentimental; they keep their sentiments of gratitude in their hearts and will allow them if an opportunity arises. During the Japanese occupation of Cambodia, all the French community were sent to jail by the Japanese authorities. The Cambodian unexpectedly came to the help of their former rulers at the risk and peril of their lives.

They are also very frank and sometimes show openly what they think and this makes people believe they are not flexible. Actually, for many of them, a thing must be black or white with nothing in between. This feature is especially true for the people of the rural areas.

In short, the Cambodians are generally characterized as very happy, very cheerful, and very affectionate. They have a relaxed manner of their approach to life, and tend to love to sing and dance. They are perhaps slow and passive, but have excellent dispositions and show you they are industrious. Once you get their confidence, they will become very loyal to you.

THE INFLUENCE

The value system of the Cambodians derives from several different cultural traditions (Khmer, Indian, French) and shows the influence of Brahmanism and Theravada Buddhism.

The first set of values derives from a combination of ancient Khmer culture with Indian Hinduism, oriented toward a system of fixed class with ascribed status and important rank distinctions. Each person is supposed to have a definite place in the social order and a clearly prescribed role to go with it .

The second set is influenced by the Theravada Buddhism (or Small Vehicle). The basic concepts are the unity of all life and the ultimate spiritual perfectibility and equality of all mankind. The concepts also stress the acceptance of the secular social order, religious detachment from worldly affairs, the individual's responsibility for his own status in life, and the possibility of altering one's status through a combination of individual merit and reincarnation.

The Third derives from the cultural tradition carried on as a result of the French presence. This influence has penetrated Cambodian society through government education and the way of thinking. The tradition places a high value on the individual's ability to raise his/her own status in life through the direct and practical means of secular education and economic advancement. It stresses active rather than passive aspects of achievement and the accumulation of material wealth as a means of achieving both personal and social ends. This tradition is strongest among the civil servants and the upper class, who served in the previous French-like administration of Cambodia.

SOCIAL RELATIONSHIP

In general, Cambodians prefer to have their social relationship clearly defined so that each person involved has a distinct status and a prescribed role to play. There is security in thus knowing precisely where an individual stands, what is expected of him and others, what he and others can or cannot do. The rules of the etiquettes between people of different status and rank are carefully spelled out, and every status and rank has its appropriate and circumscribed roles for every situation. Once the situation has been recognized and the appropriate formal courtesies exchanged, individuals are willing to shift to a more informal kind of interchange, but the basic definition of the situation and the limits of behavior must still be adhered to.

Conversely, if a Cambodian wants to assume a role which his current status does not permit him to assume in particular situations, he cannot simply extend his role informally, as Americans for instance do. He must first formally shift his status, then assume the appropriate role. This shift must be clear and abrupt, and must be publicly announced. (And he does not view such a shift in status as evidence or irresponsibility). Here are a few examples:

When King Norodom Sihanouk felt that his status as king did not permit him to play the role of the kind he wanted in Cambodian politics, he abruptly abdicated the throne and switched to another status (Head of the State) that allowed him more latitude in dealing directly with his people

When a man becomes a bonze, he severs his connections with his family, and his future relationship with his parents is that of any young person to older people rather than that of parents and child. In political life, rebel leaders who surrender and formally announce their previous roles, become eligible for at least some kind of high posts in the government. For the same reason, a criminal, one he has served his prison time, may resume his status as free citizen without prejudice.

It is said that Cambodians in general never really negotiate and instead they enter into parleys with goals they do not intend to modify, or with basic principles they do not intend to relinquish. Cambodians do not actually have the western concept of "negotiation" on which the objectives are based. In fact, if there are persistent disagreements between themselves, generally it is because each of the parties involved feels that the other side does not understand the situation. The disagreement could be resolved only through mutual probation and explanation that enables the parties to reach a common definition of the situation. If this is impossible, both parties withdraw and leave the problem unresolved, with the hope that the time and the circumstances with remove the issue altogether, or that one side will ultimately see the light.

It is also said that Cambodians in general are too fond of entering into legal proceeding and spending their money on the fees even if they have to ruin themselves in the process. The main concern is that they don't "lose face". Some disagreements have been known to last many years.

PERSONAL CONDUCT

Cambodians feel that the individual should be attuned to Buddhist code of personal conduct. Nonviolence is another important precept, and crimes of violence such as an assault, murder, and rape are extremely rare. In general, temperance, diligence, thrift, and self-discipline are stressed.

If you ask Cambodians whether one should ever lie, everybody would unanimously say it is not good to lie and they hate to lie. But some people would probably answer "of course." For it is acceptable to do a little "social lying" and still keep one's integrity. For instance, you have to say to a hostess' quiche is delicious even when it is soggy, and that somebody's dress is pretty even if it looks terrible. A girl sometimes has to lie to a man for her confidential reason, etc...

In Cambodia, this kind of "social lying" seems very common. Furthermore, "social lying" as a means of avoiding embarrassment or shame to oneself or to others, is considered normal and is widely accepted. But that does not mean lying is the rule. On the contrary, the Buddhist precepts teach people since childhood to despise lying as being incompatible with their natural pride.

In the past, it has been true that Cambodians have felt little compulsion to succeed in a material sense or to gain more power as individuals. Acquisitiveness is not a dominant characteristic. Adequacy is the objective in life. For instance, if a rice farmers finds that he has more than enough money for himself and his family, he gives the surplus to the pagoda for charity. Nevertheless, at the present time, more Cambodians are beginning to examine their values in light of the realities of the modern world. For many then, the only way to attain a prominent position in the accumulation of wealth as a means of attaining economic and political power.

THE RHYTHM OF LIFE

Cambodia is a predominantly agricultural country and, as in most agricultural areas in the world, sowing time and harvesting time are highly important in the life cycle. Festivities and marriages can be postponed, but no one can afford to court disaster by sowing his rice late, by transplanting the tender shoots when the soil has hardened, or by bringing in the harvest late.

These laws affects other activities as well. Idle farm labor become available for other tasks, such as building roads, after the harvest is in. The Cambodian farmer will use the dry season to repair his house, an oxen cart, or build a boat. He may decide to go into the city to work for a while or visit friends and relatives; he has disposed his crop, made payments on his debt, and has spare cash on hand to spend on the Water Festival. His mind is at ease.

The period between the beginning of October and the end of January is one of big times in Cambodia. It is the time that the government generally chooses for major political or national events. The average people, unworried by major material problems, are now receptive to all matters which may provide a break in the routine in their daily life.

The formal Cambodian calendar is a combination of the lunar and solar calendar That is the months are based upon the movement of the moon, but the yearly cycle of months is corrected every three years so to bring them to accord with the movement of the sun.

The lunar months are also the basic units for the Cambodian religious calendar. There are alternately months with 29 and 30 days; the former are known as "female" (Ko Bei) months; the latter as "male" (Ko Buon). Some times the 29-day months are referred to as "Khae Khaat" adn the 30-day months as "Khae Penh." The status of the month is of great importance in Cambodian life; for instance, marriages cannot be celebrated during the 29-day month.

The exact date of the new year changes every year according to the calculations of Buddhist clergy, but usually the civil calendar begins the 13th of April.

The Cambodians, like the Chinese, use a twelve-year cycle calendar which is also used in other countries in Southeast Asia. It carries the symbols of 12 animals (rat, ox, tiger, hare, dragon (Naga), snake, horse, goat, monkey, rooster, dog, and pig). The months are divided into two fortnights : one from the new to the full moon (Kneut), the other from the full month to the end of lunar cycle (Ronoch). The days are numbered from one to 14 or 15 with the addition of the word "Kneut" for the first fortnight of the month, and the word "Ronoch" for the second fortnight of the declining moon.

The 8th, and the 15th days of the first fortnight and the 8th and the last day of the second fortnight are sacred days (Thngai Sel). During the two sacred days of the first fortnight, the faithful go the pagodas where Buddhist texts are explained to them by the bonzes, and during the two sacred days of the second fortnight, the bonzes must publicly confess their shortcomings and the laity engage in merrymaking.

The weekdays correspond exactly to the solar calendar, with the same stars and planets representing the days of the week. But for each day, a special color is supposed to predominant, and during an official ceremony, the dress must have the color of the day. Following are some examples:

Khmer (lunar) days	Western (solar) days	planet	color
Thngai Atit	Sunday	Sun	Red

Thngai Chan	Monday	Moon	Orange
Thngai Angkea	Tuesday	Mars	Violet
Thngai Put	Wednesday	Mercury	Green
Thngai Prohohs	Thursday	Jupiter	Cloud grey
Thngai Sok	Friday	Venus	Blue
Thngai Sao	Saturday	Saturn	Black

ANGKOR. FACTS AND FIGURES

The temples at Angkor are spread out over some 40 miles around the village of Siem Reap, about 192 miles from the Cambodian capital, Phnom Penh. They were built between the eighth and 13th centuries and range from single towers made of bricks to vast stone temple complexes. There are two main sites where the Khmer temples are located. The first is at Roluos which is about 10 miles south east of today's village of Siem Reap, where only a few of the earlier temples were built. This was the first Khmer capital in the Angkor area. In the late ninth century, Yasovarman I moved the capital to the immediate vicinity of Siem Reap. This is a much larger site, where the majority of the Khmer temples are located. It is officially known as the City of Angkor. There are other temples located in the area, some up to 20 miles away from Siem Reap. Khmer temples can also be found in many other parts of Cambodia, as well as China, Thailand, Laos and Vietnam.

Today, a great deal of restoration work has been done on many of the temples. However, because of the lack of security in Cambodia and the continuing rebel insurgency around the Angkor region, some of the temples are closed to tourists. The major temples, as listed below, are usually open to tourists

MAJOR TEMPLES AT ANGKOR:

ANGKOR WAT:
Regarded as the supreme masterpiece of Khmer architecture, it is a huge pyramid temple built by Suryavarman II between 1113 and 1150. It is surrounded by a moat 570 feet wide and about four miles long. The mass of bas-relief carving is of the highest quality and the most beautifully executed in Angkor.

BAKONG:
The central temple in Indravarman I's city of Hariharalaya. It is a large pyramid temple, measuring 180 feet square at the base. It was built towards the end of the ninth century.

BANTEAI SREI:
A delicate and small temple around 15 miles from the village of Siem Reap. It was built by Jayavarman V and finished in AD968. It is an example of the idea of making a temple complex comprised of several buildings, and features some very fine carvings in pink sandstone.

THE BAPHUON:
A large pyramid temple built by Udayadityavarman II between 1050 and 1066. It features beautiful carvings including a 131-foot reclining Buddha.

THE BAYON:
A massive temple complex built by Jayavarman VII between 1181 and 1220. It features 3,936 feet of superb bas-relief carving and mysterious Buddha faces carved on the towers of the third level.

PREAH KO:
An early temple at the Roluos site about 10 miles from Siem Reap. It was built by Indravarman I in the late ninth century.

PREAH KHAN:
Built by Jayavarman VII in the late 12th century, this large temple is very well preserved and features excellent carvings.

TA PROHM:
A very large temple complex enclosed by a moat. It is one of the most beautiful of the Khmer temples as it has not been restored, but has been left surrounded by jungle. It was built by Jayavarman VII in the later 12th century.

TA KEO:
A sandstone temple built by Jayavarman V between AD968 and 1001. It has a large central tower surrounded by four smaller towers.

APSARA DANCE

It is one of two major forms of Khmer dancing, and incorporates parts of the other - much older traditional or popular dancing, which has its roots in animism and primitive magic -with Hindu forms introduced during the time of Indian influence beginning in the 1st Century. Classical dance took on its own unique form, adding movements and meaning, during the reigns of kings Jayavarman II to VII. By the 13th Century, it was more Khmer than Indian, unlike any other dance form in the world. At the heart of the classical form is the apsara, the joyful, almost wanton dancer whose images are everywhere. Apsara dancing goes back to the 1st Century. The graceful movements of the apsara dancer, adorned with gold headdresses and silken tunics and skirts, are carved on the walls of many of the temples at Angkor. Estimates are that there were 3,000 apsara dancers in the 12th Century court of King Jayavarman VII.

Over the centuries Khmer dancing lent its influence to the classical ballet of neighboring countries and some of its postures and movements are similar to other Southeast Asian dance forms. But according to Princess Buppha Devi, "The Khmer Kingdom started its traditions in the 8th century, 500 years before Thailand." In 1400, with the sacking of the Angkor Empire, the apsara dancers were seized and taken to Thailand.

Apsara dancing is one of two elements of classical ballet, the other being "tontay" dancing, the depiction of early myths. Many of the dances involve performing a fragment of the Ramayana, the ancient Indian epic that is one and a half times as long as the Odyssey.

Others are based on the legendary battles and mythical sagas carved in bas relief in the walls of the temples of Angkor-including the Churning of the Ocean of Milk, the great battle between gods and demons for the holy liquid that gives immortality. There are some 100 Cambodian dances and dramas. There are four typical roles in Khmer dancing -the male, the female, the monkey and the giant. Women and girls usually play the male and female and giant roles. Males often play the monkey role. In the early days, all dancers were women, and females still dance most of the roles in the Royal dance troupe today.

In December 1995, Cambodia revived its Ramayana tradition after 25 years with a performance of the epic at Angkor Wat. Dancers came from six countries as part of a Southeast Asia cultural exchange. The dances are full of meaning, with each gesture symbolizing something, from great concepts such as love and peace to small. A finger to the sky means "today" arms crossed over the chest "very happy," and the left arm stretched out behind the dancer's right hand held up before the chest with three fingers up and index finger touching the thumb depict the Naga, the great many-headed snake that symbolizes the spirit of the Cambodian people.

A hand up means "dead," one down "alive," and fast switching up and down depicts two of the four parts of human life in Buddhist teaching: birth, life, sickness and death. Besides the life of a human, formal kinds of apsara dancing also honor spirit of Cambodia -and immortality. Princess Buppha Devi says that over the centuries "The hand gestures have changed very little," although the organization or the Royal troupe has changed often, with each reigning King. As she puts it, "The ballet belongs to the kingdom and His Majesty the King is in charge."

Like much of classical dance, the hand gestures were born in the other major form of Khmer dancing, popular or traditional. This dates back to the earliest days, before Indian influence, and has roots in early animism, the worship of the spirits of trees, animals and other natural things. You can readily see traditional dancing at almost any social gathering, when Khmer people dance slowly in a circle, gesturing gracefully with their hands. Other kinds of traditional dancing are peacock and wedding dances.

Traditional dancing never died out in Cambodia, unlike classical dance, which since the decline of Angkor was revived within the past century by Queen Kossomak and Princess Buppha Devi, who became one of many teachers of apsara dance. Both forms thrive now. Queen Kossomak modernized many traditions, and she herself went to the primary schools to seek out girls with the fine bones and graceful limbs who would make good dancers. These young girds were trained initially at school outside the palace, and eventually trained inside the palace, a system that remains in place today.

Today children selected for dance training are taught to do hand exercise at an early age to loosen their joints. Dancers must be trained while the bones are still supple. Apsara dancers' fingers are extraordinarily elastic, they can bend their fingers back wards almost to the wrist. One of the most prominent choreographers on Cambodia today is Proeung Chhiebg, 47, a former member of the Royal dance troupe who used to perform with Princess Buppha Devi. His grandmother was a member of the Royal dance troupe and he and his sister, also a Royal dancer, used to follow her around the palace grounds while she trained. At age 8 he went into formal training under his grandmother. "I always played the monkey role because of its acrobatics," he said. The Royal dancers weren't paid particularly well. He said his first salary was 25 riel or about 1 cent. At 17 he became a dance teacher. He is one of only a handful of dance teachers to have survived the Khmer Rouge era, a regime that resulted in the deaths of most of the intellectuals and artists. Today he is the Dean of the Choreographic Arts Faculty at the Royal University of Fine Arts in Phnom Penh.

In addition to classical, traditional dancing is also taught at the Royal University of Fine Arts, along with masked drama, shadow puppets classical Cambodian music and circus arts.

As in the old days, technical training is given in the morning and regular schooling takes place in the afternoon. Although now retired from professional dancing, today at age 53 Princess Buppha Devi continues to dazzle audiences through her work as director of the 300 dancers who belong to the modern Royal ballet. Today, apsara-dancing performances are no longer relegated to the gods and kings. Performances can been seen at the major hotels, and at Chatomuk Theater near the Royal Palace. With the tinkling of xylophones and a euphony of gongs and drums, the apsara dancers, dressed in their tightly fitted silk tunics embroidered in gold and silver, barefoot but with elaborate headdresses, and outstretched arms symbolizing the naga and glistening with jewelry, enter the stage to perform with incredible grace. Dancing holds great significance for the Khmer people and the government considers the Royal ballet in particular to be a national treasure.

POLITICAL AND GOVERNMENT SYSTEM

The Kingdom of Cambodia is a constitutional monarchy with a market economy. Cambodia's constitution was adopted in 1993 and provides for a constitutional monarchy and for separation of powers between the executive, legislative and judicial branches of government. King Norodom Sihanouk is Cambodia's constitutional monarch. According to the Constitution, he reigns, but does not govern. Norodom Sihanouk was Cambodia's constitutional monarch from the time Cambodia became independent from France in 1953 to the republican coup of 1970. Sihanouk was also nominal head of state during the notorious Khmer Rouge regime, 1975-79.

The current system of government emerged from the Paris Peace Accords in 1991, in which four warring factions agreed to put aside hostilities and allow the United Nations to set up a transitional authority (UNTAC) in Cambodia which would administer the country until Cambodia could draft a new constitution and hold democratic elections. The elections took place in 1993, resulting in a coalition government between the royalist FUNCINPEC Party of Prince Norodom Ranariddh, and the Cambodian People's Party (CPP) lead by Hun Sen, which had ruled Cambodia since 1979.

The 1993 coalition government collapsed during factional fighting in July 1997, during which Second Prime Minister Hun Sen ousted First Prime Minister Norodom Ranariddh. Many FUNCINPEC and opposition party the country, but returned to participate in national elections in July 1998. Four months after the election, CPP and FUNCINPEC formed the current coalition government. Hun Sen is Prime Minister. Prince Norodom Ranarridh is president of the National Assembly. Cambodia's 24 government ministries are split between the two parties, except for the Ministries of Defense and Interior, which have co-ministers from each party. The CPP has 64 seats in the National Assembly, FUNCINPEC 43 seats, and the opposition Sam Rainsy Party, lead by the former Finance Minister of the same name, has 15 seats. In March 1999, Cambodia created a Senate with two members appointed by the King, and 59 others appointed by the various parties in proportion to their representation in the National Assembly. The Senate is led by President Chea Sim (CPP), who acts as head of state in the king's absence.

Cambodia is divided administratively into 20 provinces (Khaet) and 4 municipalties (Krong). Each province is divided into districts (Srok), and further into over 1600 communes (Khum) nationwide. Provincial and district leaders are appointed by the central government, and are currently split between the two coalition parties. Commune leaders are mainly the same individuals who the CPP appointed in the 1980s. However, Cambodia is currently drafting legislation to allow for elections for commune officials, which are planned for 2001.

Since the UNTAC period, Cambodia has undertaken an aggressive economic and political reform program with the assistance of the International Financial Institutions and various multilateral and bilateral donors. Reforms slowed down during the period of instability beginning in mid-1997, but resumed in late 1998. Donors expressed their confidence in the government's commitment to reform at the World Bank-chaired donors' Coordinating Group meeting in Tokyo in February 1999 with pledges of about $470 million in assistance, but intensified their monitoring of Cambodia's progress. Donors also instituted regular consultations with the Cambodian government on key reform areas including military demobilization, forestry reform, fiscal reform, administrative reform and various other issues. Cambodia performed well on its reform program in 1999, and donors pledged a total of $548 in assistance at a Coordinating Group meeting in May 2000.

The United States of America has full diplomatic relations with Cambodia and normal trade relations. Cambodia received MFN status from the U.S. under the terms of a 1996 agreement on Trade and Intellectual Property Rights, and received GSP benefits from the U.S. in 1997. Cambodia signed a ground-breaking textile agreement with the United States in 1999, which offers increased textile quota if the U.S. determines that Cambodia is in substantial compliance with internationally recognized core labor standards. Cambodia has begun the process of accession to the WTO, and is a member of the Asean Free Trade Area.

The Cambodian government has adopted a free market, pro-investment economic policy. The state role in the economy is minimal and the government offers significant incentives to attract foreign investors. The government has recently begun regular consultations with the business community. However, significant gaps in the legal system, the weakness of key financial institutions such as the banking sector, and problems of non-transparency and corruption continue to deter investment. One notable exception has been the garment industry, which has attracted over 160 new factories since 1994 and now accounts for over 90 percent of Cambodia's exports. This industry was drawn to Cambodia by the availability of textile quota for the U.S. market, and Cambodia has not yet repeated this degree of success in any other industrial sector.

POLITICAL AND ADMINISTRATIVE STRUCTURE

In the transitional period between the signing of the Paris Peace Agreements in October 1991 and a free and fair national elections conducted by the United nations Transitional Authority in Cambodia (UNTAC) in May 1993, Cambodia was governed by a Supreme National Council (SNC), regrouping all four major political parties.

In September 1990, the Security Council (resolution 66811990) welcomed "the agreement reached by all Cambodian parties at Jakarta to form a Supreme National Council as the unique legitimate body and source of authority in which, throughout the transitional period, the independence, national sovereignty and unity of Cambodia is embodied". This development was also welcomed by the General Assembly which noted in its resolution 4513 of 16 October 1990 that the Supreme National Council "will therefore represent Cambodia externally and occupy the seat of Cambodia at the United Nations, in the United Nations specialized agencies and in other international institutions and international conferences ".

Administration of the country was temporarily entrusted to UNTAC, which successfully organized the elections with a large turnout of the population. Following the installation of a Provisional National Government, the elected Constituent Assembly adopted and promulgated on September 24, 1993 the nation's constitution, which proclaimed King Norodom Sihanouk as Head of State and established the Royal Government of Cambodia (RGC) within a framework of parliamentary democracy. Two Prime Ministers were appointed to represent the two major parties that won the elections. This same date marks the official end of UNTAC's mandate. 30th September marks the date of easing of the activities of the various UNTAC components and 15th November, the date provided for the end of withdrawal of the "Blue helmets".

THE CONSTITUTION

On 22nd September, after 5 days of intensive debate, the Constituent Assembly adopted by secret ballot, the Constitution of the Kingdom of Cambodia" by 113 votes for, 5 votes against and 2 abstentions. On 24th September, the Head of State promulgated the basic charter. A few hours later, during a ceremony characterized by dignity and great simplicity, it pronounced the oath which made Norodom Sihanouk the first Constitutional King of Cambodia. The Constituent Assembly became the National Assembly and the King on the proposal of the President and Deputy Presidents of the Assembly, designated by virtue of Article 138 of the Constitution, H.R.H. Prince Norodom Ranariddh and H.E. Mr. Hun Sen, First and Second Prime Ministers respectively. From then on, the life in the country is governed by one hundred and thirty-nine articles spread over 14 chapters in the Constitution.

SOVEREIGNTY

The Constituent Assembly attempts to define in six articles Cambodia's sovereignty and its policy of neutrality and non-alignment. It also attempted to define with great determination the national territory limits with specific reference made to "1/100,000 scale maps made between the years 1933-1953 and internationally recognized between the years 1963-1969".

THE KING

His Majesty King NORODOM SIHANOUK

and Her Majesty Queen NORODOM MONINEATH SIHANOUK

Twenty-four articles define the royal role as being one of a symbol of unity and permanence of the Nation and a guarantee of national independence, sovereignty and territorial integrity of the Kingdom. The King is the Head of state for life. He holds the throne but does not hold power. "The King reigns but does not Govern". He appoints the Prime Minister(s) and the Council of Ministers. Upon presentation by the Council of Ministers, the King signs decrees of appointment., transfer and dismissal of high civil and military officials, extra-
ordinary and plenipotentiary ambassadors and delegates, and upon presentation by the Supreme Council of Magistracy, he signs decrees to appoint, transfer or dismiss judges.

As the Supreme Commander of the Royal Khmer Armed Forces, the King appoints -the Commander-in- Chief of the Royal Khmer Armed Forces, declares war upon approval of the National Assembly, and upon approval of the Prime Minister(s) and the President of the National Assembly, the King declares the state of emergency. The King receives letters of credentials from foreign ambassadors extraordinary and plenipotentiary to the Kingdom of Cambodia, and upon the approval of the National Assembly, he signs and ratifies international treaties and conventions.

The wife of the reigning King holds the royal title of Queen of Cambodia. She does not have the right to engage in politics, to assume the role of leader of state or government, or to assume other administrative or political roles. The Queen of Cambodia exercises activities that serve the social, humanitarian and religious
interests, and assists the King with protocol and diplomatic functions.

In the absence of the King, the President of the National Assembly assumes the powers as acting Head of State. In case of serious illness, the President of the National Assembly performs the duty of Head of State as "Royal Delegate' and in the event of the King's death and before the appointment of the new King the
President of the National Assembly shall take over the responsibility as acting Head of State until the new King is elected by the Royal Council of the throne. As to the succession to the throne, in accordance to the tradition, the Cambodian monarchy is elected. However, the King does not have the power to appoint his
successor to the throne. A Council of the Throne chooses the new Sovereign from among the male descendants, aged at least 30, of the Kings Ang Duong, Norodom and Sisowath. No member of the Royal Family sits in his official capacity on this body which consists of 6 people: the President and the two first Vice Presidents of the National Assembly, the Prime Minister, the Supreme Patriarch from each of the two Buddhist orders. The King cannot designate his successor.

LEADING GOVERNMENT OFFICIALS

Samdech Chea Sim
Chairman of the Senate

Samdech Hun Sen
Prime Minister

Samdech Krom Preah Norodom Ranaridh
Chairman of the National Assembly

H. E. Hor Nam Hong
Minister of Foreign Affairs and International Cooperation

RIGHTS AND DUTIES OF THE KHMER CITIZENS

Twenty articles list the fundamental rights enjoyed by Khmer citizens: They have equality before the law and have the same rights, freedoms and obligations, regardless of race, color, sex, language, religious belief, political tenancy, ethnic origin, status, or other social position. Citizens of both sexes enjoy the right of active participation in the political, economic, social and cultural life of the nation, the rights to privacy and the freedom to travel . They have the right to vote at age 18, and to be candidates in elections at age 25.

Citizens have freedom of expression and association. They have the right to set up associations and political parties, participate in mass organizations, and form and to be members of trade unions. Although Buddhism is the state religion, citizens have the right to practice other beliefs unless they affect other beliefs and public security. A citizen, accused of a crime, is presumed innocent until proven guilty by a competent court. Any citizen can file actions for damages for the illegal acts of state institutions and social institutions .

THE RE-ESTABLISHMENT OF RIGHTS TO PRIVATE OWNERSHIP AND OF A FREE MARKET ECONOMY

The constitution emphasizes the re-establishment of rights to private ownership and of a free market economy. It provides that all persons, individually or collectively, have the right to ownership, but that only individuals or legal entities with Khmer nationality can have the right to own real estate. Just compensation is require d for any taking by the State. Furthermore, it specifies that Cambodia will, inter alia: allow,citizens to sell their products freely; provide production materials, protect the price of products and help producers to find markets; help regulate the market to guarantee appropriate living conditions for the people; promote economic development; and protect and manage the environment. The Constitution gives both sexes "the right to choose employment appropriate to their ability and the needs of society", "the same remuneration for the same job", "the right to obtain social security", the right to form and be members of trade unions".

THE NATIONAL ASSEMBLY

In this parliamentary monarchy the Constitution gave the National Assembly important legislative power. Elected for five years, it can be dissolved only under very specific circumstances (article 78): if, on two occasions in twelve months, the government has been in a minority. Then upon the agreement of the Chairman of the National Assembly the Prime Minister(s) and the King are required to dissolve it. This is a mechanism which, while greatly limiting the right of dissolution, nevertheless helps to avoid paralysis in the event of a prolonged political crisis. Another sign of the. importance of the parliamentary institution, the Chairman of the National Assembly is one of the most important figures in the Kingdom. A member of the Council of the Throne, his agreement is required in the event of possible dissolution and for the appointment of, the Prime Minister. Another classical function of the parliament to control the government is provided for in the Constitution (article 96) by means of written questions or questioning.

The National Assembly consists of at least 120 members. National Assembly members shall be elected by universal election, through a free, equal, direct and secret ballot. National Assembly members may stand for re-election. Candidates must be Khmer citizens of both sexes, aged at least 25 years old, and who have the right to vote. In the case of war or other specific circumstances where an election cannot be held, the National Assembly may extend its term for one year at a time, at the request of the-King. Extension shall require a two-thirds vote of the entire National Assembly.

National Assembly members shall have parliamentary privilege. The can not be arrested, intercepted or detained because of ideas expressed in carrying out their jobs. The arrest, interception or detention of a National Assembly member can be done only with the agreement of the National Assembly or its permanent committee between sessions except in cases of criminal offenses.

The National Assembly have an independent budget. The National Assembly members receive a parliamentary salary. Before starting its function, the National Assembly must decide the validity of each member's mandate. the National Assembly must hold a separate election to select the Chairman, Vice Chairmen and all members of the National Assembly committees. This election must be decided by two third majority vote of all members of the National Assembly. A two thirds majority vote is required for adoption of the internal regulations of the National Assembly. All members must take an oath of allegiance before holding their position or function.

The ordinary session of the National Assembly is held twice per year, Each session lasts at least three months. If there is a proposal from the King, Prime Minister or one-third of the National Assembly members, the permanent committee of the National Assembly can call an extraordinary session. Between sessions, the permanent committee shall manage the work of the assembly . The National Assembly's permanent committee consists of the President of the National Assembly, both Vice-Chairmen of the National Assembly and the heads of all National Assembly committees.

If the country is in a state of emergency, the National Assembly must meet every day- The National Assembly has the right to terminate the state of emergency if the situation permits. If the National Assembly cannot meet because of circumstances such as the occupation by foreign forces or other circumstances the declaration of the state of emergency must be automatically extended. During the state of emergency the National Assembly must not be dissolved.

The National Assembly session is held in public. The National Assembly can meet in closed session at the request of the Chairman of the National Assembly or at least one tenth of the National Assembly members, or the King or the Prime Minister. The quorum of the National Assembly- is seven-tenths of all members. Up on the proposal of at least one-tenth of its members, the National Assembly may invite a high dignitary to clarify or discuss important issues. The National Assembly is the only organ to adopt laws. This right is not transferable to any other organ.

The National Assembly approves the national budget; the state planning, the permission of the State to borrow and to lend, and the creation, changes or annulment of tax. The National assembly approves or annuls treaties or international convention, and may declare a state of war. The adoption of the above mentioned laws must be decided by a simple majority of all members. The National Assembly may pass a vote of confidence or no-confidence in the Royal Government by a two-thirds majority of all members.

National Assembly members or the Prime Minister shall have the right to propose laws. But these proposals are unacceptable if they aim to reduce public assets or to increase the burden on citizens. Laws adopted by the National Assembly which run counter to the principles of national sovereignty and affect the political unity or the administrative management of the nation is annulled. The Constitutional Council is the only organ which can approve this annulment. Laws approved by the National Assembly and signed by the Head of State is effective in Phnom Penh within ten days after signing and within twenty days throughout the country.

Urgent laws shall become effective immediately after the signature by the King. National Assembly members have the right to submit written questions to the Royal Government through the Chairman of the National Assembly. Replies can come from one or more ministries according to the issue raised, if the issue raised concerns general policies within the Royal Government. The Prime Minister ca n reply verbally or in writing.

All replies must be given within seven days after receipt of the question. The Chairman of the National Assembly can decide whether the Assembly discusses the issue in open debate. If there is no discussion, the matter is settled. If there is open discussion, the questioner, Minister or Prime Minister may discuss their views within the time of one meeting. The National Assembly sets aside one day a week for responses to questions. However, the session for answering questions shall not lead to a vote.

National Assembly committees can invite ministers to give explanations on their field of responsibility. The National Assembly can dismiss a minister or members of the cabinet or government from his/her position by a vote of two-thirds of the National Assembly members. A vote of no-confidence can be put to the National Assembly by thirty members of the full assembly to decide.

THE CONSTITUTIONAL COUNCIL

The constitutional Council consists of 9 members, 3 of which are appointed by the King, the National Assembly and the Supreme Council of the Magistracy respectively It judges, without appeal, the constitutionality of the laws. It deliberates with authority on the Internal Regulations of the National Assembly and the organic laws.

THE JUDICIARY

Asserted through UNTAC impetus and confirmed by the Constitution, the power of the courts is one of independence. The courts maintain impartiality and protect the rights and freedoms for the people. The courts cover all cases, including administrative ones. The power of the courts is given to the Supreme Court and other courts of all levels. The Cambodian judicial system is built on provincial and municipal 21 tribunals, a Court of Appeals and a Supreme Court. Being the legacy of the former State of Cambodia, this judicial system lives on and will be the basis of future Cambodian judicial system. Cambodian magistrates and court clerks are few in number, approximately 80 and 200 respectively.

THE POLITICAL SYSTEM

Five articles describe the characteristics of the system installed: a "pluralist liberal democracy". All the powers belong to the people who can exercise their power through the National Assembly, the Royal Government, and the courts. There are provisions relating to the neutrality of the country which exclude any adherence of Cambodia to any alliance or any regional organization which has a military purpose. However, Cambodia keeps its right to receive foreign aid as military materials, weapons, ammunitions, military training and other assistance for its self-defense, its public order and security throughout the country.

THE ROYAL GOVERNMENT

The council of Ministers is the Royal Government of the kingdom of Cambodia. The Royal Government is the executive organ of the State led by H.R.H. Prince Norodom Ranariddh and H.E. Samdech Hun Sen, First and Second Prime Ministers respectively. The Royal Government, with its armed forces and its administration, governs the State. It is in charge of the overall execution of all national policies and programmes and is responsible and accountable to the National Assembly.

The two Prime Ministers are assisted by two deputy Prime Ministers, each of whom are also in charge of a separate ministry, the Ministry of Public Works and Transport and the Ministry of Interior. The other members of the Council of Ministers are:

6 Senior Ministers or Ministers of State, three of whom are in charge of separate ministries, the Ministry of Economy and Finances, the Ministry of Public Works and Transports, and the Ministry of Justice. The other 3 are in charge of specific mandates of Rehabilitation and Development, of General Inspection, and of Culture, Arts, Land Use Planning and Urbanization.

15 Ministers share the responsibilities of 12 ministries, with the exception of two who are in charge of the Cabinet of the Council of Ministers, an institution whose task is to

prepare the decisions for the Council of Ministers both from the political and administrative side.

9 Secretaries of State, 4 of whom hold autonomous ministerial responsibilities. The other 5 are in charge of State Secretariats but directly reporting to the Council of Ministers.

12 Secretaries of State attached to different ministries.

In addition, there are more than 50 Under Secretaries of State who, although not being part of the Royal Government, art also considered as political appointees. Out of them, 2 hold ministerial attributions (Civil Service and Civil Aviation).

The two Prime Ministers, by virtue of Article 138 of the Constitution, share the same rights, prerogatives and privileges to run the Royal Government. The Constitution call s for a weekly meeting of the members of the Government under the Chairmanship of the Prime Ministers (article 104). Plenary sessions are called Council of Ministers. They can take full decisions concernant any types of activities of the government. Restricted sessions are called Interministerial Meeting. In these sessions, membership selection are restricted according to the need and wish of the Prime Ministers and their chairmanship can be delegated to a Deputy Prime Minister or to a member of the Royal Government. Their decisions do not bind the government as a whole but only on the well defined matters.

The Prime Ministers, through their regulatory authority., execute all decisions adopted by the Council of Ministers. They presented the Decrees (Kret) to the King for his signature. They can also exercise their own regulatory authority by way of Sub-decree (Anu-kret), after the approval of the Council of Ministers, or by way of Decisions and Circulars. All regulatory acts, whether from the Royal Government or from a ministry, are published in the Official Gazette once they are signed. The Prime Ministers can lead the negotiations of treaties., international conventions, economic, technical, cultural, and defense cooperation. The ratification and promulgation of these treaties and conventions will be done by the King after approval by the National Assembly.

The Prime Ministers can present for nomination by the King by way of a Royal Decree (Reach-Kret) the following high ranking civilian and military officials: members of the Royal Government; Governor and Deputy Governor of the National Bank of Cambodia, Under Secretaries of State; Advisors to the Royal Government and to the Prime Ministers; Secretary Generals of the Royal Government; Secretary Generals and Director Generals of ministries, Delegates of the Royal Government; Governors of provinces and municipalities;
Ambassadors; Extraordinary and Plenipotentiary Envoys; Military Chief of Staff, and Generals. They can appoint with a Sub-decree (Anu-Kret) other high ranking civilian, military and foreign service officials, Deputy Governors of provinces and municipalities, Chiefs of District (Srok) and urban divisions (Khan).

ORGANIZATION OF THE ADMINISTRATION

Two articles only announce the division of the national territory into provinces and municipalities. The provinces (Khet) are subdivided into districts (Srok)l and districts into communes (Khum). The municipalities are subdivided into sections (Khan), and sections into quarters (Sangkat). Administratively,. the country comprises 20 provinces and two municipalities (Phnom Penh, Sihanoukville). The provincial administration is headed by a governor, assisted by two or three deputy governors, one of whom is in charge of agriculture. Provinces and municipalities are divided into districts (172), which have their own administrative staff and district-level ministry staff.

The average population per district is about 50,000 people. Districts are further sub-divided into 1,400 communes,, with a total 6f about 11,700 villages (Phum) . While funds were provided by the central Government to pay salaries of public servants in the provincial administration provincial taxes were collected and held in the provincial treasury at the disposal of the governor. The resulting misallocation of resources and loss of technical control by the central ministries have been a concern of the new Government. In a recent major political move, governors have been replaced in a number of provinces and in late December 1993, the National Assembly passed a new Financial Structure Law which strips provincial authorities (as well as central ministries and powerful individuals) of the right to collect taxes independently.

RESTRUCTURING THE STATE FOR AN EFFICIENT CAMBODIA

The country is experiencing the commencement of rehabilitation and development after two decades of political, economic, and social disruption. This reconstruction is intended to be based on market economy principles, a liberal, democratic society, and an "Etat de Droit". None of these frameworks can successfully be put in place without a strengthened Government machinery oriented along these frameworks, accompanied by a public service trained and oriented toward these frameworks, and backed by fair revenue generation that can sustain the Government machinery and programme delivery designed to lead to equitable development for all Cambodians.

The development objective of the public administration reform programme is to transform the administrative machinery so as to be capable of establishing a stable climate for investment and private sector development, providing necessary infra-structures, developing human resources, and more generally implementing Government policies.

The specific objectives are to strengthen the State machinery and "rule of law", to increase productivity and service delivery of the public administration,, to improve the legal and organizational structure of the public service, to increase the abilities of the public servants, and to strengthen provincial administration.

The National Program for Public Administration Reform (NPPAR) is an integral part of the National Program to Rehabilitate and Development (NPRDC), and was agreed to in February 1994, by a meeting of the Council of Ministers. The Program was presented to the March, 1994 meeting of the International Committee for the Reconstruction of Cambodia. The Government's NPRDC was launched in 1994. It is considered necessary to reform the public administration institutions and personnel in order to carry out

economic reforms and sectoral projects. The Government has legally constituted the Interministerial Technical
Commission for Administrative Reform to serve as the focal point for policy and implementation of public administration reforms.

Number of Civil Service Employees (as of September 1995)

Agency	**Number of Employees**
Administration	143,855
Central Government	28,646
Health	4,114
Education	2,555
Social Welfare	776
Information	1,377
Industry & Energy	765
Tourism	226
Planning	518
Foreign affairs	637
Civil Service	72
Religions	96
Justice	316
Environment	526
Commerce	51
Agriculture	5,020
Post & Telecommunications	833
Public Works & Transport	2,236
Economy & Finance	3,823
Civil Aviation	386
Cabinet	585
Royal Palace	242
National Assembly	293
Others	2,732
Provincial Government	115,209
Health	12,844
Education	72,060
Social Welfare	1,535
Information	2,468
Other Administration	26,302

The National Program for Public Administration Reform is expected to lead to a variety of improvements:

(a) Government institutions will have substantially strengthened their capability to deliver services to the people, and to under- take continuous public administration reform,

(b) the absorptive capacity of the ministries and agencies will be improved. Output, both tangible and non-tangible, will increase on a cost-effective basis, making public services available in a more efficient manner,

(c) the structures and the human resources of the central and local administrations will be adapted to the needs and means of the State. The public service will be afforded an effective system of administration and financing for human resources. A new legal framework will strengthen the neutrality and the motivation of the public service,

(d) the capacities of public servants from a wide range of ministries and institutions will have been strengthened in administrative management, personnel management, budgeting, and individual and organizational performance management through training in modern techniques,

(e) the provincial administrations will be strengthened and central-local relations will be clarified, and

(f) the institutional capability to define, manage and coordinate the public administration reform, will be established by strengthening the Interministerial Technical Commission for Administrative Reform in the Bureau of the 'Council of Ministers, and leading to the creation of a core of management analysis experts who will contribute to the public administration reform process, as well as to continuous management improvement.

EVIDENCE OF EARLY COMMITMENT OF THE GOVERNMENT TO ITS PUBLIC ADMINISTRATION REFORM PROGRAM

The Council of Ministers has already undertaken a review of the structure of the ,State and its administration, the results of which are embedded in draft laws, now just being reviewed in the National Assembly. These draft laws begin to clarify the structure of the State, and the responsibilities of ministries and other State organizations. Other required laws, decrees and related documents are also being drafted. The Council of Ministers has established the Interministerial Technical Commission for Administrative Reform (ITC/AR), in order to place emphasis on building capacity for management and coordination of reform programs, continuous monitoring of conditions, for policy development, for evaluation of implementation efforts, and for management of these change processes. The ITC/AR is composed of 18 members, representing the Council of Ministers and key ministries. The ITC/AR has an Executive Secretariat composed of eight members, representing the Council of Ministers, the State Secretariat of the Public Service and the Ministry of the Interior.

Other salient points of reform involve, for example, reform of the budgetary process which was taken in December 1993 through passage of the new public finance law and the 1994 Budget. This budgetary reform is a decisive step towards achieving greater control over public expenditures. The Ministry of the Interior has begun a process of renovating provincial administrations, including an effort to strengthen program delivery through clearer delineation of responsibilities, improved communications and training. Many operational ministries have prepared two-yea action plans. Sectoral programs have been endorsed at national symposiums an conferences in areas such as commerce health and education.

REFORM OF THE ADMINISTRATION

The National Program to Reform the Administration (NPRA) outlines the objectives and operational modalities of the initiatives to be carried out over the long term, It is the result of work undertaken since the election, and undertaken in consultation with various specialized international institutions and other organizations. The NPRA was endorsed at an interministerial work- shop in February 1995.

The NPRA consists of 5 operational fields which were developed within the NPRD itself. The Interministerial Technical Committee to Reform the Administration (ITC/RA), together with its Executive Committee and Permanent Secretariat are the architects of the interministerial consensus on the implementation strategy. The urgent, immediate operational priorities are to complete the structure of the management of the reform program itself, which includes facilities to mobilize and coordinate external assistance; to clarify roles and responsibilities; and to inform and seek the support of the population. In order to ensure the long-lasting effects of reform, it is also essential to satisfy two conditions

(i) A firm long-term commitment from contributing countries and international organizations, because a reform of the breadth envisaged will take many years and will be costly- UNDP estimates that the essential elements of reform will cost around US$8 million in technical assistance for the first five years of the program. This is excluding the cost of training and reintegration which adds up to tens of mil- lions of US dollars. For the moment, only US$4 million have been promised and are about to be committed. However, the World Bank has extended a line of credit of US$17 million of which a small part could be used to finance initiatives relating to the remodeling of the civil service.

(ii) The existence of efficient, motivated State officials because reform can be successful only if officials are motivated, take part and sustain the anticipated reform, and if they have the necessary ability and equipment. Adequate, incentives and remuneration are therefore preoccupation's of prime importance.

The NPRA has identified the approach and nature of the required actions in each of five sections:

RESTRUCTURING THE STATE APPARATUS

The objective of this component is essentially to organize governmental work efficiently thus contributing to the strengthening of the effectiveness of the Administration. It. principally involves the strengthening of the state-run superstructure to manage and coordinate governmental action, to clarify ministerial attributions., and to restructure the services necessary for administrative effectiveness and propriety. The structural laws and regulations - those of attribution and operation of ministries and agencies - are on the road to completion. Already, the law on the organization and function of the office of the Council of Ministers has been adopted. Others, such as the law on the creation of the ministries and secretariats of state and their organization and functions, are recently submitted to the National Assembly for approval. The next stage will therefore focus on strengthening the Council of Ministers' services, the formalization of procedures and instruments of decision, and of coordination and follow- UP., and the clarification of mandates in order to delineate roles and responsibilities.

STRENGTHENING OPERATIONAL MINISTERS

The objective here is to improve operational ministries' performances and the quality of services offered. The Royal Government is implementing a targeted program to strengthen management capability and to improve administrative techniques and procedures. The Government, while it is mapping out a national strategy, is outlining programs adapted to particular circumstances, needs and abilities of targetted ministries (Health, Education, Agriculture and Social Welfare). The experience acquired will be applied to the remaining ministries in accordance with their needs. A vast program for strengthening the management and administration of health services across the Kingdom has just been launched; a similar exercise in education is starting; and a unit in public management counseling will be established without further delay to help the ministries carry out these reforms.

REFORM OF THE CIVIL SERVICE

This component of the NPRA is made up of three parts with the objective of transforming the public service into a unified,, transparent., neutral and efficient service: namely, reshaping the civil service; reforming the framework for current management; and reforming regulations. Much has happened in the last year, in particular: the introduction of the Common Statute for the Civil Servants which establishes both the State's rights and obligations as an employer, and those of its employees; stops the automatic hiring of students; and undertakes to reduce manpower by 20 per cent by 1997. There was also a first headcount of staff in February 1995. The next priorities cover a large area: undertaking a qualitative and quantitative census of civil servants; feasibility studies on reintegration measures; and reforming personnel management It practices and processes, including all relevant basic statutes. The Royal Government also intends to develop a policy regarding State officials' remuneration which is compatible with the sustainability of the reform, and thus that of the NPRD itself.

DEVELOPMENT OF HUMAN RESOURCES

The plan is to create a permanent program for improvement and training with a view to strengthening the capability of officials to meet operational priorities. In particular, the Royal Government intends to create a framework for managing such a program and to implement short-term training to meet the most urgent needs. This program aims to increase competence quickly and, therefore, the absorptive capacity of the Administration. Several seminars and information sessions have been held. Intensive training is underway for officials from the Ministry of Economy and Finance and other specialized services, such as disaster management.

The Royal School-for Administration has undertaken an accelerated program to address the most pressing needs. The Royal Government intends to accelerate its action and extend it to a wider spread of priority needs. Seminars, workshops and apprenticeships or tutoring in the workplace would be preferred over more traditional methods. In the short term, there- fore, the object is to create a center specialized in the development of human resources; and to formulate and implement a short-term training program in the design and management of projects, in finance and in other administrative techniques, for instance.

STRENGTHENING PROVINCIAL ADMINISTRATION

The object of this component is to reinforce the capacity of territorial administration by defining the framework for decentralizing the administration, developing the capacity of the Ministry of Interior to exercise a territorial administrative function, and progressively improving the organization and capacity of provincial administrations. The Ministry of Interior has already undertaken a vast work program extending from a definition of administrative parameters to an exhaustive inventory of State assets. The Ministry has also organized important information and familiarization sessions for provincial officials.

In the course of the next 18 months, attention will be drawn particularly towards the strengthening of interministerial ties in the provinces; the improvement of communication between the capital and the provinces; the dissemination of information on laws, regulations, and procedures; and the training of provincial officials. Diagnostic studies will be completed on the required structure, procedures and practices for the decentralization of the administration.

REFORM OF THE JUDICIAL APPARATUS

The restoration of l'Etat de Droit - the rule of law - is an ambitious goal, and it presupposes that different powers and instruments of administration can act only within the limitation authorized by law. It requires some kind of jurisdictional empowerment. In order to institute the rule of law, it is necessary that both the effectiveness of laws and the legality of acts be the object of control and eventually sanctioned by institutional units such as tribunals.

Complementing the legal framework necessary, the Royal Government is seeking to implement mechanisms for the application of adequate legal control. The Royal Government wishes that judicial power be endowed with the means and the people to apply the decisions of the tribunals. Strictly speaking, it is therefore necessary, and in parallel with legislative work, to envisage the restructuring of the judicial system first in quantitative terms which will then enable an improvement to be made in the quality of the judiciary. Magistrates should have the means to sit on the bench, respect privacy in deliberating verdicts, and know how to draw up and pass judgment.

THE ROYAL GOVERNMENT ENVISAGES THREE MAJOR PRIORITIES:

(i) the training of magistrates and clerks;

(ii) the provision of office equipment for the tribunals; and

(iii) the rehabilitation of tribunals.

REFORM OF THE SECURITY APPARATUS

This reform is the most complex and politically sensitive. At the same time, it is also essential and fundamental to the success of NPRD. The Royal Government has already embarked on this work via two main thrusts:

1. POLICE AND PUBLIC SECURITY

The Ministry of Interior has embarked on a series of initiatives for reforming the administration of the police force and for rearranging the network of detention centers. During the course of last year, efforts were principally focused on training and acquiring basic skills.

2. DEMOBILIZATION OF THE ARMED FORCES

The Royal Government has pledged to reduce the number of military staff from 130,000 to 90,000 over three years. A study mission should reveal the main routes of action. Very rapidly, feasibility studies should be completed to determine the modalities and financing of demobilization. Mechanisms for demobilization and reintegration into civilian occupations should be compatible with those for remodeling the civil service. In both cases, technical and financial assistance is indispensable to the success of the operation. For its part, the Royal Government has decided to appoint civilian authorities to undertake the process of demobilization. most probably the Ministry of Social Welfare, Labor and Veteran's Affairs.

U.S.-CAMBODIAN RELATIONS

The United States recognized Cambodia on February 7, 1950, and between 1955 and 1963 provided $409.6 million in economic grant aid and $83.7 million in military assistance. This aid was used primarily to repair damage caused by the first Indochina war, to support internal security forces, and for the construction of an all-weather road to the seaport of Sihanoukville, which gave Cambodia its first direct access to the sea and access to the southwestern hinterlands.

Relations deteriorated in the early 1960s. Diplomatic relations were broken by Cambodia in May 1965 but were reestablished on July 2, 1969. US relations continued after the establishment of the Khmer Republic until the US mission was evacuated on April 12, 1975. During the 1970-75 war, the United States provided $1.18 billion in military assistance and $503 million in economic assistance.

The United States condemned the brutal character of the Khmer Rouge regime between 1975 and 1979. At the same time, the United States opposed the military occupation of Cambodia by Vietnam and supported ASEAN's efforts to achieve a comprehensive political settlement of the problem. This was accomplished on October 23, 1991, when the Paris Conference reconvened to sign a comprehensive settlement. The United States opened a Mission in Phnom Penh on November 11, 1991, headed by Mr. Charles H. Twining, Jr., designated U.S. Special Representative to the SNC. On January 3, 1992, the U.S. embargo was lifted, normalizing economic relations with Cambodia. The U.S. also ended blanket opposition to lending to Cambodia by international financial institutions. When the freely-elected Royal Cambodian

Government was formed on September 24, 1993, the United States and the Kingdom of Cambodia immediately established full diplomatic relations. The United States continues to support efforts in Cambodia to build democratic institutions, promote human rights, foster economic development, eliminate corruption, improve security, achieve the fullest possible accounting for POW/MIAs, and to bring members of the Khmer Rouge to justice for their crimes.

DEMOCRACY AND HUMAN RIGHTS

A new coalition Government was formed on November 30 between the Cambodian People's Party (CPP) and the National United Front for a Neutral, Peaceful, Cooperative, and Independent Cambodia (FUNCINPEC). CPP leader Hun Sen is Prime Minister and Prince Norodom Ranariddh of FUNCINPEC is President of the National Assembly. A 1993 coalition government had collapsed when forces loyal to Hun Sen ousted then-First Prime Minister Prince Ranariddh from power in July 1997. In July, in the first national elections since 1993, the CPP won a plurality of votes.

The electoral campaign and its aftermath were marked by protests, voter intimidation, and partisan violence, some of it government-directed. Despite the incidents of political violence, intimidation, and election irregularities, the formation of the new Government reflected the will of the electorate. King Norodom Sihanouk remains the constitutional monarch and Head of State. Most power lies within the executive branch, and the National Assembly does not offer a significant check to executive power. The judiciary is not independent and suffers from corruption.

The seriously weakened Khmer Rouge continued to wage a low-level guerrilla insurgency against the Government. From July 1997 until November, Khmer Rouge troops cooperated with resistance forces loyal to FUNCINPEC against government troops. Former Khmer Rouge leader Pol Pot died in April. At year's end, following mass defections and the surrender of Khieu Samphan and Nuon Chea, the only remaining Khmer Rouge leader at large was General Ta Mok.

The National Police, an agency of the Ministry of Interior, have primary responsibility for internal security, but the Royal Cambodian Armed Forces (RCAF), including the military police, also have domestic security responsibilities. Government efforts to improve police and RCAF performance were hampered by political factionalism within the forces and by budgetary limitations. Members of the security forces committed numerous human rights abuses.

Cambodia has a market economy in which approximately 80 percent of the population of 11 million engage in subsistence farming, with rice as the principal crop. Annual per capita Gross Domestic Product is approximately $300. Foreign aid is an important component of national income. Economic growth stalled following the July 1997 political violence, with decreases in business, investment, and tourist activity; the economic slump continued through the year.

There were numerous, serious problems in the Government's human rights record. Military and civilian police were responsible for at least five extrajudicial killings. Members of the security forces regularly tortured, beat, and otherwise abused persons in custody. There were credible reports that members of the security forces tortured, beat, or killed some opposition party supporters before and after the elections in July and during demonstrations in August and September.

Police were responsible for at least two deaths during the postelection demonstrations. In the days after the demonstrations, 24 unidentified bodies were discovered; most showed evidence of torture or violent death. The Government rarely prosecuted members of the security forces for such abuses. Prison conditions are harsh. Arbitrary arrest and detention, prolonged detention, and infringement on citizens' privacy rights were problems, particularly during the September demonstrations. Immunity for those who commit human rights abuses is a continuing problem.

The Government lacked the political will and the financial resources to act effectively against persons, particularly members of the military services who were suspected of being responsible for human rights abuses. Democratic institutions, especially the judiciary, remain weak. The judiciary is subject to influence by the executive branch and is marred by inefficiency, a lack of training, a shortage of resources, and corruption related to low wages. Politically related crimes rarely were prosecuted. Citizens effectively were denied the right to a fair trial.

The Government sometimes limits press freedom and fear of government-directed violence against the press created a climate that encouraged self-censorship by some journalists. However, the number of newspapers critical of the Government remained high, with frequent vehement criticism of the CPP. The Government permitted some freedom of assembly during the election period, but at times restricted this right. The Government allowed large demonstrations to protest against claimed election irregularities in August and September. However, police forcibly dispersed a public protest critical of Hun Sen that had been organized by the FUNCINPEC and Sam Rainsy parties following the demonstrations. Over 2 dozen opposition figures left the country temporarily after the inauguration of the National Assembly in September.

The Government at times restricted freedom of association and movement. Domestic violence against women and abuse of children are common. Trafficking in women and children for forced prostitution is a problem. The ethnic Vietnamese minority faced widespread social discrimination and some acts of violence perpetrated by the Khmer Rouge and persons loyal to the FUNCINPEC and Sam Rainsy parties; discrimination against the disabled persists. The Government sometimes does not enforce existing legal provisions against antiunion discrimination adequately. Forced labor, including forced labor by children, remains a problem. Child labor persists. Mob violence against ethnic Vietnamese resulted in a number of deaths.

Khmer Rouge forces committed a number of abuses, including killings, and committed violence against the ethnic Vietnamese minority.

RESPECT FOR HUMAN RIGHTS

RESPECT FOR THE INTEGRITY OF THE PERSON, INCLUDING

A. POLITICAL AND OTHER EXTRAJUDICIAL KILLING

There were numerous political and extrajudicial killings. The United Nations Center for Human Rights (UNCHR) documented 49 reported killings carried out in connection with the electoral process. Of these, the UNCHR found that three likely were committed by police or local government authorities and 13 others by remnant Khmer Rouge soldiers. UNCHR investigation of most of the remaining reported cases disclosed either no political motive or mixed political and personal motives. The Government has made no arrests in connection with these crimes.

On June 19, the body of Em Iem, a Sam Rainsy Party district official, was exhumed in Kompong Cham province. He had been arrested by the village chief, having left his home 9 days earlier to travel to the district headquarters of his party. Witnesses reported that police handcuffed and blindfolded Em Iem and took him in the direction of a nearby rubber plantation where his body later was found. His death followed several documented threats against him and other Sam Rainsy party members by local Kompong Cham government officials for anti-CPP political activities.

On June 24, Som (Thong) Soi, a Reastr Niyum party representative, was shot and killed by a concealed gunman while returning from work in Kompong Chhnang province. He earlier had left his position as a CPP group leader recently to join the Reastr Niyum Party and had expressed fear for his life in the days prior to his killing, naming two local officials whom he believed would be responsible if he were killed. Although he had known personal conflicts with other villagers, the balance of evidence suggested a political motive for his death.

On June 27, the badly mutilated body of FUNCINPEC commune electoral observer Thong Sophal was found in Kandal province after he had been missing for 10 days. According to fellow villagers and relatives, he had no known problems with neighbors or others and was a respected member of his community. Party colleagues confirmed that he had been a FUNCINPEC supporter for several years, but his wife and son had participated in a CPP gift distribution in April, when she registered him with the CPP. According to the UNCHR, the evidence collected about his FUNCINPEC political activities immediately prior to his disappearance, the attitude of the national police and local authorities, and the circumstances of his disappearance suggested a political motive for his killing.

In addition to killings during the election period, there were credible reports of political and extrajudicial killings during the period of opposition protests in August and their subsequent suppression by government security forces in September. According to the UNCHR, at least 34 persons were killed in August and September, including 2 deaths prior to the demonstrations, 2 deaths that occurred when security forces intervened to halt the demonstrations, and 2 other unrelated deaths. There were four killings of Vietnamese residents targeted specifically because of their ethnicity (see Section 5). No direct link was established by the UNCHR between the remaining 24 deaths and involvement in the demonstrations or other political activities; however, investigations showed that most of these unidentified bodies bore signs of torture or violent death.

On September 7, Chem Pich was killed by gunfire in front of the Cambodiana Hotel where he had gone to participate in a demonstration. He reportedly also was beaten by a person using a rifle butt. He died on the way to a hospital.

On September 11, Chun Samnang was shot and killed in Phnom Penh, apparently by security personnel during a political demonstration.

On September 30, Vorn Meak was killed by police outside his village in Kompong Cham province following his arrest earlier in the day. The arresting officer accused him of being a FUNCINPEC party member and of having been involved in an armed robbery. His hands were tied behind his back and he was taken to a police post before being taken into a jungle area where he was killed.

In December two senior Khmer Rouge leaders, Khieu Samphan and Nuon Chea, ceased resistance to the Cambodian Government and moved to Pailin, a town nominally under the control of the national Government. Hun Sen initially stepped back from earlier government commitments to bring senior Khmer Rouge leaders to justice by questioning the need for an international tribunal for the two leaders. After public criticism, Hun Sen and other public officials indicated their willingness to cooperate with the international community in bringing the Khmer Rouge to justice.

From July through September, at least four ethnic Vietnamese persons were killed in mob violence. Some were killed during postelection demonstrations; others were killed by mobs that suspected that Vietnamese had engaged in food poisonings. Police investigations uncovered no evidence. No persons were prosecuted or punished (see Section 5).

On August 20, Sieng Sean, a driver for the Kyodo News Agency, was killed outside the Interior Ministry in Phnom Penh by a hand grenade during a protest against alleged election fraud; the protest was led by opposition leader Sam Rainsy inside the Interior Ministry compound. Sieng Sean was standing outside the compound in the street when the perpetrators fired from a passing car and threw a grenade toward the gate of the ministry. The perpetrators escaped.

On September 7, Orn Saphorn was beaten to death by a truck driver or a mob shortly after a hand grenade attack at the city residence of then-Second Prime Minister Hun Sen. Saphorn appeared to be one of two persons involved in a traffic accident close to Hun Sen's residence and was suspected of involvement in the grenade incident. No arrests were made.

On September 24, Sar Chan Rithy was killed in Siem Reap when a propelled grenade aimed at a Hun Sen motorcade detonated in his family's house. The motorcade was traveling to the opening of the National Assembly.

The UNCHR reported that 13 of 49 killings carried out in connection with the election process likely were committed by remnants of the Khmer Rouge.

In April Khmer Rouge soldiers killed 23 persons in Kompong Chhnang Province (see Section 5).

In July the Khmer Rouge reportedly killed 3 persons in Kratie province (see Section 5).

On July 17, a driver named Mon and a militia guard named Ngor were killed when a group transporting election materials was attacked near a village close to the former Khmer Rouge stronghold of Anlong Veng. Available evidence indicates that the attackers were either remnant Khmer Rouge forces or Khmer Rouge defectors from Anlong Veng.

On election day, July 26, 11 persons were killed during an attack by suspected Khmer Rouge soldiers near Anlong Veng. Seven of those killed were civilians; two were RCAF soldiers; and two others were attackers. All evidence indicated that the incident was aimed at disrupting the election process.

B. Disappearance

There were at least 53 credible reports of politically motivated disappearances during and following the August and September demonstrations, including 4 Buddhist monks. The U.N. High Commissioner for Refugees (UNHCR) reported the presumed arrests of 6 persons whose whereabouts could not be determined; 47 other persons not known to be detained also remain unaccounted for. As of year's end, the UNHCR's efforts to establish the whereabouts of all 53 persons were continuing.

C. Torture and Other Cruel, Inhuman, or Degrading Treatment or Punishment

The Constitution prohibits torture and physical abuse of prisoners; however, torture, beatings, and other forms of physical mistreatment of persons held in police or military custody continued to be a serious problem. The problem is compounded further by government impunity, whereby perpetrators of torture frequently are protected from prosecution or disciplinary action by government authorities, despite some recent government efforts to address problems of accountability.

There were credible reports that military and police officials used torture and severely beat criminal detainees, particularly during interrogation. According to the UNCHR, municipal police in the Serious Crimes Department in Phnom Penh beat or tortured persons routinely, and nearly half the 60 detainees interviewed in Koh Kong province complained of torture in police custody. One human rights nongovernmental organization (NGO) received credible reports of 50 incidents of torture or beatings in custody through November.

One local NGO documented five cases of beatings in Battambang province in February. In each case, militia or police officials hit the persons in custody on the back and head with a stick or a rifle butt until the victims bled or lost consciousness.

In a case documented in May by the UNCHR, three young boys held in the youth rehabilitation center of Phnom Penh were whipped with an electric cable on several parts of their bodies by a police officer and another official while in detention. The beatings occurred in the presence of a group of child prisoners sharing their open cell; a subsequent medical examination confirmed the beatings.

In another case documented by a local NGO in November, a female prisoner in Phnom Penh was beaten severely in an unsuccessful effort to obtain a confession to a robbery. Prison police officials repeatedly kicked her on the chest and hips, beat her with an electric baton on her neck, and whipped her with an electric wire before she lost consciousness. While in detention, she refused to reveal the names of the officers due to continued fears for her safety.

Vorn Meak was killed by Kompong Chhnang police following his arrest on September 30 (see Section 1.a.).

Prison conditions are harsh and deteriorated during the year. Government efforts to improve prison conditions were hampered by lack of funds. Human rights organizations cited a number of serious problems, including overcrowding, food and water shortages, malnutrition, and poor security. Use of shackles and the practice of holding prisoners in small, dark, cells continued in some prisons. Government ration allowances for purchasing prisoners' food are inadequate, exacerbating their malnutrition.

The Government continued to allow human rights groups to visit prisons and to provide human rights training to prison guards.

D. Arbitrary Arrest, Detention, or Exile

The Constitution prohibits arbitrary arrest and detention; however, security forces continued to arrest and detain citizens arbitrarily. A penal code drafted by the UN Transitional Authority for Cambodia (UNTAC) in 1992 and approved by the Interim Supreme National Council remains in effect, as does the 1993 criminal procedure law enacted during the State of Cambodia period. The criminal procedure law in principle provides for adequate protection for criminal suspects; however, in practice the Government frequently ignored these provisions. One human rights NGO reported 32 complaints of unlawful detention and arrest by police, military, or local government authorities through October.

Although lengthy detention without charge is illegal, suspects often are held by authorities for long periods before being charged or released. Accused persons legally are entitled to a lawyer, although in practice they often have no access to legal representation. Prisoners routinely are held for several days before gaining access to a lawyer or family members. Although there is a bail system, many prisoners, particularly those without legal representation, often have no opportunity to seek release on bail. The recent introduction into the legal system of newly trained lawyers, who frequently received supplemental training by NGO's, resulted in significant improvements for those defendants who were provided with counsel, including a reduction in the pretrial detention period and improved access to bail.

The Government does not use forced exile; however, several newly elected parliamentarians fled the country in a state of self-imposed exile following their inauguration on September 24. These politicians included Prince Norodom Ranariddh (FUNCINPEC), Sam Rainsy, and over two dozen other FUNCINPEC and SRP Parliamentarians. While many of the FUNCINPEC officials returned without incident shortly thereafter, Prince Ranariddh, Sam Rainsy, and most of the SRP parliamentarians returned in November only after receiving personal assurances of security from King Sihanouk and Prime Minister-designate Hun Sen.

Prince Chakrapong remained in exile at year's end.

E. DENIAL OF FAIR PUBLIC TRIAL

The Constitution provides for an independent judiciary; however, the Government does not respect this provision in practice. The courts are subject to influence by the executive, and there is widespread corruption among judges, virtually none of whom receives a living wage.

The court system consists of lower courts, an appeals court, and a Supreme Court. The Constitution also mandates a Constitutional Council, which is empowered to review the constitutionality of laws, and a Supreme Council of Magistrates, which appoints and disciplines judges. The composition of both of these bodies is viewed widely as favorable to the CPP. There is a separate military court system.

The 1994 law on civil servants requires the courts to seek Ministry of Justice permission to prosecute a member of the civil service, which includes the police. The Ministry of Justice is required, in turn, to forward requests for prosecution to the relevant ministry. Although the Minister of Justice and other senior government officials sought to reform the law to make it easier for the courts to prosecute civil servants, there was no legislative effort in the National Assembly to do so. The military forces are not covered by this law.

Human rights groups indicate that, in practice ministries sometimes decline to respond to the courts, or refuse their requests for prosecution. Delays in responding to the courts' requests sometimes allow those accused of crimes to flee or otherwise escape prosecution, effectively leading to impunity for most government officials who commit crimes.

Trials are public. Defendants have the right to be present and to consult with an attorney, to confront and question witnesses against them, and to present witnesses and evidence on their own behalf. However, trials are typically perfunctory, and extensive cross-examination usually does not take place. The serious shortage of attorneys-especially outside of Phnom Penh--remains a significant impediment to broader implementation of the right to counsel in practice.

Defendants legally also are entitled to the presumption of innocence and the right of appeal. However, because of extensive corruption, defendants often are expected to bribe the judge for a favorable verdict and therefore effectively are denied the presumption of innocence.

A serious lack of resources and poor training contribute to inefficiency in the judicial branch, and in practice the Government does not ensure due process. For example, judges often lack copies of the laws on which they are expected to rule. As a result of these weaknesses, citizens often were denied the effective right to a fair trial.

Ongoing cooperation between the Government, foreign donors, and NGO's to improve the legal system remains hampered by the suspension of some assistance programs after the July 1997 violence.

In September Sam Rainsy Party (SRP) official Srun Vong Vannak, who had been convicted of the 1996 murder of Mrs. Hun Sen's brother-in-law, was released from prison after receiving a pardon from King Sihanouk. The King granted the pardon after receiving approval of the country's political leadership.

The courts often pressure victims of crimes to accept small cash settlements from the accused. When a case does make its way to court, the verdict often is determined by a judge before the case is heard, sometimes on the basis of a bribe paid by the accuser or the defendant. Sworn, written statements from witnesses and the accused usually are the extent of evidence presented in trials. Such statements by the accused often result from beatings or threats by investigating officials, and illiterate defendants often are not informed of the content of written confessions that they are forced to sign. In cases involving military personnel, military officers often exert pressure on judges to have the defendant released.

The military court system suffers from deficiencies similar to those of the civilian court system.

There were no reports of political prisoners.

Arbitrary Interference with Privacy, Family, Home or Correspondence

The Constitution protects the privacy of residence and correspondence and includes a provision against illegal search; however, there were reports that the Government monitored private electronic communications, including during police investigations of suspected criminal activity.

The police routinely conducted warrantless searches and seizures. In October in response to a surge in crime in Phnom Penh, the Government announced that it would conduct searches of private residences for illegal weapons. The searches were to be conducted without any notice, consent, or judicial authorization. After protest by legal NGO's, the Government took no action to implement the program.

Citizens largely were free to live where they wished. There were continued reports of land disputes between residents, local authorities, and business persons. Since the forced collectivization during Khmer Rouge rule before 1980 and the return of thousands of refugees, land ownership is often unclear.

The Government does not coerce or forbid membership in political organizations systematically. However, there were credible reports that government officials used intimidation and threats to force FUNCINPEC and Sam Rainsy Party members to sign oaths of loyalty to the CPP and vote for the CPP in the July elections. Moreover, FUNCINPEC and Sam Rainsy Party supporters reported several credible instances of intimidation in the days following the election, when dozens of provincial party workers from those parties fled to Phnom Penh amid a climate of fear (see Section 3).

There were reports that military officers forcibly conscripted adults and children; the Government denied that it engages in this practice (see Section 6.c.).

Membership in the Khmer Rouge, which has conducted an armed insurgency against the Government, is illegal.

G. USE OF EXCESSIVE FORCE AND VIOLATIONS OF HUMANITARIAN LAW

Sporadic fighting between government and Khmer Rouge forces continued throughout much of the year; however, negotiations in November between the Government and Khmer Rouge commanders secured the defection of most of the remaining Khmer Rouge soldiers and civilians and contributed to a cessation of armed conflict by year's end. Civilians were killed or wounded by indiscriminate shelling and by land mines deployed by all sides.

RESPECT FOR CIVIL LIBERTIES

A. FREEDOM OF SPEECH AND PRESS

The Constitution provides for freedom of expression, press, and publication; however, the Government sometimes limits press freedom in practice. Some journalists practice self-censorship. The Constitution implicitly limits free speech by requiring that speech not adversely affect public security. The Constitution also declares that the King is "inviolable." A Press Law in effect since 1995 provides journalists with a number of rights, including a prohibition on prepublication censorship and protection from imprisonment for expressing opinion. However, the Press Law also includes a vaguely worded prohibition on publishing articles that affect national security and political stability. The Government engaged in harassment and intimidation of some journalists during the election campaign, and fear of government-directed violence against the press created a climate that led some journalists to practice self-censorship.

Although limited in circulation, newspapers are a primary source of news and expression of political opinion. All major political parties have reasonable and regular access to the printed media. The press remained highly partisan, with many newspapers receiving financial support from political parties. There are approximately 40 Khmer language newspapers in Phnom Penh, of which approximately 28 are major newspapers published regularly. Of these, 14 are considered to be pro-CPP journals, 13 are considered to support either the FUNCINPEC or Sam Rainsy Parties, and 1 is considered to be antimonarchy. In addition there is one French language daily, one English language daily, and two other English language newspapers published regularly. Many of the Khmer language newspapers frequently publish reports translated from the English language newspapers.

Most newspapers criticize the Government frequently, and Prime Minister Hun Sen frequently came under strong attack by opposition newspapers both before and after the election. There were some instances of government intimidation or retribution against newspapers for their critical reporting.

On August 20, a driver for the Kyodo News Agency was killed by unknown assailants outside the Interior Ministry (see Section 1.a.).

In September the Ministry of Information suspended Moneaksekar Khmer (Khmer Conscience), a pro-Sam Rainsy Party newspaper for 30 days for its publication of an article critical of King Sihanouk.

In October the Government threatened two English language newspapers, the Cambodia Daily and the Phnom Penh Post, and one news agency, Deutsche Press-Agentur, with closure in reaction to alleged misreporting of the September 24 rocket attack on then-Second Prime Minister Hun Sen's motorcade in Siem Reap province. The Government also threatened to revoke the visas of the Western journalists allegedly responsible for the reporting. The Government rescinded the threats following diplomatic intervention.

Unlike previous years, no journalist was killed for publishing critical articles. However, there was one report of a violent attack against a journalist. On June 8, Thong Uy Pang, the editor of the pro-CPP Koh Santepheap (Island of Peace) newspaper, was wounded by gunfire from close range by unknown assailants. The shooting came after the newspaper printed a critical article about corruption of police and military authorities. The assailants escaped.

The Government, the military forces, and political parties continued to dominate the broadcast media. This domination created an imbalance in equitable access to the broadcast media during the election, which were permitted to disseminate political statements during a 1-month election campaign period. According to a report published by the UNCHR, procedures for licensing and allocation of radio and television frequencies from the media were not impartial, and decisions were made on a party political basis. In addition news about opposition politicians and their views were virtually excluded from the broadcast media during the election process.

Unlike prior years, there were no reports that authorities inhibited discussion of some political issues at the University of Phnom Penh.

The Khmer Rouge did not allow freedom of speech or press in zones that they controlled during the year.

B. FREEDOM OF PEACEFUL ASSEMBLY AND ASSOCIATION

The Constitution provides for freedom of peaceful assembly; however, the Government at times restricted this right in practice.

In April pro- and antigovernment demonstrations following Prince Ranariddh's return from abroad led to some violence among demonstrators; police injured several persons when they attempted to break up the demonstrations. In June the Phnom Penh municipal government cited security concerns in issuing a ban on public demonstrations in the period prior to the election. The ban was ignored widely and never implemented; the Government did not interfere with several demonstrations that took place. Two weeks later, the government reversed its position and only requested that political parties inform officials of planned rallies.
Several demonstrations and marches thereafter took place without incident or security incidents.

In August large antigovernment demonstrations and marches to protest alleged election irregularities were organized by opposition leaders Prince Ranariddh and Sam Rainsy. Frequent marches by thousands of persons proceeded through Phnom Penh without incident. During this period, a sit-in began near the National Assembly, which consisted of several hundred persons who remained at the site continuously. In September progovernment demonstrations contributed to fears of major violence. In September government security forces intervened to break up the demonstrations and the sit-in; at least two persons were killed during the police intervention, and the bodies of at least 24 others bearing signs of violent death were found thereafter (see Section l.a.).

In December there was a demonstration by more than 300 persons against a toxic waste dump in Sihanoukville. Demonstrators attacked the local port office, the home of the deputy governor, and a luxury hotel in protest against allegedly corrupt officials who allowed the waste to be brought in from Taiwan. One person died in a hospital after being hit on the head by furniture thrown from the ransacked home. Police fired their weapons into the air to disburse the demonstrators after appeals over loudspeakers had little effect. Two employees of LICADHO, a human rights NGO, were arrested and charged with robbery and destruction of property after protests against the Sihanoukville toxic waste dump turned violent.

LICADHO defended its employees, stating that they had no part in the riot or the protests, although the protesters had spoken with them a few days before the violence began.

Numerous groups assembled peacefully, including workers, opposition activists, peace marchers, and local groups protesting land disputes, all without incident.

The Constitution provides for freedom of association; however, the Government at times restricted this rightby interfering with political party offices during the period prior to the election (see Section 3). Government officials reportedly also forced FUNCINPEC and Sam Rainsy Party supporters to sign oaths of loyalty to the CPP prior to the elections (see Section 1.f.).

Membership in the Khmer Rouge is illegal.

C. FREEDOM OF RELIGION

The Constitution provides for freedom of religion and prohibits discrimination based on religion. The government respects this right in practice. Buddhism is the state religion and over 95 percent of the population is Buddhist. Most of the remainder is made up of ethnic Cham Muslims, who generally are well integrated into society and face no reported persecution.

The Khmer Rouge traditionally discouraged religion, and continue to do so.

D. FREEDOM OF MOVEMENT WITHIN THE COUNTRY, FOREIGN TRAVEL, AND REPATRIATION

The Government generally does not restrict domestic or international travel; however, in September it imposed a ban on international travel by opposition politicians. The ban was lifted following the inauguration of the new National Assembly on September 24, after which many politicians from the FUNCINPEC and Sam Rainsy Parties left the country without incident. At least one prominent politician, Kem Sokha of the Son Sann Party, was prevented from leaving during this period. The Government claimed that he was subject to lawful arrest as a result of his illegal activities during the demonstrations. Kem Sokha subsequently went into hiding and ignored two official documents summoning him to court for questioning. Following the agreement to form a new coalition Government in November, Kem Sokha appeared in court without incident in response to a third summons. At year's end, it was unclear whether a travel ban was still in effect for him.

Monks can move internally without restriction.

There are no longer illegal security checkpoints; however, the presence of land mines and bandits make travel in some areas perilous.

Following sporadic partisan fighting in the north and northwest, several hundred refugees left the country for temporary refugee camps in Thailand. These refugees joined the approximately 50,000 refugees who had left the country following the political violence of July 1997. There were no reports of refugees being forced by Thai authorities to return to Cambodia involuntarily. By year's end, approximately 9,000 refugees had been repatriated by the U.N. High Commissioner for Refugees (UNHCR) voluntarily, and there were no reports of persecution or discrimination against those who returned. At year's end, approximately 35,000 refugees remained in the camps. In addition to those refugees repatriated by the UNHCR, several thousand more also returned voluntarily. Internally displaced persons also were allowed to resettle in other areas of the country.

The Government allows noncitizens to apply to the UNHCR for refugee status. The Government did not provide first asylum during the year and has not agreed to UNHCR requests to issue refugee travel documents. The new Government has not formulated fully a policy regarding refugees, asylees, or first asylum; its political platform promised cooperation with international organizations to prepare for the repatriation of remaining refugees from Thailand.

There were no reports that the Government forced any persons to return to another country where they feared persecution.

RESPECT FOR POLITICAL RIGHTS: THE RIGHT OF CITIZENS TO CHANGE THEIR GOVERNMENT

The Constitution provides for the right of citizens to change their government, and most citizens exercised this right by participating in the national elections in July. Citizens could not exercise this right in areas controlled by the Khmer Rouge.

The July 26 national elections were the first since the 1993 U.N.-sponsored elections that resulted in a coalition government dominated by the CPP and FUNCINPEC until July 1997. This coalition collapsed after forces loyal to Hun Sen ousted Ranariddh from power in July 1997. Ranariddh fled the country along with other leading politicians from FUNCINPEC and other political parties. With their return in March, the campaign leading to the July elections belatedly began, and elections ultimately were held in July. More than 93 percent of the eligible electorate voted. The CPP received 41.4 percent of the vote; FUNCINPEC 31.7 percent; the Sam Rainsy Party 14.3 percent. The 36 other parties together received 12.6 percent. Following more than 3 months of political deadlock, during which government legal institutions dismissed claims of election irregularities and parties conducted large public demonstrations, a new coalition government was formed.

Until March the Government denied opposition parties their political rights and precluded them from opening offices or putting up party signs. In March the Government registered 44 parties as legal political parties, which gave them the right to operate, put up signs, receive funds, engage in political activities, and otherwise campaign freely. In June the National Election Commission registered 39 parties for the election. Although there were no significant problems associated with these procedures in the majority of places, opposition party members were unable to campaign in some remote areas because of threats or fears of violence. There were a number of attacks on party signs, which intimidated campaign workers.

There were credible reports that government officials used intimidation and threats to force FUNCINPEC and Sam Rainsy Party members to sign oaths of loyalty to the CPP and to vote for that party's candidates in the elections (see Section 1.f.).

The UNHCR received 18 reported cases of killings and two cases of attempted killings during the preelection period. Of these, only three were determined to have been clearly politically motivated, and two others were perpetrated by Khmer Rouge forces. Of the 18 cases, at least 5 involved the killing of CPP officials. The UNHCR also received numerous reports of illegal arrests, physical abuse, threats, harassment, and intimidation during the period. Intimidation claims frequently involved threats to party sign boards, but not persons. Many of the suspected perpetrators were members of local security forces or local CPP officials; in many cases, the perpetrators were not identified.

Voter registration generally was considered a success by election monitors, as very large numbers of eligible voters registered. However, some problems were reported that may have limited the rights of persons to vote. They included reports of armed soldiers, police, militia, and local officials in and around registration stations in violation of the election law. There were also reports that illegal registration took place before and after official hours and of expedited registration of large groups of persons transported to registration sites by party
officials, raising questions about their eligibility. Widespread but unconfirmed opposition reports claimed that there was mass registration of ethnic Vietnamese persons who were not Cambodian citizens.

Structural problems with registration included: Confusion over opening and closing dates for registration; the very short period for registration (22 to 23 days); lack of information about the registration process; and confusion about where registration must take place. No arrangements were made to allow the significant number of eligible voters among Cambodian citizens in refugee camps in Thailand to register. In addition no provisions were made for the large number of citizens living abroad to register.

The Government dominated the broadcast media during the election campaign, as news about opposition politicians and their views were virtually excluded from coverage during the election process (see Section 2.a.).

In National Assembly elections, each province elected members through a system of proportional representation. Three of the 39 parties that took part 3 won seats: The CPP won 64 seats; FUNCINPEC won 43 seats; and the Sam Rainsy party won 15 seats. Over 93 percent of the eligible persons cast ballots.
Despite the incidents of political violence and intimidation and the failure of legal institutions to resolve complaints of election irregularities sufficiently, most international observer groups certified the election as acceptable. The formation of the new Government reflected the will of the electorate.

However, the political opposition was harassed after the election. According to Human Rights Watch, there was "a wave of reprisals by officials and security forces" affiliated with the CPP. Local officials, forces loyal to the CPP, and others reportedly coerced members of opposition parties to flee their villages, sometimes firing on them (see Section 1.f.). An atmosphere of fear and political intimidation prompted dozens of opposition politicians to flee the country temporarily after the National Assembly inauguration (see Section 1.d.).

After more than 3 months of political negotiation, the CPP and FUNCINPEC, the two parties that won the largest number of votes and seats in the National Assembly, entered into a coalition government in November that provided for a roughly equal power sharing between the parties, with Hun Sen as Prime Minister and Prince Ranariddh as President of the National Assembly. Of the 9 National Assembly committee chairs, four were allocated to the CPP, four to FUNCINPEC, and one to the SRP. The National Assembly approved this coalition government in November, and the government portfolios were announced in December along with a political platform for the new Government.

The legislature remained weak in comparison with the executive branch. The previous government appointed the provincial governors and their deputies, who generally are divided between the CPP and FUNCINPEC parties; by year's end, new appointments had not yet been made. District and commune officials also were appointed by the previous government; most of these officials are appointees from the previous regimes, the People's Republic of Kampuchea and the State of Cambodia. Communal elections were scheduled for 1999, but the National Assembly has not enacted the communal election law.

Traditional cultural practices inhibit the role of women in government. In its political platform, the Government in November pledged to promote women's development in politics. Women took an active part in the elections, and 5 of the 39 political parties vying for National Assembly seats were headed by a woman.

Representation of women in the National Assembly and Cabinet increased slightly following the election. There are 10 women among the 122 members of the National Assembly and 2 ministers and 4 state secretaries in the Cabinet.

The Government established a new cabinet Ministry of Women's and Veteran's Affairs in December and appointed a woman as minister and to both state secretary positions. The Government also appointed a woman to head the Ministry of Culture and appointed women as state secretaries in the Justice and Social Affairs and Labor Ministries.

There are several members of ethnic and religious minorities in the Cabinet and the National Assembly (see Section 5).

Section 4 Governmental Attitude Regarding International and Nongovernmental Investigation of Alleged Violations of Human Rights

The large domestic and international human rights community that began operating during the UNTAC period remained active and engaged in diverse activities. Numerous human rights organizations and the UNCHR conducted human rights training for election observers, military officers, villagers, the legal community, and other groups. There are approximately 40 NGO's involved in human rights activities, but only a small portion were involved actively in organizing training programs or carrying out investigations of abuses. The Government generally cooperated with human rights workers in performing their investigations, but one local NGO reported limited cooperation from some provincial authorities in conducting inspections of prison conditions.

The Government established the Cambodian Human Rights Committee in June to conduct investigations of individual cases of alleged human rights violations. The committee also is charged with improving the administration of justice and drafting a law establishing an independent permanent national human rights commission. By year's end, the national commission had not been established.

In May the Government and the UNCHR agreed to an extension until March 2000 of its activities in the country. The UNCHR maintains a head office in Phnom Penh and has six provincial offices. The U.N. Special Representative for Human Rights continued to work with government officials at all levels, as well as with representatives of political parties and NGO's.

DISCRIMINATION BASED ON RACE, SEX, RELIGION, DISABILITY, LANGUAGE, OR SOCIAL STATUS

The Constitution prohibits discrimination based on race, color, sex, language, religious beliefs, or political views. Although the Government does not engage in discrimination systematically, it often fails to protect these rights in practice.

WOMEN

International and domestic NGO workers report that violence against women, including rape and domestic violence, is common. Although there were reports of rape and domestic abuse, accurate statistical documentation is not available. Authorities normally decline to become involved in domestic disputes, and the victims frequently are reluctant to complain.

Prostitution and trafficking in women are serious problems. Due in part to budgetary limitations, the Government has not enforced adequately a 1996 law against prostitution and trafficking in women. Despite sporadic government crackdowns on brothel operators in Phnom Penh that resulted in the closure of many brothels and the arrest of over 30 brothel owners, the prostitution trade continues to flourish in the capital. InJune, following an investigation by a local NGO, the owner of one of the largest brothels in Poipet was arrested for killing a young woman who refused to have sex relations with customers.

According to NGO reports, women constitute 52 percent of the population, 60 percent of agricultural workers, 85 percent of the business work force, 70 percent of the industrial work force, and 60 percent of all service sector workers. Women often are concentrated in low-paying jobs in these sectors and largely are excluded from management positions.

The Constitution contains explicit language providing for equal rights for women, equal pay for equal work, and equal status in marriage. In practice women have equal property rights with men, have the same status in bringing divorce proceedings, and have equal access to education and to some jobs. However, culturaltraditions continued to limit the ability of women to reach senior positions in business and other areas. There are a large number of women's NGO's, which concentrated on training poor women and widows and on addressing social problems such as spousal abuse and prostitution.

CHILDREN

The Constitution provides for children's rights, and ensuring the welfare of children is a specific goal of the Government. However, according to the U.N., 20 percent of children under 5 years of age suffer from acute malnutrition. The Government relies on international aid to fund most social welfare programs targeted atchildren, resulting in only a modest flow of funds to ameliorate problems affecting children. Children frequently suffer from the inadequacy of the health care system. Infant mortality is reported at 89.4 per thousand, and 12 percent of children do not live to the age of 5 years. Child mortality from preventable diseases is high.

Children also are affected adversely by an inadequate educational system. Despite an extensive government school construction program, schools are overcrowded and short of equipment. Less than 5 percent of primary school teachers have completed high school. The Government does not deny girls equal access to education, but in practice families with limited resources often give priority to educating boys.

Child abuse is believed to be common, although there are no statistics on the extent of the problem. Poverty and domestic violence often drive children onto the streets; local NGO's estimate that there are more than 10,000 street children in Phnom Penh alone who are easy targets for sexual abuse and exploitation.

Although sexual intercourse with a minor under the age of 15 is illegal, child prostitution and trafficking in children are common. There were reliable reports that children were kidnaped in some provinces and forced into the illegal sex trade, both in Cambodia and abroad (see Section 6.c.).

PEOPLE WITH DISABILITIES

The Government does not require that buildings or government services be accessible to the disabled. According to the Government, approximately 1 in 246 citizens is missing at least one limb. This statistic reflects the continuing effects of land mine detonations. Programs administered by various NGO's have brought about substantial improvements in the treatment and rehabilitation of amputees. However, amputeesface considerable societal discrimination, particularly in obtaining skilled employment.

RELIGIOUS MINORITIES

Muslims are the largest religious minority, and experience little or no discrimination in practice. The smallChristian community has not experienced serious or systematic discrimination. Unlike the previous year, there were no reports of local tension between Cambodian Christians and non-Christians. Christian missionary groups have not encountered significant difficulties in performing their work.

NATIONAL/RACIAL/ETHNIC MINORITIES

Citizens of Vietnamese and Chinese ethnicity have long constituted the largest ethnic minorities. Ethnic Chinese citizens are well accepted in society. However, fear and animosity continue among Khmer citizens toward ethnic Vietnamese, who are seen as a threat to the Cambodian nation and culture. The rights of minorities under the 1996 nationality law are not explicit; constitutional protections are extended only to "Khmer people," that is, Cambodians.

There were credible reports that both security personnel and ordinary citizens routinely singled out Vietnamese citizens for discrimination during the election campaign. During the registration period, many were given language tests, then refused registration because of their accent or vocabulary. At the urging of opposition parties, the National Election Commission deleted some ethnic Vietnamese citizens from voterregistration lists on insufficient evidence and without notice. Some leading opposition politicians campaigned on a theme of ethnic hatred and used ethnic slurs to urge expulsion of Vietnamese immigrants.

After the election, some opposition politicians, including Ranariddh and Sam Rainsy, made inflammatorystatements propaganda directed against ethnic Vietnamese citizens and Vietnamese residents. Many Vietnamese received verbal death threats and other harassment from both security personnel and ordinary citizens in the aftermath of the demonstrations in August and September.

Some prominent opposition politicians used racial epithets and anti-Vietnamese slogans during the antigovernment rallies. At least 4 ethnic Vietnamese were killed in ethnic violence following the demonstrations during a wave of popular suspicion that Vietnamese were responsible for a number of alcohol or food poisoning incidents. InSeptember Nguyen Van Minh was beaten to death by a crowd on suspicion that he had poisoned wine at a shop in Phnom Penh, where he had gone to buy a pack of cards. Police found no evidence of poisoning. Alsoin September, an unidentified Vietnamese woman was beaten to death on a street in Phnom Penh by acrowd after an argument over poisoning. A Vietnamese husband and wife, Nguyen Thi Muy and Tong VanHoi, sought to intervene and also were killed by the crowd. No poison was found at the scene.

The Khmer Rouge continued a calculated campaign against ethnic Vietnamese residents. In April Khmer Rouge attackers massacred 23 persons in a predominantly Vietnamese fishing village in Kompong Chhnang province, including 13 ethnic Vietnamese. In another attack blamed on the Khmer Rouge in July, 3 ethnic Vietnamese were killed in Kratie province (see Section 1.a.)

WORKER RIGHTS

The new Government's political platform announced plans to consolidate implementation of the Labor Law and international treaties relating to labor and the rights of unions.

A. THE RIGHT OF ASSOCIATION

The 1997 Labor Law provides workers with the right to form professional organizations of their own choosing without prior authorization, and all workers are free to join the trade union of their choice; however, the Government's enforcement of these rights has been uneven. Membership in trade unions or employeeassociations is not compulsory, and workers are free to withdraw from such organizations. The Government issued decrees and subdecrees clarifying the Labor Law in a number of areas, including the registration of labor unions, the election of worker representatives, the registration of collective bargaining agreements, and the calculation of overtime pay rates. However, despite these legal advances, the Government's enforcement efforts have been hampered by a lack of resources, little knowledge of the law by factory managers, and a lack of qualified labor inspectors.

There were a large number of strikes and labor demonstrations in the first half of the year, virtually none of which were carried out in accordance with the law. The Government allowed all peaceful strikes and demonstrations to take place, although police intervened in violent strikes at several garment factories. In reaction to the wave of strikes, the Government established a Strike and Demonstration Settlement Committee in February chaired by the general director of the national police. Despite concerns that the committee would become a vehicle to suppress peaceful labor demonstrations, it appeared to have little effect.

The Labor Law requires unions and employer organizations to file a charter and lists of officers with the Ministry of Social Affairs, Labor, Vocational Training, and Youth Rehabilitation. The Ministry registered approximately 25 new unions during the year, and a total of 44 unions have been registered since the Labor Law was passed in January 1997. However, most of these unions have few resources and operate at a very low level of activity. Many have close ties with the Government or management and are not independent in practice. Very few unions are able to negotiate with management as equals.

Some observers have charged that the Ministry of Labor has shown clear political bias in its administration of the April 1997 subdecree on union registration. As a result, unions that have close relations with the CPP can obtain registration easily, while the applications of unions linked to the opposition are subject to numerous delays. The Ministry registered the opposition Free Trade Union of the Workers of the Kingdom of Cambodia in December after having held up its application for more than 8 months for technical reasons. Observers also charged that the subdecree is unduly burdensome and requires unions to file an excessive number of documents.

The Ministry has held elections for shop stewards in more than 50 factories. While shop stewards in some factories have begun to represent workers to management, there is evidence that elections in other factories were conducted improperly due to collusion between labor inspectors and management.

Most workers are subsistence rice farmers and have little knowledge of trade unions. Nearly all trade union activity has been concentrated in the rapidly growing garment sector. Although there is an expanding service sector, most urban workers are engaged in low-level commerce, self-employed skilled labor, or unskilled day labor. The Labor Law does not apply to workers in the public sector.

Unions may affiliate freely, but the law does not address explicitly their right to affiliate internationally.

B. THE RIGHT TO ORGANIZE AND BARGAIN COLLECTIVELY

The Labor Law provides for the right to organize and bargain collectively; however, the Government's enforcement of these rights has been uneven.

In the two years since the passage of the Labor Law, there has been confusion over the overlapping roles of labor unions and shop stewards. The Labor Law gives unions the right to negotiate with management over wages and working conditions and allows unions to nominate candidates for shop steward positions.
However, the Labor Law gives the shop stewards the right to represent the union to the company director and to sign collective bargaining agreements.

In practice very little collective bargaining takes place. During the wave of strikes and demonstrations in the first half of the year, workers at some factories asked political figures to negotiate collective agreements on their behalf; many of these agreements are no longer honored. A successful strike in February by a union at a Phnom Penh cigarette factory represented the first known instance in which an officially registered trade union held a strike that generally conformed with Labor Law requirements.

The Labor Law prohibits discrimination against the leaders of registered trade unions and protects them against dismissal. Employers are required to obtain permission from the Ministry of Social Affairs, Labor, Vocational Training, and Youth Rehabilitation before terminating officers of trade unions. However, these provisions are not enforced adequately, and observers have charged that in several instances the Ministry of Labor has allowed the firing of union leaders. In the first decision of its kind, a court in Kandal province ruled in January that a Phnom Penh garment factory had violated the Labor Law when it fired union leader Srey Em in June 1997. The court ordered that Em be reemployed and receive back pay and compensation for damages that she has sustained. However, management at the factory defied the court and refused to rehire Em; both sides later agreed to a severance pay package.

The Government sets wages for civil servants. Wage rates in other sectors largely are based on market conditions and are set by employers.

There are no export processing zones.

C. PROHIBITION OF FORCED OR COMPULSORY LABOR

The Labor Law prohibits forced or compulsory labor, including forced labor by children; however, the Government does not enforce prohibitions against forced or compulsory labor adequately. In 1996 the National Assembly adopted the Law on the Exploitation and Trafficking of Humans. The law establishes a jail sentence of from 15 to 20 years for any person convicted of trafficking in persons under the age of 15.

There were credible reports of mandatory overtime in the garment industry as well as reports of women and girls being forced to work as prostitutes. The most recent survey of this problem, made by a human rights NGO in 1995, indicated that 31 percent of female prostitutes were between the ages of 12 and 17. Half the girls involved were sold into prostitution by their families and forced to work as prostitutes. There we also reports that children were kidnaped and forced to work in the illegal sex trade (see Section 5).

Although the institution of bonded labor does not appear to be widespread, there were credible reports ofbonded labor in the wood-processing, rubber, and brick manufacturing industries, There were also reports that military officers have implemented the forced conscription of both adults and children; the Government denies that it has engaged in this practice.

D. STATUS OF CHILD LABOR PRACTICES AND MINIMUM AGE FOR EMPLOYMENT

The Labor Law establishes 15 years as the minimum age for employment. However, the law permits children between the ages of 12 and 15 to engage in "light work" that is not hazardous to their health and does not affect school attendance. The Ministry of Social Affairs, Labor, Vocational Training, and Youth Rehabilitation has not set up an apparatus to enforce this law and has not published a list of occupations considered acceptable for minors.

In May the Government issued a subdecree that established the labor advisory committee responsible for setting industry minimum wage rates and specifying particular occupations that are hazardous to the health, safety, or morality of adolescents and that cannot employ workers under age 18. The committee is also responsible for consulting with the Ministry of Labor to determine the types of employment and working conditions that constitute "light work" for children between the ages of 12 and 15.

Children under the age of 15 routinely engage in a variety of jobs, including street trading, construction, agriculture, and small-scale manufacturing. According to an ILO study, 9.2 percent of children are"economically active." More than 90 percent of working children live in rural areas. The law prohibits forced labor by children; however, the Government does not enforce the law effectively (see Section 6.c.).

E. ACCEPTABLE CONDITIONS OF WORK

The Labor Law requires that a minimum wages be established for each sector of the economy based on recommendations by the Labor Advisory Committee. To date, a minimum wage has been set only in one sector, the garment industry, where workers must be paid a minimum of $40 (151,000 reil) per month after the conclusion of their training period. Although there have been numerous, credible reports of employers paying less than this minimum wage, enforcement of the provision improved. This wage is not sufficient to provide a worker and family with a decent standard of living.

The Labor Law provides for a standard legal workweek of 48 hours, not to exceed 8 hours per day. The lawstipulates time-and-one-half overtime pay, and double overtime pay if the overtime hours are worked at night or on the employee's day off. The Government does not enforce these standards adequately, and workers frequently complain about being required illegally to work more than 48 hours a week. Another common complaint in the garment industry is that management violates the law by paying the overtime rate only for the salary component of workers' paychecks, leaving piece rates unchanged regardless of the number of hours worked.

The Labor Law states that the workplace should have health and safety standards adequate to ensure workers' well-being. The Government issued several instructions on workplace standards during the year, but enforced these standards inadequately. Work-related injury and health problems are common. Conditions in small-scale factories and cottage industries generally are poor and often do not meet international standards. Penalties are specified in the Labor Law, but there are no provisions to protect workers who complain about unsafe and unhealthy conditions. Workers who remove themselves from unsafe working conditions risk loss of employment.

STUDYING COUNTRY TROUTH THE CONSTITUTION

CHAPTER 1 SOVEREIGNTY

Article 1- Cambodia is a Kingdom with a King who shall rule according to the Constitution and to the principles of liberal democracy and pluralism. The Kingdom of Cambodia shall be an independent, sovereign, peaceful, permanently neutral and non-aligned country

Article 2- The territorial integrity of the Kingdom of Cambodia shall absolutely not be violated within its borders as defined in the 1/100,000 scale map made between the years 1933-1953 and internationally recognized between the years 1963-1969

Article 3- The Kingdom of Cambodia is an indivisible State

Article 4- The motto of the Kingdom of Cambodia is: " Nation, Religion, King ".

Article 5- The official language and script are Khmer.

Article 6- Phnom Penh is the capital of the Kingdom of Cambodia. The national flag, anthem and coat-of arms shall be defined in Annexes 1, II and III.

CHAPTER II THE KING

Article 7- The King of Cambodia shall reign but shall not govern. The King shall be the Head of State for life. The King shall be inviolable.

Article 8- The King of Cambodia shall be a symbol of unity and eternity of the nation. The King shall be the guarantor of the national independence, sovereignty, and territorial integrity of the Kingdom of Cambodia, the protector of rights and freedom for all citizens and the guarantor of international treaties

Article 9- The King shall assume the august role of arbitrator to ensure the faithful execution of public powers.

Article 10- The Cambodian monarchy shall be an appointed regime. The King shall not have the power to appoint a heir to the throne.

Article 11- If the King cannot perform His normal duties as Head of State due to His serious illness as certified by doctors chosen by the President of the Assembly and the Prime Minister, the President of the Assembly shall perform the duties of Head of State as "Regent".

Article 12- In case of the death of the King, the president of the Assembly shall take over the responsibility as Acting head of State in the capacity of Regent of the Kingdom of Cambodia.

Article 13- Within a period of not more than seven days, the new King of the Kingdom of Cambodia shall be chosen by the Royal Council of the Throne. The Royal Council of The Throne shall consist of: The president of the National Assembly The Prime Minister Samdech the Chiefs of the orders of Mohanikay and Thammayut. The First and Second Vice- President of the Assembly. The organization and functioning of the council Throne shall be determined by law.

Article 14- The King of Cambodia shall be a member of t he Royal family, of at least 30 years, descending from the blood line of King Ang Duong, King Norodom or King Sisowath. Upon enthronement, the King shall take the oath of allegiance as stipulated in Annex IV.

Article 15- The wife of the reigning King shall have the royal title of QUEEN of Cambodia

Article 16- The Queen of the Kingdom of Cambodia shall not have the right to engage in politics, to assume the role of Head of State or head of Government, or to assume other administrative or political roles. The Queen of the Kingdom of Cambodia shall exercise activities that serves the social, humanitarian, religious interests, and shall assist the King with protocol and diplomatic functions.

Article 17- The provision as stated in the first clause of Article 7, " the King shall reign but shall not govern", absolutely not be amended.

Article 18- The King shall communicate with the Assembly by royal messages. These royal messages shall not be subjected to discussion by the National Assembly.

Article 19- The King shall appoint the Prime Minister and the Council of Ministers according to the procedure stipulated in Article 100.

Article 20- The King shall grant an audience twice a month to the Prime Minister and the Council of Ministers to hear their reports on the State of the Nation.

Article 21- Upon proposals by the Council of Ministers, the King shall sign decrees (Ret) appointing, transferring or ending the mission of high civil and military officials, ambassadors and Envoys Extraordinary and plenipotentiary. Upon proposal by the Supreme Council of the Magistracy, the King shall sign decrees (Ret) appointing, transferring or removing judges.

Article 22- When the nation faces danger, the King shall make a proclamation to the people putting the country in a state of emergency after agreement with the Prime Minister and the President of the Assembly.

Article 23- The King is the Supreme Commander of the Royal Khmer Armed Forces. The Commander -in -Chief of the Royal Khmer Armed Forces shall be appointed to command the Royal Khmer Armed Forces.

Article 24- The King is serve as Chairman of the Supreme council of national Defense to be established by law. The King shall declare war after approval of the National Assembly.

Article 25- The King shall receive letters of credentials from ambassadors or envoys extraordinary and plenipotentiary of foreign countries accredited to the Kingdom of Cambodia. The King shall declare war after approval of the National Assembly

Article 26- The King shall sign and ratify international treaties and conventions after a vote of approval by the National Assembly.

Article 27- The King shall have the right to grant partial or complete amnesty.

Article 28- The King shall sign the law promulgating the Constitution, laws (Kram) adopted by the National Assembly, and sign decrees (Kret) presented by the council of Ministers

Article 29- The King shall establish and confer national medals proposed by the Council of Ministers. The King shall confer civil and military ranks as determined by law.

Article 30- In the absence of the King, the President of the Assembly shall assume the duties of Acting head of State.

CHAPTER III THE RIGHTS AND OBLIGATIONS OF KHMER CITIZENS

Article 31- The Kingdom of Cambodia shall recognize and respect human rights as stipulated in the United Nations Charter, the Universal Declaration of human Rights, the covenants and conventions related to human rights, women's and children's rights. Every Khmer citizen shall be equal before the law, enjoying the same rights, freedom and fulfilling the same obligations regardless of race, color, sex, language, religious belief, political tendency, birth origin, social status, wealth or other status. The exercise of personal rights and freedom by any individual shall not adversely affect the rights and freedom of others. The exercise of such rights and freedom shall be in accordance with law.

Article 32- Every Khmer citizen shall have the right to life, personal freedom and security.

Article 33- Khmer citizens shall not be deprived of their nationality, exiled or arrested and deported go any foreign country unless there is a mutual agreement on extradition. Khmer citizens residing abroad enjoy the protection of the State. Khmer nationality shall be determined by a law.

Article 34- Khmer citizens of either sex shall enjoy the right to vote and to stand as candidates for the election. Citizens of either sex of at least eighteen years old, have the right to vote. Citizens of either sex of at least 25 years old, have the right to stand as candidates for the election. Provisions restricting the right to vote and to stand for the election shall be defined in the electoral for the election.

Article 35- Khmer citizens of either sex shall be given the right to participated actively in the political , economic, social and cultural life of the nation. Any suggestions from the people shall be given full consideration by the organs of the State

Article 36- Khmer citizens of either sex shall have the right to choose any employment according to their ability and to the needs of the society. Khmer citizen of either sex shall receive equal pay for equal work. The work by housewives in the home shall have the same value as what they can receive when working outside the home. Every Khmer citizens shall have the right to obtain social security and other social benefits as determined by law. Khmer citizens of either sex shall have the right to form and to be members of trade unions. The organization and conduct of trade unions shall be determined by law.

Article 37- The right to strike and to non-violent demonstration shall be implemented in the framework of a law.

Article 38- The law guarantees shall be no physical abuse against any individual. The law shall protect the life, honor and dignity of the citizens. The prosecution, arrest, or detention of any person shall not be done except in accordance with the law. Coercion, physical ill- treatment or any other mistreatment that imposes additional punishment on a detainee or prisoner shall be prohibited. Persons who commit, participate or conspire in such acts shall be punished according to the law. Confession obtained by physical mental force shall not be admissible as evidence of guilt. Khmer citizens of either sex shall respect public and legally acquired private properties. Any case of doubt shall be resolved in favor of the accused. The accused shall be considered innocent until the court has judged finally on the case. Every citizen shall enjoy the right to defense through judicial recourse.

Article 39- Khmer citizens shall have the right to denounce, make complaints or file claims against any breach of the law by the State and social organs or by members of such organs committed during the course of their duties. The settlement of complaints and claims shall reside under the competence of the courts.

Article 40- Citizens' freedom to travel, far and near, and legal settlement shall be respected. Khmer citizens shall have the right to travel and settle abroad and return to the country. The right to privacy of residence and to the secrecy of correspondence by mail, telegram, fax, telex, and telephone shall be guaranteed. Any search of the house, material and body shall be in accordance with the law.

Article 41- Khmer citizens shall have freedom of expression, press, publication and assembly. No one shall exercise this right to infringe upon the rights of others, to affect the good traditions of the society, to violate public law and order and national security. The regime of the media shall be determined by law.

Article 42- Khmer citizens shall have the right to establish associations and political parties. These rights shall be determined by law. Khmer citizens may take part in mass organizations for mutual benefit to protect national achievements and social order.

Article 43- Khmer citizens of either sex shall have the right to freedom of belief. Freedom of religious belief and worship shall be guaranteed by the State on the condition that such freedom does not affect other religious beliefs or violate public order and security. Buddhism shall be t he State religion.

Article 44- All persons, individually or collectively, shall have the right to ownership. Only Khmer legal entities and citizens of Khmer nationality shall the right to own land. Legal private ownership shall be protected by the law. The right to confiscate possessions from any person shall be exercised only in the public interest as provided for under law and shall required fair and just compensation in advance.

Article 45- All forms of discrimination against woman shall be abolished. The exploitation of women in employment shall be prohibited in marriages and matters of the family. Marriage shall be conducted according to conditions determined by law based on the principle of mutual consent between one husband and one wife

Article 46- The commerce of human beings, exploitation by prostitution and obscenity which affect the reputation of women shall be prohibited. A woman shall not lose her job because of pregnancy. Women shall have the right to take maternity leave with full pay and with no loss of seniority or other social benefits. The State and society shall provide opportunities to women, especially to those living in rural areas without adequate social support, so they can get employment, medical care, and send their children to school, and to have decent living conditions

Article 47- Parents shall have the right to take care of and educate their children to become good citizens. Children shall have the right to take good care of their elderly mother and father according to Khmer traditions.

Article 48- The State shall protect the rights of the children as stipulated in the Convention on Children, particular, the right to life, education, protection during wartime, and from economic or sexual exploitation. The State shall protect children from acts that are injurious to their education opportunities, health and welfare.

Article 49- Every Khmer citizens shall respect the Constitution and laws. All Khmer citizens shall have the duty to take part in the national reconstruction and to defend the homeland. The duty to defend the country shall be determined by law.

Article 50- Khmer citizens of either sex shall respect the principles of national sovereign, liberal multi-party democracy. Khmer citizens of either sex shall respect public and legally acquired private properties.

CHAPTER IV ON POLICY

Article 51- The Kingdom of Cambodia adopts a policy of Liberal democracy and Pluralism. The Cambodian people are the masters of their country. All powers belong to the people. the people exercise these powers through the National Assembly, the Royal Government and the Judiciary. The Legislative, Executive, and the Judicial powers shall be separated

Article 52- The Royal Government of Cambodia shall protect the independence, sovereignty, territorial integrity of the Kingdom of Cambodia, adopt the policy of national reconciliation to insure national unity, and preserve the good national traditions of the country. The Royal Government of Cambodia shall preserve and protect the law and ensure public order and security. The State shall give priority to endeavors which improve welfare and standard of living of citizens.

Article 53- The Kingdom of Cambodia adopts a policy of permanent neutrality and non-alignment. The Kingdom of Cambodia follows a policy of peaceful co- existence with its neighbors and with all other countries throughout the world. The Kingdom of Cambodia shall not invade any country, nor interfere in any other country's internal affairs, directly or indirectly, and shall solve any problem peacefully with due respect for mutual interests. The Kingdom of Cambodia shall not join in any military alliance or military pact which is incompatible with its policy of neutrality.

The Kingdom of Cambodia shall not permit any foreign military base on its territory and shall not have its own military base abroad, except within the framework of a United Nations request. The Kingdom of Cambodia reserves the right to receive foreign assistance in military equipment, armaments, ammunition, in training of its armed forces, and other assistance for self-defense and to maintain public order and security within its territory.

Article 54- The manufacturing, use, storage of nuclear, chemical or biological weapons shall be absolutely prohibited.

Article 55- Any treaty and agreement incompatible with the independence, sovereignty, territorial integrity, neutrality and national unity of the Kingdom of Cambodia shall be annulled.

CHAPTER V ECONOMY

Article 56- The Kingdom of Cambodia shall adopt market economy system. The preparation and process of this economic system shall be determined by law.

Article 57- Tax collection shall be in accordance with the law. The national budget by law. The national budget shall be determined by law The management of the monetary and financial system shall be defined by law.

Article 58- State property notably comprises land, mineral resources, mountains, sea, underwater, continental shelf, coastline, airspace, islands, rivers, canals, streams, lakes, forests, natural resources, economic and cultural centers, bases for national defense and other facilities determined as State property. The control, use and management of State properties shall be determined by law.

Article 59-

The State shall protect the environment and balance of abundant natural resources and establish a precise plan of management of land, water, air, wind geology, ecologic system, mines, energy, petrol, and gas, rocks and sand, gems, forests and forestrial products, wildlife, fish and aquatic resources.

Article 60- Khmer citizens shall have the right to sell I their own products. The obligation to sell products to the State, or the temporary use of State or properties shall be prohibited unless authorized by law under special circumstances.

Article 61- The State shall promote economic development in all sectors and remote areas, especially in agriculture, handicrafts industry, with attention to policies of water, electricity, roads, and means of transport, modern technology and a system of credit.

Article 62- The State shall pay attention and help solve production matters, protect the price of products for farmers and crafters, and find marketplace for them to sell their products.

Article 63- The State shall respect market management in order to guarantee a better standard of living for the people

CHAPTER VI EDUCATION, CULTURE, SOCIAL AFFAIRS

Article 64- The State shall ban and severely punishes those who import, manufacture, sell illicit drugs, counterfeit and expired goods which affect health and life of the consumers.

Article 65- The State shall protect and upgrade citizens' rights to quality education at all levels and shall take necessary steps for quality education to reach all citizens. The State shall respect physical education and sports for the welfare of all Khmer citizens

Article 66- The State shall establish a comprehensive and standardized education system throughout the country that shall guarantee the principles of educational freedom and equality to ensure that all citizens have equal opportunity to earn a living.

Article 67- The State shall adopt and educational program according to the principle of modern pedagogy including technology and foreign languages. The State shall control public and private schools and classrooms at all levels.

Article 68- The State shall provide primary and secondary education to all citizens in public schools The State shall disseminate and develop the Pali schools and the Buddhist Institutes

Article 69- The State shall protect and promote the Khmer language as required. The State shall preserve ancient monuments, artifacts and restore historic sites.

Article 70- Any offense affecting cultural and artistic heritage shall carry a severe punishment.

Article 71- The perimeter of the national heritage sites as well as heritage that has been classified as world heritage, shall be considered neutral zones where there shall be no military activity.

Article 72- The health of the people shall be guaranteed. The State shall give full consideration to disease prevention and medical treatment. Poor citizens shall receive free medical consultation in public hospitals, infirmaries and maternities. The State shall establish infirmaries in rural areas.

Article 73- The State shall give full consideration to children and mothers. The State shall establish nurseries, and help support women and children who have inadequate support.

Article 74- The State shall assist the disabled and the families of combatants who sacrificed their lives for the nation.

Article 75- The State shall establish a social security system for workers and employees.

CHAPTER VII THE ASSEMBLY

Article 76- The assembly consists of at least 120 members. The deputies shall be elected by a free, universal , equal, direct and secret ballot. The deputies may be re-elected Khmer citizens able to stand for election shall be the Khmer citizens of either sex who have the right to vote, at least 25 years of age, and who have Khmer nationalities at birth Preparation for the election, procedure and electoral process shall be determined by an Electoral Law.

Article 77- The deputies of the Assembly shall represent the entire Khmer people, not only Khmers from their constituencies. Any imperative mandate shall be nullified.

Article 78- The legislative term of the Assembly shall be 5 years and terminates on the day when the new assembly convenes. The assembly shall not be dissolved before the end of its term except when the Royal government is twice deposed within a period of twelve months. In this case, following a proposal from the Prime Minister and the approval of t he Assembly President, the King shall dissolve the Assembly. The election of a new assembly shall be held no later than 60 days from the date of dissolution. During this period, the Royal government shall only be empowered to conduct routine business. In times of war or other special circumstances an election cannot be held, the Assembly may extend its term for one year at a time, upon the request of the King. Such an extension shall require at least a two- third vote of the entire assembly.

Article 79- The assembly mandate shall be incompatible with the holding of any active public function and of any membership in other institutions provided for in the constitution, except when the assembly member(s) is (are) required to serve in the Royal Government. In these circumstances, the said Assembly members shall retain the usual assembly membership but shall not hold any position in the Permanent Standing Committee and in other assembly commissions.

Article 80- The deputies shall have parliamentary. No assembly member shall be prosecuted, detained or arrested because of opinions expressed during the exercise of his or her duties. The decision made by the Standing Committee of the assembly shall be made only with the permission of the assembly or by the Standing Committee of the Assembly between sessions, except in case of flagrante delicto. In that case, the competent authority shall immediately report to the assembly or to the Standing Committee for decision. The decision made by the Standing Committee of the assembly shall be submitted to the assembly at its next session for approval by a 2/3 majority vote of the assembly members. In any case, detention or prosecution of a deputy shall be suspended by a 3/4 majority vote of the Assembly members.

Article 81- The assembly shall have the autonomous budget to conduct its function. The deputies shall receive a remuneration.

Article 82- The assembly shall hold its first session no later than sixty days after the election upon notice by the King. Before taking office, the assembly shall decide on the validity of each member's mandate and vote separately to choose a President, Vice-Presidents and members of each Commission by a 2/3 majority vote All assembly members must take the oath before taking office according to the text contained in Annex 5.

Article 83- The assembly shall hold its ordinary sessions twice a year. Each session shall last at least 3 months. If there is a proposal from the King or the Prime Minister, or at least 1/3 of the assembly members, the Assembly Standing Committee shall call an extraordinary session of the assembly. In this case, the agenda with the conditions of the extraordinary, shall be disseminated to the population as well as the date of the meeting.

Article 84- Between the assembly sessions, the assembly Standing Committee shall manage the work of the assembly. The Permanent Standing Committee of the assembly consists of the President of the Assembly, the Vice- Presidents ,and the presidents of assembly commissions.

Article 85- The assembly sessions shall be held in the royal capital of Cambodia in the Assembly Hall, unless stipulated otherwise in the summons, due to special circumstances. Except where so stipulated and unless held at the place and date as stipulated, any meeting of the assembly shall be considered as illegal and void.

Article 86- If the country is in a state of emergency the assembly shall beet every day continuously. The assembly has the right to terminate this state of emergency whenever the situation permits. If the Assembly is not able to meet because of circumstances such as the occupation by foreign forces the declaration of the state of emergency must be automatically extended. During the state of emergency, the assembly shall not be dissolved.

Article 87- The President of the assembly shall chair the assembly sessions, receive draft bills and resolutions adopted by the assembly, ensure the implementation of the Internal Rules of procedure and manage the assembly relations with foreign countries. If the President is unable to perform his/ her duties due to illness or to fulfill the functions of Head of State ad interim or as a Regent, or is on a mission aborad, a Vice- President shall replace him. In case of resignation or death of the President or the Vice-President(s), the Assembly shall elect a new President or Vice- President(s).

Article 88- The assembly sessions shall be held in public. The assembly shall meet in closed session at the request of the President or of at least 1/10 of its members, of the King or of the Prime Minister. The assembly meeting shall be considered as valid provided there is a quorum of 7/10 of all members.

Article 89- Upon the request by at least 1/10 of its members, the assembly shall invite a high ranking official to clarify important special individual

Article 90- The assembly shall be the only organ to hold legislative power, This power shall not be transferable to any other organ or any individual.

The assembly shall approve Administrative Accounts.

The assembly shall approve the law on amnesty.

The assembly shall approve or annul treaties or international conventions.

The assembly shall approve law on the declaration of war.

The adoption of the above-mentioned clauses shall be decided by a simply majority of the entire assembly membership.

The assembly shall pass a vote of confidence in the Royal Government by a 2/3 majority of all members

Article 91- The deputies and the Prime Minister shall have the right to initiate legislation. The deputies shall have the right to propose any amendments to the laws, but the proposals shall be unacceptable if they aim at reducing public income or increasing the burden on the people.

Article 92- Laws adopted by the Assembly which run counter to the principles of preserving national independence, sovereignty, administration of the nation shall be annulled. The Constitutional Council is the only organ which shall decide upon this annulment.

Article 93- Any law approved by the Assembly and signed by the King for its promulgation, shall go into effect in Phnom Penh 10 days after signing and throughout the country 20 days after its signing. Laws that are stipulated as urgent shall take effect immediately throughout the country after promulgation. All laws promulgated by the King shall be published in the Journal Official and published throughout the country in accordance with the above schedule.

Article 94- The Assembly shall establish various necessary commissions. The organization and functioning of the assembly shall be determined by the assembly Internal Rules of Procedure.

Article 95- In case of death, resignation, or dismissal of an assembly deputy at least 6 months before the end of the mandate, a replacement shall be appointed in accordance with the Internal Rules of Procedure of the National Assembly and the Electoral Law.

Article 96- The deputies have the right to put a motion against the Royal Government. The motion shall be submitted in writing through the President of t he assembly. The replies shall be given by one or several ministers depending on the matters to the accountability of one or several ministers. If the case concerns the overall policy of the Royal Government, the Prime Minister shall reply in person. The explanations by the ministers or by the Prime Minister shall be given verbally or in witting. The explanations shall be provided within 7 days after the day when the question is received. In case of verbal reply, the President of t he assembly shall decide whether to hold an open debate or not. If there is no debate, the answer of the minister or the Prime Minister shall be considered final. If there is a debate, the questioner, other speakers, the ministers, or the Prime Minister may exchange views within the time frame not exceeding one session. The assembly shall establish one day each week for questions and answers. There shall be no vote during any sessions reserved for this purpose.

Article 97- The assembly commissions may invite any minister to clarify certain issue under his/her field of responsibility.

Article 98- The Assembly shall dismiss a member or members of the Royal Government or the whole Cabinet by the adoption of a motion of censure by 2/3 majority of the entire Assembly. The motion of censure shall be proposed to the Assembly by at least 30 assembly members in order for the entire Assembly to decide.

CHAPTER VIII THE ROYAL GOVERNMENT

Article 99- The Council of Ministers is the Royal Government of Cambodia. The Council of Ministers shall be led by one Prime Minister assisted by Deputy Prime Ministers, and by State Ministers, Ministers, and State Secretaries as members.

Article 100- At the recommendation of the President and with the agreement of both Vice- Presidents of the Assembly, the King shall designate a dignitary from among the representatives of the winning party to form the Royal Government. This designated Assembly or members of the political parties represented in the from the Assembly. After the Assembly has given its vote of confidence, the King shall issue a Royal decree (Kret) appointing the entire Council of Ministers. Before taking office, the Council of Ministers shall take an oath as stipulated an Annex 6.

Article 101- The functions of members of the Royal Government shall be incompatible with professional activities in trade or industry and with the holding of any position in the public service.

Article 102- Members of the Royal Government shall be collectively responsible to the Assembly for the overall policy of the Royal Government. Each member of the Royal Government shall be individually responsible to the Prime Minster and the Assembly for his/her own conduct.

Article 103- Members of the Royal Government shall not use the orders, written or verbal, of anyone as grounds to exonerate themselves form their responsibility

Article 104- The Council of Minister shall meet every week inn plenary session or in a working session. The Prime Minister shall chair the plenary sessions. The Prime Minister may assign a Deputy Prime Minister to preside over the working sessions. Minutes of the Council of Ministers' meeting shall be forwarded to the King for His information.

Article 105- The Prime Minister shall have the right to delegate his power to a Deputy Prime Minister or to any member of the Royal Government.

Article 106- If the post of Prime Minister is permanently vacant, a new Council of Ministers shall be appointed under the procedure stipulated in this Constitution. If the vacancy is temporary, an acting Prime Minister shall be provisionally appointed.

Article 107- Each member of the Royal Government shall be punished for any crimes or misdemeanors that he/she has committed in the course of his/her duty. In such cases and when his/her duty, the Assembly shall decide to file charges against him/her with competent. The Assembly shall decide on such matters though a secret vote by a simple majority thereof.

Article 108- The organization and functioning of the Council of Ministers shall be determined by law.

CHAPTER IX THE JUDICIARY

Article 109- The Judicial power shall be an independent power.

The Judiciary shall guarantee and uphold impartiality and protect the rights and freedoms of the citizens.

The Judiciary shall cover all lawsuits including administrative ones.

The authority of the Judiciary shall be granted to the Supreme Court and to lower courts of all sectors and levels.

Article 110- Trials shall be conducted in the name of the Khmer citizens in accordance with the legal procedures and laws in force. Only judges shall have the right to adjudicate. A judge shall fulfill this duty with strict respect for the laws. wholeheartedly, and conscientiously.

Article 111- Judicial power shall not be granted to the legislative or executive branches.

Article 112- Only the Department of Public Prosecution shall have the right to file criminal suits.

Article 113- The King shall be the guarantor of the independence of the Judiciary. The Supreme Council of the Magistracy shall assist the King in this matter.

Article 114- Judges shall not be dismissed. The supreme Council of the Magistracy shall take disciplinary actions against any delinquent judges.

Article 115- The Supreme Council of the Magistracy shall be established by an organic law which shall determine its composition and functions. The Supreme Council of the Magistracy shall be chaired by the King. The King may appoint a representative to chair the Supreme Council of the Magistracy. The Supreme Council of the Magistracy shall make proposals to the King on the appointment of judges and prosecutors to all courts. The Supreme Council of the Magistracy shall meet under the chairmanship of the President of the Supreme Court or the General Prosecutor of the Supreme Court to decide on disciplinary actions against the judges or prosecutors.

Article 116- The statuses of judges, and prosecutors and the functioning of the judiciary shall be defined in separate laws.

CHAPTER X THE CONSTITUTIONAL COUNCIL

Article 117- The Constitutional council shall have the duty to safeguard respect for the Constitution, to interpret the Constitution, and the laws passed by the Assembly. The Constitutional Council shall have the right to examine and decide on contested cases involving the election of assembly members.

Article 118- The Constitutional Council shall consist of nine members with a nine-year mandate. One third of the members of the Council shall be replaced every three years. Three members shall be appointed by the King, three members by the Assembly and three others by the Supreme Council of the Magistracy. The Chairman shall be elected by the members of the Constitutional Council. He/she shall have a deciding vote in cases of equal vote.

Article 119- Members of the Constitutional Council shall be selected among the dignitaries with a higher-education degree in law, administration, diplomacy or economics and who have considerable work experience.

Article 120- The function of a Constitutional Council member shall be incompatible with that of a member of the Royal Government, member of the assembly, President or Vice-President of a political party, President or Vice- President of trade-union or in-post judges.

Article 121- The King, the Prime Minister, the President of the Assembly, or 1/10 of the assembly members shall forward draft bills to the Constitutional Council for examination before their promulgation. The Constitutional Council shall decide within no more than thirty days whether the laws and the Internal Rules of Procedure are constitutional.

Article 122- After the law is promulgated, the King, the prime Minister, the President of the Assembly, 1/10 of the assembly members or the courts, may ask the Constitutional Council to examine the Constitutionality of that law. Citizens shall have the right to appeal against the Constitutionality of the laws as through their representatives or the President of the Assembly as stipulated in the above paragraph.

Article 123- Provisions i any article ruled by the Council as unconstitutional shall not be promulgated or implemented. The decision of the Council is final.

Article 124- The King shall consult with the Constitutional Council on all proposals to amend the Constitution.

Article 125- An organic law shall specify the organization and operation of the Constitutional Council.

CHAPTER XI THE ADMINISTRATION

Article 126- The territory of the Kingdom of Cambodia shall be divided into provinces and municipalities. Provinces shall be divided into districts (srok) and district into commune (khum). Municipalities shall be divided into Khan into Sangkat.

Article 127- Provinces, municipalities, districts, khan, khum, and sangkat shall be governed in accordance with organic law.

CHAPTER XII THE NATIONAL CONGRESS

Article 128- The National Congress shall enable the people to be directly informed on various matters of national interests and to raise issues and requests for the State authority to solve. Khmer citizens of both sexes shall have the right to participate in the National Congress.

Article 129- The National Congress shall meet once a year in early December at the convocation of the Prime Minister. It shall proceed under the chairmanship of the King.

Article 130- The National Congress shall adopt recommendations for consideration by State authorities and the Assembly. The organization and operation of the National Congress shall be defined by a law.

CHAPTER XIII EFFECTS, REVISION AND AMENDMENTS OF THE CONSTITUTION

Article 131- This Constitution shall be the Supreme law of the Kingdom of Cambodia. Laws and decisions by the State institutions shall have to be in strict conformity with the Constitution

Article 132- The initiative to review or to amend the Constitution shall be the prerogative of the King, the Prime Minister, the President of the Assembly at the suggestion of 1/4 of all the assembly members. Revision or amendments shall enacted by a Constitutional law passed by the Assembly with a 2/3 majority vote

Article 133- Revision or amendment shall be prohibited when the country is in the State of emergency, as outlined in Article 86.

CHAPTER XIV TRANSITIONAL PROVISION

Article 134- Revision or amendment affecting the system of liberal and pluralistic democracy and the regime of Constitutional Monarchy shall prohibited.

Article 135- This Constitution, after its adoption, shall be declared in force immediately by the Head of State of Cambodia.

Article 136- After the entry into force of this Constitution, the Constituent Assembly shall become the National Assembly. The Internal Rules of Procedure of the assembly shall come into force after adoption by the assembly. In the case where the assembly is not yet functional, the President, the First and Second Vice-Presidents of the Constituent Assembly shall participated in the discharge of t duties in the Throne Council if so required by the situation in the country.

Article 137- After this Constitution takes effect, the King shall be selected in accordance with conditions stipulated in Article 13 and 14.

Article 138- After this Constitution take effects, and during the first legislature, the King of the Kingdom of Cambodia shall appoint a First Prime Minister and a Second Prime Minister to forma Royal Government after securing the consent of the President and the two Vice-Presidents of the assembly. The Co-President existing before the adoption of this Constitution shall participate as members of the Committee and in the Throne Council as stipulated in Articles 11 and 13 above.

Article 139- Laws and standard documents in Cambodia that safeguard State properties, rights, freedom and legal private properties and in conformity with the national interests, shall continue to be effective until altered or abrogated by next texts, except those provisions that are contrary to the spirit of this Constitution.

This constitution was adopted by the Constitutional assembly in Phnom Penh on 21 September 1993 at its second plenary session.

SELECTED OFFICIAL MATERIALS

EXECUTIVE SUMMARY OF THE INTERNATIONAL CONFERENCE ON SMALL ARMS PROLIFERATION AND TRADE IN THE ASIA PACIFIC

Following is the Executive Summary of the International Conference on Small Arms Proliferation and Trade in the Asia Pacific, held in Phnom Penh on 19-20 February 2001 presented by the Cambodian Institute for Cooperation and Peace and the Friedrich-Ebert-Stiftung at the ARF CBMs Seminar on Conventional Arms and Light Weapons, held in Phnom Penh on 21-22 February 2001:

Background

The Cambodian Institute for Cooperation and Peace and the Friedrich-Ebert?Stiftung jointly organized an International Conference on "Small Arms Proliferation and Trade in the Asia Pacific" on February 19?20, 2001, in Phnom Penh. The conference was well attended by more than 100 participants, from most of the ASEAN countries, as well as representatives of the EU, the UN, China, Japan, Germany, Russian Federation, and the United Kingdom. The conference was organized at the track?two level. Overall, while the meeting raised many key issues concerning proliferation and trade of small arms and light weapons, the timing of the conference was important in relations to: (1) the Cambodian government's ongoing efforts to curb the use and trafficking of small arms and lights weapons; (2) the track?one ARF CBM Seminar on Light Weapons and Conventional Arms; and (3) the upcoming International State Conference on the illicit trade in small arms and light?weapons in all its aspects scheduled on 9?20 July 2001, in New York.

Below is a concise summary of the outcomes of the two?day conference. The summary is not intended to capture every point. Rather, this concise summary only highlighted the key issues raised at the conference.

1- General

* small arms and light weapons are part of conventional arms
* address both supply and demand sides
* not only focus on illicit trade but also focus on all aspects of small arms and light weapons (including ammunition)
* Cope with the root causes in the intra?state conflicts; combat the proliferation of small arms.

2- Imperative of Cooperation

* international cooperation is necessary
* closer cooperation and consultation between and among ASEAN states are essential
* problems cannot be handled successfully by individual countries, not even regions alone. But, ultimately the responsibility rests * ith individual

states
* the situation in neighboring country directly affects the situation in another country
* prevention before conflicts (prevention of new destabilizing accumulation)
* parliamentary oversight

3- Interdependence between arms reduction measures and development

* easy availability of small arms poses threat to development
* availability of arms is a major source of insecurity,
* the prevalence of weapons increases the lethality or violence of conflicts

4- Respect for Legitimate Security Needs (question of interference in internal affairs)

* small arms cannot be prohibited as a category because of legitimate needs for self?defense
* legitimate security needs (arms for self?defense) should serve as a benchmark, the rest is surplus
* intentionally or unintentionally, efforts in other countries are easily undermined
* non-state actors should not be supplied with weapons at all

5- Agreement or Consensus on Definitions

* use precise definitions or concepts in order not to leave loopholes
* concentrate on military weapons
* Address the question of ammunition (in a way it's easier to tackle: perishable, difficult to manufacture, is needed in large quantities)

6- Arms Control, Trade Control, Export Trade Control

* monitoring of arms trade is vital
*focus not only on illicit trade but also on legal production and trade (norms setting and standardization)
* focus both on new and used arms (recycle of small arms from one place to another)
* prevent the diversion of small arms to illegal channels (means: see transparency)
* reduction of existing surplus is crucial (political decision or leadership)

7- Post-Conflict Policies: Demobilization, Disarmament, Reintegration (DDR)

* registration of arms, safe storage (prevent leakage from officially stored weapons), and (public) destruction 3
* DDR should be included in peace agreements
* disarmament should be mandatory, rapid and transparent
* disarmament should be done immediately, using the existing chains of command; later arms are dispersed in the population and owned by individuals

* disarmament using the chain of command first, later offer incentives for voluntary disarmament (more complicated)
* important: address the topic of surplus weapons (industrialized nations are also affected, should set examples)
* long-term measures: confidence-building (establish confidence and trust in security situation) by training of police, reform of security sector, and establishing rule of law
* key factors: capacity to enforce control and inspire confidence
* capacity building (local inputs), especially local communities
* reconciliation and justice (reintegration not at the expense of justice)
* institutional building
* challenge and reverse culture of violence (e.g., it's dishonorable to possess arms)
* development assistance

8- Transparency

* information exchange (as a first step: government to government transparency)
* exchange information on export policies, export control, pass on information to UN arms register
* marking of weapons in order to be able to trace them
* registration of weapons
* accurate and sustained record keeping
* information exchange can reinforce or enhance sovereignty, not undermine sovereignty

9- Participation or Involvement of the Track Two and Civil Society

* inputs from think tanks or the track two are essential (such as ASEAN?ISIS or CSCAP)
* active support from civil society is required, especially for disarmament

10- Recommendations for Cooperation: Possible First Steps

* establish national commission for management of weapons and ammunition
* information exchange (state-to-state, but also establishment of networks) concerning national laws and regulations, the *arking system, which authorities are in charge
* network for cooperation between law enforcement officials
* closer regional cooperation on customs, police, border controls
* support programmes for reduction of weapons in post?conflict situations (e.g. EU in Cambodia)

OPENING REMARKS BY SENIOR MINISTER AT ARF CBMS SEMINAR

Following is the integral text of the opening remarks made by His Excellency Mr. HOR Namhong, Senior Minister, Minister of Foreign Affairs and International Cooperation, at the ARF CBMs Seminar on Conventional Weapons Transfers held in Phnom Penh on 21-22 February 2001:

Mr. Co-Chairmen,
Excellencies
Distinguished Guests,
Ladies and Gentlemen,

It gives me, indeed, great pleasure to extend a warm welcome to all distinguished guests and participants to this significant seminar on Conventional Weapons Transfers in order to make joint actions for preventing their illegal spread.

I wish to take this opportunity to sincerely thank the Governments of Japan and Canada and the United Nations for their precious assistance, which has made this Seminar possible.

Our meeting today is as it were the extension of the International Conference on Small Arms Proliferation and Trade in the Asia Pacific, held on 19-20 February 2001. These two meetings complete one another the inseparable issues of conventional weapons transfers and small arms proliferation and trade.

I hope that this meeting will produce fruitful recommendations on the issue of conventional weapons transfers, paving the way for the future actions of the United Nations and for the ARF Ministerial Meeting next July in Hanoi to deal with this crucial issue.

This seminar is held at a time when the international community is facing serious problems caused by the uncontrolled transfer of conventional weapons and the illicit trade of small arms and light weapons which pose a severe threat to peace and security throughout the world and constitute a source of insecurity and terrorism in many countries and regions.

Taking into account the current intensity of transnational crimes affecting many parts of the world today, the transfers of conventional weapons and the trafficking of small arms and light weapons are alarming issues that the entire international community must join hands to solve. It requires from all of us a more efficient cooperation and coordination of actions between national, regional and international law enforcement agencies.

Today everyone knows that mass-production of conventional arms, especially small arms and light weapons are manufactured and traded in abundance. The problem is how to prevent that production and export of these weapons would not contribute to encouraging war and terrorism in many parts of the world, in particular in the developing countries.

Excellencies,
Ladies and Gentlemen,

Nowadays, many societies in developed and developing countries are plagued by a growing level of criminal activities, terrorism and lawless actions due to the excessive and uncontrolled accumulation and spread of small arms and light weapons. Their proliferation has aggravated the violence associated with organized and transnational crimes.

In the last decade alone, conflicts fought with only small arms have killed over three million people among them are overwhelmingly unarmed civilians.

In the face of this grave problem, I guess that there is an obvious need for all to take very concrete measures to eliminate the illegal transfer of conventional weapons, small arms and light weapons. This is a problem for the whole international community and not for any specific country or region.

The Kingdom of Cambodia has acted very transparently when dealing with arms issues, because we believe that it is an important element and example to contribute to the reduction of arms traffic, criminal and terrorist actions.

The Royal Government of Cambodia (RGC), in the last few years, has taken severe measures to strictly control the use and circulation of small arms and ammunitions, eliminate their illegal procurement and sales by destroying those seized arms. It has so far confiscated 91,269 pieces of assorted small arms and light weapons, out of which 37,009 pieces were publicly destroyed.

Moreover, recently we have sent to the United Nations a list of conventional weapons and ammunitions for the purpose to be put into the United Nations Conventional Arms Register (UNCAR). We have also produced a White Defense Paper, which have been distributed just yesterday to all of you.

In the same vein, Cambodia is committed to strongly and actively support the initiatives of the EU on 17 December 1998 called " Joint Action ", to combat destabilizing accumulation and spread of Small Arms and Light Weapons (SALW).

Cambodia expresses also its full support to the convening of the UN Conference on Illicit Trade in Small Arms and Light Weapons (SALW) in All Its Aspects in July 2001. It views this Conference as an opportunity to address the problem in a more systematic and holistic manner in order to move ahead in shaping of a more peaceful, secure and stable world.

Cambodia, therefore, would like to add its voice to calls for a draft of actions plan to combat the illicit trade of conventional weapons, small arms and light weapons, aiming at strengthening national, regional and international security for all. This should lead towards more transparent armament issue encompassing production, transfer and legal use.

Finally, I hope that this seminar will contribute for sure to identifying concrete measures for diminishing the illegal transfer of conventional arms as well as traffic of small arms and light weapons paving the way for the success of the UN Conference in next July on this issue for a better world in this third millennium.

May I wish the Seminar a fruitful exercise.

CLOSING KEYNOTE ADDRESS BY SENIOR MINISTER AT THE INTERNATIONAL CONFERENCE ON SMALL ARMS PROLIFERATION AND TRADE IN THE ASIA PACIFIC

Following is the text of the closing keynote address delivered by His Excellency Mr. HOR Namhong, Senior Minister, Minister of Foreign Affairs and International Cooperation, at the International Conference on "Small Arms Proliferation and Trade in the Asia Pacific", held in Phnom Penh on 19-20 February 2001:

Your Highness Prince Sisowath Sirirath, Co-Minister of National Defense,
Your Royal Highness Sdech Krom Khun Norodom Sirivudh, Supreme Privy Counselor to His Majesty the King of Cambodia and Chairman of the Board of Directors of the Cambodian Institute for Cooperation and Peace,
Dr. Erfried Adam, Director of the Office for Regional Cooperation in Southeast Asia of the Friedrich-Ebert-Stiftung,
Excellencies,
Distinguished Participants,
Ladies and Gentlemen,

First of all, I wish to express my sincere thanks to both the Cambodian Institute for Cooperation and Peace and the Friedrich-Ebert-Stiftung for inviting me to give this closing keynote address at this very important international conference. The issues of small arms and light weapons are key problems that have been discussed at both regional level especially at the ASEAN Regional Forum (ARF) and the international levels, the EU as well as the United Nations itself. The conference is highly relevant because of its social values, insights and contributions to peace and security to the world at large. It depends on how best we should work together more effectively in order to address the common challenges of the danger of the proliferation and illicit traffic of small arms and light weapons.

Although I have not been able to attend during the past two days of this International Conference, nevertheless, I have been fully informed on the outcomes of the meeting. The conference had raised a number of essential issues concerning the need to curb the illicit and trafficking of small arms and light weapons. But it is important, as underlined by several speakers, that the Asia Pacific region must take the leadership in managing the Basic issues of small arms and light weapons. At the same time, a number of speakers and participants have raised the issues of the growing profile of the problems and challenges arising from the uncontrolled small arms and light weapons in our region, which could have devastating effects. I strongly share the views that this issue has serious implications for peace, security, stability and development at national, regional and international levels.

Many speakers, starting from the opening session to the last session this afternoon, emphasized the need to build greater trust and confidence between and among the countries in this region and beyond, as well as between and among key players and actors on the imperative to promote not only greater public awareness but also the imperative of engaging in transparency and accountability in this area. I believe that this must be done by both sides-supply and demand. At the same time, we need to build better database of information and documentation of small arms and light weapons, as well as their transfers and transactions. We need certainly to share more information, although this may pose the question of political sensitivity, confidentiality and security. However, we will be able to overcome these problems only by doing so.

For Cambodia as a country only just emerging from a long period of war, conflict and destruction, we still have fresh memories or smells of the sounds of the guns or small arms. As H.E. Sok An, Senior Minister and Minister of the Council of Ministers, and H.E. Tea Banh, Senior Minister and Co-Minister of Defense, stated yesterday the commitment and determination of the Royal Government of Cambodia to the complete ban and elimination of small arms and light weapons which we do not need. The Cambodian government is committed to work constantly to contain and restrict the use, sale and transfer of these weapons throughout the country and to concentrate its entire efforts and resources on national reconstruction and development. Cambodian competent authority has so far, since 1997, confiscated 91, 269 pieces of assorted small arms and light weapons, out of which 37, 009 pieces were publicly destroyed.

Excellencies,
Ladies and Gentlemen,

I am very pleased to note that this international conference has been attended by top people from both the track-one and track-two levels of the ARF and from a wide spectrum of participants. I wish to underline the issues of small arms and light weapons are the fundamental issues at the heart of His Excellency Samdech Hun Sen, who has strongly committed to build a more stable, more peaceful, small arms-free society for Cambodia. Reduction of small arms and light weapons is very much linked to sustainable development and economic progress.

Taking into consideration the discussion during these two days, I wish to share with you some of my thoughts on some of the ways in which we should do together in order to move the agenda of stopping the illicit trafficking of small arms and light weapons in our region and in the world at large.

First, we should continue to raise the profile of small arms and light weapons as the way we had done with respect to landmines. This is vital, as we need to mobilize the global public opinions worldwide to succeed in this area.

Second, we need to promote and consolidate confidence-building measures (CBMs) at the track-one level of the ARF. In this context, I am very happy to say that Cambodia is very supportive of the current efforts to move ahead on the need to curb small arms and light weapons, as illustrated in hosting of the upcoming track one meeting on the ARF, following this track-two conference. Trust and confidence are vital to the exchanges of not only ideas but more importantly information and data. We should work in a gradual approach on this as each one of us will have to proceed at a comfortable pace.

Third, we must promote good governance in the area of small arms and light weapons-especially the basic questions of accountability, and transparency. While recognizing the sensitivity and the politics of the issues, I strongly believe that we can share the common views on the importance of enhancing regional stability as well as international peace and security. Moreover, given the danger and negative effects of the transnational crime, we have to make every effort to closely cooperate and interact with one another more effectively and in the spirit of joint responsibilities.

Fourth, combating illicit trafficking of small arms and light weapons are not only just the responsibilities of the national governments alone but also the share responsibilities of regional organizations and the international institutions such as the United Nations. In this respect, I am very pleased to note that the ASEAN Regional Forum, the European Union and the United Nations will continue to cooperate on this issue. In particular, I share the view of His Excellency Mr. Jayantha Dhanapala, Under-Secretary-General for Disarmament Affairs of the United Nations, that the regional organizations such as ASEAN should play a leading role in addressing the issues and implications of small arms proliferation and illicit trade. However, I am of the view that these crucial problems require cooperation from all countries and international organizations in the world.

Fifth, I believe that we need to work at all levels-local, national, subregional, regional and international-in order to manage these growing problems in its multidimensional aspects. This is vital for building a peaceful and stable world for all.

In essence, this two-day conference has raised many challenging problems that we will continue to ponder on how we should move ahead in coming up with more practical plans of actions, policy options and alternatives for dealing with these crucial questions. This is, I guess, our individual and collective responsibility.

Finally, I wish to take this opportunity to thank all the participants for taking time and making every endeavour to actively participate in this very important international conference. I am also very pleased to congratulate the Cambodian Institute for Cooperation and Peace and the Friedrich-Ebert-Stiftung for organizing this very successful conference.

SPEECH BY SAMDECH PRIME MINISTER ON "CAMBODIA'S ECONOMIC RECONSTRUCTION AND REGIONAL COOPERATION"AT THE INTERNATIONAL CONFERENCE ON THE FUTURE OF ASIA

Imperial Hotel, Tokyo (Japan), June 8, 2001

Excellencies, Ladies and Gentlemen,

It is a great honor and pleasure for me to address the international conference on **"The Future of Asia: Beyond Globalism, Ways to Harmonize Competition and Cooperation".** "Cambodia's Future in Southeast Asia: Problems, Potentials and Perspectives of the Asian-Pacific Networks". I would like to take this opportunity to express my appreciation to Japan's Nikei newspaper for organizing this conference.

Today, I wish to take the opportunity provided by this conference to share with Your Excellencies, Ladies and Gentlemen some of my thoughts on our efforts to rehabilitate and develop Cambodia in this geo-politically strategic part of Southeast and East Asia.

We are gathering today, at the time when the world and regional economies are facing major challenges. Overall, the world economy turned in an impressive performance since 1999. At that time the underlying fundamentals of the world economy have more generally strengthened and a more sustainable pattern of growth has been created. At the same time, the Southeast Asian economies continue to recover rapidly from the cataclysm that had wrecked havoc many countries in the region a few years ago. However, the global outlook for 2001 is becoming significantly more adverse, with the unexpected economic slowdown in the United States, lower growth in Europe and problems in the Japanese economy. This is compounded by weakness in the global IT sector, with some ASEAN economies heavily depend on the production and exports of electronic goods. The current situation has created some problems and difficulties for the economies of Southeast Asia.

Therefore, we can consider past achievements and experiences, envision the challenges to our future and together put in place effective measures to overcome these challenges. The above factors have made the outlook for the economies of Southeast Asia and East Asia more uncertain.

I am sure that this meeting will provide East Asian countries with much needed opportunities to discuss ways to sustain the recovery of regional economies, to build up business and investor confidence and to mitigate the impact of China joining the WTO on the regional economies. It also provides forum to discuss ways to turn these developments into "win-win" opportunities for the development and progress of the whole East Asian region. It is my conviction that it is important to sustain the momentum of growth in our individual countries and the region, thereby securing greater economic stability and resilience of the region, which is crucial for long-term, sustainable development.

In this context, I believe that we should focus mainly on the following issues :

1-coping with regionalism and globalization;

2-reducing and eradicating poverty of our populace, in particular bridging economic disparities and igital divide in the region and the world; and

3-enhancing economic cooperation based on our country's comparative advantages and mutual benefits.

Let me now turn to the issues that are of utmost importance for Cambodia and how we will cope with regional and global affairs.

First, in the areas of international affairs, Cambodia has given priority to strengthening its international relations and deepening its commitment to open markets and trade as a member of ASEAN. Cambodia's joining ASEAN is the necessity of the geo-politics and geo-economics. For Cambodia, ASEAN's attractions are fourfold:

1. The principle of non-interference in each other's internal affairs is the pillar of ASEAN existence since its inception.

2. The consensus principle in ASEAN's decision making process. This principle provides each nation with the status of equality and equal rights regardless of its size.

3. Even though so far some ASEAN members have faced with many economic challenges, including the financial turmoil a few years ago, ASEAN remains the economic center, which is capable to generate high growth over the long- term. Through its involvement in regional affairs and cooperation, Cambodia
will be able to succeed in achieving this potential and share the win-win situation with its ASEAN partners.

4. ASEAN has long tradition of cooperation with its dialogue partners and therefore is a major international gateway and the arena for diplomacy for Cambodia, provides opportunity for economic cooperation with other countries and open access to international markets.

In this sense, Cambodia is looking forward to participating in all regional endeavors aimed at establishing and ensuring an environment of security, peace and stability, which constitutes the instrumental foundation for sustainable development and prosperity of the people. The commitments to democracy, the respect for human rights, the safeguard of peace and national reconciliation, especially the dismantling of the Khmer Rouge's political and military organization - which constitute long-term instability for the country and the region - are invaluable contribution to ASEAN and East Asia.

On the economic front, the Royal Government of Cambodia (RGC) has taken considerable strides to boost economic growth and reduce poverty. Hence, even after the most severe flooding in 70 years, the Royal Government of Cambodia (RGC) is committed to taking necessary measures in order to reach the GDP growth target of 5.5 percent. According to our latest estimate, real GDP growth was 5.4 percent in 2000 against the projected 5.5 percent. This testifies to the fact that the growth momentum, which commenced in 1999, was maintained. It is necessary to recall that, according to our official data, after tepid growth of 3.7 percent and1.5 percent in 1997 and 1998 respectively growth rate for 1999 reached 6.9 percent against 4 percent projected. According to government's forecast, real GDP growth will be 6.1 percent in 2001 and 2002. Inflation will be kept at a low level and the exchange rates will be broadly stable.

In the regional context, we are actively involved in ASEAN's affairs and cooperation projects,such as the ASEAN Free Trade Area (AFTA), the ASEAN Industrial Cooperation Scheme (AICO) and the ASEAN Investment Area (AIA). This cooperation also helps strengthen economic and trade relations and promotes investment across the borders.

Second, strengthening relationships with countries of Northeast Asia (Japan, China and South Korea) within the framework of ASEAN plus three is of paramount importance for Cambodia. At the recent fourth ASEAN Informal Summit in Singapore, ASEAN plus three leaders raised the possibility of holding the East Asian Summit instead of the

ASEAN plus three and plus one Summit. In fact, the recent financial turmoil in the region more than three years earlier has shown that the future of countries in East Asia is inextricably linked together and the debate on "the East Asian Free Trade Area" or " the East Asia Community" is no longer a taboo. The Chiang Mai Initiative (CMI), - through the expansion of the ASEAN Swap agreement (ASA) to all ten ASEAN members and the establishment of Bilateral Swap Arrangements (BSA) and the Repurchase Agreements (Repo) between ASEAN members and the plus three countries (Japan, China and South Korea) - constitute a remarkable progress for strengthening financial cooperation. It also provides a financial underpinning for East Asian economic integration. This self-help mechanism is expected to become an effective instrument to prevent and resolve economic and financial crisis in the future. These initiatives testify to the fact that East Asia has actively endeavored to establish a regional financial architecture, which is to supplement and complement the existing world architecture. Cambodia voices full support for the commitment and the initiatives to strengthen the East Asian cooperation in all fields, including political and security cooperation.

Third, we will also intensify our cooperative involvement within the framework of the Mekong River Commission (MRC) and Greater Mekong Sub-region (GMS) project. The two developments will have great repercussions for emerging economies in Southeast Asia. This kind of cooperation is very important and imperative for countries in the sub-region, since the Mekong River is the lifeblood of agriculture, inland fishery and river navigation in each country and the whole sub-region. Any development upstream might have far-reaching environmental and economic consequences on the downstream countries. Moreover, the development of the Greater Mekong Subregion (GMS) is instrumental for ASEAN, given its great potential for economic growth and development. In terms of geo-economics, the GMS is an important "economic gateway", linking Southeast Asia to China, a political and economic superpower in East Asia. More importantly GMS countries consist mainly of ASEAN new members with lower level of economic development, compared to more developed old members. This huge economic disparity is the main cause and impediments to regional economic integration. Therefore, concerted efforts in promoting the development in the GMS are the only effective resolution in addressing the problem of economic gaps within ASEAN and building up capacity of new member nations. This will remove the impediments to regional economic integration. In this spirit, I have proposed a number of initiatives to strengthen cooperation in the sub-region, especially the proposed establishment of a joint working group consisting of members from ASEAN countries, Republic of Korea, China, Japan, ADB, the Economic and Social Commission for Asia and the Pacific (ESCAP) and other donors to evaluate all existing initiatives, studies and projects and draw up a comprehensive, realistic master plan to set the direction for cooperation and development in the GMS over 20 to 25 years. At first, I believe that efforts should be geared toward developing a network of physical infrastructure linking regional countries and turning them into agricultural, industrial, trade and investment zones. Cambodia is ready to be fully involved in all these endeavors, aimed at turning the GMS from a region stricken by poverty to a center of prosperity in the 21st century. It is my conviction that the GMS deserves this and can materialize this aspiration.

Fourth, Cambodia will also strengthen its engagement with the international system through accession to the World Trade Organization (WTO), the Asia-Pacific Economic Cooperation (APEC) and the Asia-Europe Meeting (ASEM). APEC has grown into a very promising regional organization. It is not an economic grouping in the same mould as the European Union, the WTO or the North American Free Trade Area (NAFTA). It has elements of each of the above, yet has maintained its unique character and identity. APEC is often referred to as an "open economic association" or "open regionalism". It is open because it does not seek to discriminate against non-members. It is economic because it deals basically with economic growth, trade and investment. The recent Singapore ASEAN Informal Summit voiced support for Cambodia and other non-APEC members of ASEAN to participate in the APEC Working Group Meeting on Human Resource Development. Cambodia warmly welcomes this initiative. The Asia-Europe Meeting (ASEM) is also on our next agenda. Although ASEM is a consultative process and not a formal mechanism for cooperation, it provides an important forum for furthering relations between ASEAN and the European Union. It also brings added value to bilateral and multilateral arrangements. Cambodia continues to increase its international participation not least because discussions and rules on such issues as trade, foreign investment and the international financial architecture have implications for Cambodia's efforts to strengthen her national capacity for active involvement in the regional and worldwide cooperation. It also allows the country to share appropriately the win-win situation in the current wave of regionalism and globalization. Moreover, the engagement with the international system is the key to ensure that Cambodia is not excluded from such negotiations and cooperation because of lack of capacity or lack of access to negotiations.

Fifth, human resource development should play a key role in implementing the strategy for cooperation in East Asia. This is especially important for intra-ASEAN integration. At the Singapore Summit ASEAN leaders paid special attention to the problem of integrating the economies of the four new ASEAN members into ASEAN. In this regard, attention is given to human resource development based on the principle of "prospering your neighbors". Cambodia enthusiastically welcomes all initiatives that have been proposed in this area.

Sixth, the revolution in information technology and telecommunications has created a new development paradigm, which makes the economy to become digitalized and knowledge-based. The intellectual capital has become an important production factor in the 21st century. In this sense, highly qualified and skilled human resources are key to gaining competitive advantages in the newly structured world economy. We are therefore required to give high priority to the development of information and communications technology (ICT) and the use of Internet for conducting studies, research and training and to promote the use of English language to enable the Cambodian people to benefit from globalization and regionalism. In the regional framework, attention is given to these issues. At the recent ASEAN Informal Summit, the 10 ASEAN Heads of State and Government signed the E-ASEAN Framework Agreement, which we intend to use as our main instrument to bridge the digital divide in the region. Moreover, I believe that ASEAN should take advantage of all opportunities presented by Japan's initiative at the G-8 Summit in July 2000 to provide US$15 billion over the period of five years to assist developing countries in information technology and telecommunications. Particularly for Cambodia the priority areas for government interventions are to promote the learning of English and the use of Internet. Cambodia is prepared to take an active part in the work of the ASEAN + 3 Working Group on IT Development with a view to reducing the digital divide among countries in the region.

Cambodia also welcomes the initiative to establish a communication link among countries in East Asia, which ultimately connecting East Asia with Europe and America. It is my conviction that human resource development and the promotion of IT will help Cambodia reduce poverty, ameliorate the living standards of the people and enhance the country's capacity in engaging in the regional and world affairs, while boosting Cambodia's competitiveness in the current of globalization.

I have spent some time elaborating on some important issues relating to the government's visions, strategies and policies, which determine Cambodia's position in the regional and world affairs. I expect that the deliberations during this conference would contribute to promoting cooperation and creating a bright future for Asia. In this sense, I would like to wish for successful completion of this conference.

In conclusion, I would like to extend to Your Excellencies, Ladies and Gentlemen and all participants to this conference good health, success in your missions and happiness. I sincerely thank all of you for your attention.

STATEMENT BY SENIOR MINISTER HOR NAMHONG AT THE APAP SIEM REAP FORUM

Following is the integral text of a Statement by Senior Minister HOR Namhong, Minister of Foreign Affairs and International Cooperation, delivered on 28 February 2002 in Siem Reap:

Prof. Tadashi Yamamoto, President of the Japan Center for International Exchange,
Professor HAN SUNGJOO,
Distinguished Participants,
Ladies and Gentlemen,

1- I wish to take this opportunity to express my most sincere appreciation to the Japan Center for International Exchange (JCIE) and the Cambodian Institute for Cooperation and Peace (CICP) for inviting me to participate in this very important gathering of intellectuals from the Asia-Pacific region under the framework of the Asia-Pacific Agenda Project (APAP). I am deeply honored and pleased to be here and to share my view in the debate on the subject "Asia Pacific Regional and Global Order in the Post 9-11 World." I wish to congratulate the organizers for choosing this timely and relevant theme for the APAP Siem Reap Forum.

Impact of Terrorism

2- Since the tragic terrorist attacks on the United States in September 2001, there have been many discussions on various aspects related to terrorism, including root causes, strategies for combating terrorism, and implications of terrorism at national, regional and global levels. Certainly, besides the discussions, there have been military actions against Taliban and Al-Qaida network in Afghanistan, suppression of financing system of terrorism and the breakup of al-Qaida networks worldwide. The terrorist attacks on the United States have affected global peace and stability and have undoubtedly changed the conduct of international relations, especially the relationship between the major powers of the world.

3- There is no doubt that terrorists will continue to engage actions around the world; and many nations have, and will continue to engage in counter-terrorism actions. Discussions on various issues related to terrorism and counter-terrorism will also continue, as in the case of this APAP Siem Reap Forum. The intellectual exchange of views here in Siem Reap is very important for our region, as the notion of security has been more or less changed since the September 11 terrorist attacks on the U.S.

What Should Be Done to Fight Terrorism?

4- In this context, I wish to share with you some of my views on what I believe we should do together, regionally and internationally, in order to avoid further tragedies and violence. Given the far-reaching impacts of the September 11 terrorist attacks, not only on the United States but also on the world as a whole, fighting against terrorism need to be carried out in the form of global anti-terrorism against a globalized terrorism.

5- However, in order to be effective and meaningful in our cooperative efforts, we must have a comprehensive strategic approach in this fight against terrorism. In my view, military action is not the only viable option. One should look to other options, such as political, economic, social and cultural dimensions. In other words, we may need to understand the several root causes of terrorism. This approach is vital in mobilizing world opinions and global efforts against terrorism.

6- However, the difficult problem is how we can unanimously agree on what the terrorism is. Otherwise, there will be misunderstanding, misperception and suspicion in combating terrorism regionally and internationally. I believe that it should not be double standards in the fight against terrorism.

7- Moreover, we must understand that there is a need to distinguish between what is terrorism and what constitutes struggle for national salvation. It's obvious that a clear distinction between these two notions is important but sometimes difficult to make, because the concept and the policy framework to be conducted depend on this distinction.

8- In my view, to eliminate terrorism we must absolutely tackle its root causes. One of the root causes of terrorism that I strongly believe is the increasing poverty in the developing countries and the widening gap between the rich and the poor at national, regional, and global levels. Aggravated by the globalization, therefore, one way of eliminating the sources of terrorism is to fight poverty and promote development in those societies whose vulnerability is a source for terrorist networks recruitment.

9- In this regard, more efforts, and I mean international financial resources, should be spent on poverty reduction programs around the world. Therefore, promoting people's access to better living standard could significantly contribute to the fight against terrorism. In this sense, the realization of the U.N. Millennium Declaration in 2000 and the Commitments by the G8 leaders could help to bring about the success of the fight against poverty.

10- Another approach in addressing terrorism is to promote greater dialogue and communication across societies, nations, and regions. Constructive dialogue and effective communication could help prevent the terrorists from spreading and assist us to better contain it.

11- I also believe a win-win policy in combating terrorism at national, regional and international levels could be a solution to eliminate terrorism. In other words, there is no single approach to the fight against terrorism. We should explore all other possible options and attempt to bring all stakeholders on board in the crusade against global terrorism.

12- I am convinced that if there are no political and economic approaches in combating the root cause of terrorism, as I said earlier, there will be no global consensus on actions against terrorism today. I still believe that the success of military action in Afghanistan today will not be sustained over the terrorists and their al-Qaida networks worldwide, if we do not resort to other viable options.

13- In the face of the military action taken so far by the U.S., the terrorists may have taken only a concealment tactic for now. They may revive their actions some day when the situation is more favorable. In this regard, we should not be overconfident about the current military action against terrorism.

The Case of Cambodia

14- I wish to inform you that Cambodia has played its role in the fight against terrorism. In fact, Cambodia has been also victim of terrorist attacks as well, although at a much lesser level. As you may have been aware, Cambodia was attacked by a group of terrorists, the so-called Cambodian Freedom Fighters (CFF), in November 2000. The CFF is comprised of mainly Cambodians with American citizenship based in California. The CFF attacked the government buildings and killed a number of Cambodian police officers.

15- Since the 9-11 terrorist attacks, Cambodia has been fully cooperating with the United States in sharing information and intelligence, in controlling financial transactions which may lead to the terrorist networks, and in providing the US aircraft's access to our airspace in the performance of their mission in the region. Cambodia's commitment to combating terrorism has been unequivocally clear.

16- In addition, Cambodia had ratified four international conventions which are relevant to the fight against terrorism and signed one convention on suppressing the financing of terrorism. Cambodia is also in the process of acceding to seven other key international conventions, which are essential steps in combating terrorism not only in Cambodia but also in the region.

17- In my view, an overall Convention on terrorism derived from the World Summit organized by the United Nations, is absolutely necessary for the whole world to join hands and combat against terrorism.

The Role of ASEAN and the ARF in Combating Terrorism

18- I believe that both ASEAN and ARF could do more to play their meaningful role in the fight against terrorism both in the region and in the world. ASEAN has clearly condemned the 9-11 terrorist attacks on the United States, as specified in the Declaration on Combating Terrorism at the 7th ASEAN Summit in Brunei in November 2001. In addition, the ARF Chairman issued a statement in support of the fight against terrorism several weeks following the terrorist attacks on the United States. In December 2001, ASEAN and the United States held a bilateral dialogue in Washington, D.C., which entered mainly on the need to combat terrorism.

19- I wish also to inform you that at the ASEAN Foreign Ministers' Retreat in Phuket, on February 21, terrorism and the imperative of intensifying cooperation in the fight against terrorism is one of the topics of discussion. ASEAN is very much conscious of the fact that terrorism is a real threat to the region as a whole. We are also determined to deepen cooperation and reaffirm political commitment in the fight against terrorism. As I have said, terrorism is an international problem with globalized network. This means that to fight terrorism more effectively there is a need for a global approach.

20- I think that if even ASEAN is committed conscientiously to eliminate terrorism in the region, it will not be able to do it alone, because terrorism with its global network will threat the whole world and dictates subsequently the necessity of regional, inter-regional, and international cooperation.

21- Given the important role of the ARF in Asia-Pacific security policy, I think we need to strengthen our proactive actions among the ARF members. ARF should not rely on its current perception of security in Asia-Pacific. To be timely relevant in an increasing complicated regional and global security order prevailing in the world today, needs to strategically deal with a new concept of security policy in Asia-Pacific. Therefore, I believe that ARF cannot evolve in the future on the basis of its current perception, which is essentially relying on the phases of confidence-building measures, preventive diplomacy and approach to conflict resolution among Asia-Pacific nations, due to the increasing widespread problems of terrorism after September 11, 2001. This terrorist attacks had significantly changed the notion of security, making it more broadly defined and at the same time brought about fundamental changes in international relations.

CAMBODIA FIGHTS AGAINST TERRORISM

Following is the integral text of a report presented by the Kingdom of Cambodia to the Committee of the Security Council on the implementation of paragraph 6 of the Security Council Resolution 1373, dated 28 September 2001:

In accordance with the United Nations Security Council's Resolution 1368 (2001) of 12 September 2001 and 1373 (2001) of 28 September 2001, the Kingdom of Cambodia has been committed to work together with the international community to combat all acts of international terrorism.

Cambodia has been one of the victims of terrorism dedicated to upset peace and stability of the country and to the overthrow of the elected government. The recent terrorist attacks occurred on 24 November 2000 by a well-armed and foreign-funded group, which called themselves "Cambodian Freedom Fighters " or CFF.

Indeed, this terrorist group of about 100 men launched an attack in the evening of 24 November 2000 on the Ministry of Defense, the Council of Ministers which is the seat of the Royal Government and on other strategic locations of the capital city. It was fortunate that they caused few loss of life and minor damage to property. They were quickly rounded up and captured and put on trial. Some of the terrorists are still serving their prison terms. But their leaders escaped by crossing into neighboring countries and returned to their hometown in California-USA.

In the national front against terrorism, Cambodia adopted a law on the punishment of terrorism in 1992. In the international arena, Cambodia ratified a number of international conventions and protocol related to terrorism suppression such as:

1. Convention on Offences and Certain Other Acts Committed on Board Aircraft;
2. Convention for the Suppression of Unlawful Seizure of Aircraft;
3. Convention for the Suppression of Unlawful Acts against the Safety of Civil Aviation;
4. Protocol for the Suppression of Unlawful Acts of Violence at Airports Serving International Civil Aviation, Supplementary to the Convention for the?Suppression of Unlawful Acts against the safety of Civil Aviation,

Cambodia signed and is in the process of ratification of:

1. Convention for the suppression of the Financing of Terrorism.

Moreover, Cambodia is also in the process to accede to other anti-terrorism conventions such as:

1. Convention on the prevention and Punishment of Crimes against Internationally Protected Persons.
2. Convention against the Taking of Hostages.
3. Convention on the Physical Protection of Nuclear Material.
4. Convention for the Suppression of Unlawful Acts against the Safety of Maritime Navigation.
5. Protocol for the Suppression of Unlawful Acts against the Safety of Fixed Platforms Located on the Continental Shelf.
6. Convention on the Marking of Plastic Explosives for the purpose of Detection.
7. Convention for the Suppression of Terrorist Bombings.

The Royal Government of Cambodia extends its full cooperation to the international community to fight against international terrorism by whatever means at its disposal. In this regard, it provides flyover and landing facilities to U.S. Aircrafts in mission to fights international terrorism in the region.

Further more, the National Bank of Cambodia (NBC) has circulated nationwide the UN Security Council and the U.S. lists of individuals and entities involving in terrorism. The NBC has officially instructed all financial and banking institutions operational in Cambodia to scrutinize and freeze the assets of persons and entities whose names appeared on the above?mentioned lists. Up to this moment, there has been no evidence of financial linkage of those wanted entities and institutions. The NBC however continues to investigate and closely watch for financial elements and activities of any suspected terrorists. The NBC also issued orders prohibiting transactions with persons or entities considered as having committed or threatened to commit or having supported terrorism.

The National Police Authorities have also improved their surveillance system to crack down any terrorist activities.

Cambodia is a member of the International Police Forces (Interpol) and closely cooperates with other members of this Organization to fulfill its obligation, including the information sharing.

Cambodia is ready to cooperate further with the International community by all lawful means to fulfill its international obligation in the fight against terrorism and for the purpose of suppression of terrorist network.

Samdech Prime Minister's Comments on International Women's Day

Following is the integral text of Samdech Prime Minister's Comments on International Women's Day, delivered on 04 March 2002:

Please allow me to elaborate a bit out of the prepared speech. Just now Lok Chumteav Minister of Women and Veteran Affairs has expressed her thanks to men and on behalf of all the men here I wish to reciprocate in kind, including my dear wife. She is looking at the sentence written above: "Men saving women is like saving own selves" - by Samdech Prime Minister Hun Sen. Women and Men is an issue that one could not separate at all. We are all in a situation of interdependence between men and women.

Samdech Hun Sen and Madame pose for a photo with women on the celebration of the International Women's Day

I wish to offer my appreciation for the efforts made by HE Ministers, Secretaries of States as well as Under-State Secretaries in their work. In this new term of Government I have noticed a strong leadership of the Ministry of Women's Affairs. I welcome their efforts and their strivings to demand inclusion of gender principles in good governance matter.

May I give a recommendation on how to challenge with men in work. I have agreed already that the Ministry of Women's Affairs conducts discussions with related Ministries so that their agendas and objectives could be included in those ministries' five-year plan. I have approved in principle. What remains to be done is that each ministry takes actual step in incorporating the demands by the Ministry of Women's Affairs. Take for example, the constitution stipulates that the Cambodian children and citizens have to complete a nine-year education. So we have to invest in education. Of course we have activities in parallel to prevent household violence, trafficking of women and children.

Based on what is stipulated in the constitution, the Ministry of Education, and their provincial system has to work with the Ministry of Women's Affairs in drafting out a geography of education. We used to say about inequality between women and men, boys and girls. In most of my speeches in the last year, I have suggested that parents pay attention to their daughters because they would do for their sons. In fact the girl, especially if she is the eldest, would do a lot of work to assist the family, which ranges from kitchen stuff to taking care of younger ones. So it most likely that she is to drop school to help work at home and it is true that her brothers would go to school. This is the reality in our family life. This happens mostly in rural areas.

Why do I talk about geography for education? Because if the girl students finished their 06-year study in the primary education, and if the junior high school is far away from residence, it is very likely that their parents would bar them from continuing their studies. Therefore the rate of school dropout after completion of primary education is high. So it is seen as a solution to bring the junior secondary education closer to the community. This would in anyway respond to what has been stipulated in the constitution. This should help bring down the number of school dropout among the girls.

Looking at the gap between the number of girls knowing how to read and write and those of boys, I am still keeping my thought of building a hostel for girl students in post higher education and higher education so that their number could be increased in the tertiary education. As of now we have some women in the Senate, the National Assembly and the Royal Government. So help me to plan a strategy that would solve this problem because as long as our women are illiterate, the infringement of their rights is there.

In the communal election, 900 out of 12,000 women candidates have been voted in the commune councils. These 900 women are a commencing figure. They would have higher percentage if their names are moved upwards on the list. I hope that in the next election they move women candidate upward in the list. Anyhow this number of women in the commune councils is a great success and it clearly indicates the efforts pooled by women in the state institutions as well as in the civil society. We must nurture this path.

The Royal Government considers investment in health helpful in reducing the mortal rate of women and children. So
HE Minister of Women Affairs should sound out whatever sector you wish to have collaboration I will offer my support in the move to incorporate gender concepts in those demanded institutions. Like in the process of making women heads of the water use groups, it is the best decision. Women know the problem better than men. Take for instance in the boat race season, men are out boating while women are staying home and doing double duties. So care and consideration should be taken in offering women leading roles to any communities to be set up at the local level. Already implemented were community of water use and management, village development, fishing, etc. I would see that women are more capable in rural credit in the future.

Address by Samdech Prime Minister to the Fourth Government-Private Sector Forum

Following is the integral text delivered by Samdech Prime Minister HUN Sen at " the Fourth Government-Private Sector Forum":

Excellencies,
Ladies and Gentlemen,

It is a great honor and pleasure for me to be here with you at the third Government-Private Sector Forum, held as we have agreed during the last meeting. We are gathering here at the time when a synchronized worldwide recession has become a serious danger. The US economy is still sluggish and showed no signs of an imminent rebound. Japan's economy is already in the doldrums, while Europe's slow growth could get slower and a financial crisis is threatening Argentina and possibly other nations in Latin America. In Asia only China is doing quite well. But other regional economies are being badly affected by the slowdown in the high-tech industry and the dot.com meltdown. The current situation has an impact on investment decisions worldwide.

The Cambodian economy has experienced an upward growth momentum, which runs counter to the slowdown observed throughout Southeast Asia. Our country has been undergoing a period of accelerated transformation and reforms. The main thrust of the implementation of the financial reform package in 2001 focused on maintaining macroeconomic stability, strengthening the banking and financial institutions, implementing additional fiscal reform measures, ensuring a sound management of public property and increasing public investment in physical and social infrastructure and human resource development. While the results of these reforms are now tangible, they are far from complete. Moreover, much remains to be done to allow reforms to take a firmer root. It may take another three years of strict implementation of the reform programs as scheduled to put Cambodia firmly on the track of sustainable growth and poverty reduction.

The restructuring and adjustment that we have put in place and actively implemented are now starting to pay off. Performance of the Cambodian economy in 2000 and the first half of 2001 is strong, with continued growth, low inflation, and further progress in the areas of fiscal reforms. Economic activity was buoyed by good performance especially in the tourism sectors. The manufacturing sector, particularly the garment industry, had displayed a strong dynamism, albeit the slowdown of the US economy has resulted in the drop in garment orders, thus negatively affecting Cambodian exports in 2001. Hence, diversification is critical to improving the health of our economy by encouraging other export-oriented, natural-resource-based and tourism-related industries, which Cambodia has a great potential. It is also crucial at the initial stage of development to gear the industrial development policies to build on the country's comparative advantages by developing natural factor of production, including natural resources, historical assets, arts and culture, physical heritage, skilled labor and entrepreneurship of the people. At the same time, Cambodia should strive to attract, as much as possible, the investment relocation from neighboring countries in the region, which have graduated from the GSP program with developed countries, while attaining a higher degree of development. With the efforts to develop physical infrastructure and the increase in skilled labor, Cambodia's industry can progressively move towards more technologically-sophisticated and capital- using activities.

At present, a number of companies have used computers, the English language and the Internet to create employment in Cambodia. This signals Cambodia's possible entry into a world of new development paradigm, where private companies could use English language, the Internet and the computer skills of Cambodia's ambitious and yearning youth to provide basic information services to US and Canadian corporations. At the same time, I urge the Ministry of Education, Youth and Sports and relevant government ministries to closely cooperate with the private sector to reset the directions of training, especially by developing good curricula for general education, language and basic skill training in response to market demand.

One of Cambodia's biggest challenges is to provide training that meets market demand. Even though during the past decade the Royal Government of Cambodia (RGC) has opened up education for the private sector's participation, Cambodia is still being considered as lacking skilled labor. Therefore, the RGC will make further efforts to reform the education system, both public and private, by focusing on vocational training and developing appropriate curriculum. This will help investors secure skilled labor, while providing well-trained youth to find relevant jobs. I am confident that all investors should play an active part in this important endeavor.

The drop in new investment approval by the Council for the Development of Cambodia (CDC) is worrisome for all of us. In 2000, a total of 96 investment projects with US$269 million fixed assets were approved, a decline by 40 percent as compared to 1999. During the first half of 2001, 27 investment projects were approved with US$56 million in fixed assets, a further decline by 36 percent, compared to the first half of 2000. We have however noticed that expansion of old projects and investments in tourism-related sector, such as expansion of the airport and hotel construction in Siem Reap, are still vibrant. Overall, even though the new investment approvals decreased, FDI inflows into Cambodia were estimated at US$150 million per annum. Moreover, total investment consisting of FDI and domestically funded private investments, which are not reflected in the CDC figures, did not drop, but increased by 7 percent in 2000 compared to 1999.

Nevertheless, what is the signal for Cambodia? Even though Cambodia can secure sustainable development over the short to medium term, with the increase in public investment and ODA inflows, the declining FDI poses a serious concern for the prospect of economic growth over the long term. Indeed, the decline does not happen only in Cambodia. The drop in new investment approvals can be observed throughout Southeast Asia, which has experienced a net outflow of funds. Net FDI outflows from Singapore alone were US$10 billion in 2000. But China could attract US$40 billion last year, buoyed by the prospect of the country's accession to the WTO and investors' rush to get a share of this huge market. Nevertheless, this should not be used as a pretext to circumvent our efforts to improve the investment and business climate in the Kingdom of Cambodia. Attracting and promoting investments, both domestic and foreign, is a pre-requisite to achieving sustainable development and poverty reduction.

In this sense, I would like to turn this Government-Private sector forum into a brainstorming session on how to make Cambodia attractive to investments. The RGC recognizes that improving the business climate and establishing an enabling environment for private sector development is a key prerequisite for fostering growth-reducing poverty and achieving sustainable economic development. The RGC recognizes that there is somewhat of a herd effect with would-be investors following where others are already operating successfully. This is the reason why that as the Head of the Government I pay much attention to improving business environment for the existing investors. This is the reason why the seven, sectoral, joint Working Groups with the private sector were established and meet on a regular basis in order to improve investment environment and address investors' concerns. The RGC hopes that this initiative will allow private sector's effective participation in the efforts to improve the quality of policy making with respect to investment and to ensure its consistency. In this sense, policies with respect to the private sector should be based on the following:

First, supporting the massive small and medium enterprises (SMEs) and the unrecorded economy; and

Second, promoting and facilitating big investors.

The SMEs and the informal, unrecorded sector play an increasingly important role in the Cambodian economy, creating substantial employment for Cambodia's poor. The lack of credit for establishing new or expanding the existing enterprises is currently one of the biggest challenges. Hence, as the Head of Government I urge the Rural Development Bank to conduct a study as soon as possible on fostering cooperation between commercial and specialized banks and microfinance operators, which are capable of providing loans to small and medium enterprises (SMEs) and the small-scaled, unrecorded sector involving in rice milling, food processing, animal feed production, furniture-making and handicraft production, which are important sources of revenue generation for the poor.

At this morning's meeting, apart from listening to the presentations by the representatives of the seven working groups, I wish to set the tone and the direction of the discussions during this forum and within the working groups, which are operational between the fora. I would like to take this opportunity to consider together how best we - government and the private sector -could do to improve the regulatory and legal regime and ensure a level playing field for both existing and prospective investors, whether domestic or foreign. I understand that the private sector has aired their concerns and made suggestions to relevant government bodies through our joint working groups to ensure an equitable and fair treatment, as well as fair competition.

In this sense, the RGC has a role to play to ensure free, fair and transparent competition. In this regard, it is important to have an Accounting Law and an Audit Law applicable for private firms based on international standards. This law should ensure transparent operations, and fair and equitable distribution of tax burdens on private companies. In this sense, the RGC has encouraged thorough discussions of this draft law with wide participation from experts, the private sector and regulators, especially within the framework of the Working Group on Legislation, Tax, Governance and SMEs. It was a time consuming process, but it ensures that the job was well done, thus facilitating smooth implementation.

Most investors have expressed their legitimate concerns with regard to the proposed amendment to the Law on Investment, which will impose on investment firms appropriate tax burdens, used to finance government's efforts to upgrade the physical infrastructure, in exchange for improved governance, facilitation and services. The later includes streamlining of bureaucratic red tapes and irrelevant procedures, improved customs and tax administration and eradication of corruption, for which the RGC needs resources and time to do. It is true that sometimes it is very difficult to weigh between immediate costs and future benefits.

You may have seen that the RGC has taken very seriously the problems facing the private investment sector and businesses, such as:

i. high operating costs, in part brought about by poor infrastructure and overpriced utility services;

ii. excessive layers of bureaucracy that add to production costs and introduce uncertainty;

iii. 'hidden' transaction costs and smuggling -a heavy burden for investors and business people; and

iv. a lack of transparency and accountability, especially a sound legal and regulatory framework.

Though most problems are long-term in nature, thus time is needed to address all the impediments. With strong determination, the RGC has achieved encouraging results. In my address to the third forum, I elaborated on government's efforts to rehabilitate the country's infrastructure and measures to reduce electricity and telephone tariffs. There is a progress in this area. Road and bridge infrastructure has been rehabilitated. The telephone tariffs were reduced. The RGC has made massive investments in the electrical power sector with improved institutional capacity. This has been done to facilitate and promote economic activities and investments in Cambodia. The RGC needs substantial financial resources to rehabilitate, build and maintain these works. In this sense, the RGC relies on active and appropriate participation of the private sector in this endeavor.

At the same time, the RGC recognizes that much remains to be done, especially those related to governance. To this end, we have adopted and implemented with strong determination the Governance Action Plan (GAP), aimed at improving the efficiency of public services, ensuring transparency and predictability of the public services. In this context, the RGC is implementing a US$6 million Strengthening the Economic and Financial Management Project by closely cooperating with the international financial institutions and a number of donors in order to accelerate the reforms, strengthen customs and tax administration, and public expenditure and treasury management. The objectives of this project also include expanding the tax base and establishing an equitable and modern tax system. Overall, the RGC will make further efforts to implement the four- pronged reform package with a view to creating an enabling environment for private sector development.

Nevertheless, I wish to clarify the main principles for the review of the Law on Investment.

First, it will be proposed as a package, which offers investment facilitation and the review of tax incentives;

Second, the review of tax incentives will be carried out with caution to a certain degree that ensures a transparent, fair and equitable treatment, acceptable to all and without discrimination. This is the most important factor, which maintains Cambodia's attractiveness as compared to countries in the region.

Third, the RGC will continue intensive consultations with the private sector and other players concerned with the review of this Law on Investment.

Excellencies,
Ladies and Gentlemen,

One cannot talk about improving the legal and regulator framework for investment without reforming the Council for the Development of Cambodia (CDC). In this sense, I signed on 27th July a subdecree to strengthen the organization and the functioning of the CDC by appointing the Minister of Commerce as another CDC Vice Chairman and expanding the composition of the CDC to include representatives from all government ministries, agencies and provincial/municipal governors. The main objectives of this restructuring are to enhance the one-stop shop for investment by expanding the scope of this coordination to the provinces and municipalities, where investment projects are being implemented. Moreover, it will ensure a close coordination between policies and strategies on trade, industry and investment, including the establishment of a Free Trade Area, an Export Processing Zone and a Special Industrial Zone. It also reflects government's strategy to link investment to exports, which have played a critical role in employment creation for our population and accelerating economic growth.

Within the context of the restructuring, the CDC should organize a workshop with the participation of representatives from all government ministries and agencies, as well as provincial/municipal governors -members of the CDC to raise awareness and facilitate investments in Cambodia. The government's philosophy with regard to investment is facilitation and provision of all kinds of services to investors at all stages. Using commercial and marketing terms we should provide investors with the after-sale and after-care services. Thus, I urge the CDC to pay attention to this new concept, redirect and re-adjust its own mechanism, structure and workplace to strengthen efficiency. As H.E. KEAT CHHON, Chairman of the Council for the Development of Cambodia (CDC), has stated in his address to the forum, the efforts deployed by the RGC, especially the CDC, are geared to improving the legal and regulatory framework and procedures to strengthening the government's institutional capacity. This is to promote and facilitate investment and business activities in the Kingdom of Cambodia in line with this philosophy. From this report I have noticed that all working groups have met regularly and have made some positive results. I strongly hope that through this close cooperation a wise partnership between the government and the private sector will be further strengthened.

Today I want to talk less, but to listen more. Thus, I think that it is time to give you the floor so that you can air in a frank and candid manner your grievances, concerns and suggestions, so as to help the RGC to re-shape policies and improve further the business environment in this country.

I encourage all my colleagues in the government present here and the representatives of the private sector to continue our good tradition of close partnership and to discuss in an open and candid manner all issues and challenges, and explore ways to establish favorable conditions to attract investments to Cambodia.

My colleagues and I will be happy to answer to your questions and provide comments on any issues that have been your concerns or that you consider as impediments to doing business or undertaking investments in Cambodia. As in previous fora, most members of the RGC, senior officials and provincial/municipal governors are in attendance. Thus, I will consider the decision to be made today as those made legally made during the Cabinet meeting and the meeting of the CDC.I would like to sincerely thank you all for your kind attention.

SAMDECH HUN SEN ADDRESSES FORUM FOR DISSEMINATION OF GOVERNANCE ACTION PLAN AND PUBLIC ADMINISTRATION REFORM

Following is the integral text of an opening address delivered on 11 December 2001, by Samdech HUN Sen, Prime Minister and Chairman of the Supreme Council for State Reform, to the Forum for Dissemination of the Governance Action Plan and the Public Administration Reform :

Excellencies, distinguished representatives of the donor community,
Excellencies members of the Royal Government,
Excellencies, Ladies and Gentlemen,

First of all, I am pleased to extend a warm welcome to all of you today at the forum for dissemination of the Governance Action Plan (GAP) and the Public Administration Reform (PAR).

After the Consultative Group (CG) Meeting held in June 2001 in Tokyo, the Royal Government of Cambodia (RGC) has taken serious strides to rigorously implement all reform programs, especially to strengthen governance, which constitutes the backbone of its reform programs with the view to achieving sustainable development and rapid alleviation of poverty. The RGC has actively implemented actions to strengthen governance as specified in the GAP, as it strongly believes that good governance is the prerequisite to sustainable socio-economic development and social justice. This is crucial for ensuring that the fruits of economic growth, which has been achieved through considerable efforts and hardship, will trickle down to all social strata of Cambodia.

The GAP identifies two categories of governance reform where action will be critical to Cambodia's development over the near- and the medium-term. The first category involves four cross-cutting areas:

First, Legal and judicial reforms: improving the legislative process, promoting dissemination of laws and regulations, developing a legal framework for private sector, developing human and material resources and infrastructure, enhancing the integrity of the judiciary and meeting private sector's needs for the arbitration of commercial disputes.

The RGC recognizes that there is a significant correlation between effective legal and judicial systems and sustainable economic growth. Legal and judicial change is necessary to support the evolutionary process of social and economic change. The legal systems should be adjusted to support our new economic strategy. Experiences of developed countries in the world have shown that the market economy cannot be developed without adequate legal underpinnings. Our efforts therefore are being concentrated on putting in place basic elements of the legal framework to underpin the development of a vibrant market economy - laws on property, the creation and winding-up of business entities, contract and a fair marketplace, banking, tax, accounting and audit. Moreover, since it is necessary to create and ensure a favorable environment for private sector development, the RGC strives to create and enforce a transparent legal framework with clear rules of the game for eventual dispute resolution.

Second, *public finance*: streamlining customs control, combat smuggling, developing a modern customs administration, improving VAT refunds, developing a regulatory framework for tax on profits, undertaking a comprehensive reform of investment incentives, ensuring integrity of the budgetary process, improving performance of spending units and strengthening the public investment management program.

The RGC has continued to rigorously implement economic and fiscal reforms with the view to strengthening macroeconomic stability by ensuring sustainable economic growth, keeping inflation at a low level, maintaining a stable exchange rate and increasing the international reserves of the banking system. Strengthening governance in public finance will encourage strict respect for budgetary discipline, enhance revenue collection and increase the efficiency and rationalization of expenditure. This is crucial for strengthening the foundation for sustainable economic growth and for Cambodia's decisive march towards eternal peace and lasting progress. To this end, it is important to promote gradual poverty reduction, developing democracy and promoting the respect for human rights.

Third, *civil administration reform*: rationalization of employment structure, review of remuneration and establishment of management system, enhancing productivity and motivation, reinforcing transparency and participation, ensuring a close link between administrative and financial decentralization and developing human managerial and human resources at the municipal, provincial, district and commune levels.

The RGC clearly understand that successful implementation of the reform programs in all fields depends on institutional capacity, which can be assured through public administration reform and increasingly efficient public service delivery. The development of highly skilled human resources is not sufficient for strengthening institutional capacity. It is important to establish a viable mechanism to ensure efficient utilization of these valuable resources. I however have observed that both the government agencies and the partners from the donor community have not thoroughly considered and have not given due priority to use our scarce human resources as efficient and reasonable as possible.

In administrative reform, the RGC has shifted from a centralized to a decentralized management system by introducing technical devolution of power from the central to the local levels, enhancing democracy, strengthening public services, increasing public participation in management and development process, especially promoting the status and role of women at the local level. In the Interim Poverty Reduction Strategy Paper (IPRSP) the RGC has highlighted these factors, which would ensure social cohesion and sustainable economic growth. These are the ingredients for achieving government's strategy of poverty reduction. Moreover, the government is not only concerned about the rate of growth, but also the quality of economic growth. The later can be achieved through growth with equity, the respect for the dignity and the basic rights of people from all walks of life, narrowing the gaps between the rich and the poor, promoting the status of women and strengthening democracy.

Fourth, *anti-corruption:* setting ethical standards for political appointees and civil servants, enacting special anti-corruption legislation, enforcing the sub-decree on public procurement and strengthening enforcement and scrutiny. The RGC recognizes that without credible actions in these areas, the basic virtues of good governance will not take hold in Cambodia. Indeed, while pushing for the implementation of these measures, we cannot cut off from the situation and the reality of Cambodia.

In addition to these cross-cutting issue areas, the RGC has identified two specific policy issues on which governance reforms must be implemented:

The first is natural resource management, including land management and forestry management. Fair resolution of land disputes is essential to peace, social stability and environmental sustainability, which are, in turn, fundamental to poverty reduction and sustainable social and economic development. The RGC considers the protection and conservation of the environment and natural resources as the main parts of its strategy for promoting sustainable development and combating poverty of the Cambodian people. To ensure the efficiency and sustainability of environmental protection, we must double our efforts to develop legal and regulatory framework and strengthen institutional capacity in this sector.

Second, the other policy issue is demobilization of the armed forces. The objectives are to transfer non-productive resources to the priority sector by transforming all demobilized soldiers into productive forces. This would have positive impact on economic development and poverty reduction in Cambodia. Therefore, the demobilization program would create favorable conditions for the government to implement the public expenditure reform, which will focus on shifting investment priorities to physical infrastructure and social and economic sectors, such as education, health, agriculture and rural development with the view to creating a socially connected, educationally advanced, and culturally vibrant society in Cambodia. This is a " New Social Policy Agenda " adopted by the government in order to liberate the majority of our people from the shackles of poverty, illiteracy, and disease.

This is our first meeting to disseminate the GAP and it is also an opportunity to do joint stock-taking of government's tremendous efforts over the past years to implement this action plan. In this sense, I am confident that the members of the RGC, governors and deputy governors, government officials and representatives of all categories of the armed forces would be able to draw on the best experiences and lessons from the way the RGC has implemented GAP and determine the strengths and weaknesses, share with us what is difficult and what is easy to do in implementing the GAP. This will allow us to take new measures to boost the momentum that has been successfully established.

Today's program is entirely for the Royal Government. It is a testimony to the fact that we own our reforms, which are a life and death issue for Cambodia. We will spend the whole day discussing these matters in the presence of the members of the Royal Government, provincial governors and deputy governors, senior government officials and will listen to their views and comments. The presentation on "Decentralization and the Commune Elections" will be delivered by H.E. Sar Kheng, Deputy Prime Minister, Co-Minister for Interior and Deputy Chair of the Supreme Council for State Reform. This will be followed by a presentation on the "Concepts, Achievements and Implementation of the Governance Action Plan" to be made by H.E. Sok An, Senior Minister, Minister for the Council of Ministers, Permanent Member of the Supreme Council for State Reform and Chair of the Council for Administrative Reform. H.E. Sok An will also sum up today's discussions. H.E. Keat Chhon, Senior Minister, Minister of Economy and Finance, will address the issues of "Fiscal Policies and Reforms within the Context of Good Governance". H.E. Im Chhun Lim, Minister of Land Management, Urbanization and Construction, will make a presentation on "Governance-related Land Policy". H.E. Chhay Than, Minister of Planning and Chair of the Council for Social Development, will touch upon the "Social Development Policy within the Context of Good Governance". And H.E. Sum Manith, Secretary of State of the Council of Ministers and Secretary General of the Council for Administrative Reform, will make a presentation on the "Strategy to Combat Corruption".

I urge all colleagues from the Government and senior government officials to discuss frankly and candidly the issues and challenges facing our reform and good governance. I welcome any good ideas and suggestions, aimed at directing and moving Cambodia forwards to a bright future through poverty alleviation and sustainable development. I wish successful discussions at this forum to disseminate the Governance Action Plan and the Public Administration Reform.

SAMDECH HUN SEN'S ADDRESS AT THE OPENING CEREMONY OF THE WORKSHOP ON PUBLIC AWARENESS ABOUT INFORMATION TECHNOLOGY

Following is the integral text of an Address delivered on 11 September 2001 by Samdech Prime Minister HUN Sen at the Opening Ceremony of the Workshop on Public Awareness about Information Technology:

Excellencies,
Ladies and Gentlemen,

It is a great pleasure for me to attend the workshop on Public Awareness about Information Technology, which is being held during the next three days. I would like to express my sincere appreciation to the National Authority for Information Technology for organizing this seminar, while efforts are being deployed by the Royal Government of Cambodia (RGC) formulate policies and strategies aimed at reducing a digital divide between Cambodia and the region and the rest of the world in order to promote poverty alleviation and sustainable development and to reap appropriate benefits from globalization. I also take this opportunity to sincerely thank UNESCO, UNDP, IBM, Mobitel and Big Pond for their assistance in organizing this seminar to raise public awareness about the benefits of information technology (IT) in our day-to-day life, management and business, as well as the need for the introduction of IT in government business.

This conference on IT Awareness is of great significance, since it is a timely response to the immediate needs and requirements of Cambodia and helps the country to bring about the introduction of IT in all sectors, to join the bandwagon of development and to catch up with the region and the world. To this end, an Authority was established to consider the benefits and implications of IT use and to study and establish appropriate institutional organization to meet Cambodia's current conditions. Its objectives also include human resource training, introduction of international standards and the establishment of a sound legal and regulatory framework. At the same time, I am confident that the papers to be presented by all presenters and the brainstorming on each topic will become a comprehensive database, information and a strong foundation for the development of a vision for the IT development. This will play a key role in building up Cambodia comparative advantages in the world of globalization.

Taking this rare opportunity, may I share with you all my own views, which hopefully could be instrumental in developing the vision of IT development in Cambodia.

If we look beyond the horizon towards a future, we can see that at the dawn of the new millennium the world is moving very fast, fuelled by globalization, towards a new, unfettered IT development. The miraculous development of new high tech and computers has shortened the distance of the world and is giving way to the emergence of a new, digitalized and knowledge-based economy. Information, broadcasting and telecommunications have increasingly become an important factor, which underpins the development of human civilization. Relationships and exchange between communities and countries on arts, culture, politics and scientific achievements are conducted by using the state-of-the-art telecommunications. The radio, national and international TV networks, and the Internet are being recognized as the most efficient communication medium, which speed up the dissemination of information. The use of multi-media technology and IT has become an imperative and a large number of countries have used these technological achievements to facilitate business, commensurably with the pace and the magnitude of market operations.

Therefore, technological revolution has rapidly changed the world. Transactions are being made on-line. Almost all products and services, including banking, consultant and accounting services, can be purchased on line using the Internet. Moreover, the current state of technology allows us to codify knowledge and know-how and transfer them through e-mail, fax or the Internet. Thus, almost all human beings in the world can obtain assets, goods, services and resources almost at the same time from different places. In this context, electronic commerce has emerged as a dynamic, modern form of transactions, which has received adequate attention, especially from the World Trade

Organization (WTO). E-commerce has become one of the most important forms of cooperation in ASEAN.

At the ASEAN plus three Summit Meeting held in Singapore, on 28 November 2000, I stated that the world has recognized that in the current of globalization concerted efforts to reduce the digital divide is key to poverty alleviation, improvement in people's well-beings and the strengthening of each nation's comparative advantages in order to promote sustainable development. The development of IT and telecommunications has an important role to play in this process. Then, I welcome and voiced a strong support for Japan's initiative at the G-8 Summit in July 2000 to provide US$15 billion over the period of five years to assist developing countries in information and telecommunications technology. Moreover, within the ASEAN framework, all members are in the process of implementing ASEAN IT development projects, such as the E-ASEAN project and the projects to build up IT capacity for new members.

This shift in the development paradigm imposes a new development scenario for Cambodia. In the long run, key factors of production will shift from land and natural resources to information, knowledge and innovation embodied in Cambodia's human capital. In other words, knowledge, skills and expertise of the Cambodian people will become increasingly crucial to the country's future economic growth. Extensive economic growth and development will be gradually giving way to intensive economic growth. This type of growth requires more added values from ideas and innovation. Cambodia should not be marginalized from the development of human civilization. Thus, the RGC has endeavored to promote the use of modern technology in Cambodia's e-mail systems to enable the country to respond to the current needs in all sectors, especially to the development of e-commerce.

However, the government's top priority is to use IT to serve and to meet the day-to-day needs of the people. IT should become as an efficient means for the public to exercise their rights to get information related to the decisions made by the government and the conduct of government business in accordance with the principles of transparency and good governance. In the long run, the introduction of decentralization and deconcentration as part of the government's administrative reform efforts will require the increasing use of IT to link the communes and local communities with Phnom Penh with a view to promoting efficient management and facilitating timely exchange of necessary information. Thus, from the point of view of the political and administrative aspects, IT will help strengthen democracy, ensure transparency, promote good governance in government and community businesses. With regard to the economic and social aspect, IT will improve major public service delivery to the local people and allow them to monitor and receive regularly and timely all kinds of information, especially the necessary information about the markets, which will facilitate their economic decision making.

The experiences of many neighboring countries show that human resource development is key to promoting IT developments. IT development should be linked to the increase in labor productivity and the knowledge of the people, the transfer of expertise and technology, diversity and access by the people to health care and education, the development of entrepreneurship and the accumulation of new cultural assets.

To achieve the above objectives, Cambodia needs a long-term IT development strategy, which responds to the realities of the country, the changes and new developments in regional and world economies. This vision should be supported by a detailed action plan for implementation. The common vision for IT development, with all the supporting policies, strategies and multi-discipline measures to be elaborated by the government, as well as concrete actions being undertaken at the national level, should guide Cambodia towards a bright future, strengthen the culture of peace, promote virtues, knowledge and living standards of our people, and more importantly Cambodia's prestige in the international arena.
As the Head of the Government and as a Cambodian, I wish to make a humble contribution to the development of this vision by drawing your attention to the following:

First, the sine qua non conditions for the increased use of IT is the development of telecommunication infrastructures through the policy of liberalization, strengthening the authority responsible for the supervision and regulation and open access to instill fair competition. In this sense, attention has been given by the RGC to formulate policies and establish a legal and regulatory framework for the development of the telecommunication sector. At the same time, the RGC is committed to provide incentives to attract investments in the telecommunications sector. As a result, Cambodia is being recognized as a country with the state-of-the-art telecommunication network, which will pave the way for further development of the sector. Nevertheless, much more remained to be done with our partners to ensure that Cambodia will not be marginalized from the telecommunication and IT revolution.

Second, expanding the coverage for the use of the Internet by considering measures to attract private investments and modern technology, and by ensuring free and fair, market-based competition. This will create necessary conditions for cost reduction, improvement in public services, so that the government, the private sector, the educational and research universities and the Cambodian people in general will be able to use of this instrument as efficient as possible.

Third, Language is an important vehicle to promote development and IT transfer. The use of IT in Khmer language will open access to millions of people who will be able to benefit from these technological developments. Therefore, standardization of Khmer language in computers will improve efficiency and capability of this sector and facilitate communications at all levels. I suggest to the Authority for ICT Development to pay considerable and immediate attention to this problem. Nevertheless, improvement in English language is of critical importance in terms of acquiring and deepening IT knowledge. To become competitive in the future within the context of ASEAN and globalization we should promote English as the second or working language of Cambodia, while Khmer langue should always be Cambodia's official language. In general, I support the idea that every Cambodian should know at least four languages (Khmer, English, French and a language of one of the countries of East Asia). In the future, language skills will become an important comparative advantage for Cambodia.

Fourth, computer literacy, as is the case with foreign languages, must be promoted among Cambodians. Computer literacy is currently one of the most important tools that exist for communications, economic management, trade, domestic and international investment, as well as for knowledge accumulation and management expertise. This is true for every country in the world, and Cambodia is no exception to this. The most important direction is to include computer literacy in the curriculum of every secondary school, faculty and university throughout Cambodia.

Fifth, continuous efforts should be given to promote the activities and encourage the participation of the private sector in IT development. This is also related to government's policies to ensure the sound management of foreign direct investment. It should provide sufficient incentives for companies to transfer to Cambodia technical skills and new technology for the country's development while at the same time allowing other companies and individuals to access the ideas that flow from the research.

Sixth, attention should be given to protect intellectual capital and use the Internet for development purposes by preventing the use of such technology for committing crimes or other purposes, which are contrary to morality, traditions and good mores of the society.

These are the main elements of our strategy, which should be taken into account while considering the preparation of a long-term vision for IT development in Cambodia. In all these endeavors, human resource and effective and efficient use of these resources are the key to success. I am confident that this conference will provide opportunity for lively discussions on this very important topic and contribute in a concrete and substantial manner to raise public awareness and formulate a vision for IT development in Cambodia.

In concluding, I would like to extend to you all, Excellencies, Ladies and Gentlemen, as well as all participants, a success and prosperity in all your endeavors. I would like to declare that the *"workshop on Public Awareness about Information Technology".*

ADDRESS BY SAMDECH PRIME MINISTER TO THE FOURTH GOVERNMENT-PRIVATE SECTOR FORUM

Following is the integral text delivered by Samdech Prime Minister HUN Sen at " the Fourth Government-Private Sector Forum":

Excellencies,
Ladies and Gentlemen,

It is a great honor and pleasure for me to be here with you at the third Government-Private Sector Forum, held as we have agreed during the last meeting. We are gathering here at the time when a synchronized worldwide recession has become a serious danger. The US economy is still sluggish and showed no signs of an imminent rebound. Japan's economy is already in the doldrums, while Europe's slow growth could get slower and a financial crisis is threatening Argentina and possibly other nations in Latin America. In Asia only China is doing quite well. But other regional economies are being badly affected by the slowdown in the high-tech industry and the dot.com meltdown. The current situation has an impact on investment decisions worldwide.

The Cambodian economy has experienced an upward growth momentum, which runs counter to the slowdown observed throughout Southeast Asia. Our country has been undergoing a period of accelerated transformation and reforms. The main thrust of the implementation of the financial reform package in 2001 focused on maintaining macroeconomic stability, strengthening the banking and financial institutions, implementing additional fiscal reform measures, ensuring a sound management of public property and increasing public investment in physical and social infrastructure and human resource development. While the results of these reforms are now tangible, they are far from complete. Moreover, much remains to be done to allow reforms to take a firmer root. It may take another three years of strict implementation of the reform programs as scheduled to put Cambodia firmly on the track of sustainable growth and poverty reduction.

The restructuring and adjustment that we have put in place and actively implemented are now starting to pay off. Performance of the Cambodian economy in 2000 and the first half of 2001 is strong, with continued growth, low inflation, and further progress in the areas of fiscal reforms. Economic activity was buoyed by good performance especially in the tourism sectors. The manufacturing sector, particularly the garment industry, had displayed a strong dynamism, albeit the slowdown of the US economy has resulted in the drop in garment orders, thus negatively affecting Cambodian exports in 2001. Hence, diversification is critical to improving the health of our economy by encouraging other export-oriented, natural-resource-based and tourism-related industries, which Cambodia has a great potential. It is also crucial at the initial stage of development to gear the industrial development policies to build on the country's comparative advantages by developing natural factor of production, including natural resources, historical assets, arts and culture, physical heritage, skilled labor and entrepreneurship of the people. At the same time, Cambodia should strive to attract, as much as possible, the investment relocation from neighboring countries in the region, which have graduated from the GSP program with developed countries, while attaining a higher degree of development. With the efforts to develop physical infrastructure and the increase in skilled labor, Cambodia's industry can progressively move towards more technologically-sophisticated and capital- using activities.

At present, a number of companies have used computers, the English language and the Internet to create employment in Cambodia. This signals Cambodia's possible entry into a world of new development paradigm, where private companies could use English language, the Internet and the computer skills of Cambodia's ambitious and yearning youth to provide basic information services to US and Canadian corporations. At the same time, I urge the Ministry of Education, Youth and Sports and relevant government ministries to closely cooperate with the private sector to reset the directions of training, especially by developing good curricula for general education, language and basic skill training in response to market demand.

One of Cambodia's biggest challenges is to provide training that meets market demand. Even though during the past decade the Royal Government of Cambodia (RGC) has opened up education for the private sector's participation, Cambodia is still being considered as lacking skilled labor. Therefore, the RGC will make further efforts to reform the education system, both public and private, by focusing on vocational training and developing appropriate curriculum. This will help investors secure skilled labor, while providing well-trained youth to find relevant jobs. I am confident that all investors should play an active part in this important endeavor.

The drop in new investment approval by the Council for the Development of Cambodia (CDC) is worrisome for all of us. In 2000, a total of 96 investment projects with US$269 million fixed assets were approved, a decline by 40 percent as compared to 1999. During the first half of 2001, 27 investment projects were approved with US$56 million in fixed assets, a further decline by 36 percent, compared to the first half of 2000. We have however noticed that expansion of old projects and investments in tourism-related sector, such as expansion of the airport and hotel construction in Siem Reap, are still vibrant. Overall, even though the new investment approvals decreased, FDI inflows into Cambodia were estimated at US$150 million per annum. Moreover, total investment consisting of FDI and domestically funded private investments, which are not reflected in the CDC figures, did not drop, but increased by 7 percent in 2000 compared to 1999.

Nevertheless, what is the signal for Cambodia? Even though Cambodia can secure sustainable development over the short to medium term, with the increase in public investment and ODA inflows, the declining FDI poses a serious concern for the prospect of economic growth over the long term. Indeed, the decline does not happen only in Cambodia. The drop in new investment approvals can be observed throughout Southeast Asia, which has experienced a net outflow of funds. Net FDI outflows from Singapore alone were US$10 billion in 2000. But China could attract US$40 billion last year, buoyed by the prospect of the country's accession to the WTO and investors' rush to get a share of this huge market. Nevertheless, this should not be used as a pretext to circumvent our efforts to improve the investment and business climate in the Kingdom of Cambodia. Attracting and promoting investments, both domestic and foreign, is a pre-requisite to achieving sustainable development and poverty reduction.

In this sense, I would like to turn this Government-Private sector forum into a brainstorming session on how to make Cambodia attractive to investments. The RGC recognizes that improving the business climate and establishing an enabling environment for private sector development is a key prerequisite for fostering growth-reducing poverty and achieving sustainable economic development. The RGC recognizes that there is somewhat of a herd effect with would-be investors following where others are already operating successfully. This is the reason why that as the Head of the Government I pay much attention to improving business environment for the existing investors. This is the reason why the seven, sectoral, joint Working Groups with the private sector were established and meet on a regular basis in order to improve investment environment and address investors' concerns. The RGC hopes that this initiative will allow private sector's effective participation in the efforts to improve the quality of policy making with respect to investment and to ensure its consistency. In this sense, policies with respect to the private sector should be based on the following:

First, supporting the massive small and medium enterprises (SMEs) and the unrecorded economy; and

Second, promoting and facilitating big investors.

The SMEs and the informal, unrecorded sector play an increasingly important role in the Cambodian economy, creating substantial employment for Cambodia's poor. The lack of credit for establishing new or expanding the existing enterprises is currently one of the biggest challenges. Hence, as the Head of Government I urge the Rural Development Bank to conduct a study as soon as possible on fostering cooperation between commercial and specialized banks and microfinance operators, which are capable of providing loans to small and medium enterprises (SMEs) and the small-scaled, unrecorded sector involving in rice milling, food processing, animal feed production, furniture-making and handicraft production, which are important sources of revenue generation for the poor.

At this morning's meeting, apart from listening to the presentations by the representatives of the seven working groups, I wish to set the tone and the direction of the discussions during this forum and within the working groups, which are operational between the fora. I would like to take this opportunity to consider together how best we - government and the private sector -could do to improve the regulatory and legal regime and ensure a level playing field for both existing and prospective investors, whether domestic or foreign. I understand that the private sector has aired their concerns and made suggestions to relevant government bodies through our joint working groups to ensure an equitable and fair treatment, as well as fair competition.

In this sense, the RGC has a role to play to ensure free, fair and transparent competition. In this regard, it is important to have an Accounting Law and an Audit Law applicable for private firms based on international standards. This law should ensure transparent operations, and fair and equitable distribution of tax burdens on private companies. In this sense, the RGC has encouraged thorough discussions of this draft law with wide participation from experts, the private sector and regulators, especially within the framework of the Working Group on Legislation, Tax, Governance and SMEs. It was a time consuming process, but it ensures that the job was well done, thus facilitating smooth implementation.

Most investors have expressed their legitimate concerns with regard to the proposed amendment to the Law on Investment, which will impose on investment firms appropriate tax burdens, used to finance government's efforts to upgrade the physical infrastructure, in exchange for improved governance, facilitation and services. The later includes streamlining of bureaucratic red tapes and irrelevant procedures, improved customs and tax administration and eradication of corruption, for which the RGC needs resources and time to do. It is true that sometimes it is very difficult to weigh between immediate costs and future benefits.

You may have seen that the RGC has taken very seriously the problems facing the private investment sector and businesses, such as:

i. high operating costs, in part brought about by poor infrastructure and overpriced utility services;

ii. excessive layers of bureaucracy that add to production costs and introduce uncertainty;

iii. 'hidden' transaction costs and smuggling -a heavy burden for investors and business people; and

iv. a lack of transparency and accountability, especially a sound legal and regulatory framework.

Though most problems are long-term in nature, thus time is needed to address all the impediments. With strong determination, the RGC has achieved encouraging results. In my address to the third forum, I elaborated on government's efforts to rehabilitate the country's infrastructure and measures to reduce electricity and telephone tariffs. There is a progress in this area. Road and bridge infrastructure has been rehabilitated. The telephone tariffs were reduced. The RGC has made massive investments in the electrical power sector with improved institutional capacity. This has been done to facilitate and promote economic activities and investments in Cambodia. The RGC needs substantial financial resources to rehabilitate, build and maintain these works. In this sense, the RGC relies on active and appropriate participation of the private sector in this endeavor.

At the same time, the RGC recognizes that much remains to be done, especially those related to governance. To this end, we have adopted and implemented with strong determination the Governance Action Plan (GAP), aimed at improving the efficiency of public services, ensuring transparency and predictability of the public services. In this context, the RGC is implementing a US$6 million Strengthening the Economic and Financial Management Project by closely cooperating with the international financial institutions and a number of donors in order to accelerate the reforms, strengthen customs and tax administration, and public expenditure and treasury management. The objectives of this project also include expanding the tax base and establishing an equitable and modern tax system. Overall, the RGC will make further efforts to implement the four- pronged reform package with a view to creating an enabling environment for private sector development.

Nevertheless, I wish to clarify the main principles for the review of the Law on Investment.

First, it will be proposed as a package, which offers investment facilitation and the review of tax incentives;

Second, the review of tax incentives will be carried out with caution to a certain degree that ensures a transparent, fair and equitable treatment, acceptable to all and without discrimination. This is the most important factor, which maintains Cambodia's attractiveness as compared to countries in the region.

Third, the RGC will continue intensive consultations with the private sector and other players concerned with the review of this Law on Investment.

Excellencies,
Ladies and Gentlemen,

One cannot talk about improving the legal and regulator framework for investment without reforming the Council for the Development of Cambodia (CDC). In this sense, I signed on 27th July a subdecree to strengthen the organization and the functioning of the CDC by appointing the Minister of Commerce as another CDC Vice Chairman and expanding the composition of the CDC to include representatives from all government ministries, agencies and provincial/municipal governors. The main objectives of this restructuring are to enhance the one-stop shop for investment by expanding the scope of this coordination to the provinces and municipalities, where investment projects are being implemented. Moreover, it will ensure a close coordination between policies and strategies on trade, industry and investment, including the establishment of a Free Trade Area, an Export Processing Zone and a Special Industrial Zone. It also reflects government's strategy to link investment to exports, which have played a critical role in employment creation for our population and accelerating economic growth.

Within the context of the restructuring, the CDC should organize a workshop with the participation of representatives from all government ministries and agencies, as well as provincial/municipal governors -members of the CDC to raise awareness and facilitate investments in Cambodia. The government's philosophy with regard to investment is facilitation and provision of all kinds of services to investors at all stages. Using commercial and marketing terms we should provide investors with the after-sale and after-care services. Thus, I urge the CDC to pay attention to this new concept, redirect and re-adjust its own mechanism, structure and workplace to strengthen efficiency. As H.E. KEAT CHHON, Chairman of the Council for the Development of Cambodia (CDC), has stated in his address to the forum, the efforts deployed by the RGC, especially the CDC, are geared to improving the legal and regulatory framework and procedures to strengthening the government's institutional capacity. This is to promote and facilitate investment and business activities in the Kingdom of Cambodia in line with this philosophy. From this report I have noticed that all working groups have met regularly and have made some positive results. I strongly hope that through this close cooperation a wise partnership between the government and the private sector will be further strengthened.

Today I want to talk less, but to listen more. Thus, I think that it is time to give you the floor so that you can air in a frank and candid manner your grievances, concerns and suggestions, so as to help the RGC to re-shape policies and improve further the business environment in this country.

I encourage all my colleagues in the government present here and the representatives of the private sector to continue our good tradition of close partnership and to discuss in an open and candid manner all issues and challenges, and explore ways to establish favorable conditions to attract investments to Cambodia.

My colleagues and I will be happy to answer to your questions and provide comments on any issues that have been your concerns or that you consider as impediments to doing business or undertaking investments in Cambodia. As in previous fora, most members of the RGC, senior officials and provincial/municipal governors are in attendance. Thus, I will consider the decision to be made today as those made legally made during the Cabinet meeting and the meeting of the CDC.I would like to sincerely thank you all for your kind attention.

SAMDACH PRIME MINISTER HUN SEN'S ADDRESS AT THE SIXTH GOVERNMENT-PRIVATE SECTOR FORUM AT THE COUNCIL FOR DEVELOPMENT OF CAMBODIA

The following is the integral text of Samdach Prime Minister HUN Sen's Address at the Sixth Government-Private Sector Forum at the Council for development of Cambodia on 07 August 2002 :

Your Excellencies,
Ladies and Gentlemen,

Today,I take great pleasure and honor in participating with Your Excellencies, Ladies and Gentlemen in this Sixt Government-Private Sector Forum. On behalf of the Royal Government of Cambodia, I wish to express my warm greetings to all of you who are here today.

Allow me to take this opportunity to make an overall assessment of the status of our economy and our performance in the management of development in Cambodia since our last forum and up till now. I wish also to comment on the affectivity of this Government-Private sector Forum as a mechanism to share experiences and collaboratively improve our performance.

Overall, during the last sixth months the Royal Government of Cambodia has exerted serious efforts to ensure our country's take-off toward sustainable economic development. Recognizing the positive developments, the Executive Board of the International Monetary Fund completed on 22 July 2002 the fifth review of Cambodia's economic performance under the Poverty Reduction and Growth Facility program (PRGF.) This review was encouraging and this achievement has enabled the immediate release of an additional US$ 11.2 million for the support of Cambodia's balance of payments.

The International Monetary Fund noted:

The Cambodian government has continued to make good progress in implementing its economic reform program. Inflation remains low and economic growth is being sustained despite a weaker external environment. Progress in the implementation of structural reforms has also been broadly satisfactory...

Thus, the IMF agrees with us that Cambodia has performed quite well during the first half of 2002. However, the IMF also noted that:

"... but reform efforts need to be strengthened in key areas, particularly revenue administration, public expenditure management, forestry policy and civil service reform."

Therefore, while we have performed well during the first semester of this year, we should not relax. We should work even harder for accelerated development and the improvement of the welfare of our Cambodian people.

We are ensuring that the Royal Government is well prepared for calamities, and is setting out measures to prevent such disasters from constraining our economic growth as well as the livelihood of the people. For example, Cambodia has experienced drought that could badly impact on the agricultural sector. As you know, agriculture contributes about 40 percent of our Gross Domestic Product (GDP), and the production of rice and other crops together contribute about 15 percent of GDP.

In order to achieve our economic growth targets, the Royal Government has been taking actions to reduce the impact of drought and flood. The Government has been mobilizing resources from domestic as well as offshore sources, donor countries as well as international finance institutions. We must stop any declines in rice and crop production while promoting growth in other sectors through further reforms. Together, all these measures are further accelerating the socio-economic development of Cambodia.

This year, Cambodia will host several very important international meetings and conferences. All these meetings will contribute to the improvement of the credibility of Cambodia in the region and in the international arena as a whole. This heightened profile and credibility will further promote the socio-economic development of Cambodia.

You all know we hosted in June 2002 the meeting of the Consultative Group (CG) of Donors in Cambodia. This was a historic event since it was held for the first time in Cambodia. At this meeting, the donor community discussed and assessed the progress and setbacks in the performance of the government's reform programs. Based on their assessment, they pledged a total of US$ 635 million in new assistance to Cambodia - exceeding the US$ 50 million pledged by NGOs.

This pledge far exceeds the government request for only US$ 486 million for the year 2002. It is an important encouragement for the government's efforts in bringing peace and political stability, strengthening the foundations for democracy and respect for human rights in our society, and especially in promoting sustained economic growth and substantially reducing poverty. Indeed, the success of the CG signifies the approval and support of the international community for the appropriateness and success of the government's reform policies and program.

In the next few months, Cambodia will be honored to host the summit of the Greater Mekong Subregion (GMS), the ASEAN Heads of State, the ASEAN + 3 and ASEAN + 1, and also the ASEAN-India Summit. In addition, we are preparing for other important events such as the ASEAN Cultural Week for 2002 and the ASEAN Tourism Forum in early 2003. Note that during the ASEAN tourism Forum, the ASEAN Framework Agreement of Tourism (T-ASEAN) is expected to be signed.

All of these major meetings will certainly raise our profile in the international sphere and over time provide Cambodia with positive effects leading to further growth of the trade, investment and the tourism sector.

You all know that in recent years, the Royal Government has been quite successful in maintaining macroeconomic stability. We have maintained the annual average growth rate of 7% during the last three years, from 1991-2001. In fact, although Cambodia suffered some difficulties in 2002, we were still able to achieve our forecasted rate of growth of 5-5.5%! Furthermore, inflation rates of the last three subsequent years were close to zero and the exchange rate has remained firm.

However, despite such stability in our macroeconomy, the Royal Government is very much worried to see only a slight increase in approvals of new investments by the Council for the Development of Cambodia (CDC). Investment approvals for the first half of 2002 increased by only 7 percent or US$ 60 million compared to the same period last year. While these investments will create jobs for more than twenty thousand Cambodians, still we want to see more employment.

In the second half of this year 2002, we expect to approve the proposed investment in Build-Operate-Transfer (BOT) contracts. These include the construction of Route 68, Route 10 and Route 72 for a total investment of US$ 42 million. Moreover, we expect to see investment of US$ 46 million in mobile phones by S Telecom Ltd.

The key sources of our economic growth continue to be tourism and the garments industry. Thus the Royal Government has taken major steps to build and strengthen the foundations and prerequisites for the accelerated growth and competitiveness of the tourism and garment sectors. These include programs to rehabilitate and develop roads and bridges, airports, ports and related facilities such as water and power supplies and telecommunications. We need this entire infrastructure to transform Cambodia's tremendous tourism and garments potentials and comparative advantages into economic reality, sustained through the medium and even long term.

Therefore, so far in 2002, there have been some improvements in investments compared to 2001. However, we are not satisfied even with such a positive result, since we believe we can and should do much better. Our philosophy is to make and enable private investment play a more pivotal role in spurring greater economic growth. With such a goal in mind, the Royal Government has focused on major policy actions to intensify legal and judicial reforms that will ensure an enabling environment for business and improve Cambodia's competitiveness as an investment destination.

Indeed, a basic thrust of our economic development policy is on reducing the costs of doing business and streaming the regulatory environment. With this conception, the Cambodian Government is also taking systematic actions to encourage and facilitate investment in the country. Certainly, we expect that the satisfactory amendment of the Law on Investment, with broad participation from all stakeholders specially from the private sector, should build greater confidence among investors and make Cambodia attractive for investment, trade and business.

I am pleased to report that after the extensive consultations, the Royal Government finalized the amendments to the Law on Investment in the middle of 2000. The amended version is now being reviewed and debated at the National Assembly.

An important point of our conception in amending the Law on Investment is to facilitate investments by streamlining procedures and paperwork in the processing of investment applications and approvals. Streamlining will also cover imports and exports of goods and equipment covered under the framework of the investment project. The main objective is to simplify and reduce paperwork and promote transparency and predictability in the process of approval, monitoring and implementation of investment projects.

In connection with the systematic approach of revising the Law on Investment, we have also arranged for the amendments of the Law on Taxation, which will be reviewed by the Cabinet soon. The same process of consultation with private sector and broad participation from stakeholders has been applied to the amendments of this law. I learned that, during the process, the private sector has raised some concerns. At this point, I assure you that the Cabinet will review the provisions of this Law very carefully, taking into account all the arguments raised.

The Cabinet is now working on the new Customs Code since it was submitted by the Ministry of Economy and Finance to the Council of Ministers on 31 July 2002. There is another important step forward which should be recognized, since it deals with another area of business-related legal reform - the Law on Corporate Accounting and Audit, which entered into force on 8 July 2002.

Indeed, there is much that has been done, but admittedly much more work that needs to be done! But we must say that all the progress so far achieved reflects strong commitment and decisive efforts of the Royal Government in the legal and economic reforms necessary to build an enabling environment for investment and business in Cambodia.

Furthermore, the Royal Government is actively implementing structural reforms aimed at improving and streamlining the procedures in investment approval and monitoring. As a result, we have now been succeeding in reducing the time required for review and approval of investment projects by the CDC Executive Committee to only seven working days.

Moreover, the approval of projects subject to the "one-stop-shop" mechanism is now a maximum of fourteen working days. It is encouraging that many positive changes have taken place. To this end, we will continue to work on a broad range of policies aimed at reducing transaction costs and removing impediments to effective competition.

We are conscious that the introduction of tolls for route 4 and the container scan result are additional costs for business in Cambodia. However you must realize that the collection of tolls would improve our capacity to maintain the roads and thereby help keep transport costs low in the long run.

We should accept the reality that Cambodia would always request aid for road repair. In addition, we cannot leave our roads in damaged condition. Without repair, bad road leads to high transport costs, damage to vehicles, slow traffic and even more dangerous travel. In the end, poor maintenance will take us back to where we started 15 years ago. Let me ask you: which is better and more sensible - build the road, or buy a car? Just like the problem of the chicken or egg, when we have good roads then our car will last longer. But when the roads are poorly built, the service life of the road is much shorter. We should take into account economic efficiency, time and accident implications of road design and building. Under such circumstances, we are formulating mechanism to ensure sustainability. This is to ensure good roads and the shift in our approach from aid dependency to managing road maintenance by ourselves.

As for the CT scanner, if properly managed, it will help improve the efficiency and effectiveness of the Customs in performing their job with regard to goods and commodities control as well as the fights against illegal acts especially the tax evasion. The CT scan will also be an effective measure for risk management, which will help improve trade by greatly improving safety and risk-management measures against criminal acts.

We should discuss these and related issues carefully to find a mutually satisfactory solution, particularly in the setting of a transparent and rational price setting formula. I ask the working group on Law, Taxation and Governance to discuss possible solutions with all the stakeholders as soon as possible.

There is another important, related matter that I want to inform all of you here today. We have found through careful review and consultation with many companies that the high transaction costs in Cambodia is mainly caused by illegal charges. According to the recently established Government Commission to oversee the matter, the illegal charges are collected at 27 different points in the Sihanoukville port, which involve some authorities, and dramatically increases transaction costs.

Specifically, we found that for a tax-exempted 20-foot container, the illegal charges amount to US$ 113. For a 40-foot tax-exempt container the charges total US$ 130. For a container subjected to taxation, the illegal charges amount to US$ 138 for a 20-foot container and US$ 155 for a 40-foot container.

The situation of the collection of high and illegal charges cannot be allowed to continue. I have taken a personal interest in this matter and have given instructions to the heads of all the concerned authorities, especially the CamControl, the Customs, the CamSab, and the Immegration Police and the Port authorities to take immediate actions to wipe out such illegal practices. I request for further follow-up of the progress on this matter at the level of the working groups concerned.

Over the past six months, the Royal Government has established and supported an inter-ministerial task force to fight against tax evasion. The task force, comprising of officials at central and provincial levels, the armed forces, the national military police, the police and local authorities, works closely with the Department of Customs and Excise in combating and cracking down on tax evasion activities. I think it is time to assess the progress and the performance of this measure! I welcome comments and recommendations by all of you regarding this matter.

Ensuring the availability of a skilled, flexible, and reliable workforce is another priority of the Royal Government. Reform of the education and training system is required to build such a labor force. Such reforms leading to improved quality of education are being pursued through the following key initiatives:

1. increased focus on professional and language skills, especially in English language skills for students;
2. greater utilization of information technology as a learning tool; and

Therefore, the Royal Government has strongly encouraged companies to give priority to the training of their employees. Companies are also encouraged to set up on-the-job training facilities so that they are assured of labor that meets their specific requirements. The Royal Government has also taken a liberal policy with regard to private sector training and education so that many private schools and institutes have emerged to respond to the demand for labor and the deep hunger among our people for skills for personal employability, growth and advancement.

Complementing these policies and programs in support of competitiveness is more intensive attention to the promotion of tourism opportunities. In this regard, we shall work closely with the private sector to develop tourist destinations. As you know, we have given much attention to the improvement of sanitation and health services in Siemreap, to ensure the sustainability and continuing beauty of the monuments and the City.

The Royal Government has also devoted more attention to the development of the tourism potentials of areas other than Siem Reap. We should promote attractions that enable greater tourist traffic in under-served areas, as well as longer stay and increased spending by tourists. Thus, the Royal Government encourages the development of access to eco-tourism destinations such as Mondulkiri and Ratanakiri, beach tourism in our sea access areas to the South, the upgrading of Kang Keng airport in Sihanoukville and the promotion of initiatives such as the night market. We should push for all of these initiatives as we prepare to serve as hosts for the ASEAN Tourism Forum in 2003.

Just last week, on 29 July 2002, the Royal Government launched the Second Socio-Economic Development Plan (SEDP-II) for 2001-2005. The overall thrust of poverty is the accelerated creation of employment, so that each and every Cambodian will have a dignified, human livelihood. Therefore, it is a key aspect of the industrial policy of the Royal Government to give priority to the development of other labor-intensive industries such as toy-making, footwear, and the assembly of electrical and electronic appliances.

Furthermore, the development of micro and small-scale enterprises is at the heart of our plan to promote industrial development. This strategy we will apply particularly in the areas at the outskirts of Phnom Penh, and in Sihanouksille, Banteay Meanchey, and Koh Kong. In these areas, the Royal Government will enable the provision of micro-finance and marketing services, streamline procedures, provide some training on production techniques, management and the liberal supply of crucial information.

Cambodia still has vast untapped and potentials in agriculture and livestock, particularly in high-value products and processed foods. We should all cooperate to develop these potentials in a sustainable manner. Our agricultural sector can provide jobs for so many of our labor force if we develop the rural sector in a rational and substantial manner. To achieve this momentum, the resolution of land issues and the establishment of roads and irrigation systems are the priorities of the Government in the next several years.

Moreover, the Royal Government will focus on the proposed industrial and export processing zones in order to attract private investment. In these zones, priority attention will be focused on completing the road network, systems for power and water supply, ensure waste management and environmental protection, provide education and vocational training, upgrade health services, the establishment of warehouse and reduction of customs procedures, and so forth.

Indeed, the improvement of Cambodia's international competitiveness is crucially dependent on success in the upgrading of basic physical infrastructure - including water, power, telecommunications and information. However, we cannot supply all these public goods all at once and in all parts of the country as we are under tough budget constraint.

We only have limited resources, and so we have to prioritize and carefully manage and allocate these resources for investment in those projects and areas with the highest economic reforms.

Therefore, the establishment of industrial corridors or centers concentrated in the key areas in the right solution for Cambodia. I strongly believe that the private sector - who is the potentially heaviest users of the entire system of infrastructure -- is in a good position to share with the government their visions and recommendations, advice and guidance, in the management and allocation of these scarce public resources for investment in the common interest.

I am appreciative of the working group mechanism within which the Government and private sector communicates and cooperates. The working group has become a very effective mechanism for addressing the concerns of investors and in reducing the difficulties in the situations that they encounter in business. Of course, regular participation in the working group demands time and effort - an expensive proposition for all of you as executives.

However, let me assure you that your valuable time and efforts are not wasted, and the results achieved thus far confirm that it worth these efforts. This mechanism has brought the Government-private sector partnership to a new openness and mutual gain, which are all crucial for the development and poverty reduction in Cambodia. I greatly appreciate all of you who have participated in the regular meetings of the working groups to address the concerns of the private sector. I understand that some of the working groups are convened as frequently as once a month, such as the working group on Law, Taxation and Governance. Of course, between the meeting dates issues can be resolved through the secretariat.

I have received regular reports from HE Keat Chhon who is coordinator of the seven working groups of this forum. I support the proposal for transferring the "Distribution" component from working group "C" to working group "G," and the component on small and medium-scale enterprises from working group "D" to working group "C." Therefore, later on, working group "D" will be the working group on Law, Taxation and Governance, while working group "G" will be called the working group on Export Processing and Trade Facilitation.

I also welcome the establishment of a core group representing the private sector to discuss important issues with the Prime Minister during the period in between the forums, when those issues are of high priority requiring immediate solution, but could not be resolved at the working group level.

At this point, I should give way so that all of you can also take the floor. I wish that you could all express, in a frank and candid but constructive manner, your concerns, suggestions and recommendations. I encourage all my colleagues in the government who are present here and the representatives of the private sector to continue our good tradition of close partnership and together explore ways to establish favorable conditions for profitable enterprise and to attract investments to Cambodia.

Finally, I encourage all of us to take a problem-solving attitude in our dialogue. We cannot just find fault nor blame one another for problems. We should see the problems of Cambodia as our own. The problems of Cambodia are not the problems of the Royal Government alone. The problems of Cambodia are OUR problems, you and I, and all of us together. These mutual problems can only be resolved if we work together on solutions which is the end will yield better lives for our children and for all of our people.

STATEMENT BY HIS EXCELLENCY SENIOR MINISTER HOR NAMHONG ON THE 35TH ANNIVERSARY OF ASEAN

The following is the integral text of a Statement delivered by His Excellency Senior Minister HOR Namhong, Minister of Foreign Affairs and International Cooperation, at the 35th Anniversary of ASEAN in Phnom Penh on 08 August 2002 :

Your Excellencies,
Distinguished Guests,
Ladies and Gentlemen,

1.Today, it is truly an auspicious occasion for all of us to commemorate the Thirty-Fifth Anniversary of the founding of the Association of South-East Asian Nations (ASEAN). Since its inception in 1967, ASEAN has evolved significantly over the years and has undeniably built up an impressive track record of achievements. In the thirty-five years of its existence, ASEAN has created a positive climate of regional cooperation and friendship through the establishment and strengthening of close relationships among all its members. The transformation of ASEAN over the years has been real and substantive.

2. Despite some of the challenges confronting our association in recent years, ASEAN remains vibrant, dynamic and forward-looking. Cambodia's admission into ASEAN in 1999 finally realized the ASEAN founding fathers' vision of bringing together all Southeast Asian countries to cooperate in securing the region's peace, stability and development.

3.ASEAN has built a solid foundation on the key principles of "unity in diversity" and "consensus-building," which are important for responding to the increasing challenges confronting our region. However, impacted by the rapid change of regional and global political security and the overall economic outlook, I believe that ASEAN has and will face several key challenges, which will require a greater spirit of solidarity.

4.The first challenge, in my view, is how to achieve ASEAN integration, which is the most important factor today for ASEAN to be able to move forward at the same pace, and to meet the challenges of globalization and regionalization in other parts of the world in order for us to stand in partnership with the Plus Three Countries.

5.The second challenge is that ASEAN must continue to broaden and deepen its partnership with the Plus Three Countries of China, Japan and the Republic of Korea (ROK) in order to strengthen East Asian identity. This deepened relationship will enable ASEAN to move ahead toward the establishment of the East Asia Summit in the future. At the moment, ASEAN should do its utmost to push forward the Initiative for the Development in East Asia (IDEA) and the recommendations of the East Asia Study

Group (EASG), which will be endorsed by the ASEAN+3 Summit in Phnom Penh this year.

6.The third challenge, I believe, is the strategic importance of ASEAN to look west. Given the economic and strategic importance of India in the world today, ASEAN will not only need to pay greater attention to India, but will also need to strengthen overall relations with this country. The strengthening of relations between ASEAN and India, particularly after the upcoming inaugural ASEAN-India Summit in Phnom Penh in November this year, would be mutually beneficial.

7.As the current Chairman of the ASEAN Standing Committee (ASC), Cambodia is very much committed to do its best to mobilize our common endeavors to address the challenges I mentioned earlier.

8.Regarding the ASEAN Regional Forum, I believe that the ARF has significantly evolved over the course of time. While the ARF concentrated much of its efforts on confidence-building measures successfully in the early years, it has since moved on to preventive diplomacy (PD) by adopting the "Concept and Principles of Preventive Diplomacy" and the "Enhanced Role of the ARF Chair" last year in Hanoi. The challenge now is how to move progress further in the future.

9.To be sure, the concept of security has changed dramatically since the September 11 terrorist attacks on the U.S. As a result, there have been far-reaching implications on our region and the world at large. In this context, the concept of security in the Asia-Pacific is different than that of nearly a decade ago. We all know that the threats of terrorism remain real and serious despite the preventative measures and plans of action that have been put in place, both collectively and individually, by ASEAN and ARF. Thus, there is a need to redefine our security concept to tackle the threat of terrorism.

10.In conclusion, based on the successes and experiences achieved in the past thirty-five years, in addition to the collective will and strong commitment in the spirit of solidarity, unity and integration of all members, I believe that ASEAN will be able to successfully overcome the difficulties and deal effectively with the present and future challenges.

11.The road ahead toward the realization of ASEAN Vision 2020 is still long however, the prospects are extremely promising. Collectively, we have already achieved some successes in reaching the goal of this Vision through the Hanoi Plan of Action (HPA). The implementation of the HPA, although not yet completed, has contributed much to the realization of this Vision, which is based on the ideas of "A Concert of Southeast ASEAN Nations," "A Partnership in Dynamic Development," and "A Community of Caring Societies and An Outward-Looking ASEAN."

12.Finally, I wish to take this opportunity to thank each and every one of you for being present at this joyful ASEAN night in the commemoration of the Thirty-Fifth Anniversary of the founding of ASEAN. I wish you all happiness, good health, and longevity. Happy ASEAN Anniversary.

Thank you very much.

SENIOR MINISTER HOR NAMHONG PARTICIPATES IN IDEA MINISTERIAL MEETING IN TOKYO

His Excellency Senior Minister **HOR Namhong**, Minister of Foreign Affairs and International Cooperation, led a delegation of the Kingdom of Cambodia to participate in the **Initiative for Development in East Asia (IDEA) Ministerial Meeting** , held in Tokyo on 12 August 2002 at the initiative of His excellency Junichiro KOIZUMI, Prime Minister of Japan. Attending this meeting were Foreign Ministers and Ministers in charge of development of ASEAN countries, China, Japan, and Republic of Korea.

The meeting had a frank exchange of views and experiences on coordination of cooperation in East Asia that led to economic growth by recovering from economic crisis in ASEAN countries, China, Japan and Republic of Korea.

The meeting focused on poverty reduction, including equitable income distribution and social development.

During one day discussion, the Ministers examined the current challenges facing East Asia, including the accelerated economic globalization, technological revolution, and global economic climate.

Participated Ministers highlighted the importance of and supported the Regional and Sub-Regional Cooperation, such as Greater Mekong Sub-Region Cooperation (GMS) and the realization of the Initiative for ASEAN Integration (IAI).

The meeting emphasized on the significance of maintaining adequate Official Development Assistance (ODA) as a tool for strengthening regional cooperation. Meanwhile participated Ministers urged the developed countries to open the market for poor countries and encouraged Foreign Direct Investment (FDI) to those countries in South East Asia which would lead to economic sustainable development and prosperity in the whole region.

In his address to the meeting, Senior Minister HOR Namhong had successfully gathered support for regional and sub-regional cooperation such as Greater Mekong Sub-Region, Initiative for ASEAN Integration and the encouragement of FDI to South East Asia, especially to the less developed countries in the region.

Finally, the meeting passed a Joint Ministerial Statement, which would be submitted to the upcoming ASEAN + 3 Summit in Phnom Penh.

STATEMENT BY HIS EXCELLENCY SENIOR MINISTER HOR NAMHONG AT IDEA MINISTERIAL MEETING

Here is the integral text of a Statement delivered by His Excellency Senior Minister HOR Namhong, Minister of Foreign Affairs and International Cooperation, at the IDEA Ministerial Meeting in Tokyo on 12 August 2002 :

Excellency Madam Chairperson,
Your Royal Highness,

Excellencies,
Distinguished Colleagues,
Ladies and Gentlemen,

1. First of all, allow me, Madam Chairperson, to express my most sincere appreciation to you and your colleagues for the warm hospitality and the excellent arrangement of our meeting today.

2. First, 1 believe that IDEA is a bold and a very important and positive initiative for the development of our entire East Asia region, based on our common understanding that this in the interest of all of us, East Asia as a whole. I also believe that we will have much to gain, all together, North East and Southeast Asia, in pushing forward ASEAN integration as the way to enhancing East Asia cooperation.

3. I believe that the materialization of this initiative will promote economic growth, poverty reduction and sustainable development in our region. I also think that the implementation of IDEA would further strengthen peace, security and prosperity in this region. As development experience demonstrated in the past, ODA continue to play a significant role in ASEAN development and prosperity.

The ASEAN member countries achieved in the past years economic development by effectively utilizing Japanese ODA.

4. IDEA, in my view, will help pave the way for, in Prime Minister's words, "Act Together and Advance Together". Given its stated goals, IDEA could be an important catalyst for ASEAN, particularly the new members, to meet the challenges of the world today.

To act together and advance together, it should not be, I believe, a wide gap between partners within ASEAN and between ASEAN and +3 countries. Therefore, I fully share the views of our colleagues from Singapore and Malaysia regarding the importance and the necessity to realize IAI East Asia cooperation.

5. However, while talking about East Asian development experience, I wish to share with you the Cambodian perspective on development and growth. Based on our experience, believe that there are several key elements which are important for economic development in our region, such as stable macroeconomics policies, policy coherence, substantive investments in infrastructure, human resource development, and good governance.

6. Nevertheless, I believe that the official development assistance remains necessary and vital for ASEAN, particularly the new members, as they need to catch up with the development in the region. Once fully integrated, ASEAN becomes an equal partner with North East Asian countries, which would be beneficial to the whole East Asia region.

7. Equally necessary and important, I think that private investment is crucial for the development of any country. ODA alone is not sufficient. Therefore, any help from the Japanese Government in this sense would be very important for the new members of ASEAN, in particular Cambodia, where Japanese investment is very weak.

8. Finally, I think that with internal public investment, efficient and transparent use of ODA and FDI, ASEAN can continue to move ahead with stable economic growth and sustainable development in the years to come. This would ultimately help advance East Asia through narrowing regional development gap.

Allow me to take this opportunity to sincerely thank the government of Japan for helping greatly Cambodia in the economic and social development.

Thank you very much.

OPENING ADDRESS OFHIS EXCELLENCY SENIOR MINISTER HOR NAMHONG AT IAI DEVELOPMENT COOPERATION FORUM

The following is the integral text of Opening Address delivered by His Excellency Senior Minister HOR Namhong, Minister of Foreign Affairs and International Cooperation, at the IAI Development Cooperation Forum at the ASEAN Secretariat, Jakarta, Republic of Indonesia on 15 August 2002 :

- *H.E. Hassan Wirajuda, Foreign Minister of the Republic of Indonesia,*
- *H.E. Rodolfo Severino, ASEAN Secretary General,*
- *Excellencies,*
- *Ladies and Gentlemen,*

1.At the outset, I wish to take this opportunity to thank H.E. Rodolfo Severino, ASEAN Secretary General, for inviting me to speak at the opening of this important IAI Development Cooperation Forum (IDCF). It is indeed a great honor and a great pleasure for me to be here at the launching of the IDCF, which I believe is a significant gathering in advancing the implemen- tation of the IAI Work Plan, programs and projects that surely will contribute to ASEAN integration.

2.The IAI Work Plan, which is a key development framework for the new ASEAN members in the next six years, is vital for achieving ASEAN integration. As a top priority, IAI focuses on four strategic areas, namely infrastructure, HRD, ICT, and regional economic integration. The realization of the IAI programs and projects would require sufficient resources and active support.

3.On this occasion, I wish to inform you that at the Initiative for Development of East Asia (IDEA) Ministerial Meeting in Tokyo a few days ago, the ASEAN+3 Foreign Ministers discussed extensively the East Asia cooperation and they unanimously supported the IAI Work Plan and projects. I believe that the support of the Work Plan by China, Japan and the Republic of Korea (ROK) is an important step forward toward the success of IAI. In this context, I think that our meeting here in Jakarta is very timely as we attempt to seek the support of all our partners and friends represented here. Their support, in my view, would be an important guarantee for the achievement of the IAI programs and projects which have also been approved by all the ASEAN Foreign Ministers in Brunei last month. The ASEAN's Dialogue Partners also supported these projects in Brunei.

4.Nowadays, we are in the process of three important initiatives for strengthening East Asia partnership, namely the Initiative for Development of East Asia of Japan, the East Asia Study Group (EASG) proposed by ROK, and the Framework Agreement on Economic Cooperation between ASEAN and China which will be agreed by the ASEAN-China leaders at the upcoming summit in Phnom Penh in November this year. I believe that these initiatives and the IDEA meeting in Tokyo recently demonstrate a strong will of all the thirteen countries in East Asia to move ahead with the broadening of East Asia cooperation as well as in advancing East Asian integration in a long-term perspective.

5.However, to realize this cooperation policy and the vision of East Asian integration, there is an urgent need to eliminate the current two-tier ASEAN, because an ASEAN divide is a serious handicap not only for ASEAN as a whole but also for East Asia as well. Therefore, I believe that ASEAN must have a strong determination to narrow the development gap within our region. Although they need foreign assistance, I believe that the new members would have to do their utmost in enhancing the self-help first to promote development so that they can benefit from the support of other ASEAN members, as well as our partners and friends.

6.In my view, we have no other viable alternative to realize ASEAN integration and effectively addressing the imbalance of development in the region on the one hand, and move ahead in our way to enhancing and deepening East Asia cooperation, on the other hand. The disparity in ASEAN today constitutes our real major challenge, which we must overcome it at any cost. In this context, I wish to thank those original members of ASEAN for having provided assistance and support in capacity building, training and human resource development to the new members in recent years, specifically after the IAI was launched by our leaders in Singapore in November 2000.

7.While recognizing that much more can be done to reduce the development gap within ASEAN, I hope that the positive outcome of this Forum would be an important contributing factor to realize this goal. In this regard, external support is utterly necessary to assist the CLMV countries to accelerate the economic growth, poverty reduction, sustainable development and integration. I expect that this Forum will demonstrate the rationale of the Work Plan, programs and projects, as well as the impact of such projects on CLMV's development. I wish to convey our message to our friends and partners present here that we need your support and assistance to help us realize the ASEAN integration first and East Asian integration in the long-term. I believe that both ASEAN integration and the broader East Asia cooperation are very much linked to one another, as we now agreed in Tokyo to "act together and advance together," to borrow the words from Japanese Prime Minister Koizumi.

8.Although we are fully aware of the budgetary constraints of our friends and partners as well as the international organizations due to global economic slowdown and the competing needs in other parts of the world, I still hope that you all understand the necessity and importance of ASEAN integration.

9.In recognition of their generous support and assistance over the years, I wish to take this opportunity to thank all ASEAN's friends and partners for having accepted to attend this important forum. In particular, the commitment of China, Japan and ROK to support IAI which was made in Tokyo a few days ago constitutes an important factor of the success of IAI.

10.While understanding the need for greater accountability and effectiveness of using the resources provided by our friends and partners, we will work closely with everyone to ensure the effectiveness of the assistance. I also believe that the CLMV countries will play their part in ensuring the realization of the Work Plan and projects in the framework of their national plans of development. In this regard, I believe that CLMV have been and will continue strengthening the legal framework, creating an enabling environment for attracting investment, and enhancing transparency.

11.Finally, I believe that a fully integrated ASEAN will sustain its relevance, boost its competitiveness in the face of increasing challenges of globalization and regionalization, as well as be a catalyst for strengthening East Asia. Moreover, an economically strong ASEAN will not only benefit ASEAN alone but also its partners. Therefore, the integration of ASEAN, in my view, remains a critical factor which will be of significant benefits to East Asia as a whole as well as to other partners of ASEAN.

12.Once again, on behalf of ASEAN, in particular the new members, may I take this opportunity to thank you very much for your presence here. Your participation in this Forum has already indicated your support of ASEAN as well as IAI. I also wish to extend my best wishes for a successful IDCF.

Thank you very much.

LETTER TO EDITOR IN CHIEF OF THE CAMBODIA DAILY

On 22 August 2002, Senior Minister HOR Namhong, Minister of Foreign Affairs and International Cooperation, sent a following letter to the Editor in Chief of The Cambodia Daily. This letter was published in the next issue of The Cambodia Daily on 23 August 2002 .

Dear the Editor in Chief,

In the article "Annan Letter Renews Hope For KR Talks", "The Cambodia Daily" on 22 August 2002 wrote: "At various points, Foreign Minister HOR Namhong said Cambodia would never allow international control of a trial".

In this connection, I would like to clarify as follows:

1- "During the 35th AMM, ARF and PMC in Brunei Darussalam from 29 July to 1 August 2002, at the meeting between the ASEAN Foreign Ministers with the ASEAN's Partner Countries, I solemnly stated: "Cambodia would like to see the UN's involvement in the trial of former KR leaders to have a fair trial in conformity with the international standard of justice".

2- Furthermore, on my arrival at Pochentong International Airport on 02 August 2002 from Brunei Darussalam, I reiterate the same position to the reporters on this matter.

I hope that this clarification will be published in the next issue of the "The Cambodia Daily".

Please accept, Dear Editor in Chief, the assurances of my high consideration.

SAMDECH PRIME MINISTER'S ADDRESS TO THE INAUGURATION OF UNESCO/JSA PROJECT OFFICE

Following is the integral text of Samdech Prime Minister HUN Sen's address delivered on 01 July 2002 at the Inauguration of the UNESCO/JSA (Japanese Government Team for Safeguarding Angkor) Project Office built by the UNESCO/Japan Trust Fund in Siemreap Town, Siemreap Province :

Today I have great honor and great pleasure to be able to participate -- with Samdech Preah Ream, princes/s, Excellencies, ladies and gentlemen -- in the inauguration of the UNESCO/JSA project office that is a material foundation for the protection and conservation of Angkor in the province of Siemreap. I think that our meeting today in front the new building with feature of the Sambo Prey Kuh eight-dimension temple is another event of historical importance in the work to conserve and repair Angkor temple aimed at preserving and promoting the cultural heritage and national civilization...

Taking this opportunity I would like express my deep thanks to Professor Dr. Nakagawa Takeshita, General Director of the Japanese Government Team for Safeguarding Angkor (JSA) and other Japanese and Cambodian staff for their active collaboration in offering supports, repair and safeguard of Angkor temple. JSA not only makes available funds, spirit, and care in their works to repair and conserve the temple but also transfers technology and skills to the Cambodian staff making them become experts while printing and disseminating research reports and organizing symposiums on the Bayon temple. I wish to express my appreciation and high evaluation to the continuing efforts made in maintaining the terrace of the Royal Plaza of Angkor Thom, in conserving and restoring the Prasat Suor Proat towers, in repairing the Northern Library inside the outmost enclosure of Angkor Wat, and in formulating a master plan for the conservation and restoration of the entire Bayon complex to be completed by 2005.

The conservation and promotion of advancement of the national cultural heritage and civilization is an absolute will and determination of the Royal Government reflecting the actual need of development aimed at conserving and from conserving to developing the national culture and civilization that was reputed in the world for centuries. The reputation has degraded in the last decades because of internal conflicts and lack of care. In the present world, conserving and developing national cultures have become a prerequisite for all the weak nations in the strong current of globalization, for which they have to face with challenges and to stand influences of foreign cultures that have more economic and technological power than them. In this context the Ministry of Culture and Fine Arts together with every Cambodian have not only the task to conserve but also to develop and advance their national culture through the collaboration of idea and wisdom of our intellectuals and knowledgeable person.

Political crisis and the stalemate of internal war over the past three decades not only destroyed the foundation of our social and economic infrastructure to naught but also devastated severely Cambodia's culture while degrading the national morale, originating increase of violence, and demolishing various pagodas, temples and feature sculptures. Some bad people have taken advantage by making excavation in search of national archeological objects and export them illegally for sale to foreign merchants.

Successes in the implementation of the triangular strategies of the Royal Government has brought us peace and full territorial unity for the first time on the land of Cambodia in decades. This is a prime condition for opportunities to take place, especially in the creation of a solid base for major changes in all fields - politically, economically and socially - in Cambodia. The realization of peace and territorial unity also constitutes the most important factor in the rehabilitation of the national culture.

To make use of this rare chance, as Prime Minister of the Royal Government, I had issued a comprehensive policy aimed at safeguarding and promoting national cultural heritage and civilization by curbing illegal exports of archeological objects, restoring and reconstructing pagodas, historic sites and old temples of our nation. At the same time we have gathered resources of all kinds inside and outside the country for the sake of safeguarding, maintaining, repairing, registering an inventory list, making projects and plans to conserve and restoring the cultural heritage of our nation. We have for instance implemented various conservation and development of the national cultural patrimonies such as temples, resorts and historical parks as well as all sorts of natural culture property like forest, sea, rivers, lakes, canals and valleys since the 1980s with participation of conservation experts from India and Japan. In the 1990s and the present, experts from France, Japan and other countries have arduously in the conservation of the national cultural heritage of Cambodia. I wish to take this opportunity to express my gratitude to all the experts for making their efforts physically and spiritually in contribution to the maintenance of Cambodia's cultural property.

The passing decades of wars had brought about declining morale, culture and knowledge of our people, which culminated in various negative phenomena in Cambodia's society. Education is key for the uprooting of all these problems. Education is the most effective measure in the combat against ignorance. Every Cambodian has to understand clearly that the Khmer culture is the Khmer national identity and soul. Destruction of the national culture and civilization is therefore destruction of own selves. In this meaning we all have a noble task in training and raising awareness of all Cambodians to understand about historical, artistic, cultural, scientific and architectural values of all the temples that are spreading throughout Cambodia. Each and every Cambodian have to know that the Khmer patrimony possesses invaluable value and the world has included it as one of the world wonders.

To effectively respond to the policy of promotion of the cultural heritage and sustaining the civilization, the Royal Government has made effort in increasing resources from within its limited availability consecutively for the purpose of supporting and developing culture and fine arts. In the last five years, our budget reserved for culture has increased from Riel 3 billion in 1998 to over Riel 11 billion in 2002. So in just five years, the budget for cultural sector has risen three-fold. At the same time the Royal Government has tried and is trying to increase investment in area of culture through the Government-direct-investment budget as gathered from foreign assistance and to encourage contribution from private sectors.

Culture has contributed and is contributing to the country's development through its promotion of cultural tourists. Cambodia possesses a number of comparative advantages and potentials in area of tourism and other services relating to tourism. More importantly, tourism is not only a high potential area in offering jobs and providing income. Tourism is also providing potential for mental progress of our people through the increase of education and mutual understanding, making them aware of and appreciating any differences from own national or country's identity, while promoting inter-relation, encouragement of respect and conserving natural environment. It is also true that tourism contributes in the strengthening of peace and creating favorable condition for different nations and cultures to co-exist.

The Royal Government clearly realizes that the infrastructure and physical adapting mechanism like communication, water supply and electricity as well as telecommunications is foundation for transforming these great potentials and comparative advantages into reality. Looking into the speed of current external assistance and investment we hope that in just four or five years ahead we will realize an appropriate physical infrastructure in response to the basic need of development in tourism. One other important work is the training of human resources to a level of high knowledge and with sufficient capability in both national and international standards so that they can respond to our need in coping with globalization. It is an urgent task that every institution pays due attention and advances the making use of existing human resources by placing them in jobs that are corresponding to their skills, working practice and learning while taking experience and making improvement. They have to refrain from narrow-mindedness so as to fulfil our objectives of conserving and developing for an equitable society. Human resource training for the cultural and fine arts sector has to be conducted in conformity with the construction process of cultural infrastructure, which also includes the conservation site in Angkor area, Koh Ke area, Boeung Mealea, Preah Vihear temple area, Sambo Prey Kuh area, and other cultural tourist resorts.

Achievements in area of culture and fine arts that we have realized so far have illustrated clearly active participation by Samdech Preah Ream, leaders and staff of the Ministry of Culture and Fine Arts, local authorities at all levels, the APSARA authority, UNESCO and other national and international organizations. It is true that there are more works to be done. The Royal Government has specially pushed for the making of laws, sub-decrees, and various norms so that they could efficiently and comprehensively serve in a timely manner to urgent needs of our people, producers and private companies in making decision to invest in areas of culture and cultural tourism.

SENIOR MINISTER HOLDS DISCUSSION WITH SINGAPOREAN FOREIGN MINISTER

His Excellency Senior Minister **HOR Namhong**, Minister of Foreign Affairs and International Cooperation, held on 26 August a bilateral discussion with His Excellency Prof. **S. Jayakumar**, Minister of Foreign Affairs of the Republic of Singapore, who had been in Cambodia for a working visit on 26-27 August 2002.

Both Ministers expressed satisfaction with the excellent relations of friendship and cooperation between the two countries andshared the same wishes for their further promotion, especially the flow of more Singaporean investments to Cambodia.

Senior Minister HOR Namhong holds Discussion with Singaporean Foreign Minister Jayakumar

As far as the ASEAN Integration is concerned, Senior Minister HOR Namhong stressed on the necessity to move the Initiative for ASEAN Integration (IAI) forwards in order to reduce the development gap between the original and the new members of ASEAN.

Senior Minister HOR Namhong and Minister Jayakumar also had discussions and exchange of views on how to move forwards the Initiative for Development in East Asia (IDEA) as well as the ASEAN + 3 cooperation and the cooperation between ASEAN and its partner countries.

SENIOR MINISTER HOR NAMHONG SIGNS TWO EXCHANGES OF NOTES WITH AMBASSADOR OF JAPAN

On 27 August 2002, at 16:30, at the Ministry of Foreign Affairs and International Cooperation, Samdech Prime Minister HUN Sen of the Kingdom of Cambodia presided over the signing by His Excellency Senior Minister HOR Namhong, Minister of Foreign Affairs and International Cooperation, and His Excellency Mr. Gotaro OGAWA, Ambassador Extraordinary and Plenipotentiary of Japan to the Kingdom of Cambodia, on two Exchanges of Notes of Japan's Grant Aid up to ¥ 2,422,000,000 (equivalent to 20 million US dollars).

Senior Minister HOR Namhong Signs Exchanges of Notes with Ambassador Gotaro OGAWA

The Royal Government of Cambodia would use the Japanese Grant Aid for human resource development scholarship project (¥ 366,000,000) to be carried out by 31 March 2003 and for flood protection and drainage improvement in the Municipality of Phnom Penh (¥2,056,000,000) to be executed by 31 March 2004.

SECRETARY OF STATE UCH KIMAN HOLDS CONSULTATION WITH HUNGARIAN COUNTERPART

His Excellency Mr. BÁRSONY András, Political State Secretary of the Ministry of Foreign Affairs of the Republic of Hungary told Secretary of State UCH Kiman that Hungary might help Cambodia in agriculture, tourism and human resource development. Hungary would consider the Cambodian requests through bilateral relations, added the Political State Secretary in the consultation held on 16 August 2002 at the Ministry of Foreign Affairs and International Cooperation during his visit to Cambodia from 16 to 18 August 2002.

Secretary of State UCH Kiman holds Consultation with His Excellency Mr. BÁRSONY András

His Excellency Mr. BÁRSONY András also told Secretary of State UCH Kiman that Hungary would help Cambodia in its efforts to become ASEM member and study the possibility in providing assistance to Angkor Foundation.

His Excellency Mr. UCH Kiman recalled the good relationship enjoyed by the two countries and shared the views expressed by his interlocutor for the sake of the promotion of bilateral relations. He also said that in order to reach this goal, a delegation of the Ministry of Foreign Affairs and International Cooperation would visit Hungary and other countries in Central Europe in early 2003.

SECRETARY OF STATE UCH KIMAN SIGNS AN EXCHANGE OF NOTES ON OFFICE EQUIPMENTS AID WITH AMBASSADOR OF CHINA

On 28 August 2002, at 11:00 a.m, at the Ministry of Foreign Affairs and International Cooperation, a signing ceremony of an Exchange of Notes on Office Equipments Aid provided by the Government of the People's Republic of China was held between His Excellency Mr. UCH Kiam, Secretary of State of Foreign Affairs and International Cooperation, and His Excellency Mr. NING Fukui, Ambassador Extraordinary and Plenipotentiary of the People's Republic of China to the Kingdom of Cambodia.

Secretary of State UCH Kiman Signs Exchange of Notes with Ambassador of China NING Fukui

Those office equipments valued at RMB 1,000,000 Yuan will be used by the Royal Government of Cambodia in its prepara- tion for the 8th ASEAN Summit to be held on November 4-5, 2002 in Phnom Penh.

ECONOMY AND ECONOMIC DEVELOPMENT

ECONOMIC TRENDS

Cambodia is a developing country with a market economy. GDP in 1999 was 11.96 trillion Cambodian riel (about $3.1 billion), or $268 per capita, among the lowest levels in the world. Informal estimates in terms of purchasing power parity put the standard of living in the range of $1500 per year. Once one of south east Asia's most stable and prosperous countries, Cambodia's social and economic institutions were severely disrupted by the agrarian collectivist policies of the Khmer Rouge regime from 1975-79, and the period of communist central planning that followed under the Vietnamese-backed People's Republic of Kampuchea. The Cambodian government officially adopted market economics in 1989, but it was not until after the 1991 Paris Peace accords, which led to the re-establishment of the constitutional monarchy in 1993, that the economy began to grow.

From 1993 to 1996 Cambodia's GDP grew at an average rate of 7.2% from $1.9 to $3.1 billion. However, GDP growth slowed substantially in mid-1997 following the July 5-6 factional fighting in Phnom Penh and the onset of the Asian financial crisis, increasing by just one percent in real terms in 1997 and 1998. The slowdown in economic growth coupled with continued high population growth led to a decline in Cambodia's per capita GDP from $292 in 1996 to $252 in 1998. Political stability returned to Cambodia in late 1998 with the establishment of the current coalition government, and economic growth resumed at a rate of 4.3% in 1999, exceeding government expectations. The Ministry of Economy and Finance (MEF) forecasts a higher rate of 5.5% for the year 2000.

Since 1993, the Royal Government of Cambodia has undertaken a serious program of economic reform with assistance from the IMF, World Bank, ADB, UNDP and other bilateral and multilateral donors. Even during the period of political disruption and poor economic performance in 1997-98, the government maintained macroeconomic stability through generally tight monetary and fiscal policies. Although inflation increased from its 1995 low of 3.5 percent, it remained under control at 9 percent in 1997 and 13.5 percent in 1998. MEF reports that there was zero inflation in 1999. Cambodia's currency has been relatively stable since 1993, with the exception of a sharp depreciation in 1997-98. The annual average exchange rate for 1999 was 3,800 riels/US$1. Maintaining a stable exchange rate is a priority of Cambodia's current IMF program. Cambodia's economy is also heavily dollarized, with the U.S. dollar accounting for an estimated 70 percent of total liquidity in the country.

The Cambodian government's reform program is highly detailed and closely monitored by the donor community. Cambodia made considerable progress in 1999 in improving control of the forestry sector, beginning with a successful crackdown on illegal logging which the government has sustained into 2000. The Cambodian government is now in the process of re-defining its entire forestry management system. Cambodia also made considerable progress toward reducing the size of its military. A pilot demobilization in May 2000 kicked off a three year effort to demobilize over 30,000 soldiers, a step which is necessary in order to free up budgetary resources for social sector spending. The government improved its revenue collections through the successful implementation of a value added tax in early 1999, but at about 12% of GDP Cambodian government revenues are low even by developing country standards. This impediment to increased public spending investment means that Cambodia remains heavily reliant on foreign assistance for every aspect of national reconstruction. In October 1999, Cambodia secured the first installment of an $81.6 million IMF Poverty Reduction and Growth Facility loan, and the World Bank approved a Structural Adjustment Credit worth $30 million in February 2000.

At a donors' Coordinating Group meeting in May 2000, donors pledged $548 million in support for the Cambodian government's reform program for the coming year. The subject of "good governance" became a major theme of the reform process in 1999, and the government has produced an action plan to address such issues as civil service reform, judicial and legal reform, improving the quality of public services and attacking corruption. Donors will monitor progress on these issues, as well as the more traditional aspects of economic reform, as conditions for their continued assistance.

Cambodia ran a trade deficit of $341 million in 1999. With no energy and little domestic industry, Cambodia's major imports include petroleum products, cement and construction materials, vehicles, tobacco and broad range of consumer products. Garments dominate Cambodia's exports, accounting for over $640 million in 1999, or 89% of total exports. More than three quarters of Cambodian garment exports go to the United States. The garment industry has been Cambodia's greatest success, growing from seven factories exporting $4 million in 1994 to about 200 factories today, employing roughly 100,000 workers, mostly young women. Other principal Cambodian exports include timber and wood products, latex and rubber, and fishery products.

Cambodia and the U.S. have full and expanding trade relations. The U.S. lifted the embargo on trade with Cambodia on January 2, 1992. After legislative action by Congress in September 1996, Normal Trade Relations (NTR) were established between the U.S. and Cambodia in October 1996 upon the signing of a comprehensive Agreement on Trade Relations and Intellectual Property Rights Protection. President Clinton subsequently designated Cambodia as a Least Developed Beneficiary Developing Country under the U.S. Generalized System of Preferences (GSP) program on May 30, 1997. Cambodia and the U.S. signed a three-year bilateral textile agreement on January 21, 1999 that sets export limitations on 12 categories of textile and apparel products. This textile agreement is likely to slow the growth of Cambodian apparel exports to the United States. U.S. exports to Cambodia are likely to remain modest for the near term. The U.S. exported approximately $37.5 million worth of goods to Cambodia in 1999, including used vehicles and spare parts, cigarettes, and used clothing.

A key component of the Cambodian government's reform program is to improve Cambodia's attractiveness as a destination for foreign direct investment (FDI) in order to enhance economic growth. Although Cambodia's Law on Investment establishes an open and liberal foreign investment regime, FDI dropped substantially with the political instability of 1997, and has not fully recovered. The Council for the Development of Cambodia, the government's investment agency, reports that new investment commitments dropped significantly to only $482 million in 1999, compared to over $800 million per year between 1996 and 1998, and that figures for the first three months of

2000 totaling $31.6 million, are far below commitments in the same period of 1999. Some analysts attribute at least some of this decline to the CDC's improved screening of investment licenses, but a particularly steep drop in new garment factories is also evident, a result of the U.S. decision to impose quota on Cambodian garment products.

According to the MEF, Cambodia attracted $160 in FDI flows in 1999, an improvement over 1998, which probably reflects a surge of investment in the tourism industry. U.S. investment in Cambodia to date has been modest, with the largest investors including Caltex for a chain of service stations and a terminal in Sihanoukville, Northbridge Associates for an international school and residential property, and Shelby corporation for a glove manufacturing facility. There are currently over 100 U.S. companies and companies representing U.S. products and services operating in Cambodia.

Cambodia is a member of ASEAN and the Asian Free Trade Area. Cambodia has begun the process of accession to the WTO.

PRINCIPAL GROWTH SECTORS

Agriculture: The agricultural sector, including rice farming, livestock, forestry, and cultivation of other crops, provides direct employment to more than 75 percent of Cambodia's labor force. According to the MEF, agriculture accounted for 37% of GDP in 1999. Excellent rice harvests in 1999 contributed to Cambodia's better-than-expected economic growth. With its large amount of arable land, ample rainfall, and close proximity to the major ASEAN markets of Thailand and Vietnam, Cambodia has strong growth potential in the agriculture sector. A number of plantation agriculture projects are already underway in the areas of palm oil, cashew, coffee, tea, and vegetable production.

The Government has taken note of the growth potential of the sector as well as the important role increased agricultural production can play in reducing rural poverty in Cambodia, and has designated the Ministry of Agriculture, Forestry, and Fisheries as one of four priority ministries to receive expanded budgets. Factors limiting agricultural production include unclear land ownership, a lack of irrigation infrastructure, inadequate transportation infrastructure, inefficient marketing, poor farming practices and poor public sector support services.

Services: The services sector represented an estimated 43.2 percent of GDP in 1999, and grew by 8.1 percent during the year, and the government forecasts continued strong growth in the services sector for 2000. The Cambodian tourism industry is still relatively undeveloped, but the Ministry of Tourism estimates that tourist arrivals in Cambodia will grow by 20 percent annually from 1999-2000 and 35 percent annually from 2001-2002. Tourist arrivals increased 11% in 1999 over the previous year. Tourism is a preferred sector under Cambodia's foreign investment regulations.

Industry: Industrial growth has been dominated by the expanding garment manufacturing industry. As noted above, growth in the sub-sector is likely to slow in 2000 with the imposition of quota on Cambodian garment imports to the United States in 1999. Construction is a also a strong player in the industrial sector, accounting for about a third of all industrial activity. Although construction only grew 4.9% in 1999, the MEF projects that the sub-sector will grow by about 12% a year for the next several years. Spending for infrastructure projects and for office and residential construction and rehabilitation will continue to fuel the growth of this sub-sector.

GOVERNMENT ROLE IN THE ECONOMY

Cambodia has a free market economy. It has eliminated most non-tariff barriers to trade and screens investments only to award investment incentives. Cambodia's legal structure and government policies are intended to promote exports and attract investment.

Even in the communist era, the state-owned industrial base was never extensive, and the government began to sell and lease government assets as early as 1989. Under the terms of a privatization agreement worked out with the IMF in 1994, a few additional state-owned enterprises were sold and many more were leased. The role of state-owned enterprises in the economy is not significant today.

Since its establishment in 1993, the Royal Government of Cambodia has adopted a budget statute and significantly increased the transparency of Government budget operations. On the other hand, more than 30 years of conflict have left Cambodia with a government budget heavily skewed toward defense and security expenditures, which together accounted for 42.7% percent of government spending in 1999. Freeing budget resources to address poverty reduction is the overriding goal of the government's reform program, and the Government has committed to significantly increase spending on the priority social sectors of health, education, agriculture, and rural development. However, line ministries complain that budgetary disbursements in these sectors lagged significantly in 1999, especially at the provincial level.

Cambodia is still in the process of developing a regulatory framework that will assure the health, safety, and well-being of individuals and companies operating in the free market economy. In the health sector, Cambodia has legislation regulating pharmacies and pharmaceuticals. In may 2000, the national assembly passed a law on quality of goods and services, comprising food safety, consumer protection and product liability. Government priorities for 1999 include passage of a new Land Law, a new Forestry Law, a Business Organization Law and a Trademark Law by the end of the year.

BALANCE OF PAYMENTS

According to MEF, Cambodia's 1999 current account deficit, excluding official transfers (grant aid) was $362 million, or 11.6% of GDP. The deficit was financed mainly by official development assistance grants ($191 million) and loans ($45 million), and foreign direct investment ($160 million). As of the end of 1999, Cambodia's gross official reserves were equivalent to 3.5 months of imports.

Cambodia's foreign debt is equal to approximately $1.3 billion, the majority of which it owes to Russia for debts incurred to the countries of the former Council for Mutual Economic Assistance, including the Soviet Union. Cambodia has not yet reached agreement with the Russian Federation on repayment of its debt. Cambodia's second largest creditor is the United States. Cambodia signed a Terms of Refernce with the

Paris Club of creditor nations in 1995 awarding Cambodia's official debt the Club's most favorable terms (Naples terms). Based on these terms, the U.S. Government presented a draft bilateral debt rescheduling to the Cambodian government in 1995, but Cambodia has not yet signed the agreement.

The Cambodian government follows a market-oriented exchange rate policy. The National Bank of Cambodia (NBC) performs periodic foreign exchange auctions. Since the first auction in 1993, the spread between the official and free market rates has been kept to no more than 2 percent.

INFRASTRUCTURE

Cambodia's infrastructure, which was almost completely destroyed after more than 20 years of warfare, civil strife and neglect, is slowly being restored. Power supply to the city of Phnom Penh has improved dramatically since 1993, and approximately 50 megawatts of power were added to serve the city during 1995 and 1996. Plans for Cambodia's first independent power production project, scheduled to provide another 60 megawatts of electrical power to the city, are nearing completion. According to the Cambodia Power Sector Strategy (1999-2016) developed by the Ministry of Industry, Mines, and Energy (MIME), annual electricity demand in Cambodia is projected to rise from 522GWh in 1998 to 2,634 GWh in 2016. To meet this demand, the government plans to develop $1 billion worth of hydro, gas turbine thermal, and combined cycle base load thermal generating plants in Phnom Penh, Sihanoukville, Battambang, and other cities from 2000 to 2010. The Cambodian government also plans to build a nation-wide transmission system during the same period. How Cambodia will finance development in the energy sector remains an open question.

The Cambodian government has not allocated significant budget resources to repairing the country's roads, nor has it worked out plans for private financing of road construction and repair. The highway system is therefore being rehabilitated through bilateral foreign assistance projects and multilateral loans, as they become available. Completion of the USAID-funded Route 4 rehabilitation project in late 1996 improved links between Phnom Penh and the deepwater port of Sihanoukville. Japan has rebuilt portions of routes 6 and 7 between Phnom Penh and Kampong Cham and is constructing a $57 million bridge over the Mekong River at Kampong Cham. The Asian Development Bank (ADB) has provided a $40 million loan to reconstruct Route 1 from the Neak Luang Ferry to the Vietnamese border by 2002. Other plans are in the works to rehabilitate portions of routes 3, 5, 6 and 7 with loans from the ADB and World Bank. The Cambodian government also seeks investors to repair other portions of the national highway system under build-operate-transfer (BOT) terms. A Thai contractor is currently repairing route 5 between Poipet, on the Thai border, and Sisophon on BOT terms.

The river port of Phnom Penh has been upgraded, and Japan has provided assistance to improve the cargo terminal at the deepwater port of Sihanoukville. The upgrade will include a new, 1000-meter-long, 12-meter-deep pier designed for oil tankers up to 30,000 tons.

Reliable fixed line and mobile telephone service are available in Phnom Penh and most provincial cities, but is expensive compared to other countries in the region. Fixed-line service is provided by the Ministry of Posts and Telecommunications, where as three cellular and one wireless local loop systems compete for mobile service. There is one international gateway, the operation of which MPTC has licensed to Telstra of Australia. In October 2000, MPTC intends to open a second international gateway. Long distance telephone rates have fallen, with calls to the U.S. now costing approximately $3.80 per minute.

MPTC maintains a monopoly on internet service in Cambodia, which it has licensed to two operators; its own subsidiary, Camnet, and a Bigpond, a joint venture with Telstra. The cost of internet service has fallen to about $3 per hour, but still remains far above the means of most Cambodians. The potential for e-commerce in Cambodia is further constrained by the relative unreliability of the postal system, and fact that few Cambodians have credit cards.

ECONOMIC PROSPECTS:

Cambodia has resumed its economic expansion, and is working with donors to develop the economic, legal and government institutions to support an investment-friendly open market economy. This transformation should continue, as long as political stability is maintained, and the government remains willing and able to implement the reform program it has committed to.

CAMBODIA ECONOMY AND MODERN ECONOMIC POLCY

1. Cambodia is an integrated territory under one government for the first time in three decades. In this more stable political environment, the government--formed in November 1998--is now in a position to renew its economic and structural reform program. With substantial support from the international community, progress was made in the first half of the 1990s in restoring financial stability and beginning economic reconstruction. However, much remains to be done to build basic economic and social institutions and attain sustainable development. As a legacy of the past, administrative and institutional capacities are weak, and Cambodia's need for external support remains considerable.

2. The goals of the government's reform program are poverty alleviation and the achievement of sustainable economic growth. This program is premised on strengthening the rule of law and governance, and tackling corruption. The overall agenda and strategy were endorsed by the National Assembly on November 30, 1998. The objectives of this agenda are: (i) safeguarding social stability and security; (ii) building human capacity; (iii) strengthening infrastructure and fostering an environment for private investment; (iv) fully protecting and preserving the natural environment; (v) enhancing national revenues in the context of a fully accountable and transparent fiscal policy; and (vi) encouraging the private sector as the engine of growth, investment, and employment creation. Within this agenda, this paper sets out the government's economic policy strategy and structural reforms for the period 1999-2002.

RECENT DEVELOPMENTS AND POLICY PERFORMANCE

3. **Macroeconomic performance deteriorated in the period leading up to the July 1998 elections and their aftermath, reflecting political instability and the impact of the regional crisis.** In this difficult environment, the government made strong attempts to contain the economic deterioration. Economic growth slowed, but remained positive, and inflation increased moderately. Fiscal performance reflected shortfalls in revenue and external financing, as well as overspending on the military. As a result, development expenditure was compressed, urgent increases in social spending were not achieved, and substantial bank financing of the budget was needed for the first time in four years. Moreover, there was limited progress in key structural areas such as forestry, budgetary management, and civil service and military reforms.

4. **With emerging political stability and returning confidence, economic prospects for 1999 and beyond have improved significantly**. The government is determined to break from the past, and has already initiated reform measures, announced in late 1998 and early 1999, against illegal logging and corruption, and to strengthen fiscal management. Moreover, the 1999 budget provides for important tax reform measures, increased social sector spending, and envisages no domestic financing. With these policies, and based on early indicators, economic growth in 1999 is expected to rise to 4 percent (on the strength of a rebound in agriculture and a recovery in tourism), and inflation is projected to decline to 5 percent. The external current account deficit is expected to widen to 12 percent of GDP reflecting a recovery in imports and a sharp curtailment of illegal logging activity.

5. **Building on recent initiatives, the government's medium-term strategy will focus on achieving lasting improvements in the structure of the public finances and in public resource management, in particular forestry**, all in close collaboration with international financial institutions, bilateral donors, and civil society. The program will also aim at rebuilding basic institutions, and undertaking related structural reforms, to create a secure environment for the private sector. The government has recently taken additional measures to reinforce its commitment to the reform program in the areas of tax administration, civil service and military reform, and forestry policy. However, the government fully recognizes that further actions will be needed to deepen these reforms (as indicated in the attached policy matrix).

MACROECONOMIC AND STRUCTURAL FRAMEWORK AND POLICIES

6. **The objectives of macroeconomic and structural policies are to raise economic growth and per capita income, and reduce poverty**. The key elements of the strategy are:

- Major efforts to strengthen revenue collections and enhance the transparency of fiscal operations, combined with reforms of the civil service and military;
- A substantial increase in public investment aimed at rehabilitating the country's poor social and physical infrastructure, and increased spending for health, education, and rural development;
- A strengthening of the legal framework and economic institutions.

7. The medium-term macroeconomic framework for 1999-2002 will aim at: raising economic growth to 6 percent; lowering annual inflation to 4 percent; containing the external current account deficit to 12-13 percent of GDP; and increasing gross official reserves to about four months of import coverage. The projected increases in output growth are premised on rising investment and savings. These will require a fiscal reform that increases revenues by 4 percentage points of GDP over the period, and redirects spending priorities away from defense toward social and economic reconstruction.

FISCAL POLICIES

8. The fiscal agenda aims at strengthening the role of the budget for economic management, and generating the resources needed to fund increased spending in priority areas. The main goals are to raise government saving to finance the public investment program and to avoid bank financing.

9. Revenue mobilization will be the key element in this strategy. To achieve the targeted increase in the revenue ratio from 9 percent of GDP in 1998--one of the lowest in the world--to 13 percent by 2002, the government will act on three fronts: full implementation of the remaining provisions in the 1997 Law on Taxation, strengthening the administrative capacity to collect taxes, and further broadening of the revenue base.

10. The main focus will be on a strengthening of tax and customs administration, and on ensuring full collection of nontax revenues, including arrears. Administration and enforcement of tax compliance will be enhanced through the exchange of taxpayer information between government departments; intensified on-site tax audits; and through further technical assistance from the Fund. The current practice of disqualifying investors from tax exemptions unless they are current on their tax obligations will be reinforced and extended to other taxpayers.

11. In addition, the revenue base will be broadened through:

- Tightening and strictly monitoring tax and duty exemptions provided under the Law on Investment (by revising the Law and its implementing regulations where necessary).

Strictly avoiding ad hoc tax or duty exemptions, subjecting imports to preshipment inspection, and reinforcing customs administration.

- Extending VAT coverage in terms of the number of taxpayers and the sectoral coverage.
- Strengthening financial controls by bringing all extrabudgetary revenues under the control of the Treasury, including those collected through line ministries, through strict implementation of the December 1997 Prime Ministerial Order for the transfer of revenue collected by line ministries to the Treasury, and the recent cabinet decision that empowers the Ministry of Economy and Finance (MEF) to directly collect proceeds from the sale and lease of state assets.

- Incorporating into the budget all revenue arising from garment quota auctions and management fees, and, in accordance with the Prime Ministerial Order of May 3, subjecting all new quotas to auction.

12. **The government attaches importance to achieving a substantial shift in public expenditure toward priority social areas and economic infrastructure**. With recent improvements in the security situation, the government will aim at a significant and durable reduction in defense and security spending from 4.2 percent of GDP in 1998 to 2.5 percent of GDP in 2002. This will require sustained reductions in operational expenditures and in the military wage bill in line with the planned removal of ghost soldiers and the demobilization program. The civilian wage bill (1.7 percent of GDP in 1999) will be contained and any further increases in wages will be tied to progress in implementing civil service reform.

13. **Adequate funding for priority sectors will be ensured, in line with the government's Socio-Economic Development Plan, and the World Bank's Public Expenditure Review (PER)**. Annual reviews of the three-year rolling Public Investment Program (PIP) will be strengthened to ensure that capital spending is supportive of development needs. Moreover, the government will mobilize the required local-currency counterpart of externally financed capital spending to facilitate timely disbursements of project assistance.

14. **To improve budgetary performance and transparency, the government will ensure that all issues relating to taxation are prepared in a transparent manner**, with the MEF given the responsibility for drafting, implementing, and administering tax legislation. Ad hoc spending decisions outside the budget framework will be minimized, ministries' technical and financial management capabilities will be strengthened, and responsibility for performance at the level of spending units will be promoted. A National Audit Authority will also be established by mid-2000.

FORESTRY POLICIES

15. **The government's objective in forestry is the development of an environmentally sustainable, socially responsible and economically viable sector**. Initial measures have been taken to curtail illegal activity, strengthen governance, and improve overall monitoring. These measures will be reinforced by overhauling concession management, formulating a legal framework for forestry, establishing a permanent forest estate, and strengthening intersectoral oversight and accountability.

16. **The government is committed to fighting forest crime**, through all elements of society including the military, police, provincial authorities and local communities. Above all, effective forest management, as outlined below, will serve to prevent forest crime. In addition, to better detect forest crime, monitoring capacity is being strengthened in the key agencies, and a forest crime monitoring unit has been established with the participation of outside independent experts. The government will publish the reports of this unit on a quarterly basis.

17. **The government is reforming the concession system to ensure appropriate revenue for the budget, consistent with sustainable logging**. Performance of concessionaires is being reviewed against their contracts and action will be taken to terminate those concessions in serious breach. In the first half of 1999, out of a total of

31, 11 concession contracts covering 2.2 million hectares have been cancelled and the remaining concessions are under review. The review of all concession contracts will be completed by early 2000. The government also intends to improve the practices and procedures for the management and control of any new concessions. Retendering of forest areas for concessions will be based on rational criteria, and will be supported by prior public notice and disclosure of contract terms and conditions. Concessionaires will be required to operate in accordance with standards for forest practice, as defined by the draft Sub-Decree on Forest Concession Management to be submitted to the Council of Ministers by mid-October 1999.

18. New concessions will be awarded on the basis of competitive and transparent procedures. To ensure appropriate forestry revenue, royalty provisions will be kept under review. Furthermore, to promote efficient processing and marketing of timber, the current log export ban policy will be reviewed commensurate with improvements in the enforcement of forest law.

19. Recognizing the national and global significance of Cambodia's natural heritage, the government is committed to the preservation of a representative range of the country's natural ecosystems and biodiversity. In addition to requiring concessionaires, and park and protected area managers to adhere to strict standards, the government supports community forestry as part of an approach to rural development and forest resource management. Mechanisms will be initiated for the award of long-term tenure rights to forest resources to local communities, indigenous peoples, and other targeted groups including demobilized soldiers and their families.

ADMINISTRATIVE AND MILITARY REFORM

20. Following increases in the size of the civil service in recent years, the government's objective is to rationalize and downsize the civil service. The precise number and status of civil servants needs to be ascertained and for this purpose, the government will fully implement the computerized payroll and management system. This system is now operational in eight ministries, and will be extended to all ministries by March 2000. On this basis, the government will strictly limit the number of new hires and reduce the number of civil servants in 1999 through elimination of all redundant workers and through normal attrition. Further reductions will be made in 2000-2002 following a functional review of all ministries and adoption of a comprehensive civil service reform program, all aimed at containing the wage bill to within 1.7 percent of GDP while upgrading the civil service.

21. Demobilization will be vital. Under the recently updated program for demobilization--the Cambodian Veteran's Assistance Program (CVAP)--the overall objective is to reallocate funds from defense to social and economic sectors, through reducing, over a five-year period, the size of the Royal Cambodian Armed Forces (RCAF) from 142,308 as of June 1999 to about 80,000-100,000. Total defense spending (excluding security) would be reduced from 2.9 percent of GDP in 1998 to no more than 2 percent of GDP by 2002. As the first phase of the CVAP, the identification and registration process will be completed by late 1999 and the pilot implementation will begin early in the year 2000. Full-scale implementation of the CVAP will start thereafter, following an evaluation of the pilot implementation. In the interim, the government will make full use of all possibilities for reducing the military wage bill through elimination of ghost soldiers and their dependents. In addition, other personnel with irregular status, including those identified in the registration process, will also be eliminated.

PRIVATE SECTOR DEVELOPMENT AND PUBLIC ENTERPRISE REFORM

22. For transparency and a level playing field, the government is reforming the legal and institutional frameworks for the private sector. Cambodia has made steady progress in developing the legal and regulatory framework, but substantial gaps and inconsistencies need to be rectified. For this purpose, a comprehensive Commercial Code is being prepared to strengthen the regulatory framework for business organization, contracts, intellectual property rights, and product liability. Two commercial laws will be submitted to the National Assembly by December 1999, and the remainder by end-2000. Measures will also be taken to strengthen the rule of law and transparency, including modernizing the judiciary.

23. Building on the progress in defining a strategy and a regulatory framework for public enterprise reform, further steps will be taken to establish a more efficient and streamlined public enterprise sector. The government intends to corporatize the eleven (mainly infrastructure) SOEs to remain in the public sector in accordance with the Law Regulating the Public Enterprises. Furthermore, restructuring plans for seven rubber plantations and a privatization schedule will be prepared, aimed at privatizing at least one selected plantation by December 2001.

BANKING AND EXTERNAL SECTOR POLICIES

24. The banking system must be strengthened to better meet the development needs of the economy. The new Financial Institutions Law will be adopted by October 1999, under which banks will be subject to relicensing and the provisions of the law. The Foreign Trade Bank, in which the National Bank of Cambodia (NBC) is still a major shareholder, is being restructured and will be privatized by end-2001. On-site inspections of banks through internationally recognized audit firms will be continued and their frequency increased. Further improvements in banking supervision capacity will also be made by increasing and training NBC staff. Credit policy will be geared to reducing inflation through avoiding recourse to bank financing of the budget. Issuance of treasury bills at market determined interest rates will be initiated to promote intermediation and provide the NBC with a monetary policy instrument, thereby contributing to dedollarization.

25. The government will maintain its market-based exchange rate policy and a liberal exchange system. The official exchange rate will continue to be adjusted flexibly. To signal its commitment to a liberal exchange and payments system, the government intends to accept the obligations under the Fund's Article VIII, Sections 2, 3, and 4, during the program period.

26. Under an outward-oriented growth strategy, the government is committed to intensifying Cambodia's integration into the regional and world economy. Cambodia joined ASEAN in April 1999 and preparation is well advanced for Cambodia's participation in the ASEAN Free Trade Area (AFTA) and for accession to the World Trade Organization (WTO). Membership in the Multilateral Investment Guarantee

Agency (MIGA) has been ratified in the National Assembly, and efforts are continuing to conclude bilateral investment agreements with partner countries.

27. In the context of AFTA and WTO, a credible trade reform over the period 2000-2002 will be an important start to liberalization. Currently, Cambodia's tariff structure consists of a maximum rate of 50 percent with a few exceptions, five bands including the zero rate, and an average tariff rate of 17 percent. The government aims to further rationalize and reduce import tariffs, by progressively lowering the maximum tariff rate to 30 percent by January 2002 and the number of tariff bands to four. On this basis, and taking into account technical assistance from the Fund to help define alternative revenue sources, it is envisaged that the average tariff rate could be reduced to a range of 13-14 percent by 2002.

28. Given Cambodia's limited debt servicing capacity, the government will not contract or guarantee foreign currency debt on nonconcessional terms over the period 1999-2002. In addition, concessional external debt will be closely monitored, and will be contracted only after the economic viability and prospective returns have been assured. The Minister of Economy and Finance will continue to have the sole authority over the contracting and guaranteeing of all public external borrowing. The MEF's external debt management unit will be strengthened further with technical assistance from the World Bank and the Asian Development Bank (AsDB). The government will also make its best effort to conclude the one remaining bilateral agreement under the 1995 Paris Club agreement, and the agreement with Russia within the framework of the Paris Club, as well as seeking comparable treatment by other bilateral creditors.

STATISTICS

29. The government will continue to improve the coverage, quality, and timeliness of economic data. To enhance public confidence, the trend of greater openness through regular and timely publication of data will be continued. Particular attention will be paid to improving the coverage of fiscal data to include donor-financed expenditures, and to more frequent publication of comprehensive fiscal data over the three-year ESAF period. The government will also seek to participate in the IMF's *General Data Dissemination System.*

SECTORAL POLICIES FOR ECONOMIC AND SOCIAL DEVELOPMENT

30. The government accords high priority to agricultural and rural development, as agriculture contributes half of Cambodia's GDP and employs 80 percent of the labor force. Moreover, poverty remains predominantly rural, demanding accelerated public investment and social services to the rural areas. The main objectives in the agricultural sector are: to improve food security through expanding rice production and diversifying crops; increase income-earning opportunities for farm households by facilitating production of cash crops and non-farm rural enterprises; and enhance the contribution of agriculture and agro-processing to economic growth and exports.

31. To achieve these objectives, the following key policy actions will be taken:

- Increase public investment in rural infrastructure, including upgrading and maintenance of secondary and tertiary roads, and rehabilitation of irrigation and water supply systems based on cost sharing of operating and maintenance costs;

- Increase agricultural productivity (especially rice) through production and marketing of improved seed varieties, appropriate pest management and water control, and strengthening of technical services, conservation, and management;

- Promote agricultural export earnings through research, surveys and pilot projects for the development of commercial agriculture and agro-processing;

- Develop sound rural finance institutions, and create a transparent and secure land market by adopting, after appropriate national consultations, a revised land law and its implementing regulations, with adequate protection for the rights of small-scale producers.

32. Despite recent improvements, access to good quality health care remains a priority, as government spending in health is still inadequate. The policy actions in this sector are:

- Expand the network of health centers and referral hospitals, increase the package of services to focus on maternal and child health and national disease control, and extend these services to the rural areas;

- Increase government health spending to 2 percent of GDP and establish a program of cost recovery (including user charges and community based pre-paid insurance schemes);

- Phase in a sector-wide approach, by addressing reform issues such as decentralization, financial management, local capacity, and monitoring.

33. The goals of education reform are to improve quality and to achieve equity in opportunity, through the following actions:

- Allocate a minimum of 15 percent of government revenue to education, mainly to improve the provision of books and materials, training, and teacher incentives, and focus spending on basic and lower secondary education, while encouraging private sector involvement in upper secondary and tertiary education.

- Ensure more efficient deployment of teachers and staff, and develop transparent and equitable means for nongovernment financing (e.g., school community partnerships, private education).

- Monitor results in terms of the increases in the net enrollment of children in basic education and in terms of the closing of the gender gap.

34. The focus for transport infrastructure will remain rehabilitation of high-priority trunk and feeder roads and bridges, in order to realize the potential of agriculture, tourism and trade in the rural areas. There is also the need to develop a comprehensive transport policy framework, addressing issues such as development of a balanced construction and maintenance program; increased involvement of the private sector over time; and financing of road maintenance and cost recovery mechanisms. With regard to institutional strengthening, the Ministry of Public Works and Transport will formulate strategies to improve its capacity to plan, manage, and implement road operations.

35. To improve water supply and sanitation services, steps have been initiated towards formulating a sectoral strategy. The government plans to finalize, over the next few years, sectoral policies on tariffs, financing, and institutional arrangements. Based on this strategy, the government will develop institutions to provide services based on consumer demand; develop financing policies that leverage private and community investments; encourage outsourcing of utility operations to the private sector; and promote investment in sanitation.

36. To commercialize and strengthen the power sector, and attract private sector investment, the government aims to: re-establish an adequate supply of electricity nationwide, through direct support of donors and private participation; enact an Electricity Act and establish a regulatory body (Electricity Authority of Cambodia); commercialize EDC through a performance- based contract; strengthen sector managerial and implementing capability; formulate procedures for the selection and contracting of private generators; and formulate strategy for rural electrification and initiate the first project.

37. The strategy for the environment is outlined in the National Environmental Action Plan (NEAP) approved by the Council of Ministers in 1998. The NEAP provides action plans to deal with issues related to forest policy, fisheries and floodplain agriculture in the Tonle Sap, coastal fisheries, biodiversity and protected areas, energy development and the environment, and urban waste management. Immediate priority is being given to the strengthening of forest policy, biodiversity, and the protected areas management. The Ministry of Environment, with technical assistance from the World Bank, is preparing a pilot project at the Virachey National Park to demonstrate a model approach to protected areas management that can be applied to the other 22 protected areas in the country.

EXTERNAL FINANCING REQUIREMENTS

38. Implementation of the reform program described above will contribute to a strengthening of the external position. Over the program period, export growth in dollar terms is projected to accelerate to an average annual rate of 10 percent, while import growth is projected to rise to about 9½ percent annually, reflecting increases in project aid and FDI as confidence returns. Accordingly, the current account deficit (excluding official transfers) would be contained to a sustainable level of 12-13 percent of GDP, and official reserves would rise moderately to about four months of import coverage.

39. On this basis, the total external financing requirement for the period 1999-2002 is projected at $3.5 billion (Table 3). Total disbursements from official grants and loans are projected at $1.3 billion and foreign direct investment at $0.5 billion. The residual financing gap, estimated at $0.2 billion, could be covered by prospective disbursements of the Bank's Structural Adjustment Credit (SAC), possible co-financing and other bilateral loans, and prospective drawing under the IMF's ESAF. Since new debt would be contracted on highly concessional terms, the debt service ratio is projected by the Fund staff at 5½ percent in 2002.

TECHNICAL ASSISTANCE REQUIREMENTS

40. Successful implementation of the reform program requires substantial technical assistance in the period ahead, including more attention on capacity building and training. As noted in the PFP matrix:

- The Fund will provide further technical assistance in broadening the revenue base and strengthening revenue administration, in central bank operations and banking supervision, and in the external debt area.

- The Bank will provide assistance in VAT implementation; expenditure management; civil service census, and a functional review of all ministries; governance, commercial law, and the rule of law; the power and water sectors; and in implementing the national environment action plan; and along with other donors, in the forestry area, public investment program, demobilization, and on poverty monitoring.

- Bilateral and multilateral donors are providing assistance in the key structural areas such as forestry, infrastructure, and social sectors.

41. Further technical assistance will be needed, inter alia, to develop a transparent and market-based mechanism for timber royalties; to implement an action plan for civil service reform (including social safety nets for retrenchment); to restructure and modernize the rubber sector; to develop a comprehensive transport sector policy; to implement and review pilot programs for cost recovery in the health sector; and to regularize the current informal cost recovery program in the education sector.

THE STRUCTURE OF THE ECONOMY

AGRICULTURE

he main domestic activity on which most rural households depend is agriculture and its related sub-sectors. Agriculture contributes about half of the country's GDP and employs about 80 percent of the labor force. Agriculture has been growing at an average rate of 2 percent over 1991-94. Not only is agriculture the largest primary sector of the Cambodian economy (compared with industry and services), but in the last few years its pace of development has been satisfactorily in-creasing. Not surprisingly, however, because of the long - term
influence of administered pricing and output targeting arrangements,. the current production performance of different commodities is mixed. In terms of the recorded current values of both gross and net output, crops (63 percent), livestock (26 percent), fishing (8 percent), and forestry (3 percent) represent the broad subsector ranking in order of the importance of their contribution to agricultural value added.

CROPS AND COMMODITIES

Among crops, rice (representing approximately 74 and 66 percent, respectively, of gross and net crop values) makes by far the most important contribution to value added. This is followed by vegetables, including soybean and mungbean., jute, tobacco, sugar cane, and maize in current values. Rubber, as a raw material tree crop, is also important.. but not as important as it was a generation ago when organized private plantation production provided the bulk of the output.

LIVESTOCK

It is unusual for the South East Asia region that, in Cambodia, cattle is more important than swine, principally because buffalo and oxen are valued for the wide scope of their contributions to output. Cattle are also exported informally (on the hoof) to both Viet Nam and Thailand, but there is no clear measure of the value of these sales. Pork and poultry, on the other hand, are slaughtered predominantly for domestic consumption.

FISHING

Value added contributed by fishing is less than a third of that contributed by livestock. Commercial fishing operations remain relatively small scale, but a limited export potential certainly exists. As the economy opens up, it can be expected that Cambodia will take advantage of new opportunities to exploit both domestic and overseas markets. The scope of development, however, may be limited by the traditional fishing methods in place, particularly where freshwater catches (which are by far the most important) are concerned. It is reported, however, that traditional freshwater fish habitats are becoming increasingly subject to environmental degradation and over-fishing.

FORESTRY

Officially, forest products represent only a small share of value added, but it is well known that a significant amount of unreported logging takes place and that logs are shipped regularly across Cambodia's borders, both to the west and to the east. Logging in Cambodia is a rapidly growing industry, and concerns regarding over- exploitation are being increasingly expressed. Forest cover in Cambodia has fallen from 73 percent of land area to less than 50 percent in the last two decades. While this rate is considerably slower than Thailand's, it is, nonetheless proving ecologically harmful. As has been implied above, deforestation has led to significant siltation in the Mekong and Tonle Sap Rivers, and the denudation of previously wooded hillsides is also believed to be one of the causes of increasingly severe flooding in lowland areas, particularly during the monsoon period. A nationwide campaign of forestation has been organized by the Royal Government in order to pressure Cambodia's natural resources.

INDUSTRY

Industrial value added remains at a relatively low 17 percent of GDP, although it is growing at a more rapid pace than agriculture (over 10 percent on. average over the last four years).

MANUFACTURING

Manufacturing output is varied but not very extensive and is mostly conducted on a very small-scale and informal basis. Many prospering local activities such as brickmaking and ceramics are linked. to the fortunes and performance of the construction sector. Among the industrial products made in Cambodia, agricultural implements (ploughs) show a steady rise in output, but the greatest increases in the last year or two have occurred in building-related products and bicycle/motorcycle inner tubes (tire output., on other hand, has fallen
- presumably,, in part because of the recent large jump in imports of new motorcycles and cars and the resultant temporarily reduced demand for tire replacements). Compared with the mid-1980s, however, output in this industry is running at a high level and there is a small, but improving, export trade the garment industry - thanks to GSP trade preferences - is booming with exports growing from $3.8 millions in 1996 to $26.4 millions in 1995. The electricity and water sector shows a slightly declining share of GDP, consistent with the
reported performance in the manufacturing sector and reflecting, also serious equipment-related capacity constraints in the electricity generating industry. A substantial price rise in electricity was introduced in 1991 designed, in part, to ration demand more effectively and to provide a margin for improved maintenance and repair. Almost all other industries, with the exception of a few minor goods intended for final domestic consumption (for example, glassware,, cigarettes,. vegetable oil, and local wine)., show a significant decline in output since 1985.

MINING

Mining activities are minimal. In the early 1970s, the following were being mined: clay (for ceramics), dolomite (for glassmaking), gold, limestone (for cement), pagodite,, phosphate, quartz, sapphire, ruby, silica sand, and other precious stones. Extraction was on a very small scale. With the exception of gemstones (Pailin mine) and gold, exploitation of most of these minerals has now reverted to artisanal methods and goes largely unreported. The only mineral exploration on any significant scale is that of oil and gas off the Gulf of Thailand and possibly in the mainland.

SERVICES

The service sector has shown robust growth over the last four years. It accounts for about 35 percent of GDP, and is heavily concentrated on trading activities (15 percent of GDP) and on catering-related services. The growth has been driven by the expansion in wholesale and retail trade as the economy has moved toward a more open market system. Somewhat surprisingly, the increase in output of the transport and communications sector (over 10 percent per year in 1991-93) did not keep pace with distribution services, tending instead to develop almost exactly in line with the trend in real GDP.

Physical supply constraints,, the lack of security, or simply under-reporting may account for this. The Government, although a major employer, contributes comparatively little to GDP (roughly 4 percent), partly because salaries - which form a large share of total official outlays - have remained depressed. Although official statistics do not fully reflect its status, the hotel and restaurant trade has shown considerable buoyancy over the past few years because of the sheer need to deal with a new urban work force and to accommodate the large influx of nonresidents associated with the peace process, the transitional administration, and development support in general.

US AND INTERNATIONAL ASSISTANCE

US ASSISTANCE TO CAMBODIA

U. S. national interests in Cambodia include promoting democracy, political pluralism and improved human rights; addressing global problems of infectious diseases including HIV/AIDS and poor maternal and child health; and providing humanitarian assistance to large numbers of Cambodians who suffered the effects of civil war, genocide and foreign occupation.

DEVELOPMENT CHALLENGE

Cambodia's development challenge is formidable. Ranked 140th of 174 countries on the United Nations Development Program's Human Development Index, Cambodia's social and economic indicators resemble those of western nations a century ago. Annual per capita GDP is less than $300. Life expectancy at birth is 53 years. Infant, child and maternal mortality rates are the highest in Asia, and Cambodia's HIV/AIDS epidemic is Asia's fastest growing. Years of war and neglect have ravaged the country's physical infrastructure. The educated group of teachers, managers, doctors, nurses and other skilled professionals, which was almost entirely wiped out by the Khmer Rouge, is just now being rebuilt. The result is a population aged 18-36 which lacks the basic skills necessary for more than subsistence living and a structure which is unable to support economic growth and the establishment of democratic processes -- a situation which contributes to keeping the population in a state of poverty. Added to this has been the failure to achieve a stable political environment, peace and security since the signing of the 1991 Paris Peace Accords.

Subsequent to the formation of a Royal Government of Cambodia (RGC) in 1993, USAID's program shifted from emergency relief and rehabilitation to reconstruction and long-term sustainable development. By FY 1997 the program had reached an annual level of $38 million with cooperation in democracy and human rights, rural economic growth, health and population, primary education, war and mine victim assistance, environment and HIV/AIDS prevention. Following the political events of July 1997, two-thirds of U. S. assistance, and all bilateral assistance, was suspended. That suspension remains in effect.

USAID is responding to, and has achieved significant progress toward, meeting the development challenge by building civil society structures in order to promote human rights and which support the delivery of basic humanitarian and social services.

In democracy, NGOs played major roles in restoring democratic momentum, in completion of a national election in July 1998 with 93% voter turnout, in election and human rights monitoring and in providing legal aid through a public defenders program. Management and advocacy training was also provided to build NGO capacity and strengthen civil society.

In maternal and child health, NGOs provided maternal and child health services to more than 120,000 women and children; rural health centers staff in six districts learned skills which resulted in better client care and the percentage of population with access to clean water in one Northeast Cambodia target area increased from 13% to 30%.

In HIV/AIDS prevention, assistance is designed to decrease HIV transmission in high-risk populations. In 1998, 11.7 million condoms were sold, with 30% of the sales in brothels and bars where the target population is best reached. The Khmer HIV/AIDS Alliance (KHANA) is supporting 18 Cambodian community-based organizations to raise AIDS awareness and to provide AIDS prevention and care services.

In microfinance, USAID strives to make formal savings and credit programs available to the rural poor. In 1998, 85,000 clients, over 90% of them women, received loans totaling $5.5 million from 12,500 village banks.

Under the program of assistance to war and mine victims, in 1998 over 3,400 amputees were fitted with prosthetic devices and nearly 1,000 orphans and poor youth were given vocational training and other assistance to help them seek gainful employment. Growing out of decades of war and trauma, mental illness is common in Cambodia. Under a model community-based mental health program, 104 physicians have been trained to provide these much-needed services nationwide.

Since suspension of the aid program in July 1997, major positive changes have taken place. A national election was held; a coalition government was formed and seated; the National Assembly has reconvened; and all but one of the Khmer Rouge leaders and most of its troops have abandoned warfare. In addition, the repatriation of the remaining 37,000 refugees and their reintegration into society, along with internally displaced persons, offers opportunities for cooperative efforts with USG-funded demining programs. Plans are underway for a renewed donor forum on international assistance for Cambodia at the World-Bank-chaired Consultative Group (CG) meeting currently scheduled for late February 1999. The RGC's development agenda for the CG and the World Bank's analysis of that plan will provide a framework for the provision of development assistance by the international donor community. If circumstances permit, high priorities for USAID assistance include reinstituting programs in primary education, environment and rural economic growth.

OTHER DONORS

Many bilateral donors drastically cut back their assistance progams due to the events of July 1997. Prior to the 1997 aid suspension, the U.S. was the second largest bilateral donor after Japan. Other donors include France, Australia, the European Union (EU), Netherlands and Sweden. Cambodia also receives assistance from the World Bank and the Asian Development Bank. The International Monetary Fund suspended its program in Cambodia due to illegal logging activities and a lack of transparency in the collection of forestry revenues. With the formation of a new government, other donors have recently signaled their intention to resume development cooperation with Cambodia. While new levels of donor assistance won't be known until after the February CG, the RGC request for the 1999-2001 period is about $449 annually, and indicative levels are known for Japan ($50.3 million), Australia ($32 million), and the Asian Development

Bank (ADB - $100 million). Assistance is primarily in the health, education, microfinance and other basic services sectors and for infrastructure.

PROGRAM

USAID's FY 2000 program assumes a continued humanitarian assistance program through NGOs. In democracy and human rights, programs will focus on further strengthening civil society and indigenous institutions that promote human rights, the rule of law and the provision of social services. Maternal-child health and HIV/AIDS prevention programs will fine tune existing interventions to maximize achievement of results. USAID will continue to fund NGO activities that address basic needs of war and mine victims, with a special emphasis on women. In microfinance, USAID will continue support for, and expansion of, financial services for the rural poor, particularly women.

SELECTED PROGRAMS

Strengthened Democratic Processes and Respect for Human Rights, 442-SO01

STATUS: Continuing
PROPOSED OBLIGATION AND FUNDING SOURCES: FY 2000: $8,000,000 ESF
INITIAL OBLIGATION: FY 1992 **ESTIMATED COMPLETION DATE:** FY 2000

Summary: In the course of over two decades of civil war and foreign occupation, virtually all of Cambodia's principal institutions of democratic governance were destroyed or dismantled. Rehabilitation of these institutions -- including the judiciary, the national legislature, electoral processes, and local-level governance -- is a fundamental prerequisite for Cambodia's transition to a sustainable and economically viable democratic society. The purpose of this Strategic Objective (SO) is to help Cambodians build those democratic principles and practices. The fragility of and the hopes surrounding the current juncture are shown by recent events -- the most outstanding of which are the violence of July 1997, the national election of July 1998, and the formation of a coalition government in November 1998.

In this volatile climate, USAID is focusing on increasing awareness of the rule of law, strengthening civil society, and creating greater governmental accountability (two cross-cutting themes are human rights and women). Beneficiaries directly involved in grant-funded training include eight Cambodian human rights/public policy NGOs and five women's rights associations. Beneficiaries of legal aid include indigent Cambodians accused of crimes and those in need of assistance with civil disputes. Additionally, over five million Cambodians benefit by receiving democracy-oriented public service announcements through the media. If current restrictions on direct assistance to the government are lifted, additional beneficiaries will include members of the National Assembly and the judiciary.

Key Results: Three key intermediate results have been designed to meet this SO: (1) Legal sector: increased respect for the rule of law and the upholding of citizens' rights by strengthening legal aid and public defender services, and reducing pretrial detentions and other violations of due process in the courts; (2) Elections: efforts must continue to build a system for transparent, multi-party elections (local-level elections are currently scheduled for late 1999); and (3) Human rights: strengthening the sustainability and impact of local human rights organizations by educating the public on human rights issues and by increasing the percentage of human rights abuses reported and successfully resolved.

Performance and Prospects: In response to the July 1997 violence, the U.S. Government suspended two-thirds of its $38 million aid program in Cambodia and imposed corresponding legislative and policy restrictions on all remaining assistance. These restrictions included a prohibition against assisting or working with the RGC, e.g., the courts, the National Assembly, or the various ministries. In light of these continuing restrictions, and given the nature of Cambodia's current political environment, performance with respect to this SO over the past year has been relatively successful, even if narrowly focused. USAID assistance, even on the current limited basis, continues to play a pivotal role in the country's democratic transition.

USAID-funded grantees continued to promote government accountability and strengthen civil society. This was accomplished by increasing the presence of public defenders in Cambodian courtrooms; introducing internationally recognized labor practices; building a successful community legal education program; strengthening human rights and public policy organizations, including the most visible indigenous human rights organizations and the nascent Cambodian Bar Association; and strengthening civil society by building NGO capacity. USAID-supported Cambodian NGOs were also prominent in supporting preparations for the 1998 parliamentary elections in the areas of voter-education and monitoring. In addition, the National Democratic Institute (NDI) and the International Republican Institute (IRI) provided election support that emphasized long-term popular participation in, and sustainability of, the election process rather than a particular political outcome.

The majority of funds allocated for FY 2000 under this SO will be used to strengthen the rule of law, governance, government accountability, respect for human rights, and civil society. In addition to any new projects identified in an upcoming strategy assessment, The Asia Foundation (TAF) -- currently the largest grantee under the program -- will continue supporting local organizations engaged in protecting human rights, furthering public policy making, and implementing nationwide good governance programs aimed at the local level. USAID intends to focus its ongoing rule of law program in Cambodia towards its successful programs, notably the Cambodia Project of the International Human Rights Law Group (IHRLG), and concentrate on efforts to help end the continuing climate of impunity, including efforts to strengthen the formal legal system.

Prospects in these areas will depend much on developments in the local political situation; the direction of USAID/Cambodia's democracy program will in part depend on response to those developments from Washington.

Possible Adjustments to Plans: The events of the past year and a half have delayed USAID's intensive review of its democracy and rule of law strategy. Given the recently improved local political climate, USAID is now planning a major sector strategy assessment to determine its second generation democracy and rule of law programs. The activities identified for assistance will be competed and are planned to be underway as of January 1, 2000. This assessment -- and possible redesign of the SO -- will be done in conjunction with USAID/Washington.

In addition, limited funding is available to support the local (commune-level) elections anticipated for late 1999. These elections will force previously appointed local officials to run for election.

Other Donor Programs: The United States, Japan, France, Australia, the European Union (EU) and various United Nations agencies are the major donors working in the democracy sector in Cambodia. Coordination of assistance plans and activities between the donors in specific areas has been good. A specific example of this is the close cooperation of the many donors that came together to support the 1998 parliamentary elections.

Principal Contractors, Grantees or Agencies: Current grantees include TAF, IHRLG, Private Agencies Collaborating Together (Pact), and the University of San Francisco (USF).

Improved Maternal and Child Health, 442-SO02

STATUS: Continuing
PROPOSED OBLIGATION AND FUNDING SOURCES: FY 2000: $7,000,000 ESF
INITIAL OBLIGATION: FY 1995 **ESTIMATED COMPLETION DATE:** FY 2000

Summary: When USAID began work on this objective in 1995, Cambodia had no reliable data on important measures of health status such as infant mortality, maternal mortality or contraceptive prevalence. Cambodia is still an extremely data-poor country, but the data that are available point toward significant progress in improving maternal and child health over the past four years. In target areas, USAID implementing partners have made important contributions to that progress. For example, in target areas, health facilities have been re-established, equipped and staff trained. On the national level, key health policies that will benefit the entire country are at varying stages of development and implementation.

As this five-year strategic objective nears completion, it appears that the most important targets will have been achieved, perhaps by a significant degree in some cases. However, despite the fact that the objective's targets are likely to be met, health status in Cambodia will remain at one of the lowest levels in Southeast Asia.

Key Results: The three key results for this objective are: (1) improved leadership exercised by public sector officials; (2) improved service delivery in the public and private sectors; and (3) improved MCH commodity accessibility and rational management.

Performance and Prospects: Performance on this objective has been good. With just three private clinics, one of USAID's grantees provided reproductive health, birth spacing or antenatal care services to more than 15,000 clients during the first six months of 1998, in addition to serving the birth spacing needs of more than 10,000 new clients in five provinces through community based distribution systems. USAID partners provided approximately 30,000 residents in remote provinces with improved access to water and sanitation facilities while primary health care services were strengthened and/or reintroduced in at least 43 health care facilities in target areas. On the national level, USAID implementing partners provided important technical assistance for the development and implementation of an informed consent policy for surgical contraception, pharmaceutical logistics management systems, and improved quality of care for childhood illnesses. In addition, USAID partners have contributed to developments on the national vitamin A distribution system, salt iodization plans and the introduction and adaptation of the Integrated Management of Childhood Illness initiative.

As a result of these activities, the population of the target areas has benefited directly from improved services or access to services, while at the national level, the population benefits from improved health policies and quality of services.

Possible Adjustments to Plans: With this strategic objective nearing conclusion, USAID/Cambodia will re-evaluate its approach to maternal and child health over the coming months to ensure that the interventions implemented remain the most effective and the ones most likely to achieve desired improvements in the health of women and children.

Other Donor Programs: The United Nations Children's Fund (UNICEF) supports the national immunization and essential drugs programs, as well as provincial health advisors in four provinces. The World Health Organization (WHO) supports national-level vector control programs as well as providing technical advisors for health sector reform and the provincial health management teams in a number of provinces. UNICEF and WHO, together with the Ministry of Health (MOH), have taken the lead on the introduction and adaptation of the Integrated Management of Childhood Illness initiative.

The United Nations Population Fund (UNFPA) supports a national-level reproductive health and birth spacing project in collaboration with the MOH as well as continuing analyses of the recently-collected national census data. The World Bank and Asian Development Bank support provincial-level health systems strengthening projects. Germany provides technical support for the National Public Health Research Institute. Australia provides technical support for primary health care activities at the provincial level. A coordination committee of host government, donor, international and implementing agencies meets monthly for joint review, planning and monitoring.

Principal Contractors, Grantees or Agencies: USAID/Cambodia implements its MCH activities through U.S., international, and local NGOs and centrally-managed cooperating agencies. Grantees include CARE International, Helen Keller International, Medecins Sans Frontieres, Partners for Development, Reproductive Health Association of Cambodia, Population Services International, and World Vision International. Global Bureau partners include AVSC International and John Snow.

Selected Performance Measures:

Enhanced Assistance for War and Mine Victims, 442-SpO01

STATUS: Continuing
PROPOSED OBLIGATION AND FUNDING SOURCES: FY 2000: $2,500,000 ESF
INITIAL OBLIGATION: FY 1993 **ESTIMATED COMPLETION DATE:** FY 2001

Summary: Cambodia's tragic history of war and civil unrest has resulted in an estimated 158,000 disabled persons (of whom 45,000 are land mine amputees), 200,000 impoverished youth and war orphans and 600,000 widows. These individuals face tremendous social barriers, e.g. stigmatization, lack of skills, and lack of mobility, thus precluding their effective participation in family life and in productive social and economic activities. In addition to the problem of large numbers of war-affected individuals, the inadequate health care system, widespread poverty and lack of a social safety net push war and mine victims to the extreme margins of Cambodian society.

USAID partners are implementing rehabilitation, training, and service provision activities to allow these individuals to participate more fully in society and lead productive lives. In addition, USAID implementing partners have been instrumental in the formation of 15 specialized coordination and training mechanisms to address the different activities in this sector. Given the limited capacity of the RGC and other Cambodian institutions, support for war and mine victims will continue to require significant international donor and NGO assistance for quite some time.

Key Results: The two key results for this objective are: (1) increasing access to rehabilitation care and job training, and (2) establishing ten functional coordinating and training mechanisms in government agencies and NGOs.

Performance and Prospects: Overall performance under this special objective has met expectations and some individual activities have significantly exceeded expectations. There are now 15 networks, sub-committees or other support groups working to facilitate assistance to war and mine victims as opposed to the 10 that were originally planned. Similar success was seen with prostheses and orthotics: 4,690 new and replacement prosthetic and orthotic devices were manufactured and fitted, including appropriate follow-up for patients, 53% above the annual target for 1998. Achievement of mental health care provider training and patient consultations are on target, with an additional 54 health care providers trained this year and over 1,400 patients receiving consultation or treatment in 1998. Similarly, vocational training for orphans is meeting expectations with 919 enrolling in the training courses. Over the coming years, as more Cambodians become aware of the support services available, utilization is likely to increase.

Possible Adjustments to Plans: USAID/Cambodia plans a strategic review of this sector.

Other Donor Programs: Japan, Australia, Germany and UNESCO provide support for vocational training initiatives. The EU, Australia, UNICEF, and the International Committee of the Red Cross provide support for rehabilitation programs. The International Labor Organization provides assistance for a mental health training program. The World Food Program provides food-for-work programs. The United Nations High Commission for Refugees provides assistance for internally displaced persons while the Asian Development Bank and Canada provide support for small scale economic activities. The United Kingdom provides technical assistance for demining activities. Donor assistance for this sector is about $5 million annually.

Principal Contractors, Grantees or Agencies: Current USAID grantees include Vietnam Veterans of America Foundation, American Red Cross, Salesian Mission, Harvard School of Public Health, and Handicap International.

REDUCED TRANSMISSION OF SEXUALLY TRANSMITTED INFECTIONS (STI) AND HIV AMONG HIGH-RISK POPULATIONS, 442-SPO02

STATUS: Continuing **PROPOSED OBLIGATION AND FUNDING SOURCES:** FY 2000: $2,000,000 ESF **INITIAL OBLIGATION:**FY 1998 **ESTIMATED COMPLETION DATE:** FY 2002

Summary: Cambodia is the scene of one of the most rapidly progressing AIDS epidemics in Asia. While it was only in 1991 that the first HIV infections were detected, by 1998, 150,000 Cambodians were estimated to be HIV positive. Current seroprevalence data indicate that the epidemic is still concentrated in high-risk populations such as commercial sex workers (43% HIV positive in 1998) and their clients, but that it is beginning to spread to the general population (2.4% of pregnant women were HIV positive in 1998). To head off an explosive spread of the epidemic in the general population, USAID is focusing its prevention and control efforts on the high-risk populations, and in particular the individuals (mainly men) who form bridges between the high-risk groups and the population at large.

Key Results: The three key intermediate results for this new special objective are: (1) policy makers are informed about the HIV/AIDS epidemic in Cambodia; (2) high-risk behaviors are reduced in the target areas; and (3) sexually transmitted disease (STD) and reproductive health service delivery programs for high-risk populations are piloted and replicated in the target areas.

Performance and Prospects: During the initial start-up phase, performance on this new special objective has been greater than expected. A range of formative research projects have been quickly completed, such as an STD care facility assessment and an assessment of the communications materials available in Cambodia. The results of these activities are being used not only by USAID and its HIV/AIDS implementing partners to guide further implementation activities, but also by other donors to improve their programs. USAID partners have clearly defined their respective roles and activities and are actively collaborating in their efforts. Future prospects include beginning communication interventions to bring about behavior change among high-risk men, modifying and enhancing the national HIV surveillance system, and revising treatment protocols for selected reproductive tract infections to avoid substantial overtreatment with expensive third-generation antibiotics.

Possible Adjustments to Plans: None planned.

Other Donor Programs: The National AIDS Program works closely with the United Nations Joint Programme on HIV/AIDS (UNAIDS) to plan and coordinate activities of international donors. WHO is supporting a pilot study of the 100% condom use policy in brothels, similar to the successful program in Thailand. The World Bank provides technical advisors to the National AIDS Program. The USAID program is currently the largest HIV/AIDS program in the country. Annual donor assistance is approximately $7 million. A coordination committee of host government, donor, international and implementing agencies meets monthly for joint review, planning and monitoring.

Principal Contractors, Grantees or Agencies: USAID implements its STI/HIV prevention activities through Family Health International and its partners in the IMPACT project, Population Services International and the Khmer HIV/AIDS NGO Alliance.

Selected Performance Measures:

Summary: USAID initiated this special objective to respond to the scarcity of formal savings and credit programs that are available to the rural poor. Although the number of NGO microfinance programs directed to servicing the needs of this group has increased steadily in the past five years, they are still unable to provide access to 85%-90% of the country's rural population. This lack of access to credit stifles productivity and restrains economic growth. The purpose of this special objective is to accelerate the growth of the rural poor's access to sustainable financial services. The direct beneficiaries of achieving this objective will be predominantly women, an estimated 100,000 to 200,000 of whom will be provided access to credit facilities. The indirect beneficiaries will be the children of these women.

Key Results: The four key intermediate results are: 1) an average annual growth rate of 25% in the number of clients served by the grantees funded under this special objective; 2) an average annual growth rate of 10% in the number of village banks established by these grantees; 3) an average annual growth rate of 25% in the volume of outstanding loans provided by these grantees; and 4) a steady enhancement of the quality of the enabling environment in which microfinance institutions operate.

Performance and Prospects: Prior to the development of this special objective, both USAID central funding and Mission funding for economic growth activities have been used to expand the outreach of selected microfinance programs. Their performance over the past year, reflected in the achievement of the intermediate results, has overwhelmingly exceeded expectations. The growth rates in the number of clients served (166%), the number of village banks established (189%), and the volume of outstanding loan portfolios (164%) all exceeded targeted levels by significant amounts.

Possible Adjustments to Plans: Cambodian legislation is currently proposed that will necessitate the transformation of the larger NGO credit providers in the country into licensed microfinance institutions. In order to expand the outreach of credit and savings facilities to the rural poor as rapidly as possible, USAID central funding has been obligated to provide technical assistance and training to the largest rural credit provider in the country during its transformation into a licensed microfinance institution.

Other Donor Programs: The United Nations Development Programme, the EU, and the French Development Bank have been significant providers of grants to NGO microfinance operators.

Principal Contractors, Grantees or Agencies: Current grantees receiving USAID funding include the Association of Cambodian Local Economic Development Agencies, Catholic Relief Services, and World Relief.

Expanded Access to Sustainable Financial Services, 442-SPO04

STATUS: Continuing
PROPOSED OBLIGATION AND FUNDING SOURCES: FY 2000:$500,000 ESF
INITIAL OBLIGATION: FY 1999 **ESTIMATED COMPLETION DATE:** FY 2005

UN AND INTERNATIONAL ASSISTANCE

POVERTY ALLEVIATION

UNDP's cooperation as regards Poverty Alleviation comprises a targeted series of development support activities aimed at building national capacities to plan, implement, and monitor interventions in a sustainable and participatory manner. In so doing, UNDP cooperation is aimed at having an immediate impact at the grassroots level, and, where necessary, to respond to emergency situations. One 'of the major new initiatives during 1995 will be the launching of a broad- based exercise that is to result in the design of a National Action Plan for Alleviating Poverty. This exercise is to provide the Royal Government and its development partners with an action-oriented, cross-sectoral frame- work for improving the standards of living of the poorest.

UNDP-supported projects in the areas of integrated Area Development and Employment Generation have combined their efforts to promote improved standards of living in a total of eight provinces of Cambodia (Battambang, Siem Reap, Pursat, Banteay Meanchey, Kandal, Takeo, Kompong Cham, and Kampot) and Phnom Penh. These projects , originally conceived as part of UNDP's support to the reintegration and resettlement of refugees, internally displaced persons and demobilized soldiers, now provide support to a wide range of rural and urban populations.

Specific areas of concentration and major achievements are as follows:

A. INTEGRATED AREA OF DEVELOPMENT

The UNDP/OPS-executed CARERE Cambodian Resettlement and Reintegration) program has both direct assistance and capacity-building objectives which are closely interlinked at provincial, district, commune and village level. Over the past year in particular, CARERE has undergone a significant transition in recognition of the progressively increasing role being assumed by Government bodies. Specifically, in the four northwest provinces where it intervenes, CARERE has supported since its beginning:

1. the construction of 163 km of labor-based roads and rehabilitation /maintenance of 133 km of machine-based secondary roads;

2. de-mining of access roads and abandoned villages enabling 12,000 displaced persons and returnees to resettle and take up productive activities;

3. production of over 1,350 hand-dug wells, 200 drilled wells, and excavation of 127 ponds providing access to potable water to an estimated 250,000 people;

4. rehabilitation of irrigation schemes enabling 21,000 ha of agricultural land to be brought back into production benefiting 20,000 families, and assisting land preparation and provision of agricultural inputs resulting in production of nearly 17,000 tons of rice benefiting 11,000 returnee families, and provision of vegetable seeds to 55,000 returnee families;

5. construction of 193 new schools with 737 classrooms and rehabilitation of 121 schools with 393 classrooms, with a combined capacity of over 72,000 students;

6. construction of 28 hospitals primarily at commune level and 10 health centers at district and province level serving a combined population of 320,000 persons;

7. the construction of eight new agricultural stations and training centers, and the establishment of 11 tree nurseries and a fisheries station which contribute to the production of improved varieties of rice seed and fruit trees, extension services in crop management, training, management and development planning for provincial ministry staff and farmers;

8. the formation of Provincial Water and Sanitation committees to assist Government to define standards and coordinate interventions in the sector;

9. in collaboration with UNICEF and WHO, the development of provincial health plans, patient referral services, nurse training, and the establishment of provincial health training facilities and outreach primary health care training programs; (10) the provision of training in income generation, technical and administrative fields as well as functional literacy to over 1,600 persons (70% women), training in community development and agricultural techniques to almost 500 persons, and water use education to over 30,000 school children.

Direct implementation of CARERE projects by provincial Government departments has increased up to 42% in 1994, and is expected to rise to approximately 70%, in 1995, while subcontracting with other organizations (NGOs and village groups) will continue for the remaining 30% . Already several hundred village groups have been formed through CARERE's efforts for constructing schools, managing rural credit through village banks, managing water use in irrigation schemes, and for rice seed multiplication schemes and village rice banks, as well as village work brigades for roads construction and rehabilitation. In 1995, assistance to the formation of Village Development Committees will be a major focus of CARERE capacity-building, an effort which has already begun with considerable success in Banteay Meanchey. Furthermore, CARERE will continue to emphasize capacity-building at the provincial level with the Provincial Department for Rural Development and the Provincial Rural Development Committees, both of which are strongly supported through provincial planning, sectoral meetings, and project approval exercises, intended to ensure full ownership by Government departments and provincial authorities.

While UNDP finances the technical assistance, management and operational support costs of the program, generous cost-sharing contributions from the Netherlands, the United States of America, Sweden, Norway, Finland, Australia, and the United Kingdom, as well as separate agreements with the United Nations High Commissioner for Refugees, the Caisse Franqaise de Developpement and the European Union (yet to be concluded), have financed the programme's direct interventions at the provincial level. In 1995, CARERE will open an office in Rattanak Kiri province which, funds permitting, could cover Mondulkiri in 1996.

B. EMPLOYMENT AND INCOME GENERATION

Executed by the International Labor Organization (ILO), this programme has two components, the first of which is the promotion of small or micro-business employment through a combination of skills and management training, and credit. As of January 1995, six regional vocational training centers and eight Local Economic Development Agencies (LEDAS, branches of a Cambodian NGO making up the Association of Cambodian LEDAS, or ACLEDA) are operational. Over 2,000 people participated in skills training in a variety of areas, selected on the basis of recommendations emanating from Training Needs Assessments and Business Opportunity Surveys. Many of these 2,000 people also benefited from small business training and credit. In total, over 1,700 trainees benefited from business management training, of whom over 1,000 (68% women) actually started or expanded businesses, many with the assistance of LEDA administered credit. These programs have benefited a total of over 25,000 people by raising family incomes by between 45 and 6596 for those involved in micro and small businesses. In addition, the National Training

Secretariat and the National Training Center at Tek Thla have received infrastructural, institutional, and methodological capacity- building support. Finally, a Memorandum of Understanding has been signed between the Ministry of Education, the UNDP/ILO vocational training project, and GTZ for the development of a National Vocational Education and Training (VET) Strategy which will be the precursor to the formulation of a VET Master Plan for Cambodia.

The other major component of the UNDP/ILO-supported Employment Generation Program is the use of Labor- Based Appropriate Technology (LBAT) in rural infrastructure development works. Since its beginning, this program has successfully generated more than 1.2 million days of employment. Workers have been compensated for their labor through a combination of cash remuneration and food for work provided by the World Food Program (WFP). Over 150 engineers, technicians and supervisors in the Ministry of Public Works and Transport have been trained in labor-based methods of infrastructure construction and rehabilitation, and are able to conduct such works with limited intervention from external advisors. Altogether 240 km of secondary roads and 66 km of secondary and tertiary irrigation canals covering 12,000 ha have been constructed or rehabilitated, and local village maintenance and operations systems put in place. In addition, essential clean-up work at the World Heritage site of Angkor has been organized and a cost-effective maintenance system established. It has been agreed with the Royal Government to develop a national strategy for the use of Labor Based Appropriate Technology. As one element of such a national strategy, the program is also providing support to the Institute of Technology of Cambodia (ITC) to integrate LBAT into its In addition to UNDP financing, the Netherlands has been and continues to be a generous contributor to this Program.

C. DEMINING

With UNDP assistance, considerable international support has been mobilized since last year's ICORC meeting for the cause of demining in Cambodia, which, pooled together, has enabled the Cambodian Mine Action Center (CMAC) to develop into the central national structure for ridding the Cambodian countryside of its mines. Over 6.4 million square meters of land have been demined by CMAC, over 25 million square meters have been marked as no-go zones, and tens of thousands of land mines and other explosive devices have been removed from lands utilized by Cambodia's rural populations. Mine awareness, training and mine marking conducted by CMAC (among others) have together contributed to a substantial reduction in national mine-related casualties.

Over the past year - with the assistance of 28 external technical advisors (financed by Australia, Belgium, Canada, the Netherlands, and New Zealand, as well as an additional 8 under bilateral arrangements with Norway and France) and the provision of UNDP-funded support to CMAC logistical, financial, and administrative functions - CMAC has become -an efficient and well-structured organization. With a total of 1,572 personnel, it can deploy 41 demining platoons, 16 mine marking teams and 10 explosive ordnance disposal teams in the field. A competent cadre of instructors is available at the training center to continue improving on technical demining procedures and maintaining standards. Finally, CMAC's data base currently registers over 2,000 known minefields nationwide and serves as a common resource for national and international organizations alike.

The Trust Fund target set at the beginning of the two-year program was USD20 million. To date, USD 10 million in cash contributions (as well as $2 million in equipment from the United States of America and Sweden) have been received from Japan, United States, United Kingdom, Denmark, Australia, the Netherlands, Canada, Norway, New Zealand, and the Holy See, and another $2.1 million are expected from Sweden. This leaves a total of $8 million to be mobilized between now and the end of the program of assistance in April 1996.

D. ENVIRONMENT AND NATURAL RESOURCE MANAGEMENT

Cambodia has a considerable endowment in natural resources and bio-diversity which, if managed properly, has the potential to make significant contributions to its economy and to the long term food security of the Cambodian people. UNDP has provided advisory services for the formulation of a framework environmental law and draft minerals law, concept papers for the creation of a national capacity for water quality control, the establishment of a national environmental action plan, the establishment of an integrated resource information center (IRIC) UNDP has also undertaken wide-ranging environmental education and awareness activities including eleven small-scale initiatives implemented with NGOs at village level. UNDP has received generous contributions from both Finland and Australia for a number of activities in this sector.

UNDP will continue to support the Government in the area of environmental and natural resource management, through assistance to education and awareness building, including integration of environmental education into primary and secondary school curricula, sustainable use of natural resources, health and hygiene including village-based water and sanitation projects, small-scale tree nurseries and replanting activities, sustainable fisheries, and sound advice in the use of organic and chemical fertilizers and pesticides, and on-going assistance to the sustainable management of Cambodia's water resources including the sub-regional support to the establishment of the Mekong River Commission. As regards the forestry sector, UNDP

will support the preparation of a management action plan and provide capacity building assistance in carrying out a pilot forestry inventory. Finally, the Ministry of Environment will publish in 1995,
with UNDP support, the first ever State of the Environment Report for Cambodia.

E. AGRICULTURE AND IRRIGATION

UNDP's principal achievements in the agricultural and irrigation sectors were the production of the Agricultural Development Options Review (ADOR) and the Irrigation Rehabilitation Study of 841 irrigation schemes in Cambodia. The ADOR exercise was under taken by participation of the major stakeholders, thereby promoting collaboration and common problem-solving. By highlighting the major potentials and constraints to the agricultural sector in Cambodia, the results of this process provide a sound reference for agricultural policy decision-makers over the next five years. Likewise, the Irrigation Rehabilitation Study - which, among other things, identified (at pre-feasibility phase) 10 economically viable medium-scale irrigation schemes and five capacity building projects - is of immediate relevance in guiding the allocation of resources for irrigation rehabilitation.

Furthermore, UNDP has initiated a rural credit project which targets both village-level direct assistance in the creation of local funding desks as well as capacity building at the central level to define and monitor national policy with regard to rural credit. With parallel arrangements with the Caisse Francaise de Develop-ment and UNICEF, and in cooperation with other major multi- and bilateral organizations and the NGO community, UNDP will thus support the establishment of a National Rural Credit Committee and rural credit policy
standards and practices.

In addition to on-going efforts in the context of UNDP's Area Development and Public Administration Reform programs, new support interventions will include high-level missions to assist UNDP and the Government to determine key entry points for policy-level support to the agriculture and irrigation sectors. UNDP will also provide targeted assistance to the Government for the establishment of a national, financially-sustainable and effective fertilizer distribution system in cooperation with the Caisse Francaise de Development and the Belgian Government, and will provide interim funding to the Agricultural College at Prek Leap in education management and curriculum development.

DEVELOPMENT MANAGEMENT

In order to facilitate the country's transition to a market economy, based on the rule- of law, and to assist in the re-definition of the State's mandates and functions, major UNDP support programs are being implemented to assist in the formulation of policies and reforms, and to provide capacity building support.
This comprises the following components.

MACROECONOMIC MMANAGEMENT

UNDP's program of technical assistance in the area of macroeconomic management supports the Royal Government's reform program emphasizing macroeconomic stabilization, rebuilding of institutions, and re-establishing the social and economic infrastructure. In collaboration with the Asian Development Bank, UNDP has provided advisory services and training with respect to four areas of macro-economic management, namely, macro-economic planning, fiscal reform, money and banking, and statistics. As regards the latter, the collaborative UNDP- AsDB technical assistance has supported the Ministry of Planning in preparing the first socioeconomic survey of Cambodia, based on a sample of 1,327 households.

To date, the first report has been published, providing key data on demographic indicators, labor force, migration, housing and income, as well as detailed data on consumer expenditures. UNDP has, in the process of conducting and processing the survey, provided considerable institutional capacity building. This extensive training has benefited over 50 central and provincial civil servants in survey fieldwork and analysis. UNDP funding for this program, amounts to $1.5 million, with $2.39 million in co-funding by the AsDB.

In addition, UNDP, in collaboration with the IMF, has assisted in the design of a comprehensive technical assistance program in support of fiscal and monetary management. The program of UNDP-IMF technical assistance is focused on two principal objectives:

1. the consolidation of a modem financial sector by assisting in the development of the National Bank of, Cambodia into an independent central bank with strong policy and supervisory capabilities, and

2. supporting substantive improvements in the government ability to mobilize revenue through tax and customs reform. Long-term technical support to the National Bank aims to strengthen bank supervision, operations, accounting, cash management, research and exchange functions. Support to the Ministry of Economy and Finance is focused on tax administration reform and capacity building within the Customs Department. UNDP's commitment to this program of support is USD2.6 million with additional parallel funding by the IMF of USD1.7 million.

SECTORAL POLICY AND MANAGEMENT

The common approach of UNDP support at the sectoral level, and as regards line ministries, is to strengthen policy and management functions with the aim of improving the delivery of key public services at the grass-roots level. In addition, several ministries will be selected as "pilot" cases, as part of UNDP's support to the Government's Public Administration Reform program.

In Health, a joint UN Agencies-bilateral donor initiative is under way to assist the Royal Government of Cambodia in its efforts to reform the health sector. UNDP support is aimed at assisting the Ministry of Health in defining the size, role, structure and financing requirements of the health system and in establishing management support systems. Following earlier support at, foremost, the central level, the recently implemented second phase will equally concentrate at provincial and district health systems. The Ministry of Health will be one such "pilot" case as part of the Public Administration Reform program. Initiatives instituted to strengthen capacity and improve service delivery at the Ministry of Health will provide a measure of the reform's progress and, in turn, ensure that lessons learned in this project are applied to other programs in - other sectors. Significant capacity-building to the Ministry of Health has been ensured in 1994, and will continue to be provided until 1996. UNDP's contribution amounts to $3.12 million, with additional parallel funding of approximately $2 million from UK/ODA, WHO and the American Red Cross.

In Education, UNDP, in collaboration with UNESCO, has assisted the Government in preparing an initial sector plan entitled "Rebuilding Quality Education and Training in Cambodia." The sector plan was reviewed at a national education seminar held in January of 1994. Subsequently, this plan has been utilized as part of the AsDB's sectoral planning exercise resulting in a comprehensive investment plan that was reviewed at a Government-donor meeting in December 1994.

Additionally, a second phase UNDP/UNESCO support program, which includes a UNDP contribution of $3.2 million, has been designed, and is about to be implemented. This program, funded with a $3.2 million UNDP contribution, is designed to strengthen the capacity of senior management of the Ministry of Education in planning and management capabilities for enhanced policy formulation and decision making. As regards Higher Education, UNDP support to the Institute of Technology of Cambodia (ITC) will be continued throughout 1995, with UNDP funding of in total $1.6 million.

In the Tourism sector, a preparatory assistance project was initiated in January of 1994. The purpose of this project was to provide capacity building to the Ministry of Tourism for the planning, development, marketing, and management of tourism to Cambodia. Additionally, the project assisted in the formulation of a human resource development strategy for the sector. Outputs already achieved include new regulations governing tourism services, a project proposal for the creation of a national tourism training center, surveys on arrivals and departures at Pochentong International Airport and hotels in Phnom Penh. The full UNDP-supported tourism sector project is signed and will begin in the very near future.

ADMINISTRATIVE REFORM

Following the Royal Government decision on Administrative Reform, UNDP has been instrumental in facilitating consensus building and in providing technical assistance for the actual design of the National Program of Administrative Reform (NPAR). At the same time, UNDP has assisted the design of a comprehensive support program (requiring US$ 8 million in technical assistance, including a component funded by UNDP at US$ 3.1 million), which has just recently been approved. The NPAR, and UNDP support, component comprise the following areas:

1. structuring of the Royal Government and its administration including the legal framework for the government and the roles and responsibilities of ministries,

2. strengthening administrative capacity and service delivery of key operational ministries including health, education and agriculture,

3. human resource development of government staff to include training in administration and management skills,

4. redefining and strengthening the relationship between central and provincial administrations.

Initial implementation support has so far resulted in agreement on the organization of the Inter-ministerial Committee that will be in charge of the management of the NPAR. Work Plans have been prepared for the various components of the NPAR, including further specification of support requirements. This will allow for more systematic coordination with interested donors.

Project profiles for donor support are being prepared by the Government with UNDPs assistance, while already several bilateral and multilateral donors have confirmed their intention to provide resources in support of the NPAR. In this connection, there is agreement for UNDP and the World Bank to cooperate in the design of scenarios for downsizing the public service, including social safety nets and re-training schemes. Such schemes, once designed, will be presented to donors, in addition to the above mentioned support requirements.

GOOD GOVERNANCE

UNDP in collaboration with the UN Center for Human Rights is about to finalize the design of a support Program for providing technical advice to the newly established democratic, legislative and judicial institutions. A major component of the support will be aimed at strengthening of local NGOs involved in Human Rights. UNDP will pro- vide a contribution of $2 million.

AID COORDINATION

In the context of Aid Coordination. UNDP is instituting a program of support to the Cambodian Development Council (CDC) to articulate and operationalize its mandate and functions. This support will promote and facilitate consensus building between CDC and line ministries in the implementation of the 'National Program to Rehabilitate and Develop Cambodia", thereby strengthening these national institutions to mobilize, program and implement externally provided development resources.

Policy development and strategic planning assistance will be supplemented by the development of a Management Information System on externally financed projects and assistance. This database will provide statistics on Public Development Assistance and interface with the Public Investment Program that the Royal Government is establishing in association with the development banks. These measures will contribute to dearer understanding of Cambodia's needs in matters of external assistance. UNDP is also providing assistance to the CDC to strengthen its capacity to negotiate international development- assistance agreements.

INFRASTRUCTURE

UNDP in Cambodia has launched from 1991 to 1994, several projects aimed at directly rehabilitating essential elements of Cambodia's infrastructure as well as under- taking feasibility studies to enable infrastructure rehabilitation support by bilateral donors and international credit institutions. UNDP has thus provided support for these efforts totaling $21.9, of which $14.8 have come from core UNDP resources, as summarized below. With other donors commencing sup- port in various areas of infrastructure, UNDP is in a position to phase out its direct assistance, while, focusing on management and planning support in
selected areas.

(a) Transport and infrastructure rehabilitation

Road and bridges emergency repair works on Road No.5, UNDP-managed Trust fund whose contributors were the Government of Sweden ($4.9 million), USAID ($2 million) and the Dutch Government ($113,888).

Simultaneously, a Transport Rehabilitation Study was undertaken to identify short, medium and long term needs of various modes of transport in the Kingdom of Cambodia, and to establish a Planning Unit in the Ministry of Public Works. The project's budget amounted $1.3 million with $719,400 from UNDP and a parallel financing from Sweden through AsDB of $600,000. In addition, UNDP has provided advisory services to the newly created Ministry of Public Works and Transport (MPWT) for setting technical standards and regulation for the construction and operation of the infrastructure assets and, to assist the Ministry in its coordination efforts.

UNDP/ICAO support (with UNDP funding of $2.8 million) in the area of Air Traffic Control Services has, apart from institutional and capacity building support, contributed to the establishment of regular safety standards at Pochentong (Phnom Penh) International Airport.

(b) Water and Power Utilities

UNDP and the World Bank are jointly sup- porting capacity building and initial rehabilitation- regarding the Water and the Power Utilities of Phnom Penh and Sihanoukville. This emergency assistance, with a total UNDP contribution of $7.8 million, has paved the way for major rehabilitation activities and investments amounting to, so far, $109 mil- lion for the power sector (World Bank, AsDB, Japan, France, Ireland, Belgium) and $19 mil- lion for the water sector (World Bank, Japan, France).

(c) Telecommunications

UNDP facilitated the transfer of the $28 mil- lion UNTAC satellite-based telecommunications network to -the Kingdom of Cambodia. Furthermore, UNDP/ITU technical support to the Ministry of Posts and Telecommunications of Cambodia (MPTC) has facilitated additional investment of $15 million that will generate an estimated $25 million of revenue over 8 years. In addition, UNDP/ITU support, of in total $1 million, is about to start for preparation of a 15 year Telecommunications Master Plan, including further support to strengthen the planning and management capabilities of the MPRC.

UTILIZATION OF KHMER EXPERTISE

Apart from human resources development, UNDP is actively promoting the UTILIZATION of Khmer expertise as part of all its support activities. One of the modalities being used is the TOKTEN program (Transfer of Knowledge Through Expatriate Nationals), which aims at bringing highly qualified and experienced expatriate technical and managerial professionals back to their country of origin for short-term consultancies. In 1993 and 1994, a total of 106 such consultants completed assignments in Cambodia in the fields of agriculture, health, culture, industry, education, environment, public works, tourism, administration and macro-economic management. A total of 980 Government officials and 1,100 teachers and students have benefited from training as a result of these missions. The majority of TOKTEN consultants have been drawn from France, the
United States, and Australia, and a total of 23 (or more than 20%) of these consultants have chosen to remain in Cambodia over the long term.

DIALOGUE ON LONG-TERM DEVELOPMENT STRATEGY

Building on earlier UNDP support, it is now becoming possible to work towards a longer-term framework for cooperation between the Royal Government, the UN Development System and its development partners. As part of the UN Development System, UNDP will continue to focus its dialogue with the Royal Government on such longer-term development perspective, and on the approaches that need to be developed or enhanced.

REINTEGRATION OF CAMBODIA WITHIN THE WORLD COMMUNITY

UNDP System will continue its efforts to facilitate Cambodia's re-integration in a regional and world context. Concrete impetus has been provided to the recent draft agreement on the cooperation for sustainable development of the Mekong River Basin.

Collaboration with regional institutions, like ESCAP, has already been intensified and will be further pursued. At the invitation of the Japanese Government to a Forum for the Comprehensive Development of Indochina, UNDP has supported the preparation of a Compendium on Human Resources Development requirements in the region, with a view to highlight priorities and strategies for sub-regional cooperation. It is also significant that Cambodia was represented at- the International Conference on Population and Development held in Cairo and the World Social Summit that has just recently been concluded in Copenhagen. UNDP will also continue to promote and facilitate South- South collaboration, at all levels of policy and implementation support.

TRAVELING TO THE COUNTRY

US STATE DEPARTMENT SUGGESTIONS

COUNTRY DESCRIPTION: Cambodia is a parliamentary democracy with a constitutional monarch. An agreement to form a coalition government following the July 1998 elections was reached between the two major political parties and a new government was formed on November 30.

ENTRY REQUIREMENTS: A passport and visa are required. Tourists and business travelers may purchase a Cambodian visa valid for one month at the airports in Phnom Penh and Siem Reap for a fee. All U.S. citizens departing Cambodia are required to pay a passenger service charge. Current information about entry/visa and other requirements may be obtained from the Royal Embassy of Cambodia, 4500 16th Street, NW, Washington, DC 20022, tel. 202-726-7742, fax 202-726-8381. Overseas inquiries may be made at the
nearest embassy or consulate of Cambodia.

AREAS OF INSTABILITY: There was significant political turbulence and violence in Phnom Penh in 1998. While the November 1998 formation of a coalition government has eased tensions, sporadic acts of violence remain possible. The U.S. Embassy therefore advises American citizens to avoid political gatherings or
demonstrations if they occur and also avoid the vicinity of political party, election commission, and military buildings or compounds in both Phnom Penh and the provincial capitals.

The Embassy advises its personnel who travel to Battambang and Banteay Meanchey Provinces to exercise extreme caution outside the provincial towns during the day and any place at night. Many rural parts of the country remain without effective policing and are subject to banditry.

The town of Siem Reap and the vicinity of the Angkor Wat temple complex remain officially open to tourists, but the Embassy advises U.S. citizens to travel only by air and to limit their movements to the city of Siem Reap and the main Angkor Wat temple complex. The risk of banditry and military activity continues in various parts of Siem Reap province. Illegal checkpoints, requiring cash payment to pass, have been reported sporadically on the road to the Banteay Srei temple, which is approximately 30 kilometers (about 19 miles) northeast of the town of Siem Reap and Angkor Wat. Americans are advised to consult with local police or tourist authorities before traveling to Banteay Srei.

IN-COUNTRY TRAVEL: The safety of road travel outside urban areas varies greatly. Even on heavily traveled roads, there can be incidents of banditry, so all travel should be done in daylight between the hours of 8:00 am and 4:00 p.m. Road travel at night is not advised. The U.S. embassy advises embassy personnel not to travel by train because of the high risk of banditry. Travel by boat should be avoided because boats are often overcrowded and lack adequate safety equipment. Several incidents have occurred en route to Siem Reap, including a sinking in early 1997. Owners accept no liability for accidents.

Land mines and unexploded ordnance can be found in rural areas in Cambodia, but especially in Battambang, Banteay Meanchey, Pursat, Siem Reap, and Kampong Thom provinces. At no time should travelers walk in forested areas or even in dry rice paddies without a local guide. Areas around small bridges on secondary roads are particularly dangerous. Travelers who observe anything that resembles a mine or unexploded ordnance should not touch it. They should notify the Cambodia Mine Action Center at 023-981-083 or 084.

INFORMATION ON CRIME: Crime and banditry are persistent problems in many areas; the U.S. Embassy advises its personnel to review their personal security practices regularly. The decline of the Cambodian economy has contributed to a dramatic increase in armed robberies and assaults, often during daylight hours.
A number of Americans have been robbed at gunpoint in Phnom Penh. Most of them were robbed while riding on motorcycle taxis and usually after dark. Americans should avoid traveling alone, especially after dark. They should limit outdoor activity after dark in the capital city area and return to their homes or hotels early. The U.S. Embassy advises its personnel to carry photocopies of their U.S. passport, driver's license or other important documents, rather than the actual documents, as these documents may be confiscated.

The loss or theft abroad of a U.S. passport should be reported immediately to local police and to the U.S. Embassy in Phnom Penh. Useful information on guarding valuables and protecting personal security while traveling abroad is provided in the Department of State pamphlet, A Safe Trip Abroad. It is availablefrom the Superintendent of Documents, U.S. Government Printing Office, Washington D.C. 20402, via the Bureau of Consular Affairs home page at http://travel.state.gov and autofax service at 202-647-3000, or at the U.S. Embassy in Phnom Penh.

CRIMINAL PENALTIES: While in a foreign country, a U.S. citizen is subject to that country's laws and regulations, which sometimes differ significantly from those in the United States and may not afford the protections available to the individual under U.S. law. Penalties for breaking the law can be more severe than in the United States for similar offenses. Persons violating the law in Cambodia, even unknowingly, may be expelled, arrested or imprisoned. Penalties for possession, use and trafficking in illegal drugs are strict, and convicted offenders can expect lengthy jail sentences and fines.

MEDICAL FACILITIES: The Cambodian medical system was virtually wiped out during the Khmer Rouge period and is being slowly rebuilt. Medical facilities and services in Cambodia are not up to international standards. Doctors and hospitals often expect immediate cash payment for health services, and U.S. medical insurance is not always valid outside the United States. U.S. Medicare and Medicaid programs do not provide payment for medical services outside the United States. Travelers have found that, in some cases, supplemental medical insurance with specific overseas coverage, including provision for medical evacuation, has proven useful.

MEDICAL INSURANCE: Check with your own insurance company to confirm whether your policy applies overseas, including provision for medical evacuation. Ascertain whether payment will be made to the overseas hospital or doctor, or whether you will be reimbursed later for expenses you incur. Some insurance policies also include coverage for psychiatric treatment and for disposition of remains in the event of death. Useful information on medical emergencies abroad, including overseas insurance programs, is provided in the Department of State, Bureau of Consular Affairs brochure, Medical Information for Americans TravelingAbroad, available via the Bureau of Consular Affairs home page at http://travel.state.gov and the autofax service at 202-647-3000.

OTHER HEALTH INFORMATION: Vaccine recommendations and prevention information for traveling abroad may be obtained through the Centers for Disease Control and Prevention's international travelers' hotline from the United States at 1-877-FYI-TRIP (1-877-394-8747), via its toll-free autofax number at 1-888-CDC-FAXX (1-888-232-3299), or via their Internet site at http://www.cdc.gov.

FINANCIAL TRANSACTIONS: Personal checks and credit cards are not widely accepted within Cambodia, although a number of banks in Phnom Penh accept visa cards for cash advances. Travelers' checks are accepted by banks and major hotels. The U.S. dollar and Cambodian Riel are both widely used.

DUAL NATIONALITY: Dual nationality is not prohibited under Cambodia's nationality law, enacted in 1996. Specific questions on dual nationality may be directed to a Cambodian embassy or consulate, to the consular section of the U.S. Embassy in Phnom Penh, or to the Office of Overseas Citizens Services, Department of State, Washington, D.C. 20520-4818.

AVIATION SAFETY OVERSIGHT: As there is no direct commercial air service at present, nor economic authority to operate such service, between the U.S. and Cambodia, the U.S. Federal Aviation Administration (FAA) has not assessed Cambodia's civil aviation authority for compliance with international aviation safety standards for oversight of Cambodia's air carrier operations. For further information, travelers may contact the Department of Transportation within the United States at 1-800-322-7873, or visit the FAA Internet home page at http://www.faa.gov/avr/iasa/index.htm. The U.S. Department of Defense (DOD) separately assesses some foreign air carriers for suitability as official providers of air services. For information regarding the DoD policy on specific carriers, travelers may contact DOD at 618-256-4801.

REGISTRATION/EMBASSY LOCATION: All Americans in Cambodia should register with the U.S. Embassy in Phnom Penh where they may obtain updated information on travel and security within Cambodia. The U.S. Embassy is located at no. 16, Street 228 (between streets 51 and 63), Phnom Penh, Cambodia.
The telephone number is (855-23) 216-436 or 218-931; fax (855-23)-216-437. A recording of security information is available twenty-four hours a day at telephone (855-23) 216-805.

IMPORTANT INFORMATION FOR TRAVEL

GETTING THERE

BY AIR

Cambodia's national airline, Royal Air Cambodge (VJ), operates internationally to Bangkok, Kuala Lumpur, Singapore, Ho Chi Minh City and Hong Kong. Thai International and Bangkok Airways fly to Phnom Penh from Bangkok. Malaysia Airlines flies from Kuala Lumpur, Vietnam Airlines from Hanoi, Aeroflot Russian International Airlines from Moscow, Silkair from Singapore and Lao International Aviation from Vientiane.

Approximate flight times: From London to Phnom Penh takes 12 hours 30 minutes (with a stopover in Bangkok).

International airport: Pochentong (PNH) is 12km (7 miles) from Phnom Penh. A bus service (journey time – 20 minutes) and taxis (journey time – 10 minutes) to the city are available. For pre-arranged tours a pick-up service is available.

Departure tax: US$20 levied on international departures at Pochentong airport, US$8 at Siem Reap airport.

BY SEA

The port of Phnom Penh can be reached via the Mekong delta through Vietnam. A new ocean port has been built at Sihanoukville.

BY RAIL/ROAD

The Thai border is now open, but use of this gateway is not generally recommended due to poor road and security conditions. The main highway links the capital with the Vietnam border.

GETTING AROUND

BY AIR

Internal flights operate between Phnom Penh and Siem Reap for Angkor (travel time – 45 minutes), Battambang, Koh Kong, Sihanoukville and Stung Treng.

Departure tax: US$10 at Pochentong, US$4 at Siem Reap.

BY SEA

Government-run ferries depart from the Psar Cha Ministry of Transport Ferry Landing between 102 and 104 streets and go to Kompong Cham, Kratie, Stung Treng, Kompong Chhnang and Phnom Krom. Boats are also available from Phnom

Penh to Siem Reap, a route popular with travelers. Due to the present rise in crime, inter-city boat travel should be restricted to the fast boats to Kompong Cham and Kratie.

BY RAIL

Some rail services operate, but foreigners are advised not to use them at present. There are plans to restore the international service to Bangkok, but a great deal of repair work is needed.

BY ROAD

Traffic drives on the right. Most roads are in poor condition, although the highway to Vietnam is open. It is possible to drive from Phnom Penh to Ho Chi Minh City in a day but there are formalities involved regarding the use of the same vehicle all the way. Right hand drive vehicles (quite common in Cambodia) are not allowed entry to Vietnam. Both Cambodian and Vietnamese visas must be obtained in advance and the Vietnamese visa must mention "Moc Bai" (the border point on the Vietnamese side) as a point of entry/exit otherwise travelers run the risk of being turned back. Care should be taken while driving as Cambodian drivers are prone to recklessness and accidents are relatively frequent. The safety of road travel outside urban areas varies greatly from region to region. If travel is undertaken in vehicle convoy during daylight hours only, potential risks can be reduced. Reliable information about security should be obtained before considering extensive road journeys. Bus: Buses to Phnom Penh suburbs are available from 182 Street and the bus station is open 0530-1730. Taxi: Cruising taxis are non-existent in Cambodia. However, service taxis can be hired at Psar Chbam Pao Shared-Taxi Station between 367 Street and 369 Street. Cyclo's, however, are a slow but inexpensive way to see the city and some of the drivers, especially those found outside main hotels, speak a little French or English. Car hire: Official visitors can arrange to hire a government car and driver. Enquiries about car hire should be addressed to the Ministry of Tourism. Documentation: An International Driving Permit is not recognised in Cambodia, but car hire is generally not recommended. Visitors are advised to hire a car with a driver instead which is only slightly more expensive than car hire.

VISAS

Currently, a visa is available at the airport of Phnom Penh for USD 20. It is valid for one month. Have a passport photo ready. However, there are rumours that this practice may be discontinued, so to be on the safe side, apply for a visa elsewhere.

If you enter the country by land (e.g. from Vietnam), make sure you already have a visa. You will not get one at the border.

Extensions to a visa are issued in Cambodia by the Ministry of National Security. This can be done at the Department of Foreigners (Bureaus des Etrangers) at House 32, Street 200. Opening hours are Mo-Fr 8:00-12:00. The form comes with attached stamps and costs KHR 2000. Two passport photos are required. The processing time is 10 days! Another place to extend visas is the Immigration Office at No. 5, Street 200. Opening hours are Mo-Fr, 7:30-10:00 and 14:00-16:00. Costs are: 1 week USD 20, 1 month USD 30, 6 months USD 100 (multiple entry) and 1 year USD 150 (multiple entry).

If you fail to extend your visa, you will be charged $3 for each day you overstay.

For details of how to get a visa in a certain country, have a look at the Embassy section.

MONEY

The currency is the Cambodian Riel (KHR). 1 new Riel equals 100 sen.

The going exchange rate is around 3870 KHR to 1 USD (Nov 1998)

The USD is very widely used in Cambodia. It actually serves as a second currency that is more readily accepted. Bring small denomination and clean notes with you.

There is usually no need to change money into KHR, since you will inevitably pay a lot of things in USD and receive change in KHR.

Traveler's Checks are well accepted in Cambodia. There is a commission of about 2% to change T/C into USD, less for T/C into KHR and sometimes nothing for USD into KHR. Shop around!

You can get cash advances on your credit card at several banks. The Siam Commercial Bank allows USD 1000 per day, and the Thai Farmers Bank half of that, USD 500. In every case, commissions are very high; they will have to phone Bangkok for confirmation. Shop around for the cheapest rate.

It is possible to change travelers checks and get credit card cash advances in the casinos. Of course, their motivation is to get the money "back" at the tables.

BANKS

Banks are open during weekdays from 7:30 to 14:30. Some open also at Saturday.

The Cambodia Commercial Bank, Corner of Pochentong and Monivong Boulevards cashes travelers checks and does cash advances on credit cards for no cost (unlike Thai Farmers and others which charge up to USD 20). They also get international transfers processed much faster than many other banks. They have an excellent reputation with NGOs and Ex-Pats.

The Bangkok Bank, 26 Norodom Boulevard, Phnom Penh, Tel. (23) 26593, accepts checks and Visa credit card.

The Foreign Trade Bank of Cambodia, next to the Bangkok Bank on Norodom Boulevard, Phnom Penh, changes USD travellers cheques into USD cash for a commission of 1%.

ATTRACTIONS

PHNOM PENH

The capital still retains an undeniable charm despite its tumultuous and often violent past. It has several impressive wats (temple-monasteries) that include: Wat Ounalom, Wat Phnom and Wat Lang Ka. It is also home to the spectacular Silver Pagoda, which is one of the few places in Cambodia where artefacts embodying the brilliance and richness of Khmer culture can still be viewed. There are also displays of Khmer crafts in the National Museum and the Royal Palace, King Norodom Sihanouk's official residence.

The Killing Fields of Choeung Ek are a grisly reminder of the atrocities committed by the Khmer Rouge. Some 17,000 people were killed here, just 15km south-west of the city centre, and over 8000 skulls, arranged by sex and age, are visible behind the clear, glass panel of the Memorial Stupa, which was erected in 1988.

You can sample vermicelli or frogs legs at any number of eateries, buy jewelry, antiques or the ubiquitous kramas (checked cotton scarves) at the Central Market, or purchase traditional works of art at the School of Fine Arts (Ecole des Beaux-Arts). The Central Market area, which includes Monirong Blvd, is the main center for budget travelers; it has cheap accommodation and plenty of food stalls.

ANGKOR

The celebrated temples of Angkor are Cambodia's greatest tourist attraction. The 100 or so temples are the sacred remains of what was once a much larger administrative and religious center. The temples were built between the 9th and the 13th centuries to glorify a succession of Khmer kings. Most of Angkor was abandoned in the 15th century and the temples became cloaked by forest. The site became the source of scholarly interest in the late19th century after the publication of Voyage à Siam et dans le Cambodge by French naturalist Henri Mouhot. Efforts were undertaken to clear away the jungle vegetation that threatened to completely destroy the monuments, and restoration continues today.

Apart from Angkor Wat, two other magnificent temples to visit are the Bayon and Ta Prohm. Accommodation and food can be found in the town of Siem Reap, only a few km from the temples.

UDONG

Udong, 40km north of Phnom Penh, was the capital of Cambodia between 1618 and 1866. It's generally very quiet here, and you'll often have the town's stupas to yourself (barring, of course, the armed guard who will probably want to accompany you). The ruins are sprinkled across two ridges. The smaller has two ruined buildings, several stupas and the Ta San Mosque (or at least its remains; all that's left is the building's bullet-pocked walls). From the mosque you can see a vihara, a pagoda and a building once used as a prison by Pol Pot.

A 16th century treasure is supposed to be hidden below the larger ridge, which is topped by the scattered ruins of a large vihara and Buddha statue - the Khmer Rouge blew the structures up in 1977. Surrounding the ruins are some still-intact smaller viharas, stupas and Buddhas. At the base of the ridge is a memorial to victims of Pol Pot, containing the bones of people buried in the 100 or so mass graves found in the area.

SIHANOUKVILLE

Sihanoukville (also known as Kompong Som) is Cambodia's only port. It's currently being redeveloped as a tourist attraction, with a casino planned for Naga Island. At present Sihanoukville's chief attraction is the great snorkelling and diving that can be found around the nearby islands - some of the guesthouses in town can arrange a boat trip for you. The best of the beaches around the town is probably Ochatial Beach, although its worth riding a bike down to Independence Beach, where you can check out the allegedly-haunted Independence Hotel.

RATANAKIRI

Mountainous Ratanakiri Province is best known for its isolated hill tribes. Good news for travelers is that the province is free of both landmines and Khmer Rouge activity, which means it is fairly safe to explore the surrounding countryside and visit some of the hill tribes; watch out, however, for illegal loggers, who are usually armed and not particularly welcoming to unexpected visitors. It's also best to avoid traveling here in the wet season, since the roads will be impassible and the risk of malaria and dengue fever is high.

The capital of the province is Ban Lung - it's a good base for treks, but nothing much happens here. Just 4km east of Ban Lung is Yak Lom Volcanic Lake, one of the main attractions of the region. It forms a near circle and is surrounded by forest. There are also waterfalls west of Ban Lung.

ACCOMMODATION

There are now a variety of good hotels available. The capital Phnom Penh and Siem Reap have a number of luxury hotels offering high standards and a range of recreational facilities. Hotels and guest houses are also available throughout the country, but standards generally tend to be basic. Camping is not permitted in Cambodia. For further information on accommodation, contact Diethelm Travel.

FOOD

Dietary habits appear to be basically the same among the Khmer and other ethnic groups, although the Muslim Cham do not eat pork. The basic foods are rice--in several varieties, fish, and vegetables, especially trakuon (water convolvulus). Rice may be less thoroughly milled than it is in many other rice-eating countries, and consequently it contains more vitamins and roughage. The average rice consumption per person per day before 1970 was almost one-half kilogram. Fermented fish in the form of sauce or of paste are important protein supplements to the diet. Hot peppers, lemon grass, mint, and ginger add flavor to many Khmer dishes; sugar is added to many foods. Several kinds of noodles are eaten. The basic diet is supplemented by vegetables and by fruits-bananas, mangoes,papayas, rambutan, and palm fruit-both wild and cultivated, which grow abundantly throughout the country. Beef, pork, poultry, and eggs are added to meals on special occasions, or, if the family can afford it, daily. In the cities, the diet has been affected by many Western items of food. French, Chinese, Vietnamese, and Indian cuisine were available in Phnom Penh in pre-Khmer Rouge days.

Rural Khmer typically eat several times a day; the first meal consists of a piece of fruit or cake, which workers eat after arriving at the fields. The first full meal is at about 9:00 or 10:00 in the morning; it is prepared by the wife or daughter and brought to the man in the field. Workers eat a large meal at about noon in the field and then have supper with their families after returning home around 5:00 P.M.

SUPPLEMENT

COMPOSITION OF THE ROYAL GOVERNMENT OF CAMBODIA (1998-2003)

Prime Minister	Samdech **Hun Sen**
Deputy Prime Minister	H.E. Sar Kheng
Deputy Prime Minister	H.E. Tol Lah
Senior Ministers :	
H.E. Tea Banh	H.E. Lu Lay Sreng
H.E. Keat Chhon	H.E. Chhim Seak Leng
H.E. Sok An	H.E. Dr.Hong Sun Huot
H.E. Hor Nam Hong	H.E. You Hockry
Council of Ministers:	
Minister	H.E. Sok An
Secretary of State	H.E. Sum Manith
Secretary of State	H.E. Chea Sophon
Ministry of National Defence :	
Co-Minister	H.E. Tea Banh
Co-Minister	H.H. Sisowath Sirirath
Secretary of State	H.E. Chay Saing Yun

Secretary of State	H.E. Por Bunsry
Ministry of Interior	
Co-Minister	H.E. Sar Kheng
Co-Minister	H.E. You Hockry
Secretary of State	H.E. Em Sam An
Secretary of State	H.E. Kieng Vang
Secretary of State	H.E. Prum Sokha
Secretary of State	H.E. Than Sina
Ministry of Parliamentary Affairs and Inspection	
Minister	H.E. Khun Hang
Secretary of State	H.E. Khov Meng Hean
Secretary of State	H.E. Hong Them
Ministry of Foreign Affairs and International Cooperation	
Minister	H.E. Hor Nam Hong
Secretary of State	H.E. Uch Kim An
Secretary of State	H.E. Chhoeng Chamroeun
Ministry of Economy and Finance	
Minister	H.E. Keat Chhon
Secretary of State	H.E. Uk Rabun
Secretary of State	H.E. Kong Vibol
Ministry of Information	
Minister	H.E. Lu Lay Sreng
Secretary of State	H.E. Um Daravuth
Secretary of State	H.E. Khieu Kanharith
Ministry of Health	
Minister	H.E. Hong Sun Huot
Secretary of State	H.E. Ung Phirun
Secretary of State	H.E. Mam Bun Heng
Ministry of Industry Mines and Energy	
Minister	H.E. Suy Sem
Secretary of State	H.E. Ith Praing
Secretary of State	H.E. Nhiep Bun Chinn
Ministry of Planning	
Minister	H.E. Chhay Than
Secretary of State	H.E. Ou Orhart
Secretary of State	H.E. Lay Prahoah
Ministry of Commerce	
Minister	H.E Cham Prasidh
Secretary of State	H.E. Pen Siman
Secretary of State	H.E. Khek Ravy
Ministry of Education Youth and Sports	
Minister	H.E. Tol Lah
Secretary of State	H.E. Pok Than
Secretary of State	H.E. Im Sethi

Ministry of Agriculture Forestry and Fisheries	
Minister	H.E. Chhea Song
Secretary of State	H.E. Chan Tong Iv
Secretary of State	H.E. Maey Sam Oeurn
Ministry of Culture and Fine Arts	
Minister	H.R.H. Norodom Bopha Devi
Secretary of State	H.H. Sisowath Panara Sirivudh
Secretary of State	H.E. Pen Yet
Ministry of Environment	
Minister	H.E. Dr. Mok Mareth
Secretary of State	H.E. Chhan Saphan
Secretary of State	H.E. To Garry
Ministry of Rural Development	
Minister	H.E. Chhim Seak Leng
Secretary of State	H.E. Ly Thuch
Secretary of State	H.E. Yim Chhay Ly
Ministry of Social Affairs Labour Vocational Training and Youth Rehabilitation	
Minister	H.E. Ith Sam Heng
Secretary of State	H.E Nim Thote
Secretary of State	Lok Chumteav Prak Chantha
Ministry of Post and Telecommunication	
Minister	H.E. So Khun
Secretary of State	H.E. Phan Phin
Secretary of State	H.E Lam Phu An
Ministry of Religions and Cults	
Minister	H.E. Chea Savoeurn
Secretary of State	H.E. Srey Vann Phchang
Secretary of State	H.E. Chorn Iem
Ministry of Women Affairs and Veteran	
Minister	Lok Chumteav Mov Sok Huor
Secretary of State	Lok Chumteav Ung Kunthea Thavry
Secretary of State	Lok Chumteav You Ay
Ministry of Public Works and Transport	
Minister	H.E. Khy Taing Lim
Secretary of State	H.E. Ahmed Yah Ya
Secretary of State	H.E. Tram Iv Teck
Ministry of Justice	
Minister	H.E. Uk Vithun
Secretary of State	H.E. Suy Nou
Secretary of State	Lok Chumteav Ly Vouch Leng
Ministry of Tourism	
Minister	H.E.Veng Sereyvuth
Secretary of State	H.E. Nuth Nin Doeurn

Secretary of State	H.E. Thong Khon

Ministry of Territorial Organization, Urbanization and Construction

Minister	H.E. Im Chhun Lim
Secretary of State	H.E.Ty Yao
Secretary of State	H.E. Nou Saing Khan

Ministry of Water Resources and Meteorology

Minister	H.E. Lim Kean Hor
Secretary of State	H.E. Y Ki Heang
Secretary of State	H.E. Ngor Pin

SECRETARIATS UNDER THE COUNCIL OF MINISTERS:

Secretariat of Public Service

Secretary of State	H.E. Peich Bun Chin

Secretariat of Civil Aviation

Secretary of State	H.E. Pok Sam El 0

ADDRESS AND PHONE OF MINISTRIES IN CAMBODIA

Ministry of Agriculture, Forestry & Fisheries

Address :	Norodom Blvd., Phnom Penh
Phone :	023 - 427 320
Fax :	(+855 23) 427 320

Ministry of Cult & Religious Affairs

Address :	Sisowath Blvd., Phnom Penh
Phone :	023 - 725 699, 722 699
Fax :	

Ministry of Commerce

Address :	Norodom Blvd., Phnom Penh
Phone :	023 - 723 775
Fax :	(+855 23) 426 396

Ministry of Culture & Fine Arts

Address :	Monivong Blvd., Phnom Penh
Phone :	023 - 362 647
Fax :	

Ministry of Economy & Finance

Address : Daun Penh St., Phnom Penh

Phone : 023 - 722 863

Fax : (+855 23) 427 798

Ministry of Education, Youth & Sports

Address : Norodom Blvd., Phnom Penh

Phone : 023 - 360 233

Fax : (+855 23) 426 791

Ministry of Environment

Address : Sihanouk Blvd., Phnom Penh

Phone : 023 - 426 814

Fax : (+855 23) 427 844

Ministry of Foreign Affaires & Int. Cooperation

Address : Sihanouk Blvd., Phnom Penh

Phone : 023 - 426 122

Fax : (+855 23) 426 144

Ministry of Health

Address : #128 Kampuchea Krom, Phnom Penh

Phone : 855-23-426 841

Fax : 855-23-426 841

Ministry of Interior

Address : Norodom Blvd., Phnom Penh

Phone : 023 - 724 237

Ministry of Industry, Mines & Energy

Address :: Norodom Blvd., Phnom Penh

Phone : 023 - 723 077

Fax : (+855 23) 427 840

Ministry of Information

Address : Monivong Blvd., Phnom Penh

Phone : 023 - 426 059

Fax : (+855 23) 426 059

Ministry of Justice

Address : Sothearos Blvd., Phnom Penh

Phone : 023 - 360 421

Fax :

Ministry of National Defense

Address : Pochentong Blvd., Phnom Penh

Phone : 023 - 366 170

Fax : (+855 23) 366 169

Ministry of Planning

Address : #386 Monivong Blvd.,Phnom Penh

Phone : 023 - 362 307

Fax :

Ministry of Post & Telecommunication

Address : Preah Ang Eng / Preah Ang Non, Phnom Penh

Phone : 023 - 722 823

Fax :

Ministry of Public Works

Address : Khsattreiani Kossomak St., Phnom Penh

Phone : 023 - 420 813, 752 113

Fax : (+855 23) 427 862

Ministry of Rural Development

Address : Czechoslovakia Blvd/ Pochentong Blvd., Phnom Penh

Phone : 023 - 722 425, 426 814

Fax :

Ministry of Social Welfare, Labor & Veterans

Address : #68 Norodom Blvd., Phnom Penh

Phone : 023 - 725 191

Fax : (+855 23) 427 322

Ministry of Tourism

Address : #3 Monivong Blvd., Phnom Penh

Phone : +855 23 213 911

Fax : +855 23 426 107, 426 364

Ministry of Women's Affairs

Address : Phnom Penh

Phone : 023 - 366 412

Fax :

BANKS

NBC- National Bank of Cambodia

Banque Nationale du Cambodge
Nº 22-24, Norodom, Phnom Penh
Postal code 12203

Tel 722 221/ 725 063/ 724 866
E-mail nbc@bigpond.com.kh

FTB- Foreign Trade Bank

Nº 3, Kromuon Sar (St. 114), Phnom Penh
Postal code 12203
Tel 723 866/ 723 466
Fax 426 410/ 426 108

CB- Canadia Bank Ltd.

Cambodia, Head Office
Nº 265-269, Ang Duong (St. 110), Phnom Penh
Postal code 12202
Tel 215 286/ 215 085-6
Fax 427 064
E-mail canadia@camnet.com.kh
Telex CANADIA 36188

CPB- Cambodian Public Bank Ltd.

Nº 23, Kromuon Sar (St. 114), Phnom Penh
Tel 723 664/ 426 067
Fax 426 068
E-mail campu@bigpond.com.kh
Telex (51) 94079463

ADB- Asian Development Bank

Banque Asiatique de Development
Cambodia Resident Mission
Nº 93, Norodom, Phnom Penh
Postal code 12211
Tel & Fax 215 805-6
Fax 215 807
Email adbcarm@bigpond.com.kh

DIPLOMATIC MISSIONS OF THE KINGDOM OF CAMBODIA ABROAD

COUNTRY (City)	CHIEF OF MISSION	PHONE & FAX & EMAIL	ADDRESS
AUSTRALIA (Canberra)	**H.E. Mr. HOR Nambora** Ambassador	Tel : (612) 6273 1259, 6273 1154, Fax : (612) 6273 1053 Email:Cambodianembassy@ozemail.com.au Web : www.embassyofcambodia.org.nz	Royal Embassy of Cambodia No. 5 Canterbury Crescent, Deakin, A.C.T. 2600, AUSTRALIA

BRUNEIDARUSSALAM (Bandar Seri Begawan)	**H.E. Mr. ITH Dettola** Ambassador	Tel : (673-2) 654 046 Fax : (673-2) 650 646 E-mail : cambodia@brunet.bn	Royal Embassy of Cambodia 8 Simpang 845 KG Tasek Meradum, JLN Tutong, B.S.B, BRUNEI DARUSSALAM
PEOPLE'S REPUBLIC 0F CHINA (Beijing)	**H.E. Mr. KHEK Lerang** Ambassador	Tel : (861) 06532 1889, 06532 7290 Fax : (861) 06532 3507 E-mail: cambassybeijing@yahoo.com	Royal Embassy of Cambodia No. 9 Dong Zhi MenWai Dajio 100600 Beijing, P.R.CHINA
PEOPLE'S REPUBLIC OF CHINA (Guangzhou)	**Mr. IM Sophy** Consul General	Tel : (8620) 838 79005 Fax : (8620) 838 79006 E-mail:cambodia@public.guangzhou.gd.cn	Royal Consulate General of Cambodia Room 804 - 808, The Garden Tower, Huanshi Rd. E.Guangzhou P.R..CHINA, P C : 510064
PEOPLE'S REPUBLIC OF CHINA (Hong Kong)	**Mr. CHHONG Toeun** Consul General	Tel : (852) 2546 0718, 2362 3656 Fax : (852) 2803 0570 E-mail : cacghk@netvigator.com	Royal Consulate General of Cambodia Room Nº 3606 Sigga CC 144-151, Connaught,Road West, HONG KONG, P.R.CHINA
PEOPLE'S REPUBLIC OF CHINA (Shanghai)	**Mr. OP Sisawada** Consul General	Tel : (8621) 636 1668, 636 00949 Fax : (8621) 636 11437 E-mail : tangjx@online.sh.cn	Royal Consulate General of Cambodia Huasheng Commercial Building 9th Floor, Hankou Road 400Shanghai, P.R.CHINA
REPUBLIC OF CUBA (Havana)	**H.E.Mr. CHHIM Prorng** Ambassador	Tel : (537) 241 495, 241 496, 242 333 Fax : (537) 246 400 E-mail: cambodia@ceniai.if.cu	Royal Embassy of Cambodia No. 7001 Sta AV. ESQ 70 Miramar, Havana, CUBA
REPUBLIC OF FRANCE (Paris)	**H.E. Mr. PRAK Sokhonn** Ambassador	Tel : (331) 4503 4720 Fax : (331) 4503 4740 E-mail :ambcambodgeparis@mangoosta.fr	Royal Embassy of Cambodia 4,rue Adolphe Yvon75116 Paris, FRANCE
REPUBLIC OF FRANCE	**HRH Sdech Krom Khun**	Tel : (331) 4525 1502 Fax : (331) 4525 8472	Permanent Delegation of the

(Paris)	**NORODOM Sihamoni** Ambassador	E-mail : DPCAMBODGE@wanadoo.fr	Kingdom of Cambodia to UNESCO No. 2 Place de Barcelone75016 Paris, FRANCE
FEDERAL REPUBLIC OF GERMANY (Berlin)	**H.R.H. SISOWATH Phandaravong** Ambassador	Tel : (4930) 4863 7901 Fax : (4930) 4863 7973 E-mail : REC-Berlin@tonline.de	Royal Embassy of Cambodia Benjamin-Vogelsdorf Str. 213187 Berlin, GERMANY
REPUBLIC OF INDIA (New Delhi)	**H.E. Mr. CHEANG Eng Ngoun** Ambassador	Tel : (91-11) 649 5091. 649 5092 Fax : (91-11) 649 5093 E-mail : camboemb@hclinfinet.com	Royal Embassy of Cambodia N-14,Panchsheel Park New Delhi-110017, INDIA
KINGDOM OF JAPAN (Tokyo)	**H.E. Mr. ING Kieth** Ambassador	Tel : (813) 5412 8521-2-4 Fax : (813) 5412 8526 E-mail : aap33850@hkg.odn.ne.jp	Royal Embassy of Cambodia. 8-6-9,Akasaka,Minato-Ku, Tokyo 1070052, JAPAN.
KOREA (D.P.R) (Pyong Yang)	**H.E. Mr. OUM Mannorine** Ambassador	Tel : (8502) 381 7283 Fax : (8502) 381 7625 E-mail :	Royal Embassy of Cambodia. Rue de L'université Commune Mouscou Arrondissement Daedongang R.P.D. DU COREE
KOREA REPUBLIC (Seoul)	**H.E. Mr. CHHEANG Vun** Ambassador	Tel : (822) 3785 1040 Fax : (822) 3785 1041 E-mail : camboemb@korea.com	Royal Embassy of Cambodia 653-8 Hanan Dong,Yougsan Gu, Seoul, REPUBLIC OF KOREA
P.D.R. OF LAO (Vientiane)	**H.E. Mr. MEAS Savandy** Ambassador	Tel : (8562) 131 4950, 131 4952, 131 5851 Fax : (8562) 131 4951 E-mail : recamlao@laotel.com	Royal Embassy of Cambodia Thadeua Road, KM2Vientiane, B.P. 34, LaoLAO P.D.R.
FEDERATION OF MALAYSIA (Kuala Lumpur)	**H.E. Mr. KEO Puth Rasmey** Ambassador	Tel : (603) 4257 1150, 4257 3711 Fax : (603) 4257 1157 E-mail : reckl@tm.net.my	Royal Embassy of Cambodia Nº 46,Jalan U-Than55000 Kuala Lumpur, MALAYSIA
UNION OF MYANMAR	**H.E. Mr. NIM**	Tel : (951) 541 108, 546 157	Royal Embassy of

(Yangon)	**Chantara** Ambassador	Fax : (951) 546 156 Email:RECYANGON@mptmail.net.mm	Cambodia N° 34 Kada Aye Pagoda Road Bahan Township, Yangon UNION OF MYANMAR
REPUBLIC OF THE PHILIPPINES (Manila)	**H.E. Mr. EK Sereywath** Ambassador	Tel : (632) 818 9981 Fax : (632) 818 9983 E-mail : cam.emb.ma@netasia.net	Royal Embassy of Cambodia Unit 7A/7th Floor, Country Space I Bldg., Sen. Gil Puyat Avenue Salcedo Village, Makata City, MM, PHILIPPINES
FERATION OF RUSSIA (Moscow)	**H.E. Mr. ROS Kong** Ambassador	Tel : (7095) 201 7668, 201 2115, 201 3925, 201 2234 Fax : (7095) 956 6573 E-mail : cambodia@mail.cnt.ru	Royal Embassy of Cambodia Starokonyushenny Per. 11, Moscow.
REPUBLIC OF SINGAPORE	**H.E. Mr. KEM Mongkol** Ambassador	Tel : (65) 299 3028 Fax : (65) 299 3622 E-mail : cambodiaembasy@pacific.net.sg	Royal Embassy of Cambodia 152 Beach Road, # 11-05 Gateway East Singapore 189721, SINGAPORE
SWITZERLAND (Geneva)	**H.E. Mr. SUOS Someth** Ambassador	Tel : (41 22) 0479 341 776 Fax : (41 22) E-mail : ssuos@wanadoo.fr	Permanent Mission of Cambodia to UN and International Organizations Geneva, SWITZERLAND
KINGDOM OF THAILAND (Bangkok)	**H.E. Mr. UNG Sean** Ambassador	Tel : (662) 254 6630, 253 9851, 253 7967 Fax : (662) 253 9859, 253 7961 E-mail: recbkk@cscoms.com	Royal Embassy of Cambodia N° 185 Rajdamri Road,Lumpini Patumwan Bangkok 10330, THAILAND
KINGDOM OF THAILAND (Sa Kaew)	**Mr. KER Sereyboth** Consul General	Tel : (66 37) 421 734, 421 735 Fax : (66 37) 421 736 E-mail: consulsk@cscoms.com	Royal Consulate General of Cambodia N° 666, Sovanasone Road Ampheu Meung Sa Kaew 27000, Sa Kaew Province,THAILAND

U.S.A (Washington)	**H.E. Mr. ENG Roland** Ambassador	Tel : (202) 726 7742 Fax : (202) 726 8381 E-mail : cambodia@embassy.org Web : www.embassy.org/cambodia	Royal Embassy of Cambodia 4530 16th Street N.W. Washington, D.C 20011, U.S.A
U.S.A (New York)	**H.E. Mr. OUCH Borith** Ambassador	Phone : (1212) 223 0676, 369 1369 Fax : (1212) 223 0425 E-mail : cambodia@un.int Web : www.un.int/cambodia	Permanent Mission of the Kingdom of Cambodia to the United Nations 866 U.N.O, Plaza,Suite 420 New York, NY10017,USA
U.S.A (State of California)	**Mr. Hay Yang** Honorary Consul	Tel : (213) 625 7777 Fax : (213) 625 7766 E-mail : cambodiaconsulate@usa.net	Royal Honorary Consulate of Cambodia 422 Ord Street, Suite GLos Angeles, CA 90012,U.S.A
U.S.A (State of Washington)	**Mr. Darrell Huoth** Honorary Consul	Tel : (206) 217 0830 Fax : (206) 361 7888 E-mail : consul_huoth@diplomats.com	Royal Honorary Consulate of Cambodia 1818 Westlake Avenue N., Suite #315 Seattle,WA 98109, U.S.A
SOCIALIST REPUBLIC OF VIETNAM (Hanoi)	**H.E. Mr. VAR Sim Samreth** Ambassador	Tel : (844) 942 4788, 942 4789 Mobil : 090 342 2034 Fax : (844) 942 3225 E-mail : arch@fpt.vn	Royal Embassy of Cambodia 71,Tran Hung Dao Str, Hanoi S.R.VIETNAM
SOCIALIST REPUBLIC OF VIETNAM (Hochiminh)	**Mr. LUON Kimkhuon** Consul General	Tel : (848) 829 2751 Fax : (848) 829 2744 E-mail : cambocg@hcm.vnn.vn	Royal Consulate General of Cambodia No. 41, Phung Khac Khoan, Hochiminh City, S.R.VIETNAM

DIPLOMATIC MISSIONS INTERNATIONAL ORGANISATIONS AND OTHER REPRESENTATIVES IN THE KINGDOM OF CAMBODIA

1	Algeria	Hanoi	Ambassador
2	Argentine	Bangkok	Ambassadork

3	Australia	Phnom Penh	Ambassador
4	Austria	Bangkok	Ambassador
5	Baangladesh	Bangkok	Ambassador
6	Belgium	Bangkok	Ambassador
7	Benin	Beijing	Ambassador
8	Brazil	Bangkok	Ambassador
9	Brunei Darussalam	Phnom Penh	Ambassador
10	Bulgaria	Phnom Penh	Chargé d'Affaires
11	Canada	Phnom Penh	Ambassador
12	China (People's Republic)	Phnom Penh	Ambassador
13	Croatia	Kualalumpur	Ambassador
14	Cuba	Phnom Penh	Ambassador
15	Czech Republic	Bangkok	Ambassador
16	Danish	Bangkok	Ambassador
17	Egypt	Bangkok	Ambassador
18	European Commission	Bangkok	Chargé d'Affaires
19	European Union	Phnom Penh	Coordinator
20	Finland	Bangkok	Ambassador
21	France	Phnom Penh	Ambassador
22	Germany	Phnom Penh	Ambassador
23	Ghana	Beijing	Ambassador
24	Greece	Bangkok	Ambassador
25	Guinea	Beijing	Ambassador
26	Holy See (Apostolic Nunciature)	Bangkok	Apostolic Nuncio
27	Hungaria	Hanoi	Ambassador
28	India	Phnom Penh	Ambassador
29	Indonesia	Phnom Penh	Ambassador
30	Iran	Hanoi	Ambassador
31	Iraq	Hanoi	Ambassador

32	Ireland	Beijing	Ambassador
33	Israel	Bangkok	Ambassador
34	Italy	Bangkok	Ambassador
35	Japan	Phnom Penh	Ambassador
36	Korea (D.P.R.)	Phnom Penh	Ambassador
37	Korea (Republic)	Phnom Penh	Ambassador
38	Kuwait	Bangkok	Ambassador
39	Lao P.D.R.	Phnom Penh	Ambassador
40	Libya	Hanoi	Ambassador
41	Malaysia	Phnom Penh	Ambassador
42	Mali	Beijing	Ambassador
43	Malta (S.M.O.)	Phnom Penh	Ambassador
44	Mauritania	Beijing	Ambassador
45	Mexico	Bangkok	Ambassador
46	Mongolia	Vientiane	Ambassador
47	Myannmar	Phnom Penh	Ambassador
48	Nepal	Yangoon	Ambassador
49	Netherlands	Bangkok	Ambassador
50	New Zealand	Bangkok	Ambassador
51	Nigeria	Manila	Ambassador
52	Norway	Bangkok	Ambassador
53	Pakistan	Bangkok	Ambassador
54	Palestine	Hanoi	Ambassador
55	Panama	Tokyo	Ambassador
56	Peru	Bangkok	Ambassador
57	Philippines	Phnom Penh	Ambassador
58	Poland	Phnom Penh	Ambassador
59	Portugal	Bangkok	Ambassador
60	Romania	Bangkok	Ambassador

61	Russia	Phnom Penh	Ambassador
62	Singapore	Phnom Penh	Ambassador
63	Spain	Bangkok	Ambassador
64	Slovak	Bangkok	Chargé d'Affaires a.i
65	South Africa	Bangkok	Ambassador
66	Sri Lanka	Bangkok	Ambassador
67	Sudan	Beijing	Ambassador
68	Sweden	Bangkok	Ambassador
69	Switzerland	Bangkok	Ambassador
70	Tanzania	Beijing	Ambassador
71	Thailand	Phnom Penh	Ambassador
72	Tunisia	Beijing	Ambassador
73	Turkey	Bangkok	Ambassador
74	Ukraine	Hanoi	Ambassador
75	United Kingdom	Phnom Penh	Ambassador
76	United States of America	Phnom Penh	Ambassador
77	Vietnam	Phnom Penh	Ambassador
78	Zambia	Beijing	Ambassador
79	United Nations	Phnom Penh	Representative
80	International Monetary Fund	Phnom Penh	Resident Representative
81	UNCOHCHR	Phnom Penh	Director
82	UNDP	Phnom Penh	Resident Representative
83	UNESCO	Phnom Penh	Representative
84	UNFPA	Phnom Penh	Representative
85	UNHCR	Phnom Penh	Acting Head of Laison Office
86	UNICEF	Phnom Penh	Representative
87	World Food Programme	Phnom Penh	Representative
88	World Bank	Phnom Penh	Chief of Office
89	World Health Organisation	Phnom Penh	Representative

90	ICRC	Phnom Penh	Head of Delegation
91	IFRC	Phnom Penh	Head of Delegation
92	IOM	Phnom Penh	Chief of Mission
93	MRC	Phnom Penh	Chief Executive Officer
94	Asia Development Bank	Phnom Penh	Resident Representative
95	JICA	Phnom Penh	Resident Representative

TELEVISIONS & RADIO STATIONS

TVK7-National Television Kampuchea

N°62, Monivong, Phnom Penh
Tel 714 149/ 426 761/ 430 747
Fax 426 407
HP 012 848 205
P.O. Box 984

TV5- TV Cambodia

Tchecoslovaquie (St. 169), Borei Keila, Phnom Penh
Postal Code 12253
Tel 366 061-2/ 366 064
Fax 366 063
E-mail mica.t.v.5@bigpond.com.kh

TV3- TV3 & Radio FM 103 MHz

Phnom Penh Municipality
N° 2, Confederation de la Russie, Phnom Penh
Fax 360 800
HP 012 808 849

TV11- TV Apsara (11) & Radio FM 97 MHz

N° 69, St. 57, Coner St. 360, Phnom Penh
Tel 303 002
Tel & Fax 214 302
Free Line 012 816 004

TV- BayonTV & Radio FM 95 MHz

Phnom Penh
Tel 300 231
HP 012 895 808/ 012 806 774/ 012 813 695
CTV9- Cambodia Television Station & Radio FM 107 MHz
N° 18, St. 562, Phnom Penh
Postal code 12151

Tel 880 874/ 308 212
Fax 368 212
HP 016 833 091
E-mail tv9@camnet.com.kh/ www.tv9.com.kh

FM96MHz-National Radio of Cambodia

Chamkadong, Phnom Penh
Postal code 12352
HP 012 852 741/ 012 816 001/ 011 829 011

THE CAMBODIAN GENOCIDE JUSTICE ACT

(22 U.S.C. 2656, Part D, Sections 571 - 574)

Sec. 571. SHORT TITLE.
This part may be cited as the "Cambodian Genocide Justice Act".

Sec. 572. POLICY.
(a) In General. -- Consistent with international law, it is the policy of the United States to support efforts to bring to justice members of the Khmer Rouge for their crimes against humanity committed in Cambodia between April 17, 1975, and January 7, 1979.

(b) Specific Actions Urged. -- To that end, the Congress urges the President --

(1) to collect, or assist appropriate organizations and individuals to collect relevant data on crimes of genocide committed in Cambodia;
(2) in circumstances which the President deems appropriate, to encourage the establishment of a national or international criminal tribunal for the prosecution of those accused of genocide in Cambodia; and
(3) as necessary, to provide such national or international tribunal with information collected pursuant to paragraph (1).

Sec. 573. ESTABLISHMENT OF STATE DEPARTMENT OFFICE.
(a) Establishment. -- (1) None of the funds authorized to be appropriated by this Act for "Diplomatic and Consular Programs" shall be available for obligation or expenditure during fiscal years 1994 and 1995 unless, not later than 90 days after the date of enactment of this Act, the Secretary of State has established within the Department of State under the Assistant Secretary for East Asia and Pacific Affairs (or any successor Assistant Secretary) the Office of Cambodian Genocide Investigation (hereafter in this part referred to as the "Office").

(2) The Office may carry out its activities inside or outside of Cambodia, except that not less than 75 percent of the funds made available for the Office and its activities shall be used to carry out activities within Cambodia.

(b) Purpose. -- The purpose of the Office shall be to support, through organizations and individuals with whom the Secretary of State may contract to carry out the operations of the Office, as appropriate, efforts to bring to justice members of the Khmer Rouge for their crimes against humanity committed in Cambodia between April 17, 1975, and January 7, 1979, including--

(1) to investigate crimes against humanity committed by national Khmer Rouge leaders during that period;
(2) to provide the people of Cambodia with access to documents, records, and other evidence held by the Office as a result of such investigation;

(2) to submit relevant data to a national or international penal tribunal that may be convened to formally hear and judge the genocidal acts committed by the Khmer Rouge; and

(3) to develop the United States proposal for the establishment of an international criminal tribunal for the prosecution of those accused of genocide in Cambodia.

(c) Contracting Authority. -- The Secretary of State shall, subject to the availability of appropriations, contract with appropriate individuals and organizations to carry out the purposes of the Office.

(d) Notification To Congress. -- The Committee on Foreign Relations and the Committee on Appropriations of the Senate and the Committee on Foreign Affairs and the Committee on Appropriations of the House of Representatives shall be notified of any exercise of the authority of section 34 of the State Department Basic Authorities Act of 1956 with respect to the Office or any of its programs, projects, or activities at least 15 days in advance in accordance with procedures applicable to notifications under that section.

Sec. 574. REPORTING REQUIREMENT.

(a) In General.-- Beginning 6 months after the date of enactment of this Act, and every 6 months thereafter, the President shall submit a report to the appropriate congressional committees-

(b) that describes the activities of the Office, and sets forth new facts learned about past Khmer Rouge practices, during the preceding 6-month period; and

(c) that describes the steps the President has taken during the preceding 6-month period to promote human rights, to support efforts to bring to justice the national political and military leadership of the Khmer Rouge, and to prevent the recurrence of human rights abuses in Cambodia through actions which are not related to United Nations activities in Cambodia.

(b) Definition. -- For purposes of this section, the term "appropriate congressional committees" means the Committee on Foreign Relations of the Senate and the Committee on Foreign Affairs of the House of Representatives.

THE END OF THE KHMER ROUGE[1]

Even before the post-election sound and fury in Cambodia simmers down, the new government in Phnom Penh is faced with a host of crucial issues for the future. There are dramatic contrasts between Phnom Penh and the traditional, impoverished countryside. The Asian financial crisis has damaged an already weak economy. Climate changes have reduced harvests and left the northwestern provinces on the brink of famine. The senseless political infighting and violence that have reigned in the post-election period deserve universal condemnation. All parties have been guilty of perpetuating the crimes and abuses of the past, selling out the Cambodian people in a misguided grab for power.

With the near-complete collapse of hard-line Khmer Rouge military power over the course of the last year, however, an unprecedented chance for peace has arisen. The incumbent government, led by Hun Sen, has pronounced that it is committed to bringing the leadership of the Khmer Rouge before an international tribunal to be judged for their crimes during the Democratic Kampuchea regime of 1975-1979. The new government arising out of the July 26 election must grapple with the long-standing problem of what to do about the legacy of Cambodian genocide.

As an armed movement and a political party, the Khmer Rouge is finished. The attack on polling stations in Anlong Veng, killing 10—the only act of terror and violence to mar election day—shows, pathetically, that senseless murder is the only skill the Khmer Rouge have left. But what of the masses of those who have been under the sway of the Khmer Rouge—perhaps ten thousand fighters in the west and the north, several tens of thousands of their family members, and the many thousands more ordinary Cambodians who simply had the misfortune to live in zones controlled by the Khmer Rouge? Their reintegration into Cambodian society will constitute the final stage in the dissolution of Khmer Rouge military power, and for this reason, it is imperative for the future of Cambodia that this process be given priority in Cambodian national affairs. The perpetrators of genocide, however, have largely gone unpunished.

Youk Chhang, director of the Documentation Center of Cambodia, favors indictments of at least 20 top Khmer Rouge leaders for genocide and crimes against humanity. The Documentation Center's comprehensive files on the genocide years hold more than enough data to convict fighters who have committed criminal and barbarian acts under orders from the Khmer Rouge leadership. Is it beyond the capacity of the Cambodian justice system to clearly segregate the innocent from the culpable during the process of reintegrating the rank and file Khmer Rouge? Probably. Is it beyond the capacity of the international community to handle this delicate task? Almost certainly. The process of national reconciliation in Cambodia will inevitably entail many ugly compromises. The question is, where does one draw the line?

Thus we return to the problem of the Khmer Rouge leadership, and their lingering political influence. According to recently captured Khmer Rouge leadership documents, at a June 24, 1997 KR leadership meeting on principles for negotiations with (former) First Prime Minister Norodom Ranariddh, the number one KR demand was: "1. Do not

[1] by Craig Etcheson and Andrew Wells

bring the genocide regime to justice." The choice of words here is telling; even the Khmer Rouge know the truth.

Fast forward to mid-1998, and top Khmer Rouge cadre appear to have evolved a different perspective. Almost all of the Khmer Rouge have now "defected" to the government, and few of them openly oppose the idea of a genocide tribunal for Cambodia. Even Ieng Sary, who is high on the list of potential prosecution targets for a tribunal, says that he is willing to "testify" if it will assist in national reconciliation. Senior Khmer Rouge military commander Ke Pauk was quoted in the April 10 issue of the *Phnom Penh Post* as saying "The five Standing Committee members are responsible for the killing between 1975-79.... If they want to try the five Standing Committee members, I am happy to testify." Of course, this overlooks the fact that the Standing Committee had more than five members during the KR regime, and Ke Pauk himself was one of them.

This new political line has also been disseminated among Khmer Rouge propagandists abroad. On July 5 of this year, Cambodians gathered on the Mall in Washington, DC to protest the first anniversary of the "Hun Sen coup." Mr. Prasith Kuoch, who regularly praises the Khmer Rouge in his Montreal newspaper, *Khmerajati*, and who is widely regarded in the Cambodian community as the top Khmer Rouge ideologist in North America, was one of the organizers of the July 5 protest. At the rally, he affirmed, "I do not care about the Khmer Rouge. I have no objection to an international tribunal."

So, with a majority of senior Khmer Rouge officials apparently now willing to contemplate a tribunal to judge accusations of Khmer Rouge genocide and crimes against humanity, what obstacles remain to block progress towards this long-sought objective? The Chinese government continues to defend impunity for the Khmer Rouge, but the establishment of the International Criminal Court proceeded under the authority of the United Nations General Assembly, where China cannot use its Security Council veto to block justice.

The Cambodian government has reasons to be ambivalent towards the concept of a tribunal, an attitude perhaps reflected in recent comments by Hun Sen that agitation for a tribunal in the international community is a "trick" to "prevent Cambodia from achieving real peace." Some analysts interpret this remark as indicating that Hun Sen and his People's Party intend to protect all of the "former" Khmer Rouge who have declared loyalty to the government, and will try to restrict any genocide trial to a "Gang of Three," Ta Mok, Nuon Chea and Khieu Samphan, with any extra blame assigned to the conveniently deceased Pol Pot and Son Sen. Presumably, these are the "five Standing Committee members" to whom Ke Pauk refers.

But if a genuinely independent tribunal is established, the prosecutor is unlikely to cooperate with such organized impunity; there are hundreds of suspects against whom highly damning evidence has been compiled. In the case of an independent international tribunal, paradoxically, the main threat to moving forward with genocide justice and national reconciliation in Cambodia may come from the United States.

In Washington policy circles, a bizarre double standard persists when it comes to Cambodian politics. Hun Sen and the CPP are subject to intense demonization in the American press, while abuses of the opposition, including anti-Vietnamese race-baiting and incitements to violence, have been generally ignored. Readers of the *New York Times* and *Washington Post* have been subjected to a barrage of misinformed, partisan hack jobs attacking the entire election process on the basis of sweeping judgments about the Cambodian political system.2 While the Cambodian system is far from perfect, it is arguably more democratic than most of Cambodia's Southeast Asian neighbors, such as Malaysia and Singapore. Especially given its tragic recent history, why is Cambodia singled out for special treatment?

This double standard has led to strong pressure from Washington to continue to deny Cambodia its seat in the United Nations and to isolate the Cambodian government in the international community. Congressman Dana Rohrabacher (R-CA), in a letter sent to the Clinton Administration and King Norodom Sihanouk on August 14, threatens to continue a ban on most US foreign aid until a "legitimate," defined as an opposition-led, government is formed.2 In September, Rohrabacher introduced a resolution (H.Res.533) labeling Hun Sen a "war criminal" and calling for his trial by the International Criminal Court. Under such circumstances, the Cambodian government will surely be unreceptive to US efforts to influence the mandate of a Khmer Rouge tribunal.

US hostility towards a new Hun Sen regime is not likely to be shared by most European and Asian governments, but the fact remains that without the support of the "last remaining superpower," a robust prosecution of international law in Cambodia will be politically impossible. Moreover, convening any kind of serious tribunal to judge Khmer Rouge crimes will be an expensive proposition, and if the temper in Congress continues to be focused on condemnation of the Cambodian government, then US financial assistance to support genocide justice in Cambodia will be all the more unlikely.

This is where advocates of peace and justice in the Asia Pacific can make a difference. As things now stand, Congress hears only angry voices condemning the Cambodian government. Alternative voices must be raised, reminding the Congress that an historical opportunity to achieve justice for one of the most murderous episodes of the twentieth century is within our grasp. Advocates of justice should make their views heard among US policy makers, sending a clear message that reconciliation and democracy in Cambodia can never get off the ground until the perpetrators of the Killing Fields are brought to book. We can do it, but not if the politics of division and hatred carry the day and distract the post-election agenda from refocusing on the issue of justice. When communicating with your elected representatives, please emphasize three things:

1) National reconciliation in Cambodia depends on the establishment of an international tribunal to end impunity for the Khmer Rouge leadership, and the United States should play a key role in supporting UN Ambassador Thomas Hammarberg's efforts toward this objective;

2) The prosecutor of the tribunal must be independent of all political pressures, whether they emanate from within Cambodia or from the international community; and

3) It is in the interest of the United States to provide generous financial, judicial, technical and diplomatic support for an international tribunal to judge the crimes of the Khmer Rouge regime. □

Craig Etcheson, former director of the Committee to Oppose the Return of the Khmer Rouge (CORKR), now works at the International Monitor Institute in New Haven, CT. Andrew Wells, Asia Pacific Center Program Director, served as an international monitor in the July Cambodian elections.

U.S. GOVERNMENT CONTACTS

United States Commercial Service
(Washington, DC)
Trade Information Center
Tel: (800) USA-TRADE
Fax: (202) 482-4473
(U.S. Embassy Bangkok)
Diethelm Tower A, 304
93/1 Wireless Rd.
Bangkok 10330, Thailand
Commercial Counselor: Karen Ware
Tel: [66](2)205-5090
Fax: [66](2)255-2915
E-Mail: Karen.Ware@Mail.Doc.Gov

United States Embassy Phnom Penh
(Cambodian Mailing Address)
27 St. 240
Phnom Penh, Cambodia
(U.S. Mailing Address)
Box P
Apo Ap 96546
Ambassador: Kent M. Wiedemann
Economic/Commercial Officer: Bruce Levine
Tel: [855](23)216-436
Fax: [855](23)216-811
E-Mail: Levinebj@State.Gov

Export-Import Bank Of The United States (Eximbank)
811 Vermont Ave. NW
Washington, DC 20571
Tel: 202-565-3510
Fax: 202-565-3380
Website: Www.Exim.Gov.

Overseas Private Investment Corporation (OPIC)
Mr. Bruce Cameron, Business Development Officer
1100 New York Avenue NW
Washington, DC 20527, USA
Tel: (202) 336-8745
Fax: (202) 408-5154
E-Mail: Bcame@opic.gov .

MULTILATERAL CONTACTS:

Asian Development Bank (ADB)
Box 789
0890 Manila, Philippines
U.S. Executive Director: Amb. Linda Tsao Yang
Tel: [63](2)632-6050
Fax: [63](2)632-4003
U.S. Commercial Liaison: Mr. Denny Barnes
Tel: [63](2)890-9364
Fax: [63](2)890-9713
E-Mail: Dbarnes@cs.doc.gov

International Finance Corp. (IFC)
1850 I (Eye) St. NW
Room I-11-063
Washington, DC 20433, USA
Cambodia Investment Officer: Mr. Morgan Landy
Tel: 202-473-9350
Fax: 202-676-0820

Multilateral Investment Guarantee Agency (MIGA)
1818 H St. NW
Washington, DC 20433
Tel: 202-477-1234
Fax: 202-522-2630

MARKET RESEARCH AND INVESTMENT ADVICE (LISTED ALPHABETICALLY

Dirksen, Flipse, Doran & Le (Legal Advisors)
Tel: (855-23) 428-726
Fax: (855-23) 428-227
Contact: Mr. David Doran

Ernst & Young
Tel: (855-23) 211-431/360-837
Fax: (855-23) 360-437
Contact: Mr. Senaka Fernando

International Management & Investment Consultants (IMIC)
Tel: (855-23) 362-753/362-392
Fax: (855-23) 721-756
Contact: Mr. Craig Martin, Director

Price Waterhouse Coopers
Tel: (855-23) 218-086
Fax: (855-23) 428-076
Contact: Mrs. Sally Relph

Tilleke, Gibbins, And Associates, Ltd. (Legal Advisors)
Tel: (855-23) 362-670
Fax: (855-23) 362-671
Contact: Mr. Bretton Sciaroni

STRATEGIC STATISTICS

KEY ECONOMIC INDICATORS

Population: 11.7 million (1999)
Population Growth Rate: 2.9% (1999)
Land Area: 181,035 sq. kms
Religion: Buddhist (96%), Muslim (3%)
Government System: Constitutional Monarchy
Economic Style: open market economy
Language: Khmer. (English, Chinese, French widely spoken)

GROWTH AND PRODUCTION:

(Source: Ministry of Economy and Finance. All figures in US$ millions unless otherwise indicated.)

Item	**1996**	**1997**	**1998**	**1999 (proj.)**
Nominal GDP	3,113	3,033	2,868	3,132
Nominal GDP (billions of Riels)	8,200	9,100	10,900	11,900
GDP deflator (based on 1993)-	7.1%	9.2%	18.6%	5.0%
Real GDP growth (annual increase)	7.0%	1.0%	1.0%	4.0%
Population (millions)	10.7	11.1	11.4	11.7
GDP per capita (US$)	291	274	251	267
Labor force (millions)	4.7	5.5	6.0	n/a
Official unemployment rate	1.0%	7%	2.1%	2.8%

PERCENTAGE OF GDP BY SECTOR:

Sector	1996	1997	1998	1999 (proj.)
Agriculture	42.3%	42.7%	41.9%	40.9%
Industry	18.3%	17.4%	18.0%	18.2%
Services	39.4%	39.9%	40.1%	40.9%

GROWTH RATES OF GDP SECTORS:

Sector	1996	1997	1998	1999 (proj.)
Agriculture	1.8%	1.2%	.4%	n/a
Industry	13.3%	-2.9%	1.1%	n/a
Services	8.8%	2.6%	-.9%	n/a

MONEY, PRICES AND BANKING:

Items	1996	1997	1998	1999 (proj.)
Inflation (Change in Consumer Price Index)	9.0%	9.0%	13.0%	6.5%
Exchange rate (Riels per US$, annual average)	2,643	3,000	3,820	3,800
Commercial Bank Assets	393.6	483.6	467.4	474.4

TRADE:

Items	1996	1997	1998	1999 (proj.)
Total Imports (CIF)	1,110.2	1,037.1	1,060.0	1,164.0
Total Exports (fob)	658.8	733.8	754.0	756.0
Total Trade Balance	-451.4	-303.3	-306.0	-408.0
Total Imports from U.S.	34.05	21.95	38.90	n/a
Total Exports to U.S.	2.64	70.09	292.48	n/a
Trade Surplus(+)/Deficit (-) with U.S.	-31.41	31.19	253.58	n/a

DEBT:

Items	1996	1997	1998	1999 (proj.)
External Public Debt	594.5	645.7	698.8	829.4
Debt Service Ratio (exports/debt service)	19.1	21.3	23.5	23.0

BALANCE OF PAYMENTS:

(source: National Bank of Cambodia. US$ millions.)

Year:	1997	1998	Q1 1999	Q2 1999

Trade (goods) Balance	-308.3	-391.1	-76.1	-79.7
_ Exports (fob)	784.2	705.2	212.7	235.0
_ Imports (fob)	-1,092.4	-1,097.0	-288.8	-314.7
Service Balance	-43.5	-79.9	-13.2	-16.1
Balance of goods and Services	-351.7	-471.7	-89.3	-95.8
Net Income	-53.4	-50.3	-24.8	-18.0
Private Transfers	59.9	66.0	17.5	17.5
Current Account Balance excluding official transfers	-345.2	-456.0	-96.7	-96.3
Official Transfers Net	288.5	292.9	67.7	67.7
Current Account Balance including official transfers	-56.7	-163.1	-34.2	-33.8
Official Sector Loans net (excluding IMF)	41.2	42.5	14.2	11.6
Non-official Sector Investment	122.6	80.5	27.7	16.0
_ Direct investment (net)	168.1	120.7	53.0	38.3
_ Other investment (net)	-45.6	-40.2	-25.3	-22.3
Net Errors and Omissions	-73.7	57.4	19.8	43.9
Overall Balance	33.3	17.3	27.5	37.8
Financing	-33.3	-17.3	-32.8	-43.0
_ Net foreign assets of National Bank of Cambodia	-33.7	-28.0	-33.7	-43.2
_ Exceptional Financing	0.4	10.7	1.0	0.2

KEY LABOR INDICATORS

	1998	1999	Source
Nominal GDP (US$ millions)	2,868	3,131	a
Nominal GDP (Cambodian Riel billions)	10,900	11,960	a
Per capita GDP (US$ millions)	252	268	a
Population (millions) _ in major urban areas	11.44 1.80	11.56 2.13	b b

Annual population growth (pct.)	2.49%	1.10%	c
Life expectancy at birth (years) _ male _ female	51.5 55.0	51.5 55.0	d
Adult literacy rate (pct.)	67.3%	71.2%	b
Labor force (millions) _ male _ female _ in industry (pct.) _ in agriculture (pct.) _ in services (pct.)	5.12 2.48 2.64 4.3% 77.5% 4.3%	5.54 2.64 2.90 6.4% 76.5% 6.4%	b
Unionized labor force (pct. of total) _ in garment industry (pct. of total)	.1-.2% 5-10%	.1-.2% 5-10%	e e
Unemployment rate (pct.)	5.3%	0.6%	f
Underemployment rate (pct.)	n/a	6.5%	f
person days lost to industrial disputes (1000's)	n/a	14-16	e
Minimum wage rate (US$/month - applies to garment / footwear industry only)	40	40	
Monthly compensation costs for laborer (US$) _ clerical _ mechanic _ commercial assistant	n/a n/a n/a	150 80 350	e
Average hours worked per week	48	48	e
Pct. of population below poverty level	35.9	35.9	g
Inflation (pct. change in CPI in Cambodian riel)	12.8	0.0	a

Order Code RS21289
August 21, 2002

CRS Report for Congress

Cambodia: Background and U.S. Relations

Nicole Sayres and Thomas Lum
Analysts in Asian Affairs
Foreign Affairs, Defense, and Trade Division

Summary

Although Cambodia has made some progress in establishing democratic institutions, developing export industries, and nurturing a vibrant civil society, U.S.-Cambodian relations remain strained. In response to strong-arm political tactics by the Cambodian Prime Minister, Hun Sen, the Cambodian government's delays in bringing former Khmer Rouge leaders to justice in a UN-backed international tribunal, and other issues, the United States has limited foreign assistance mostly to non-government organizations in Cambodia. This report provides background and analysis regarding U.S. policies and interests toward Cambodia, including foreign aid restrictions, trade, the bilateral textile agreement, human trafficking, illegal drugs, and HIV/AIDS. This report will be updated as warranted.

Background

After receiving its independence from France in November 1953, the Kingdom of Cambodia has seen its recent history plagued by conflict. In 1970, the military forces of U.S.-backed General Lon Nol overthrew the government of Prince Sihanouk. The Lon Nol government was then defeated in April 1975 by the North Vietnam-backed Khmer Rouge. During the Khmer Rouge's subsequent three-year brutal reign – which included imprisonment and torture, depopulation of the cities, and the establishment of a system of rural communes – an estimated 1 to 3 million people died through execution, starvation, overwork, and disease. In January 1979, an invasion by Vietnamese

CAMBODIA IN BRIEF

Population: 12.5 million
Growth rate: 2.25% (2001 est.)
Location: Borders Thailand, Vietnam, and Laos
Area: 181,040 sq. km. (about the size of Missouri)
Capital: Phnom Penh
Ethnic groups: Khmer 90%; Vietnamese 5%; Chinese 1%; Other 4% (Chams, Burmese, hill tribes)
Language: Khmer (official) 95%; French, English
Religion: Theravada Buddhist 95%; Other 5%
Life Expectancy at Birth: female 59.12 years; male 54.62 years (2001 est.)
Literacy: total 35%; female 22%; male 48% (1990)
Inflation Rate: 1.6% (2000 est.)
Gross Domestic Product: $3.2 billion (2001); *Per Capita* $257; *Growth Rate* 5.3% (2001)
U.S. Trade: exports to U.S. $964 million; imports from U.S. $ 28 million (2001)
Sources: CIA World Factbook; U.S. Department of Commerce; DRI-WEFA; U.S. Embassy Country Commercial Guide.

forces drove the Khmer Rouge from Phnom Penh into the countryside and sparked a 13-year civil war. A United Nations (UN)-brokered peace settlement officially ended the war in October 1991 and led to elections for a 120-seat Constituent Assembly in May 1993. Although the royalist FUNCINPEC (National United Front for a Neutral, Peaceful, Cooperative, and Independent Cambodia) Party won a 58-seat plurality, it agreed to form a coalition government with the Cambodian People's Party (CPP), which won 51 seats, after the CPP threatened that it would not accept the election. The establishment of the coalition government with Prince Ranariddh, head of FUNCINPEC, and Hun Sen, head of the CPP, as co-prime ministers brought fragile political stability to Cambodia. In September 1993, the Constituent Assembly adopted a new constitution, which proclaimed Cambodia a "multi-party liberal democracy" under a constitutional monarchy, headed by King Sihanouk.

In 1997, after rising tensions between the coalition partners, Hun Sen staged an armed takeover of the government. Many FUNCINPEC leaders were killed, and Ranariddh and other non-CPP politicians fled Cambodia. After considerable international pressure and the withholding of aid by donors, Hun Sen allowed Ranariddh to return to Cambodia and held new parliamentary elections in July 1998, which the CPP narrowly won. Despite charges of election irregularities, the two parties agreed to form a coalition government, with Hun Sen as Prime Minister and Ranariddh as President of the National Assembly. The coalition since then has held together, and a sense of normalcy has emerged. The death of Pol Pot in April 1998 and the subsequent collapse of the Khmer Rouge has contributed to the current period of relative stability.

Recent Developments

Local Elections. On February 3, 2002, Cambodia held its first local elections since independence, with the election of commune councils and chiefs. Prime Minister Hun Sen's party won a sweeping victory, with CPP members securing the commune chief position in 1,598 of Cambodia's 1,621 communes. FUNCINPEC and the opposition Sam Rainsy Party won 10 and 13 of the commune chief positions, respectively, as well as a combined 40 percent of the seats on the commune councils. Prior to this event, communes – administrative units consisting of four to seven villages – had been led by CPP appointees, which arguably contributed to CPP's domination of political power at the local level. According to some analysts, the overwhelming CPP victory may bring Hun Sen, who has often been vilified by the international community for his strong-arm tactics, much-needed credibility. Three critical factors will be the CPP's handling of post-election commune power-sharing, the legitimacy of the legislative elections scheduled for summer 2003, and Hun Sen's performance during Cambodia's one-year chairmanship, beginning in July 2002, of the Association of Southeast Asian Nations (ASEAN).[1]

The run-up to the commune elections was marred by allegations of political killings and intimidation. The United Nations reported 15 election-related deaths in the year leading up to January 15, 2002, and press reports indicate that four other candidates or political activists were killed in the few weeks prior to the elections, bringing the total to 19. Nearly all of the victims were from FUNCINPEC or the Sam Rainsy Party.

---

[1] ASEAN, founded in 1967, now includes Brunei, Cambodia, Indonesia, Laos, Malaysia, Myanmar, the Philippines, Singapore, Thailand and Vietnam.

According to the UN, local officials and police were responsible for most of the pre-election intimidation and violence.[2] Cambodian government officials denied that the deaths were politically motivated, attributing them to robberies, traffic accidents, and illness. Although independent monitors praised election day as peaceful, transparent, and a logistical success, these monitors also stopped short of calling the elections free and fair, citing human and political rights concerns such as pre-election deaths of candidates, intimidation of voters, and uneven access of the contending parties to the state media.

Khmer Rouge Trial. In February 2002, after almost five years of negotiation, the UN unexpectedly pulled out of the planning for a genocide tribunal for former Khmer Rouge leaders, reportedly because the court, as currently envisaged, "would not guarantee independence, impartiality, and objectivity."[3] The key issue leading to the impasse was apparently Cambodia's insistence that its August 2001 law on the joint tribunal dictate the trial process. The UN, on the other hand, argued that the law should conform to Cambodia's agreement with the UN. Supporters of the UN's pullout, including some Members of the U.S. Congress, claim that the Cambodian government – many members of which were former Khmer Rouge fighters, including Hun Sen himself – has blocked UN efforts to make the court impartial, by restricting the trials to Cambodia with a majority of Cambodian judges and attempting to limit the number of former leaders to be tried. Also, China, the Khmer Rouge's chief supporter from 1975-79, reportedly used its position on the UN Security Council to oppose the tribunal. China's actions appear to be motivated by concerns that such a tribunal would present evidence of its involvement with the Khmer Rouge, which Cambodian investigators claim includes support of Tuol Sleng prison, where an estimated 14,000 people were tortured and murdered. Other countries, including France and the United States, have pressed the UN to reconsider its decision, arguing that the international body's involvement is necessary to ensure an impartial and credible trial.[4] After initially maintaining that Cambodia would hold a trial with or without the UN's assistance, Hun Sen stated in July that Cambodia would be willing to compromise with the UN by amending the tribunal legislation.[5]

Although the top Khmer Rouge leader, Pol Pot, died in 1998, several other leaders live freely in Cambodia, including former Prime Minister Khieu Samphan, former Foreign Minister Ieng Sary, and Nuon Chea, a top member of the Khmer Rouge Politburo. Hun Sen has repeatedly stated that he will not allow prosecution of Ieng Sary, whose defection to the government in 1996 triggered the collapse of the Khmer Rouge. Two other Khmer Rouge leaders – military commander Ta Mok and Kaing Khek Iev, the commander of the Tuol Sleng prison – are in jail. No Khmer Rouge leaders have yet been tried for the atrocities committed during their rule.

---

[2] Economist Intelligence Unit Country Reports – Cambodia, May 1, 2002.

[3] Edith M. Lederer, "U.N. abandoning Cambodia talks on genocide court to try Khmer Rouge leaders,"Associated Press, February 8, 2002.

[4] Ek Madra, "Cambodia says will press ahead with K. Rouge trial," Reuters, February 8, 2002; "Key Republicans Back UN on Trial," *Far Eastern Economic Review*, March 7, 2002; "U.S. urges U.N. to resume Khmer Rouge trial talks," February 9, 2002.

[5] Chhay Sophal, "Cambodia urges U.N. to revive Khmer Rouge trial," Reuters, July 3, 2002; "U.N. wants mandate before resuming talks on Khmer Rouge trial," Kyodo News, July 30, 2002.

Economy

One of the world's poorest countries, with a per capita income of $260 (or $1,440 in purchasing power parity terms), Cambodia's economy was adversely affected in the late 1990s by the Asian financial crisis, political turmoil, cuts in foreign aid, and severe flooding. The value of foreign direct investment (FDI) in Cambodia fell from $750-$800 million per year between 1995 and 1998 to $270 million in 2000 and $233 million in 2001. Major sources of FDI include Hong Kong, China, Malaysia, Taiwan, and Thailand.[6] Key challenges for economic development include educating the population, building economic infrastructure and legal and banking systems, reducing official corruption and military spending, developing rural areas, and attracting foreign investment. Despite the above problems and difficulties, Cambodia's economy grew by 5.3% in 2001 and is expected to grow by 4.5% and 6.1% in 2002 and 2003, respectively, according to the Asian Development Bank. Two of the most promising sectors are garments and tourism.

Cambodia is negotiating to accede to the World Trade Organization (WTO). A third meeting of Cambodia's Working Party reportedly may be held in the second half of 2002. The WTO's technical assistance program, the Integrated Framework (IF), which works with other multi-national organizations such as the UNDP and IMF to help incorporate trade into national development and poverty-reduction strategies, is being tried on a pilot basis in Cambodia and two other "least-developed" countries.

Cambodia relies heavily upon foreign aid, which accounts for over half of its government budget. The United States is the third-largest foreign aid donor after Japan and Australia. Since 1996, the Consultative Group for Cambodia, a consortium of seven international financial organizations and 22 donor countries under the auspices of the World Bank, has met annually to set economic and political reform guidelines for the Cambodian government and to extend an aid package averaging $500 million per year.[7] In June 2002, the Consultative Group, meeting in Phnom Penh, pledged an aid package of $635 million. They conditioned future aid on Cambodia's progress in improving its legal, judicial, and governing systems and in protecting its environment. In addition, some donors have suggested that increased foreign aid may depend upon whether the national legislative elections, set for July 2003, are "free and fair" and whether former Khmer Rouge officials are tried in an impartial and credible international tribunal.[8]

U.S.-Cambodia Relations

Trade. In 1996, the Clinton Administration signed a trade agreement with the Kingdom of Cambodia, and the 104th Congress granted Cambodia normal trade relations status. The U.S. market is now the largest overseas market for Cambodian goods and the destination for nearly half of Cambodia's merchandise exports. In 2001, Cambodia exported almost one billion dollars worth of goods to the United States, mostly textiles

---

[6] "Foreign investment in Cambodia still low," Reuters, July 8, 2002.

[7] Kyodo News, June 21, 2002.

[8] Mike Jendrzejczyk, "Cambodia's Friends Should Get Tough," *International Herald Tribune*, June 19, 2002.

(compared to $3.6 million in 1996). Cambodian imports from the United States have remained relatively flat. The country imported $28 million worth of goods from the United States in 2001. In 2001, U.S. companies invested approximately $1 million in new economic projects in Cambodia.[9]

In 1999, with imports of Cambodian clothing items growing exponentially, the United States and Cambodia finalized a three-year bilateral textile agreement that established quotas for many apparel products and included an unprecedented provision that rewarded improvements in labor rights with increased access to the U.S. market. Under the agreement, Cambodia could receive annual, one-time "bonus" increases in its quotas if a U.S. interagency panel found working conditions in the garment sector to be in "substantial compliance" with internationally-recognized labor standards and Cambodian labor laws. Cambodia received bonuses of 9% (out of a 14% maximum) in 2000, 2001, and 2002. In December 2001, the U.S.-Cambodia textile agreement was amended and extended for another three-year period, with the potential quota bonus raised to 18%.

U.S. Foreign Assistance. The United States remains the only major donor country that has not resumed bilateral or government-to-government aid to Cambodia. Restrictions on U.S. assistance to Cambodia largely reflect congressional concerns about Prime Minister Hun Sen's seizure of power in 1997. The Foreign Operations, Export Financing and Related Programs Act, 2002 (P.L. 107-115), Section 563, prohibits U.S. assistance to the central government of Cambodia unless the Secretary of State determines and reports to the Committees on Appropriations that progress is made regarding democratic elections, human rights, and environmental protection. U.S. representatives to international financial institutions are instructed to oppose loans to the central government of Cambodia, except loans that meet basic human needs. However, U.S. assistance may be provided to non-governmental organizations (NGOs) – American, international, and Cambodian – and to local governments. Statutory exceptions allow for U.S. assistance to the central government of Cambodia for basic education, controlling human trafficking, treating and preventing HIV/AIDS, helping mine victims (Leahy War Victims funds),[10] and mitigating natural disasters. These exceptions have allowed USAID to collaborate with the Cambodian government on some assistance programs, although nearly all U.S. assistance to Cambodia is still channeled through NGOs. U.S. foreign assistance to Cambodia, which totaled $37 million in 2001, includes voter education and legal aid, child and reproductive health services, HIV/AIDS education and medical care, assistance for mine victims, and rural credit.[11]

Some U.S. lawmakers argue that foreign aid to Cambodia should continue to be restricted because they claim that Prime Minister Hun Sen's power is not legitimate. Others argue that keeping Cambodia engaged with donor nations dissuades the country

---

[9] Major U.S. investors in Cambodia include Caltex, Coca-Cola, and Pepsi. In August 2002, ChevronTexaco announced plans to begin drilling for natural gas off the coast of Cambodia in 2003.

[10] Cambodia is among the top five nations in the world for the number of land mine victims, with over 800 casualties per year.

[11] See CRS Report RL31362, *U.S. Foreign Aid to East and South Asia: Selected Recipients*, by Thomas Lum.

from turning to other benefactors such as China, which provides moderate assistance but without criticism of Hun Sen's actions. Many experts contend that Cambodian reforms and democratization need foreign assistance to succeed because of the country's lack of human and institutional capacity – the products of 30 years of warfare and genocide. If more restrictions were lifted and the central government of Cambodia were deemed to be a reliable partner, the State Department proposes using International Military Education and Training (IMET) funds for human rights and rule of law training to help professionalize the Royal Cambodian Armed Forces and Economic Support Funds (ESF) for national election programs.

Human Trafficking. In its 2002 Trafficking in Persons (TIP) Report, the State Department placed Cambodia in Tier 3, the worst category, down from its Tier 2 spot in 2001. According to the TIP Report, the Cambodian government "does not fully comply with minimum standards for the elimination of trafficking and is not making significant efforts to do so."[12] Under the Trafficking Victims Protection Act of 2000, countries placed in Tier 3 as of the 2003 TIP Report may face U.S. sanctions, such as termination of non-humanitarian, non-trade-related assistance, as well as U.S. opposition to assistance from international financial institutions. All or part of the sanctions may be waived by the President.

On December 21, 2001, the U.S. Immigration and Naturalization Service (INS) announced an immediate suspension of the processing of adoption petitions for children from Cambodia, due to concerns that, in some cases, the children were not orphans, but rather had been brought to orphanages through fraud, human trafficking, baby selling, or abduction. In order to examine the pending cases affected by the suspension, a joint U.S.-Cambodian government task force was set up in March 2002. As of June 20, the task force had cleared 142 Cambodian children for final adoption. The Department of State and the INS have stated that the suspension will remain in effect until the Cambodian government implements adoption laws and procedures that meet international norms.

Other Issues

Illegal drugs. Cambodia is a transit country for Southeast Asian (Laotian and Burmese) heroin destined for international drug markets. Parts of Cambodia have also become production centers for marijuana and methamphetamines. Criminal organizations engaged in illicit drug production or connected to foreign drug rings have reportedly defied local governments and corrupted some national-level officials. However, because there has been reportedly no evidence of heroin transiting Cambodia coming to the United States in recent years, in late 2001, the Bush Administration dropped Cambodia from the United States' annual list of major drug-producing and drug-trafficking countries. Cambodia had been on the list since 1996.

HIV/AIDS. According to USAID, Cambodia is home to the fastest growing HIV/AIDS epidemic in Asia, with an estimated 180,000 people infected. The Cambodian government is working with local and foreign NGOs to respond to the problem. The infection of pregnant women reached an alarming rate of 3 percent before falling to 2 percent following aggressive AIDS prevention efforts in recent years.

---

[12] U.S. Department of State, Trafficking in Persons Report, June 5, 2002.

Cambodia

The Development Challenge: Cambodia continues to face significant challenges in its efforts to spur desperately needed economic growth. Nonetheless, the Royal Government of Cambodia (RGC) largely met its overall targets for revenue, expenditures, and domestic financing in 2001. The Gross National Product grew 5.3 percent in real terms, with low inflation and a stable exchange rate. Budgetary allocations for social sectors have increased as expenditures for defense and security decline, albeit modestly.

Cambodia's economic growth strategy is firmly based on the private sector. The trade regime has opened up: the number of tariff areas has declined from twelve to four, and the highest tariff rate of 130 percent was reduced to 35 percent. Cambodia has been fast-tracked for accession to the World Trade Organization, a goal it expects to achieve in 2003. As chair of the Association of Southeast Asian Nations (ASEAN), Cambodia gained some international prestige when it hosted the annual ASEAN Summit in November 2002. Civil society organizations that advocate for and promote change have grown in numbers and maturity.

These positive indicators mask continuing challenges. With a low annual per capita GDP of $280, Cambodia is one of the poorest countries in Asia. Fifty-eight percent of the domestic budget is financed by donors, primarily through loans. The genocidal Khmer Rouge regime (1975-79) and occupation by Vietnam (1978-89) had a devastating impact on Cambodian institutions and human capacity. Although the trend is slowly improving, human resources capacity has not expanded sufficiently to meet needs, resulting in institutional weakness in government services and limitations for private sector growth.

About 80 percent of Cambodians are engaged in subsistence agriculture, a sector with insufficient productivity to keep up with population increases. The adult literacy rate was estimated at 37 percent by a recent UNESCO study. Health status is poor for most Cambodians. Life expectancy is in the mid-50s, population growth is 2.5 percent, and infant mortality is 95 per 1000. Half of all children under the age of five are malnourished, and 20 percent are severely stunted. The high incidence of HIV/AIDS infections, estimated at 2.6 percent of the general population, is straining the weak health care system and the economy.

Economic growth is mainly concentrated in two sectors: garments and tourism, which account for approximately one-third of GNP and 86 percent of exports. These sectors employ no more than a tenth of the labor force, and cannot provide jobs for a labor force growing at more than 5 percent per year, many of whom reside in poor rural areas. The donor agenda for economic reforms has focused on improving the legal framework, consistent application of the law in a transparent and efficient manner, financial sector reform, civil service and administrative reform, a reduction in corruption and the indirect costs of doing business, and environmental protection. Despite donor attempts to support economic reforms, private sector investment and employment generation have been disappointing. The impending abolition of the quota system globally in December 2004 poses the real danger that Cambodia may lose its market share for garments, and jobs, to lower-cost producer countries. With so few jobs currently available and legal enforcement so weak, Cambodia is a haven for trafficking in persons and child prostitution.

The coalition government consists of the dominant political party, the Cambodia Peoples Party and the National United Front for a Neutral, Peaceful, Cooperative and Independent Cambodia (FUNCINPEC). The National Assembly election in July 2003 will be the third since the Paris Peace Accords of 1991. Whether the elections will be free and fair depends on progress on issues including voter intimidation, equal access to radio and television for all political parties, and fair and impartial decisions by the National Election Committee.

The United States' main foreign policy objectives in Cambodia are to promote democratic practices, good governance and human rights; to support market-led economic growth to combat poverty; to support targeted interventions to fight the spread of infectious diseases, especially HIV/AIDS; and to improve maternal and child health.

The USAID Program: USAID requests FY 2003 and FY 2004 funds for three objectives: to increase competition in Cambodian political life; to increase the use of high-impact HIV/AIDS and family health services; and to increase the relevance and quality of basic education. The funds will also support Cambodian initiatives to engage in economic and environmental activities in the context of good governance, e.g., transparency and accountability on key economic and political issues.

USAID's democracy program supports Cambodian non-governmental organizations (NGOs) and national political parties. Years of USAID support have fostered the growth of strong, motivated NGOs. The new democracy strategy will strengthen their capacity to advocate for democratic reforms at the national level, human rights, and anti-trafficking reforms. USAID supports political parties that meet international standards for transparency and accountability, and promotes the achievement of a level playing field for all of them in the upcoming national elections in July 2003. Through its implementing partners, USAID provides technical assistance to strengthen the parties' capacities to reach voters, organize campaigns, ensure their safety and security, and gain access to media outlets in the lead-up to the elections. USAID also supports efforts by the Ministry of Women's and Veterans Affairs and Cambodian and international NGOs to prevent the trafficking of women and children.

USAID's health program supports the RGC's strong commitment to increase access to health services, and to mitigate and prevent the effects of the HIV/AIDS epidemic. USAID programs have contributed to significant reductions in infant and child mortality, as well as maternal mortality. USAID's previous support for AIDS prevention has helped to reduce HIV/AIDS prevalence significantly among key target groups and the general public. A new integrated health/HIV/AIDS program will build on innovative outreach and development approaches for the prevention and management of HIV/AIDS, and for improved coverage for child survival and maternal health programs.

Basic education activities focus on the relevance of the primary school curriculum for Cambodian children, and strengthening the school system to use new student-centered teaching methodologies. USAID collaborates well with the Ministry of Education, Youth and Sports, and participates in an effective donor coordination mechanism for this sector.

Other Program Elements: USAID/Washington programs complement and reinforce the USAID bilateral program strategy. USAID/W provides child survival grants for community-based health services, mostly in remote areas. The Leahy War Victims Fund helps to coordinate government, private, and donor activities for disabled persons, and funds rehabilitation centers to provide assistive devices, vocational training, and job placement. In the area of environmental management, programs support a university-level environmental studies program, and the protection and sustainable use of natural resources including forests, freshwater and coastal ecosystems, agricultural lands, and biodiversity.

Other Donors: The two largest donors are the multilateral banks. The Asian Development Bank finances health and education, poverty alleviation, agriculture, and roads. The World Bank funds health and education, governance and rural development. The United States is the second largest bilateral donor, after Japan. Japan focuses on a range of activities, including judicial reform, trade and investment, industrial promotion, transportation, power, telecommunications, health, education, and humanitarian aid. France is predominant in the area of higher education in law and medicine, as well as legal and judicial reform. The United Nations Development Program supports RGC programs in health, education, governance, elections and administrative reform. Australia, Germany, the United Kingdom, Sweden, and the European Union provide funds to the government for elections, governance, basic education, health, HIV/AIDS, environment, rural development, and poverty reduction. China wields considerable influence in Cambodia, but information about the size of its aid program is not available. Cambodia's small Muslim community receives assistance from Saudi Arabia and other donors. Donor coordination is effective, especially in the democracy, health, HIV/AIDS, and education sectors.

Cambodia
PROGRAM SUMMARY

(in thousands of dollars)

Accounts	FY 2001 Actual	FY 2002 Actual	FY 2003 Prior Request	FY 2004 Request
Child Survival and Health Programs Fund	9,420	15,000	22,500	22,800
Development Assistance	0	0	0	2,000
Economic Support Fund	14,967	20,000	17,000	15,000
PL 480 Title II	2,422	1,085	0	0
Total Program Funds	**26,809**	**36,085**	**39,500**	**39,800**

STRATEGIC OBJECTIVE SUMMARY				
442-001 Human Rights				
ESF	8,514	55	0	0
442-002 Family Health				
ESF	4,703	3,853	0	0
442-004 Mine Victims				
ESF	1,000	0	0	0
442-005 Reduced Transmission of Sexually Transmitted Infections and HIV/AIDS among High-Risk Populations				
CSH	9,420	0	0	0
ESF	750	0	0	0
442-009 HIV/AIDS and Family Health				
CSH	0	15,000	22,500	22,800
ESF	0	5,519	0	0
442-010 Democracy and Human Rights				
ESF	0	10,573	17,000	15,000
442-011 Improving Basic Education				
DA	0	0	0	2,000

Data Sheet

442-001: No Summary and/or Pillar information entered for this SO.

Data Sheet

442-002: No Summary and/or Pillar information entered for this SO.

Data Sheet

442-003: No Summary and/or Pillar information entered for this SO.

Data Sheet

442-004: No Summary and/or Pillar information entered for this SO.

Data Sheet

442-005: No Summary and/or Pillar information entered for this SO.

Data Sheet

442-007: No Summary and/or Pillar information entered for this SO.

Data Sheet

442-008: No Summary and/or Pillar information entered for this SO.

Data Sheet

USAID Mission:	Cambodia
Program Title:	HIV/AIDS & Family Health
Pillar:	Global Health
Strategic Objective:	442-009
Status:	Continuing
Proposed FY 2003 Obligation:	$22,500,000 CSH
Prior Year Unobligated:	$1,557,000 CSH; $121,000 ESF
Proposed FY 2004 Obligation:	$22,800,000 CSH
Year of Initial Obligation:	FY 2002
Estimated Completion Date:	FY 2005

Summary: This integrated family health strategic objective seeks: to increase and improve access to, and the quality of, health information and services; to strengthen the capacity of individuals, families and communities to protect and provide for their own health; and to improve the capacity of Cambodia's health systems. The program supports the expansion and addition of proven initiatives in HIV/AIDS and family health.

Inputs, Outputs, Activities:
FY 2003 Program:
HIV/AIDS and Infectious Disease ($17,000,000 CSH). USAID is increasing targeted prevention and care interventions for uniformed services (military and police), prostitutes, youth and other potentially vulnerable populations at the national, provincial, and district levels. At least half of the country's Military Police will be reached, 62,000 military personnel will participate in the peer education programs in 21 of Cambodia's 24 provinces, and a new initiative for military wives will be launched. Training and services at the provincial level are being doubled with support from USAID partners. Care and support services for AIDS patients, affected family members, and children will become more comprehensive and better linked to other services in 280 health centers, communities and non-governmental organizations (NGOs) in the seven-province 'full coverage' focus area. Institutional care for AIDS patients and peer support group activities will be established in Regional Military Hospitals in two of the seven focus provinces. HIV/AIDS and tuberculosis interaction training curricula are being adapted and provided to counselors and teams in the focus area. USAID is providing technical assistance to agencies of the Government of Cambodia to minimize stigma and discrimination, and increase gender equality. Funding will be provided to NGOs, civil society organizations, faith-based communities, and private sector entities to enable them to support key HIV/AIDS prevention and mitigation interventions, including stigma reduction for those affected by HIV/AIDS.

Family health ($2,600,000 CSH). Proven health interventions will reach a potential two to three million new and repeat clients in USAID's focus areas. These interventions include the rehabilitation of severely malnourished children, vitamin A distribution through community outreach, life saving skills for midwives, bed-net impregnation to prevent malaria, integrated maternal-child interventions, birth spacing, safe motherhood, and immunization outreach. Reproductive health peer education and services for young garment factory workers in Phnom Penh will be doubled from 15 factories in 2003 to 30 by 2005, covering more than 60,000 workers or 40 percent of the current total worker population. The number and proportion of women seeking and obtaining at least two ante-natal consultations will increase by 50 percent, a priority target for this objective. All family planning agreements will incorporate clauses that implement the President's directive reinstating the Mexico City Policy.

Health systems strengthening ($2,900,000 CSH). This component helps build the Ministry of Health's human resource infrastructure and capacity. Technical assistance in health care management and service delivery will improve the quantity and quality of Cambodia's health care delivery systems. The tangible outputs of these efforts in the first year are expected to include: a baseline evaluation for the entire strategy to define targets and finalize the performance monitoring plan; the results of community and service delivery assessments to identify strengths and gaps in coverage and in the health information system; the formulation of realistic solutions with partners and government; and collaborative operations research for examining program development and feeding back lessons learned into the redesign of programs.

Program management ($1,557,000 CSH Prior Year Unobligated; $121,000 ESF Prior Year Unobligated). Mission plans to transfer $800,000 of CSH carryover funds to Global Health for the Family Health International/IMPACT Project, and the balance to cooperating sponsors involved in tuberculosis Direct Observed Treatment Short-course (DOTS) activities at the community and health center level). ESF carryover funds will be use to fund new foreign service nationals for program management of the Strategic Objective.

FY 2004 Program:
HIV/AIDS and Infectious Disease ($15,000,000 CSH). The rapid expansion of on-going activities will ensure full coverage in the seven province focus area, partial coverage in an additional four provinces, and national coverage for key initiatives. Depending on the Ministry's progress in treatment plans, USAID plans to make anti-retroviral drugs available for preventing mother-to-child transmission in the government-selected referral hospitals and may pilot the use of anti-retroviral drugs through midwives at the Health Center level. The sale of 20 million condoms is projected for 2004. Female condoms are being added to the women-controlled options for disease and pregnancy prevention and are expected to reach sales of 15,000 in 2004. Projections for sexually transmitted infectious diseases kit sales are set at 15,000.

Family health ($5,800,000 CSH). Increased funding for the family health component will support continued expansion of interventions carried out in 2003. The requested funding will enable USAID to respond to the huge unmet need for contraception in Cambodia. Projected sales and distribution of modern contraceptives are expected to double by 2004 through social marketing networks and expanded private and public clinic services supported by USAID.

Health systems strengthening ($2,000,000 CSH). USAID will continue to help improve quality and management, building on prior year activities. Improved management will result from increased numbers of health workers remaining 'on the job' at the health centers, district and provincial supervisors providing consistent leadership, increased reliability of health information and increased utilization of public health services.

Performance and Results: Progress towards this objective by FY 2005 will be demonstrated by: sustained declines in HIV prevalence and increases in protective behaviors among high risk populations; sustained or reduced prevalence rates among antenatal clinic attendees; improved knowledge of how to prevent HIV infection from mother to child; improved and increased coverage of care and support for adults and children infected and affected by HIV/AIDS; reduced parent-to-child transmission of HIV (provided retroviral therapy can be made more widely available, pending key infrastructural improvements by the Ministry of Health); greater community tolerance for those infected and affected by HIV/AIDS; improved reliability of health information systems; improved national, provincial, and local policies to link operational guidelines and practices; and significant increases in the use of appropriate prevention and care services for reproductive and child health, HIV/AIDS and infectious diseases in both the public and private sectors.

Principal Contractors, Grantees, or Agencies: USAID's activities in FY 2003 will be implemented through collaborative arrangements with USAID/Washington Field Support and agreements with implementing organizations, including CARE, Family Health International/IMPACT, Population Services International, Engender Health/Reproductive and Child Health Alliance, International HIV/AIDS Alliance and the Khmer HIV/AIDS NGO Alliance, Reproductive Health Association of Cambodia, Partners for Development, POLICY, Helen Keller International, University Research Corporation and Population Council. USAID/Washington funds child survival grants with Partners for Development, World Vision, World Relief, ADRA and Catholic Relief Services.

US Financing in Thousands of Dollars

Cambodia

442-009 HIV/AIDS & Family Health	CSH	ESF
Through September 30, 2001		
Obligations	0	0
Expenditures	0	0
Unliquidated	0	0
Fiscal Year 2002		
Obligations	13,443	6,468
Expenditures	667	0
Through September 30, 2002		
Obligations	13,443	6,468
Expenditures	667	0
Unliquidated	12,776	6,468
Prior Year Unobligated Funds		
Obligations	1,557	121
Planned Fiscal Year 2003 NOA		
Obligations	22,500	0
Total Planned Fiscal Year 2003		
Obligations	24,057	121
Proposed Fiscal Year 2004 NOA		
Obligations	22,800	0
Future Obligations	0	0
Est. Total Cost	60,300	6,589

Data Sheet

442-00X: No Summary and/or Pillar information entered for this SO.

Data Sheet

USAID Mission:	Cambodia
Program Title:	Democracy and Human Rights
Pillar:	Democracy, Conflict and Humanitarian Assistance
Strategic Objective:	442-010
Status:	Continuing
Proposed FY 2003 Obligation:	$17,000,000 ESF
Prior Year Unobligated:	$427,000 ESF
Proposed FY 2004 Obligation:	$15,000,000 ESF
Year of Initial Obligation:	FY 2002
Estimated Completion Date:	FY 2005

Summary: This Strategic Objective seeks to strengthen elements within Cambodian society that seek equitable treatment for Cambodian citizens and to help them compete for their demands. Under a new strategy approved in 2002, USAID will support leading Cambodian and selected international human rights organizations to enable them to have a positive impact on law and governance in Cambodia.

Over the life of this Strategic Objective, "Increased Competition in Cambodian Political Life," the program will focus on: 1) creating political processes and strengthening political parties to meet international standards; 2) increased transparency and accountability on key economic and political issues, leading towards democratic reform; 3) enforcement of human rights norms through monitoring and investigation; 4) engagement of local officials on key development issues; and 5) increased capacity of future leaders to develop policies and effect change.

Inputs, Outputs, Activities:
FY 2003 Program:
Democracy and Governance ($15,200,000 ESF). USAID's primary focus in 2003 will be on "leveling the playing field" among all contending political parties for the 2003 national elections. USAID will help political parties strengthen their internal procedures to facilitate democratic participation and effective communication with their constituents. Support will be provided on how to improve their organizational capabilities, how to promote leadership and how to develop messages. Equipment and assistance will be provided to help ensure the safety and security of the political party candidates and their supporters. USAID will provide resources to civil society organizations to better identify and expose corrupt practices, and to promote active engagement by the public in monitoring government activities and advocating for changes. This will raise public awareness about corruption and also establish a basis for enforcement. Areas of focus include reform of procurement procedures and environmental management. USAID will also support indigenous business associations to advocate for economic governance reform, and enhance the capacity of future leaders from under-represented groups in Cambodia, such as women and minorities, through the Fulbright and the International Visitors Programs.

Human Rights ($1,800,000 ESF). USAID will support the enforcement of human rights, with a specific focus on anti-trafficking efforts through monitoring and investigation. The US Mission's anti-trafficking task force has developed a strategy for focusing future USG resources to address this serious issue. USAID will target resources and efforts towards changing Cambodia's climate of impunity by encouraging more arrests, prosecutions, and convictions for traffickers. In particular, USAID will help Cambodian organizations that take on important cases and issues, and that challenge the current norms.

Various activities ($427,000 ESF Prior Year Unobligated). USAID plans to use about $272,000 in carryover funds from FY 2002 for the Catalyzing Community Forestry in Cambodia activities, and the balance on the audits of several NGO grants and for the hiring a human rights project manager.

FY 2004 Program:

Democracy and Governance ($14,500,000 ESF). USAID will target resources on anti-corruption activities, focusing on increased transparency and accountability on key economic and political issues, and thus leading towards reform in problem areas. With Cambodia seeking to enter the World Trade Organization (WTO) in provisional status in 2003, corruption-related issues will receive more attention. WTO accession and implementation will require the "rule of law" and transparency in economic and business matters. We anticipate that this will place pressure on corrupt practices that adversely affect the economy. USAID will support NGOs that will advocate for a reform agenda. USAID will also work with newly-elected officials, particularly in creating opportunities for debate beyond the limited fora currently available. USAID will continue to strengthen the capacity of future leaders in Cambodia through educational programs such as the Fulbright program and the International Visitors Program.

Human Rights ($500,000 ESF). USAID will continue to support the enforcement of human rights through monitoring and investigation of human rights abuses and trafficking activities. The US Mission's anti-trafficking task force will continue to implement its anti-trafficking strategy. USAID will target resources and efforts to encouraging more arrests, prosecutions and convictions of traffickers. In particular, USAID will provide support to Cambodian organizations that take on important cases and issues, and that challenge the current norms.

Performance and Results: USAID efforts since 1992 to build and strengthen civil society organizations in Cambodia, along with the work of other donors, have been extremely successful. From only one Cambodian NGO in 1992, there were more than 1000 registered and active civil society organizations in 2002. Although many are small, grassroots organizations, a dozen or more have become influential leaders in their areas of focus. Under a new strategic plan approved in FY 2002, USAID has shifted from a focus on extending the outreach of these organizations to one of increasing their impact at the national level. Examples of the results achieved in 2002 are as follows:

-- For the first time in Cambodia, two human traffickers were sentenced to ten years each, and ordered to pay compensation to their victims.

-- Legal Aid of Cambodia won a case for victims of land grabbing in the Banteay Meanchey Province near Thailand. The dispute involved 581 families against high-ranking government and military officials who secretly obtained land ownership deeds in 1998 from the Cadastral Office, after land values increased. The villagers filed petitions to the National Assembly and the King, in vain. In 2000, they approached Legal Aid and the United Nations, whose envoy visited the area and appealed to the Prime Minister. Three high-ranking government officials in question relinquished their claim, while other claimants continued legal action. The villagers retained 33.8 of the original 45 hectares and will be assisted to acquire legal title.

Principal Contractors, Grantees, or Agencies: USAID activities are implemented by The Asia Foundation, the International Republican Institute, the National Democratic Institute, the American Center for International Labor Solidarity, and leading Cambodian human rights organizations.

US Financing in Thousands of Dollars

Cambodia

442-010 Democracy and Human Rights	**ESF**
Through September 30, 2001	
Obligations	0
Expenditures	0
Unliquidated	0
Fiscal Year 2002	
Obligations	10,573
Expenditures	0
Through September 30, 2002	
Obligations	10,573
Expenditures	0
Unliquidated	10,573
Prior Year Unobligated Funds	
Obligations	427
Planned Fiscal Year 2003 NOA	
Obligations	17,000
Total Planned Fiscal Year 2003	
Obligations	17,427
Proposed Fiscal Year 2004 NOA	
Obligations	15,000
Future Obligations	0
Est. Total Cost	43,000

Data Sheet

USAID Mission:	Cambodia
Program Title:	Improving Basic Education
Pillar:	Economic Growth, Agriculture and Trade
Strategic Objective:	442-011
Status:	Continuing
Proposed FY 2003 Obligation:	$0
Prior Year Unobligated:	$2,000,000 ESF
Proposed FY 2004 Obligation:	$2,000,000 DA
Year of Initial Obligation:	FY 2002
Estimated Completion Date:	FY 2005

Summary: The USAID basic education objective in Cambodia focuses on increasing the relevance of the basic education curriculum to everyday life, and on expanding the capacity of the school system to deliver competency-based education using student-centered teaching methodologies. Curriculum development will be the major activity in FY 2003, while improving the capacity to provide education services will be the major activity of FY 2004.

Inputs, Outputs, Activities:
FY 2003 Program:
Increased relevance of the basic education curriculum to everyday life ($1,500,000 ESF Prior Year Unobligated). Curriculum development will be the major activity in FY 2003. The funds will help the Ministry of Education develop a primary school curriculum relevant to the lives of Cambodians, especially in rural areas. This will improve learning skills, and help to reduce school dropout and high grade repetition rates. The life-skills component will focus on civic education, health and nutrition, and practical knowledge about the agro-ecosystem. The life-skills curriculum will reinforce language, math, science and critical thinking skills in the core basic education curriculum. Students will be able to apply these skills to problems faced in everyday life at school, at home and in the community. The following activities are planned:

-- Development and testing of: 1) a student-centered, competency-based life-skills curriculum and syllabi for grades one through six for civic participation, health and nutrition, and agro-ecosystems; 2) a competency-based teacher training curriculum and syllabi; and 3) pre-service and in-service training materials, including activity guidelines that will assist teachers in compiling their own teaching guides for use in the classroom.

-- Increased capacity of the school system to deliver competency-based education ($500,000 ESF Prior Year Unobligated). This component aims to strengthen the capacity to deliver effectively the life-skills curriculum at all levels of basic education, and to support its integration the primary education system. The focus will be on teacher training. Priority will be given to ensuring that education officials, school administrators, parents and local government officials, including commune council members, understand and support the life-skills curriculum. A ctivities will begin in FY 2003. Teacher training will be conducted at two levels: 1) in-service training in cluster schools as part of the response to the urgent need to upgrade the skills of existing teachers and to benefit students as soon as possible; and 2) pre-service training at the primary teacher training colleges to help the next generation of teachers acquire skills in delivering student-centered, competency-based training.

FY 2004 Program:
Increased relevance of the basic education curriculum to everyday life ($500,000 DA). The curriculum will be finalized and evaluated in FY 2004. The following activities are planned: 1) on-the-job training for Ministry of Education staff in the design and testing of student-centered, competency-based curricula and learning materials; 2) strengthening of partnerships between the Ministry and non-education organizations

and programs in the curriculum development and testing process; and 3) continued involvement of the community in supporting the life-skills curriculum through the cluster school system.

Increased capacity of the school system to deliver competency-based education ($1,500,000 DA). n FY 2004, this component will build the capacity of the education system to deliver the revised basic education curriculum. The following activities will be undertaken: 1) Education of trainers at the cluster school level to train and support to other teachers in the delivery of the life-skills curriculum; 2) Education of trainers at the teacher training schools; 3) Meetings with parent groups integrated into the implementa-tion process at the cluster school level to gain support for the life-skills curriculum, discuss ways in which parents can help their children attain competency, and to elicit feedback on the new curriculum; 4) Publicizing the new curriculum to build demand and support; and 5) Workshops and seminars on life-skills education, focusing on the rationale and approaches to student-centered learning methodologies for school principals, education sector officials, and other stakeholders at the national, provincial and cluster school levels.

Performance and Results: Activities funded under this Strategic Objective began in FY 2003. It is, therefore, not yet possible to report results.

Principal Contractors, Grantees, or Agencies: To be determined.

US Financing in Thousands of Dollars

Cambodia

442-011 Improving Basic Education	DA	ESF
Through September 30, 2001		
Obligations	0	0
Expenditures	0	0
Unliquidated	0	0
Fiscal Year 2002		
Obligations	0	0
Expenditures	0	0
Through September 30, 2002		
Obligations	0	0
Expenditures	0	0
Unliquidated	0	0
Prior Year Unobligated Funds		
Obligations	0	2,000
Planned Fiscal Year 2003 NOA		
Obligations	0	0
Total Planned Fiscal Year 2003		
Obligations	0	2,000
Proposed Fiscal Year 2004 NOA		
Obligations	2,000	0
Future Obligations	0	0
Est. Total Cost	2,000	2,000

Data Sheet

442-0XX: No Summary and/or Pillar information entered for this SO.

Data Sheet

442-XXX: No Summary and/or Pillar information entered for this SO.

USAID/CAMBODIA

ANNUAL REPORT FY 2002

March 2002

Please Note:

The attached RESULTS INFORMATION is from the FY 2002 Annual report, and was assembled and analyzed by the country or USAID operating unit identified on the cover page.

The Annual Report is a "pre-decisional" USAID document and does not reflect results stemming from formal USAID review(s) of this document.

Related document information can be obtained from:
USAID Development Experience Clearinghouse
1611 N. Kent Street, Suite 200
Arlington, VA 22209-2111
Telephone: 703/351-4006 Ext. 106
Fax: 703/351-4039
Email: docorder@dec.cdie.org
Internet: http://www.dec.org

Released on or after July 1, 2002

Annual Report Part III: FY 2001 Performance Narrative

442-001 Strengthened Democratic Processes and Respect for Human Rights

Key Achievements

Cambodian non-governmental organizations have proved to be some of the most courageous and professional groups in the country. This year USAID-funded partners investigated approximately 600 alleged human rights cases. The Cambodian League for the Promotion and Defense of Human Rights (LICADHO), which is one of the largest and most effective human rights NGOs in Cambodia, uncovered an alleged baby trafficking scheme. Human rights monitoring and investigation support by USAID-funded NGOs now reaches 73 percent of Cambodia's 184 districts, representing 84 percent of the population. More than 100,000 people received direct assistance from human rights NGOs supported by USAID through The Asia Foundation (TAF). These human rights organizations provide direct intervention, legal services, and other needed assistance to victims of human rights violations and prisoners. In addition, legal aid providers represented more than 60,000 disadvantaged families in disputes over land and fishing rights, often pitted against powerful figures.

The first-ever multiparty commune council elections were held on February 3, 2002. These elections represented another important step forward in Cambodia's attempts to democratize and decentralize. They also had the beneficial impact of involving 75,000 candidates in local politics, to elect 11,261 members, most for the first time, including a surprising number of women. As a result of the elections, more than 900 women were elected as representatives to the commune councils, an unprecedented event for Cambodia. Prior to elections, there were ten women involved in commune government. In preparing women to become more involved in politics, a USAID-funded local partner, Women for Prosperity (WFP), trained 5,527 women from five political parties. USAID-supported US and local NGOs effectively advocated the removal of regulations that would have resulted in censorship of voter education materials. In the run-up to election day, NGOs conducted thousands of village-level voter education meetings and drama performances, distributed 700,000 copies of a non-partisan voter's guide, and broadcast a series of voter education public service announcements on radio and television. USAID, with the National Democratic Institute (NDI) and the Khmer Institute for Democracy (KID), staged Cambodia's first-ever political debates. On election day, with USAID support, election monitoring organizations (EMOs) deployed more than 33,000 domestic observers to cover 12,400 polling stations. With USAID support, these EMOs have coalesced into credible election monitoring organizations and now have a legitimate seat at the table when it comes to domestic and international election discussions.

Performance

This SO met expectations in strengthening civil society as a prerequisite for the country's transition to a sustainable and economically viable democratic society. Civil society groups, which continue to monitor human rights, advocate for reforms and expose corruption, have grown in numbers and maturity. They know the limits within which they can safely act and continue to challenge those limits. Thanks to the outreach of NGOs throughout the country, Cambodians are more aware that their constitution guarantees them certain internationally accepted human rights. In FY 2001, 95% of courts throughout Cambodia used public defender services financed by USAID.

During FY 2001, LICAHDO provided critical human rights investigation and monitoring services in 64% of the districts in Cambodia and reached more than 57% of the districts with human rights education and training programs. From October 2000 to March 2001 alone, LICADHO investigated 277 cases of human rights violations. More than 12,000 citizens were reached during this period through LICADHO's human rights training and information dissemination sessions. In a six-month period, more than 62,000 people received direct assistance from human rights NGOs supported by TAF an USAID. These human rights organizations provide direct intervention, legal services, and other needed assistance to victims of human rights violations and prisoners. During the same period, Legal Aid of Cambodia represented 51,000 clients in 228 land disputes, both large-scale and on behalf of individual families.

Cambodian NGOs advocated for a Criminal Code and Code of Criminal Procedure, as well as a Civil Code and Code of Civil Procedure that would meet international standards. Four local NGOs pushed for revisions on the draft law on domestic violence, while the Cambodian Center for Social Development (CSD) continued to provide more input into the draft law on anti-corruption. An umbrella group of 16 human rights organizations, known as the Cambodian Human Rights Action Committee (CHRA), provided more than 40 contributions to draft legislation and government policies, including laws on the press, forestry, labor, media and elections, the law on arms, explosives and munitions, and on the Khmer Rouge trial. The Solidarity Center, with assistance from USAID and the State Department, worked with labor union leaders to press for far-reaching labor regulations protecting the rights of unions and workers.

KID and CSD are two excellent examples of NGOs that serve the nation through a check-and- balance function. KID runs courses on "Rule of Law and Due Process," covering issues on human rights, democracy, commune council election law, the constitution, judicial system, and administrative structures for local officials. These courses take place is different parts of the country and reach people and officials at different levels of society. KID remains extremely vocal on important public policy issues, and aims to hold the government accountable. CSD plays a prominent role in promoting transparency, accountability, and integrity in Cambodia. CSD is the leading organization working with reform-minded government officials and colleague NGOs on anti-corruption legislation and other measures to end corruption. CSD does this through what it calls Parliamentary Watch, which monitors and assesses activities within the National Assembly and Senate. It also informs the general public through public fora across the country, through a popular monthly bulletin that includes cartoons on serious issues by a well-known and respected cartoonist in Cambodia, and through a program in the formal school system. The Cambodian Institute for Cooperation and Peace (CICP) has also made a significant impact on combating corruption as well. CICP co-hosted with NDI, the first-ever Civil-Military Relations Conference, during which the usefulness and need of bringing civil society participation into the planning, evaluation and implementation of military reforms was discussed.

As a result of the 2002 commune elections, the CPP will share power with elected officials from its coalition partner FUNCINPEC and the opposition Sam Rainsy Party for the first time at the grassroots level. While the final results are not yet in, it appears that more than 900 women will be on these commune councils, and that is unprecedented in Cambodia. The Women's Media Center (WMC) has contributed significantly to women's involvement in politics. The purchase with USAID support of a new radio transmitter has given the WMC, as the only independent radio station in the entire country, the ability to reach more than 60% of the Cambodian population. WMC has been and remains the only source for Cambodians seeking access to information about the social, cultural, economic, and political challenges facing Cambodia, particularly Cambodian women.

Challenges

The lack of independent and impartial electoral authorities continues to represent a challenge for free and fair elections in Cambodia. The National Election Committee (NEC) essentially retained the same major-party-dominated membership it had during the 1998 national elections. The only changes were the replacement of a questionable coalition-partner-party representative with a genuine party representative, and the addition of a representative from the opposition Sam Rainsy Party. Echoing the private views of some donors regarding the election process, the Prime Minister has implicitly acknowledged the NEC's lack of credibility. He has publicly and privately called for a reform of the National Election Commission before the 2003 elections, after its current mandate expires in 2002.

The NEC's bureaucratic and sometimes biased handling of issues resulted in serious roadblocks to the formation and conduct of a credible election. One example is unfair and unequal media access. After promising to air a series of 15 voter education roundtables sponsored by NGOs, in which each political party would have equal time to answer questions about agreed-upon issues, the NEC reversed itself and decided not to allow the state-run (i.e., dominant-party controlled) television stations to air the programs. A similar problem occurred with regard to the airing of the commune candidate debates. Although the first-ever multiparty debates were definitely a success, they were not televised due to the NEC's arbitrary decision. In another example, the NEC decided to interpret an election law in a manner that would have resulted in the censorship of election education materials. Fortunately, USAID-supported NDI was able to mediate the situation by convening a roundtable meeting in which it and other USAID-supported NGOs successfully reasoned with the NEC to change its ruling and avoid charges of censorship.

While unions have been in existence in Cambodia since 1997, union members still do not enjoy all of the benefits that union membership would normally provide. The Solidarity Center, with assistance from USAID and the State Department, worked with labor union leaders to press for far-reaching labor regulations protecting the rights of unions and workers. Unions have also successfully fought, for the first time, to be included in this and other policy-making processes. The Solidarity Center has provided intensive training to teach union leaders building skills that not only create unions of workers but also create unions that effectively work to protect their members. This year more than 60 new garment factory unions were organized, bringing the total to 200. Workers in other sectors--teachers, restoration and construction, hotel and restaurant workers--are now following the example of garment workers in organizing and building new unions.

Human trafficking continues to be a major problem in Cambodia, one which USAID will increasingly seek to address. One of the most impressive Cambodian organizations dealing with this issue to date is the Cambodian Women's Crisis Center (CWCC). With support from USAID through TAF, CWCC produces materials to bring attention to human trafficking, conducts training programs and workshops to combat trafficking, provides confidential shelters for victims of trafficking and domestic abuse, and offers professional counseling and vocational training to trafficking victims. With USAID support, the Cambodian Defenders Project (CDP) recently established a Center Against Trafficking. CDP is one of the few Cambodian organizations that have the ability to address the issue of human trafficking from a legal perspective. CDP has worked diligently for improved legislation, advocated for implementation of existing laws, trained individuals responsible for implementing existing laws, and provided pro bono legal assistance for victims of trafficking.

Given the rent-seeking opportunities available in government positions, incumbents have strong financial and personal interests in maintaining power. Corruption remains a systemic problem running throughout the three branches of government. Politically, it undermines the credibility and authority of government and impedes the growth of democracy. Economically, it distorts the allocation of public resources and discourages private sector investment. The social costs of corruption are evident in the high correlation rates between corruption and poverty. In addition to the aforementioned corruption-fighting activities, the Cambodia Institute for Human Rights (CIHR) has specifically begun addressing this problem with the launching of its nationally recognized Good Governance training program. During the period from October 2000 to March 2001, this program reached more than 1,200 public officials delivering critical messages and information concerning transparency, accountability, responsibility, and the ethics of public service.

442-002: Improved Reproductive and Child Health

Key Achievements

On-going training in management and quality improvement skills for frontline health center workers have resulted in expanded supply, increased access and strengthened demand for RCH services in the partners' targeted geographic areas. Approximately 300 new Village Development Committees (VDCs) were created through support from USAID in 2001, committees which enabled Cambodians themselves to assess the needs of their communities and to make local decisions to meet their needs in the most appropriate manner. USAID technical assistance provided for the training of more than 8,000 health center and outreach staff throughout the country in 2001. The estimated number of beneficiaries for maternal and child health services from USAID partners was more than 4,800,000 in 2001. The Reproductive Health Association of Cambodia (RHAC) caseload alone grew by 67 percent from 215,000 clients in FY 2000 to 360,000 in FY 2001. According to the results of an internal assessment conducted by RHAC in early 2001, the contraceptive prevalence rate (CPR) in RHAC coverage areas was found to be an average of at least 30 percent. This contrasts with the national CPR average of just under 19 percent for modern methods reported in the 2000 DHS.

The Reproductive and Child Health Alliance (RACHA) has contributed substantially to capacity building efforts within communities. The number of community workers who received training in 2001 was almost twice the cumulative total for the three preceding years. In addition, more than 1,200 health center staff and more than 900 traditional birth attendants (TBAs) were trained. Equally impressive is the report that trained midwives in RACHA's target areas attended more than 30 percent of the deliveries. This represents a significant accomplishment when as recently as 1998 almost all deliveries occurred in the home with untrained TBAs.

The total CYP target for the year 2001 was 203,000. The actual level achieved by 2001 was 327,380. This represents a 75 percent increase over the previous year. While the total 2001 sales of *Number One* condoms reached 16,304,900, an increase of about 1.3 percent, this achievement fell slightly short of the expected target of 16.5 million condoms. *Number One* continues to be the country's most-recognized brand of condom, indicating the success of USAID-funded efforts to slow HIV transmission rates and deter unintended pregnancies.

In 2001, sales of the oral contraceptive brand 'OK' pill, socially marketed by PSI, reached 717,432 cycles, an increase of nearly 70 percent from the level recorded in 2000. The total volume of services provided and the increase in the demand for services in all the RHAC clinics provide an indication of the high demand for quality services and the high burden of disease in the country. This level of demand also reflects tremendous unmet need for family planning. For example, the number of clients seen at RHAC clinics for family planning services increased from 230,199 in 2000 to 306,134 in 2001, a 33 percent increase.

Performance

This SO met expectations to reduce child mortality, unintended pregnancies, and maternal mortality, as well as to improve infant and child health/nutrition. The primary activities for achieving this SO are: (1) expanded supply of reproductive and child health services (RCH); (2) increased access to reproductive and child health services; and (3) strengthened demand for reproductive and child health services. Children under five years of age and mothers are the key beneficiaries.

The official reporting source for the status of child survival activities is the 2000 Cambodia Demographic and Health Survey (CDHS), released in October 2001. The three main indicators used to illustrate progress towards meeting this SO are: the infant mortality rate, couple-years of protection (CYP), and the number of *Number One* brand condoms sold. Immunization rates are equally important. According to the 2000 CDHS, the infant mortality rate of 95 deaths per 1000 births is lower than the target set in 1996 of 100 deaths per thousand. Child mortality was expected to decrease from 181 deaths per thousand to 155 deaths per thousand by the year 2000, according to targets set in 1996. The 2000 CDHS shows that child mortality has been further reduced to 124.5 deaths per thousand. Modern contraceptive prevalence (CPR) has risen from 16 percent in 1998 to 19 percent in 2000. According to the CDHS, nearly half (42 percent) of currently married women who were not using any contraception at the time of the survey said that they intend to use family planning methods at some time in the future.

The USAID-sponsored immunization program run by CARE International has achieved remarkable increases in the percent of children fully immunized – from 18 percent in 1995 to 72 percent in 2001. As elsewhere in the world, the 2000 CDHS showed that children of mothers with secondary or higher education are twice as likely to be fully immunized (59 percent) as children whose mothers have no education (29 percent). While the steady increase in immunization coverage is encouraging, it is important to note the substantial differences in coverage between regions documented in the CDHS, ranging from as low as 12 percent in the remote coastal town Koh Kong to 63 percent in urban centers Battambang and Pailin.

The Ministry of Health has adopted a number of important tools and protocols developed by USAID-sponsored NGOS. In addition to their instrumental role in developing the current Ministry Child Health Card, Helen Keller International, in partnership with the National Prevention of Blindness office of the MOH, conducted an assessment of the pilot Primary Eye Care (PEC) program. The main purpose of the assessment was to determine the effectiveness of the PEC pilot program and to determine successes and constraints to program implementation in order that lessons may be applied prior to expansion. Finally, USAID was instrumental in the finalization of the Cambodia Demographic and Health Survey

(CDHS), the first of its kind. Future endeavors will include the further dissemination of the information published in the CDHS and possibly a series of 'mini' surveys. All USAID Cambodia partners play a key role in each of the relevant technical committees at both the national and provincial levels, contributing to improvements in specific program areas as well as in policy dialogue.

Local and international NGOs carry out USAID interventions for reproductive and child health. Legislative restrictions on working with the Royal Government of Cambodia have limited the ability to influence improvements in national policy and expand access to quality RCH services nationwide. The lack of skilled providers and trained and experienced staff at all levels are additional major constraints. In spite of these overwhelming challenges, the overall results achieved under the SO in a relatively brief period of time are encouraging. Significant progress towards achieving access to quality essential health services will take some years to achieve, given the social and political context in Cambodia.

442-005-01: Reduced Transmission of Sexually Transmitted Infections/HIV Among High-Risk Populations

Key Achievements
USAID programs focused strongly on targeted behavior change interventions in 2001 in order to motivate/enable population sub-groups currently at high risk to increase condom use, reduce commercial sex use and to seek treatment for sexually-transmitted diseases. During the year 2001, socially marketed PSI condoms reached record sales of over 16.3 million. Owing to USAID assistance, Cambodia has one of the most advanced HIV surveillance systems in Asia. The National HIV Sentinel Surveillance (since 1999) and Behavioral Surveillance Survey (since 1997) have shown declining trends in HIV prevalence and increased condom use among all sub-groups known to be engaging in high-risk behaviors. During 1997-2000, HIV seroprevalence decreased from 39 percent to 31 percent among direct sex workers, from six percent to 3.1 percent among the police, and from 3.2 percent to 2.3 percent among women attending antenatal clinics (it is still too early to report on 2001) (HSS, 1999).

Performance
This SO met expectations in 2001. As one of the poorest nations in the region, Cambodia is currently facing the most serious HIV/AIDS epidemic in Southeast Asia. Current estimates place the overall adult population HIV prevalence at 2.8 percent (HIV Sentinel Surveillance 2000), with more than 169,000 people with HIV/AIDS. UNAIDS estimates the total number of HIV/AIDS infected persons to have reached 220,000 in the year 2000. New estimates suggest that as many as 40,000 children have been orphaned as a result of HIV/AIDS. In late CY 2000, under a new Agency-wide expanded response to the global HIV pandemic, Cambodia was identified as one of four Rapid Scale-Up countries worldwide (and the only Rapid Scale-Up country outside of Africa). Cambodia's funding for HIV/AIDS activities increased significantly, from approximately $2.5 million in FY '00 to approximately $10 million in FY '01.

The HIV epidemic in Cambodia now affects men, women and children in all of the country's 24 provinces and municipalities. Dynamic population flow has been a major driving force behind the epidemic spread of HIV in Cambodia, which is spread almost entirely by sexual transmission (Injection drug use is in its early stages in Cambodia, with very little available data.). USAID-funded interventions focus on behavior change among population subgroups currently at high risk for HIV infection coupled with improved quality of and access to STD care for subgroups currently at low and high risk. Specifically, the programs' aim through 2001 was to inform policy makers about the HIV/AIDS epidemic in Cambodia; to reduce high-risk behaviors in target areas; and to pilot and replicate model sexually transmitted disease (STD) and reproductive health service delivery programs for population subgroups that engage in high-risk behaviors. The beneficiaries of USAID-funded HIV/AIDS programs are all Cambodians exposed to national social marketing campaigns promoting condom use for the prevention of HIV transmission; and specifically, people living with HIV/AIDS, as well as both infected and non-infected commercial sex workers and military personnel and police.

HIV/AIDS Education/Prevention: USAID supports a number of successful outreach interventions that target a variety of sub-groups currently at high risk for HIV. Outreach programs for female commercial sex workers (FCSW) are concentrated in urban areas where the majority of sex establishments are located.

Other prevention programs target men engaging in high-risk behaviors, such as those in military and police forces, through peer education. Training takes place in the base camps where the majority of these men work and reside. During 2001, FHI-trained peer educators trained 28,044 military staff members and 9,026 policemen on safe-sex practices, modes of transmission and methods of prevention of HIV/STDs, and HIV/AIDS stigma-reduction. By the end of FY 01, USAID programs conducted HIV outreach education for 4,187 sex workers.

HIV/AIDS Policy: In response to the recent approval from the U.S. Congress to work in closer coordination with the Royal Government of Cambodia on HIV/AIDS, USAID partners have been more active in supporting the improvement of national capacity in the multisectoral response to HIV/AIDS. FHI/Impact worked closely with the National Center for HIV/AIDS, Dermatology and STDs (NCHADS) to expand implementation of the RGC's "100 percent Condom Use Policy" to six provinces. With FHI/IMPACT support, the Cambodian Ministry of National Defense has completed its first 5-year strategic plan to respond to HIV/AIDS among the military.

USAID's POLICY Project provided technical support to the National AIDS Authority (NAA) to assist with a costing exercise for the development of the National HIV/AIDS Response Plan. The POLICY Project also provides support to the Ministry of Women's and Veteran's Affairs (MoWVA) to establish a Gender and HIV/AIDS Working Group which will build strategic networks with key partners and enable the MoWVA to provide leadership to other Ministries and civil society organizations. This will assist those agencies to include gender in their HIV/AIDS-related policies and programs. The POLICY project has also provided support to build up the capacity of CPN+ (the newly formed national network, Cambodia People Living with AIDS network) to increase the advocacy role of groups of People Living With AIDS in prevention, care and support. POLICY provides technical assistance to build the capacity of leaders among Buddhist Monks to expand the role of faith-based organizations in HIV/AIDS prevention and care.

STI Services: Through FHI/Impact, USAID support has focused on building the capacity of health care providers from government and non-government organizations, specifically on STI case management and the provision of quality 'sex worker-friendly' services. In an effort to support the expansion of the Ministry of Health's 100 percent Condom Use Policy, FHI/Impact staff have worked collaboratively with the National center of HIV/AIDS, Dermatology and STDs to finalize training guidelines, STI treatment manuals for sex workers, and STI in-service training and clinic management. The program has provided in-service training to ten health facilities and supported an NGO mobile clinic for sex workers. The achievements of this program, in terms of the number of patients assessed and treated appropriately, are presented in Table 2.

Table 1: Annual Report Selected Performance Measures

December 3, 2001

#	Indicator (all data should pertain to FY or CY 01)	OU Response			Fund Account	Data Quality Factors
Pillar I: Global Development Alliance: GDA serves as a catalyst to mobilize the ideas, efforts, and resources of the public sector, corporate America and non-governmental organizations in support of shared objectives						
1	Did your operating unit achieve a significant result working in alliance with the private sector or NGOs?	Yes	No	N/A X		
2	a. How many alliances did you implement in 2001? (list partners) b. How many alliances do you plan to implement in FY 2002?					
3	What amount of funds has been leveraged by the alliances in relationship to USAID's contribution?					
Pillar II: Economic Growth, Agriculture and Trade: USAID works to improve country economic performance using five approaches: (1) liberalizing markets, (2) improving agriculture, (3) supporting microenterprise, (4) ensuring primary education, and (5) protecting the environment and improving energy efficiency.						
4	If you have a Strategic Objective or Objectives linked to the EGAT pillar, did it/they exceed, meet, or not meet its/their targets?	Exceed	Met	Not Met		
USAID Objective 1: Critical, private markets expanded and strengthened						
5	Did your program achieve a significant result in the past year that is likely to contribute to this objective?	Yes	No	N/A X		
USAID Objective 2: More rapid and enhanced agricultural development and food security encouraged						
6	Did your program achieve a significant result in the past year that is likely to contribute to this objective?	Yes	No	N/A X		
USAID Objective 3: Access to economic opportunity for the rural and urban poor expanded and made more equitable						
7	Did your program achieve a significant result in the past year that is likely to contribute to this objective?	Yes	No	N/A X		

	Indicator (all data should pertain to FY or CY 01)	OU Response			Fund Account	Data Quality Factors
USAID Objective 4: Access to quality basic education for under-served populations, especially for girls and women, expanded						
8	Did your program achieve a significant result in the past year that is likely to contribute to this objective?	Yes	No	N/A X		
9	a. Number of children enrolled in primary schools affected by USAID basic education programs (2001 actual) b. Number of children enrolled in primary schools affected by USAID basic education programs (2002 target)	Male	Female	Total		
USAID Objective 5: World's environment protected						
10	Did your program achieve a significant result in the past year that is likely to contribute to this objective?	Yes	No	N/A X		
11	a. Hectares under Approved Management Plans (2001 actual) b. Hectares under Approved Management Plans (2002 target)					
Pillar III: Global Health: USAID works to: (1) stabilize population, (2) improve child health, (3) improve maternal health, (4) address the HIV/AIDS epidemic, and (5) reduce the threat of other infectious diseases.						
12	If you have a Strategic Objective or Objectives linked to the Global Health pillar, did it/they exceed, meet, or not meet its/their targets?	Exceed	Met X	Not Met		
USAID Objective 1: Reducing the number of unintended pregnancies						
13	Did your program achieve a significant result in the past year that is likely to contribute to this objective?	Yes	No X	N/A		
USAID Objective 2: Reducing infant and child mortality						
14	Did your program achieve a significant result in the past year that is likely to contribute to this objective?	Yes	No X	N/A		

Indicator (all data should pertain to FY or CY 01)	OU Response			Fund Account	Data Quality Factors
USAID Objective 3: Reducing deaths and adverse health outcomes to women as a result of pregnancy and childbirth					
15 Did your program achieve a significant result in the past year that is likely to contribute to this objective?	Yes	No X	N/A		
USAID Objective 4: Reducing the HIV transmission rate and the impact of HIV/AIDS pandemic in developing countries					
16 Did your program achieve a significant result in the past year that is likely to contribute to this objective?	Yes X	No	N/A		NCHADS
USAID Objective 5: Reducing the threat of infectious diseases of major public health importance					
17 Did your program achieve a significant result in the past year that is likely to contribute to this objective?	Yes	No X	N/A		
Pillar IV: Democracy, Conflict and Humanitarian Assistance					
18 If you have a Strategic Objective or Objectives linked to the Democracy, Conflict and Humanitarian Assistance Pillar, did it/they exceed, meet, or not meet its/their targets?	Exceed	Met X	Not Met		
USAID Objective 1: Rule of law and respect for human rights of women as well as men strengthened					
19 Did your program achieve a significant result in the past year that is likely to contribute to this objective?	Yes	No X	N/A		
USAID Objective 2: Credible and competitive political processes encouraged					
20 Did your program achieve a significant result in the past year that is likely to contribute to this objective?	Yes	No X	N/A		
USAID Objective 3: The development of politically active civil society promoted					
21 Did your program achieve a significant result in the past year that is likely to contribute to this objective?	Yes	No X	N/A		
USAID Objective 4: More transparent and accountable government institutions encouraged					
22 Did your program achieve a significant result in the past year that is likely to contribute to this objective?	Yes	No X	N/A		

	Indicator (all data should pertain to FY or CY 01)	OU Response			Fund Account	Data Quality Factors
USAID Objective 5: Conflict						
23	Did your program in a pre-conflict situation achieve a significant result in the past year that is likely to contribute to this objective?	Yes	No	N/A **X**		
24	Did your program in a post-conflict situation achieve a significant result in the past year that is likely to contribute to this objective?	Yes	No	N/A **X**		
25	Number of refugees and internally displaced persons assisted by USAID	Male	Female	Total		
USAID Objective 6: Humanitarian assistance following natural or other disasters						
26	Did your program achieve a significant result in the past year that is likely to contribute to this objective?	Yes	No	N/A **X**		
27	Number of beneficiaries					

Table 2: Selected Performance Measures for Other Reporting Purposes

The information in this table will be used to provide data for standard USAID reporting requirements

	Indicator (all data should pertain to FY or CY 01)	OU Response			Fund Account	Data Quality Factors
Child Survival Report						
Global Health Objective 1: Reducing the number of unintended pregnancies						
1	Percentage of in-union women age 15-49 using, or whose partner is using, a modern method of contraception at the time of the survey. (DHS/RHS)	18.5				DHS 2000, page 80 (CMW only, current use)
Global Health Objective 2: Reducing infant and child mortality						
2	Percentage of children age 12 months or less who have received their third dose of DPT (DHS/RHS)	Male 50	Female 47	Total 42.7		DHS 2000, page 151 (vaccinated by 12 mos of age)
3	Percentage of children age 6-59 months who had a case of diarrhea in the last two weeks and received ORT (DHS/RHS)	Male 20.2	Female 17.6	Total 18.9		DHS 2000, page 159 and 161
4	Percentage of children age 6-59 months receiving a vitamin A supplement during the last six months (DHS/RHS)	Male 28	Female 29.1	Total 28.5		DHS 2000, page 183
5	Were there any confirmed cases of wild-strain polio transmission in your country?	NO				WHO, Western Pacific Region (polio eradicated in region)
Global Health Objective 3: Reducing deaths and adverse health outcomes to women as a result of pregnancy and childbirth						
6	Percentage of births attended by medically-trained personnel (DHS/RHS)	31.8				DHS 2000, page 141
Global Health Objective 5: Reducing the threat of infectious diseases of major public health importance						
7	a. Number of insecticide impregnated bed-nets sold (Malaria) (2001 actual) b. Number of insecticide impregnated bed-nets sold (Malaria) (2002 target)	10,666 (distributed), 14,291 (re-impregnated), 66,873 (beneficiaries) 2001 2002 projection not available				Partners for Development (PFD)
8	a. Proportion of districts implementing the DOTS Tuberculosis strategy (2001 actual)	NA for 2001				
	b. Proportion of districts implementing the DOTS Tuberculosis strategy (2002 target)	2002 projection not available				Current case detection rate is 40%. MoH, with support from WHO is committed to nation-wide implementation of health center DOTS, based on the successful pilot. CARE will assist with training, supervision, transportation, drug security and community awareness.
HIV/AIDS Report						

Global Health Objective 4: Reducing the HIV transmission rate and the impact of HIV/AIDS pandemic in developing countries						
9	a. Total condom sales (2001 actual)	16,394,900				Data are from PSI
	b. Total condom sales (2002 target)	16,800,000				
10	a. Number of individuals treated in STI programs (2001 actual)	Male 7,614	Female 55,693	Total 63,317		These figures include individuals appropriately treated. This includes all patients tested, whether the appropriate treatment was to send them home with or without medicines. Data are from RACHA, RHAC, and FHI
	b. Number of individuals treated in STI programs (2002 target)	9,632	59,800	69,432		
11	a. Is your operating unit supporting an MTCT program?	No				
	b. Will your operating unit start an MTCT program in 2002?	No				
12	a. Number of individuals reached by community and home based care programs (2001 actual)	Male 175,130	Female 165,685	Total 340,815		Data are from KHANA and FHI
	b. Number of individuals reached by community and home based care programs (2002 target)	231,151	169,600	400,751		
13	a. Number of orphans and vulnerable children reached (2001 actual)	Male 127*	Female 98*	Total 78,525		Data are from KHANA and FHI. *Male/Female breakout was only available from CARE for 2001 data, and CARE's and FHI's projected data for 2002. Therefore, the totals for 2001 and 2002 target are greater than the sum of male and female for 2001 and 2002 targets.
	b. Number of orphans and vulnerable children reached (2002 target)	48,050*	47,950*	97,981		
14	a. Number of individuals reached by antiretroviral (ARV) treatment programs (2001 actual)	Male N/A	Female N/A	Total N/A		
	b. Number of individuals reached by antiretroviral (ARV) treatment programs (2002 target)	N/A	N/A	N/A		

Victims of Torture Report

Democracy, Conflict, and Humanitarian Assistance Objective 7: Providing support to victims of torture

15	Did you provide support to torture survivors this year, even as part of a larger effort?					
16	Number of beneficiaries (adults age 15 and over)	Male	Female	Total		
17	Number of beneficiaries (children under age 15)	Male	Female	Total		

Global Climate Change

USAID Objective 5: World's environment protected

18	Global Climate Change: See GCC Appendix			

Annual Report Part VII: Environmental Compliance

The mission does not anticipate any new or amended environmental examinations (IEEs) in the coming year. In 2001 the Mission completed an Environmental Analysis, including Bio-diversity and Tropical Forestry Assessments, as part of its Interim Country Strategic Plan, 2002-2005. This satisfied the requirements for compliance under Sections 118(e) and 119(d) of the Foreign Assistance Act. Activities planned under the Interim Country Strategic Plan are expected to continue to fall under the following classes of categorical exclusions: 1) programs involving education, technical assistance or training; 2) programs involving nutrition, health care or population and family planning services; and programs of maternal and child health.

Ongoing Strategic and Special Objectives and related activities are in compliance with their approved Categorical Exclusions.

WORLD COUNTRY STUDY GUIDE LIBRARY
2005

Ultimate guides for a correspondent country. Geography, history, people, language, culture, traditions, foreign and domestic policy, economy, government, constitution, places to visit, info for travelers...and more

Price: $99.95 each

Title
1. Afghanistan Country Study Guide
2. Aland Country Study Guide
3. Albania Country Study Guide
4. Algeria Country Study Guide
5. Andorra Country Study Guide
6. Angola Country Study Guide
7. Anguilla Country Study Guide
8. Antigua and Barbuda Country Study Guide
9. Antilles (Netherlands) Country Study Guide
10. Argentina Country Study Guide
11. Armenia Country Study Guide
12. Aruba Country Study Guide
13. Australia Country Study Guide
14. Austria Country Study Guide
15. Azerbaijan Country Study Guide
16. Bahamas Country Study Guide
17. Bahrain Country Study Guide
18. Bangladesh Country Study Guide
19. Barbados Country Study Guide
20. Belarus Country Study Guide
21. Belgium Country Study Guide
22. Belize Country Study Guide
23. Benin Country Study Guide
24. Bermuda Country Study Guide
25. Bhutan Country Study Guide
26. Bolivia Country Study Guide
27. Bosnia and Herzegovina Country Study Guide
28. Botswana Country Study Guide
29. Brazil Country Study Guide
30. Brunei Country Study Guide
31. Bulgaria Country Study Guide

32.	Burkina Faso Country Study Guide
33.	Burundi Country Study Guide
34.	Cambodia Country Study Guide
35.	Cameroon Country Study Guide
36.	Canada Country Study Guide
37.	Cape Verde Country Study Guide
38.	Cayman Islands Country Study Guide
39.	Central African Republic Country Study Guide
40.	Chad Country Study Guide
41.	Chile Country Study Guide
42.	China Country Study Guide
43.	Colombia Country Study Guide
44.	Comoros Country Study Guide
45.	Congo Country Study Guide
46.	Congo, Democratic Republic Country Study Guide
47.	Cook Islands Country Study Guide
48.	Costa Rica Country Study Guide
49.	Cote d'Ivoire Country Study Guide
50.	Croatia Country Study Guide
51.	Cuba Country Study Guide
52.	Cyprus Country Study Guide
53.	Czech Republic Country Study Guide
54.	Denmark Country Study Guide
55.	Djibouti Country Study Guide
56.	Dominica Country Study Guide
57.	Dominican Republic Country Study Guide
58.	Ecuador Country Study Guide
59.	Egypt Country Study Guide
60.	El Salvador Country Study Guide
61.	Equatorial Guinea Country Study Guide
62.	Eritrea Country Study Guide
63.	Estonia Country Study Guide
64.	Ethiopia Country Study Guide
65.	Falkland Islands Country Study Guide
66.	Faroes Country Study Guide
67.	Fiji Country Study Guide
68.	Finland Country Study Guide
69.	France Country Study Guide
70.	Gabon Country Study Guide
71.	Gambia Country Study Guide

72.	Georgia Country Study Guide
73.	Germany Country Study Guide
74.	Ghana Country Study Guide
75.	Gibraltar Country Study Guide
76.	Greece Country Study Guide
77.	Greenland Country Study Guide
78.	Grenada Country Study Guide
79.	Guam Country Study Guide
80.	Guatemala Country Study Guide
81.	Guernsey Country Study Guide
82.	Guinea Country Study Guide
83.	Guinea-Bissau Country Study Guide
84.	Guyana Country Study Guide
85.	Haiti Country Study Guide
86.	Honduras Country Study Guide
87.	Hungary Country Study Guide
88.	Iceland Country Study Guide
89.	India Country Study Guide
90.	Indonesia Country Study Guide
91.	Iran Country Study Guide
92.	Iraq Country Study Guide
93.	Ireland Country Study Guide
94.	Israel Country Study Guide
95.	Italy Country Study Guide
96.	Jamaica Country Study Guide
97.	Japan Country Study Guide
98.	Jersey Country Study Guide
99.	Jordan Country Study Guide
100.	Kazakhstan Country Study Guide
101.	Kenya Country Study Guide
102.	Kiribati Country Study Guide
103.	Korea, North Country Study Guide
104.	Korea, South Country Study Guide
105.	Kuwait Country Study Guide
106.	Kyrgyzstan Country Study Guide
107.	Laos Country Study Guide
108.	Latvia Country Study Guide
109.	Lebanon Country Study Guide
110.	Lesotho Country Study Guide
111.	Liberia Country Study Guide

112. Libya Country Study Guide
113. Liechtenstein Country Study Guide
114. Lithuania Country Study Guide
115. Luxembourg Country Study Guide
116. Macau Country Study Guide
117. Macedonia, The Former Yugoslav Republic Country Study Guide
118. Madagascar Country Study Guide
119. Malawi Country Study Guide
120. Malaysia Country Study Guide
121. Maldives Country Study Guide
122. Mali Country Study Guide
123. Malta Country Study Guide
124. Man Country Study Guide
125. Marshall Islands Country Study Guide
126. Mauritania Country Study Guide
127. Mauritius Country Study Guide
128. Mayotte Country Study Guide
129. Mexico Country Study Guide
130. Micronesia Country Study Guide
131. Moldova Country Study Guide
132. Monaco Country Study Guide
133. Mongolia Country Study Guide
134. Monserrat Country Study Guide
135. Morocco Country Study Guide
136. Mozambique Country Study Guide
137. Myanmar Country Study Guide
138. Namibia Country Study Guide
139. Nauru Country Study Guide
140. Nepal Country Study Guide
141. Netherlands Country Study Guide
142. New Caledonia Country Study Guide
143. New Zealand Country Study Guide
144. Nicaragua Country Study Guide
145. Niger Country Study Guide
146. Nigeria Country Study Guide
147. Niue Country Study Guide
148. Northern Mariana Islands Country Study Guide
149. Norway Country Study Guide
150. Oman Country Study Guide
151. Pakistan Country Study Guide

152. Palau Country Study Guide
153. Palestine Country Study Guide
154. Panama Country Study Guide
155. Papua New Guinea Country Study Guide
156. Paraguay Country Study Guide
157. Peru Country Study Guide
158. Philippines Country Study Guide
159. Pitcairn Islands Country Study Guide
160. Poland Country Study Guide
161. Polynesia French Country Study Guide
162. Portugal Country Study Guide
163. Qatar Country Study Guide
164. Romania Country Study Guide
165. Russia Country Study Guide
166. Rwanda Country Study Guide
167. Saint Kitts and Nevis Country Study Guide
168. Saint Lucia Country Study Guide
169. Saint Vincent and The Grenadines Country Study Guide
170. Samoa (American) A Country Study Guide
171. Samoa (Western) Country Study Guide
172. San Marino Country Study Guide
173. Sao Tome and Principe Country Study Guide
174. Saudi Arabia Country Study Guide
175. Scotland Country Study Guide
176. Senegal Country Study Guide
177. Seychelles Country Study Guide
178. Sierra Leone Country Study Guide
179. Singapore Country Study Guide
180. Slovakia Country Study Guide
181. Slovenia Country Study Guide
182. Solomon Islands Country Study Guide
183. Somalia Country Study Guide
184. South Africa Country Study Guide
185. Spain Country Study Guide
186. Sri Lanka Country Study Guide
187. St. Helena Country Study Guide
188. St. Pierre & Miquelon Country Study Guide
189. Sudan Country Study Guide
190. Suriname Country Study Guide
191. Swaziland Country Study Guide

192. Sweden Country Study Guide
193. Switzerland Country Study Guide
194. Syria Country Study Guide
195. Taiwan Country Study Guide
196. Tajikistan Country Study Guide
197. Tanzania Country Study Guide
198. Thailand Country Study Guide
199. Togo Country Study Guide
200. Tonga Country Study Guide
201. Trinidad and Tobago Country Study Guide
202. Tunisia Country Study Guide
203. Turkey Country Study Guide
204. Turkmenistan Country Study Guide
205. Tuvalu Country Study Guide
206. Uganda Country Study Guide
207. Ukraine Country Study Guide
208. United Arab Emirates Country Study Guide
209. United Kingdom Country Study Guide
210. United States Country Study Guide
211. Uruguay Country Study Guide
212. Uzbekistan Country Study Guide
213. Vanuatu Country Study Guide
214. Vatican City Country Study Guide
215. Venezuela Country Study Guide
216. Vietnam Country Study Guide
217. Virgin Islands, British Country Study Guide
218. Wake Atoll Country Study Guide
219. Wallis & Futuna Country Study Guide
220. Western Sahara Country Study Guide
221. Yemen Country Study Guide
222. Yugoslavia Country Study Guide
223. Zambia Country Study Guide

Printed in the United States
26515LVS00001B/152